An Introduction to Qualitative Research

Fourth Edition

*We dedicate this edition to Rachael B. Lawrence, our graduate
student and companion in developing the fourth edition. Rachael's calm
patience and diligence are, as ever, delightful. Thank you, Rachael.*

*And we dedicate this edition to our students—
past, present, and future—who inspire and teach us.*

MAGIC EYE® 3D INSTRUCTIONS: Hold the center of Magic Eye image *right up* to your nose, it should be blurry. *Stare* as though you are looking through the image. *Very slowly* move the image away from your face until you begin to see depth. Now hold the image still, try not to blink, and the illusion will magically appear. The longer you look, the clearer the illusion becomes.

An Introduction to Qualitative Research

Learning in the Field

Fourth Edition

Gretchen B. Rossman
University of Massachusetts Amherst

Sharon F. Rallis
University of Massachusetts Amherst

Los Angeles | London | New Delhi
Singapore | Washington DC | Melbourne

FOR INFORMATION:

SAGE Publications, Inc.
2455 Teller Road
Thousand Oaks, California 91320
E-mail: order@sagepub.com

SAGE Publications Ltd.
1 Oliver's Yard
55 City Road
London EC1Y 1SP
United Kingdom

SAGE Publications India Pvt. Ltd.
B 1/I 1 Mohan Cooperative Industrial Area
Mathura Road, New Delhi 110 044
India

SAGE Publications Asia-Pacific Pte. Ltd.
3 Church Street
#10-04 Samsung Hub
Singapore 049483

Acquisitions Editor: Helen Salmon
eLearning Editor: John Scappini
Editorial Assistant: Anna Villarruel
Production Editor: Kelly DeRosa
Copy Editor: QuADS Prepress (P) Ltd.
Typesetter: C&M Digitals (P) Ltd.
Proofreader: Ellen Brink
Indexer: Jean Casalegno
Cover Designer: Gail Buschman
Marketing Manager: Susannah Goldes

Copyright © 2017 by SAGE Publications, Inc.

Printed in the United States of America

Library of Congress Cataloging-in-Publication Data

Names: Rossman, Gretchen B., author. | Rallis, Sharon F., author. | Rossman, Gretchen B. Learning in the field.

Title: An introduction to qualitative research : learning in the field / Gretchen B. Rossman & Sharon F. Rallis, University of Massachusetts Amherst.

Other titles: Learning in the field.

Description: Fourth Edition. | Thousand Oaks : SAGE Publications, Inc., 2016. | Revised edition of the authors' Learning in the field, 2012. | Includes bibliographical references and index.

Identifiers: LCCN 2015043840 | ISBN 978-1-5063-0793-0 (pbk. : alk. paper)

Subjects: LCSH: Qualitative reasoning.

Classification: LCC H62 .R667 2016 | DDC 001.4/2—dc23
LC record available at http://lccn.loc.gov/2015043840

This book is printed on acid-free paper.

16 17 18 19 20 10 9 8 7 6 5 4 3 2 1

Brief Contents

Detailed Contents

1 | Qualitative Research as Learning   1

2 | The Researcher as Learner   23

3 | The Researcher as Competent and Ethical   48

4 | Major Qualitative Research Genres 77

5 | Conceptualizing and Planning the Research 100

6 | Entering the Field   127

7 | Gathering Data in the Field   146

8 | Issues That Arise in the Field — 181

9 | Our Characters' Data — 195

10 | Analyzing and Interpreting Data — 227

11 | Our Characters' Analyses   264

12 | Presenting the Learnings   279

List of Tables and Figures

Tables

Figures

Foreword

Michael Quinn Patton

This book is about learning *in the field*. What's the field? It's the world. It's wherever you find yourself. It's wherever you go. This book will help you become more effective at navigating the modern world by more intentionally paying attention to what's going on around you and learning through observation, interviewing, and making sense of what the resulting data reveal and mean. This means developing and nurturing a mind-set of learning. Such a mind-set involves ongoing inquiry, extracting lessons from experience, and application of research skills to whatever endeavors you undertake. Let me, then, preview for you six things you are going to have the opportunity to learn from this book that will serve you in good stead the rest of your life.

SIX QUALITIES OF HIGHLY EFFECTIVE LEARNERS

1. *Savvy and discriminating research consumption:* The learning mind-set involves making sense of information. Some of that information you will generate yourself. But by far, most of what you'll learn will come from information generated by others. You cannot help but be a consumer of research in this knowledge age. The challenge is becoming a *sophisticated consumer of research*. We are inundated constantly by research findings. A lot of it is junk. A lot of it is opinion disguised as research. A lot of it is biased. A lot of it is fabricated. And a lot of it provides new insights and knowledge that will make you more effective in whatever you do. The trick is to know how to tell the difference. The learning mind-set engages with new research findings by asking questions that may require digging deeper: What design produced those findings? What data were gathered and how were the data analyzed? How do these findings fit with other research in the field? Within what theoretical framework was the inquiry conducted? What are the practice implications of the findings, if any? A learning mind-set of inquiry means that you will not accept news headlines about research findings at face value but will look behind those headlines, using your research knowledge and skills, to determine the significance and relevance of the findings to your own work and life. This book addresses specifically how understanding the language and processes of inquiry will help you become a better producer as well as a more astute and critical consumer of research.

2. *Asking meaningful and important questions:* Learning in the field begins by asking questions. In everyday life, we are sloppy about how we frame questions. Learning to ask researchable questions with potentially actionable answers, the hallmark of the

learning mind-set, is a skill that will serve you well the rest of your life. You will listen more astutely to how people frame their inquiries, the questions they ask, the format of those questions, and whether the questions are posed in ways that could possibly be answered. A sophisticated learner is a sophisticated question-asker. It all begins with good questions. Moreover, learning to identify and assess the questions of other researchers will help you become more skilled and savvy about how to formulate your own inquiry questions. This book shows you how different approaches to, as well as purposes and frameworks for, conducting research are distinct, in part, because they ask different questions and reflect diverse inquiry traditions.

3. *Critical thinking skills:* Learning in the field involves critical thinking. Presumably, you already have some critical thinking skills. You may even think you're quite a rigorous thinker. Get ready to go deeper, not just to design and complete your research but in all that you do. The stakes can be quite high. Philosopher Hannah Arendt devoted much of her life trying to understand how the Holocaust could have occurred. Having experienced totalitarianism while young in Germany during World War II, then having fled as conditions worsened, she came to believe that thinking rigorously in public deliberations and acting democratically were intertwined. Totalitarianism is built on and sustained by deceit and thought control. To resist efforts by the powerful to deceive and control thinking, Arendt (*Between Past and Future: Eight Exercises in Political Thought.* New York, NY: Viking Press, 1968) believed that people needed to practice thinking. Toward that end, she developed "eight exercises in political thought." She wrote that "experience in thinking . . . can be won, like all experience in doing something, only through practice, through exercises" (p. 4). From this point of view, I invite you to consider your research inquiry as an opportunity to practice *thinking*, that is, to do what Arendt hoped her exercises in political thought would do, namely, help us "to gain experience in *how* to think." Her exercises "do not contain prescriptions on what to think or which truths to hold" but, rather, on the act and process of thinking. For example, Arendt (1968) thought it important to help people think conceptually,

> to discover the real origins of original concepts in order to distill from them anew their original spirit which has so sadly evaporated from the very keywords of political language—such as freedom and justice, authority and reason, responsibility and virtue, power and glory—leaving behind empty shells. (pp. 14–15)

Qualitative inquiry involves examining language, the meanings of labels and key concepts, and analyzing how they had been applied in the past and what is their relevance today. That is an exercise in critical thinking as will be all aspects of your inquiry. Indeed, understanding the lessons and wisdom offered throughout this book—knowing yourself; learning the terminology of research; understanding the assumptions and philosophical underpinnings of research; and appreciating the role of theory, the various designs of research, and considerations of quality and ethics—will help you become a more critical consumer of information and, in turn, a better writer and thinker overall.

4. *Advanced interviewing skills:* Becoming a skilled interviewer will enhance the validity and trustworthiness of the data you collect through interviewing. But becoming a skilled interviewer will also make you a more effective practitioner in the knowledge age. Every interaction with other human beings offers opportunities to inquire into their worldview, perspective, experiences, opinions, feelings, and behaviors. Knowing how to ask inviting and engaging questions, listen attentively, probe astutely, and follow-up on what you hear—these are the elements of effective interviewing. They will serve you well not only in conducting research but also in your relationships with family members, significant others, colleagues, and all you encounter on your life journey.

I find interviewing people invigorating and stimulating—the opportunity to enter another person's world for a short period of time. I'm personally convinced that to be a good interviewer you must like doing it. This means being interested in what people have to say. You must, yourself, believe that the thoughts and experiences of the people being interviewed are worth knowing. In short, you must have the utmost respect for these persons who are willing to share with you some of their time to help you understand their world. If you include interviewing in how you learn in the field, you will have an opportunity not only to deepen your skills but also to reflect on how you approach interactions of all kinds with other people. How good are you at asking evocative questions? How good are you at listening? How skilled are you at making it comfortable for people to tell you their stories? How confident are you as an interviewer in our modern interview society, a core aspect of the knowledge age? This book helps you develop your interviewing skills to more effectively learn in the field (in the world) throughout your life.

5. *Astute observational skills:* Every interview is also an observation. With our heads buried in our devices these days, we miss a lot of what goes on around us. All of science is based on, indeed depends on, astute, focused, deep, and discerning observation. The great thinkers all have been great observers: Aristotle, Copernicus, Newton, Darwin, Einstein, Jung, Goodall, and whoever have been the pioneers in your own specialized scholar-practitioner field. Skilled interviewing involves more than just looking. It involves *seeing*. It involves knowing what to look for. It requires distinguishing signal from noise, astute pattern recognition, and an openness to be witness to whatever is unfolding before you. In our everyday lives, we walk around in a fog, engrossed in our own thoughts, operating on preconceived ideas, immersed in selective perception, operating on biases, and generally oblivious. To move into a learning mind-set means to lift the fog, stop the internal noise and gaze outward into the intriguing panorama of complex reality, open the mind to new possibilities, and see things in new ways—in short, to become a skilled observer. Skill at

observation, like interviewing skills, will serve you well not only in conducting research but in all aspects of your life.

6. *Rigorous meaning-making skills:* All data have to be interpreted. Data do not speak for themselves. Making sense of data is a quintessential inquiry competence and skill. One aspect of analysis and interpretation, as with data collection itself, whether through interviewing or observation, involves distinguishing signal from noise. What is significant? What are the patterns and themes that are worth paying attention to? What do they mean? How do those meanings inform your understanding of the world and, through enhanced understanding, your actions in the world, *your* practice as a scholar-practitioner. One of the pitfalls of analysis is letting your preconceptions, selective perceptions, biases, and preferred ways of seeing things dominate your data interpretation. Rigorous analysis requires rigorous critical thinking. This includes triangulation: looking across different kinds of data (interviews, observations, documents) and diverse interpretive frameworks (previous research findings, alternative theories, competing conceptual frameworks) to figure out what interpretation best fits the data—not your hopes for the data, but the actual data. Rigorous analysis requires a disciplined search for data that doesn't fit the dominant pattern, for alternative explanations, and with a willingness to be the devil's advocate in your own research. As with the other skills I've previewed, becoming better at making sense of data will serve you well not only in your research but also in deciding the value of all kinds of findings and propositions that you will encounter as you are bombarded with allegations about how the world is. Astute sense-making, skilled interpretation, and rigorous meaning-making are what will move you from understanding to action in the knowledge age. This book encourages you to reflect on your worldview and orientation to research as a core part of the meaning-making exercise. Doing so will enhance your learning in the field and help make you an effective reflective practitioner in whatever endeavors you undertake.

ARE YOU READY?

The purpose of a foreword is to set the context for a book and help the reader get ready. This foreword has previewed six things you are going to have the opportunity to learn that will be essential in completing any research you undertake and, no less important, will serve you in good stead the rest of your life as you become a more *effective learner*.

1. Savvy and discriminating research consumption

2. Asking meaningful and important questions

3. Critical thinking skills

4. Advanced interviewing skills

5. Astute observational skills

6. Rigorous meaning-making skills

Being ready, in my experience, is primarily a state of mind: being open to new learning and prepared to do the work necessary to apply what you learn. This book has all the resources you need to complete your own research and become a more skilled lifelong learner. Ready. Set. **GO!**

Preface

The fourth edition of this book has a new name: *Introduction to Qualitative Research: Learning in the Field*. We transposed the title and subtitle to make salient the major purpose of the book, which remains true to each preceding edition—to *introduce* learners to qualitative research principles and practice, issues and dilemmas, joys and frustrations. We have had to resist the temptation to add more and more and more to this edition, as this would have taken us away from our *introductory* purpose. We have used the text in our teaching for more than 25 years and continue to seek critical feedback and suggestions from our students and other instructors who use the text. The development of the fourth edition benefited from engaged and insightful groups of graduate students who have taken our course on Qualitative Research Methods since the third edition was published. This edition has also benefited from the detailed and thoughtful comments of the several instructors of qualitative methods who reviewed the third edition, as well as those who reviewed a draft of this edition. Again, we have drawn on their insights and suggestions throughout the fourth edition. We acknowledge these instructors personally at the end of this preface. We have incorporated more examples from the work of our students to create illustrations with which learners can identify; many of these are about international students or conducting research in international settings. We have been privileged to work with dedicated and thoughtful graduate students not only from the United States but also from all regions of the world. As we have learned with them and through them, we honor their work by mentioning it here.

In making the revisions for this edition, we have kept firmly in mind the remark we have heard consistently over the years—both students and instructors have found the ideas and examples in the text accessible. We have been told that the principles, theoretical notions, and illustrations are grounded and that students can relate to them easily. For this reason, the style of this edition remains the same—we speak to "you," the learner, directly engaging you in dialogue. As with the previous editions, we are quite mindful of how the "voice" used throughout the text can distance the reader or bring him or her closer to the ideas. Using the term *qualitative researchers* places some distance between us, the authors, and them, the researchers, although we certainly place ourselves within that group—otherwise we would not have written this book. Using *we* to refer to qualitative researchers, however, creates distance between you, the reader, and us, the authors. We have chosen to use the term *qualitative researchers* to avoid distance between you and us, although we directly address you, the reader, from time to time. When we use the term *we*, we are referring to ourselves. And, to avoid sexist language, we alternate between *he* and *she* when referring to the researcher.

The fourth edition retains our three characters—Ruth, Marla, and Anthony—who are modeled on "real" students with whom we have worked. Critical feedback we have received suggested that the dialogues at the beginning of each chapter were not "authentic" snippets of conversation. Therefore, we have removed them. However, throughout the book, we use the characters' evolving research projects as examples, in addition to those from our own work and from that of our students over the years. We hope this makes the struggles and excitement of doing qualitative research vivid and real.

In all the classes we teach, we strive to create environments in which *communities of practice* develop. Small groups of peers working together test out ideas, critique one another's work, offer alternative conceptualizations, and provide both emotional and intellectual support. We have witnessed how such groups create powerful learning environments, and they are a central part of our teaching. For these reasons, we emphasize this notion throughout the fourth edition.

We continue to strive to find a meaningful way to describe the principles with which we end many chapters. The first edition referred to these as "habits of mind and heart," which quickly became overused and trivialized. The second edition used the phrase "principles of good practice," which, over time, did not quite fit. In this edition, we have retained, with minor modification, what we called them in the third— "dispositions and skills"—to capture important stances and practices that we hope qualitative research learners are developing. We fully anticipate, however, that this phrase will not quite capture what we are striving for; we welcome suggestions from interested readers.

The short sections on *dispositions and skills* still depict our central belief that thinking *and* feeling *and* doing in mindful ways are integral to doing competent, ethical qualitative research. These include a comfort with ambiguity, a deep respect for the experiences of others, sensitivity to complexity, humility in making claims for what you have learned, and thinking that is creative, analytic, and evocative. In these sections, we use the dispositions and skills to suggest a perspective on the puzzles and tensions raised in each chapter. Also, most chapters end with activities for *your* communities of practice and suggestions for further reading, which have been substantially updated. These are intended to offer a way to delve deeper into a selected topic.

We are pragmatists. We recognize that applied research, to be useful, often crosses epistemological divides and relies on both qualitative and quantitative methods in a single study. We are not methodological purists; in fact, we find mixed methods especially useful in evaluations (see Rallis & Rossman, 2002). While we conduct and teach qualitative inquiry, we are also quite savvy and familiar with mixed methods research and have the deepest respect for our psychometric colleagues. However, we do not provide extensive discussion of mixed methods research, as there are a multitude of excellent resources on this blended and increasingly popular approach to inquiry.

A note on the various rhetorical devices we use. Textboxes highlight key ideas, terms, or definitions. Tables and figures provide more elaboration or what are intended to be evocative images. The introductory paragraphs describe real issues that learners face and forecast some of the content of each chapter. The learning activities at the end of most chapters are for you and your community of practice to try out and to encourage and support your learning. And most chapters end with further reading suggestions as noted above.

The fourth edition incorporates many useful suggestions we have received, as we mention in the opening paragraph. We provide a much expanded discussion of *ethics* and ethical research practice, as well as an elaborate discussion of *systematic inquiry*—both leading to the central consideration of *trustworthiness* in research. The discussion of *genres* is refined, but does not provide a comprehensive listing of the many subgenres and subsubgenres housed—loosely—under the qualitative umbrella. We provide a more nuanced discussion of *conceptualizing* and developing a conceptual framework, as our own insights into the virtues of early development of this thinking have grown. We have also enhanced the discussion of data analysis and interpretation.

You may wonder why we have chosen to use a variation of a Magic Eye® picture for covers of the past few editions. We see the cover as a visual metaphor for the experience you will engage in as you learn to conduct qualitative research. Magic Eye designs hide a three-dimensional image within a two-dimensional pattern. The picture is a form of what is known as a *stereogram*, in which seeing the hidden image depends on the depth perception achieved by allowing your eyes to diverge. On the frontispiece, we provide the three-dimensional viewing instructions. However, many people have difficulty finding—or perceiving—the hidden image. Your ability to see the hidden image—or not—really doesn't matter. The Magic Eye is a metaphor for your individual perceptions and interpretations that you make of, for example, what you see while observing or hear while interviewing. In real life and in research, as eloquently described by Michael Quinn Patton in the foreword to this edition, not everyone sees, hears, or interprets exactly alike. Sometimes we see things others do not; just as often, we may not perceive an object or a phenomenon that exists for others. Whether you see the image or not, we hope you have fun with the cover.

This edition proceeds as follows. Chapter 1 develops three central ideas. First, that qualitative research is all about *learning*. We continue to see that very few texts on research methods emphasize this obvious (to us) idea. Second, that qualitative research is typically implemented through one of *three strategies:* (1) an analytic descriptive study that builds knowledge, (2) an evaluation or policy study that contributes to sound decision making, (3) and action research that builds participatory involvement to change existing (often oppressive) practices. Third, that research, to be ethical, should be conducted with its *potential usefulness* for various audiences in mind. We describe four ways of using research: instrumental, enlightenment, symbolic, and transformative.

Chapter 2 defines the qualitative researcher as a learner, discussing *reflexivity* as a central aspect of becoming a competent researcher. We discuss the assumptions undergirding all inquiry, qualitative research specifically. These assumptions shape your perspective—your stance—as the learner in a research project. Chapter 3 discusses considerations for the competent and ethical conduct of qualitative studies. We claim that trustworthiness entails observing *standards for competent practice* and *ethical principles*. We present four ethical theories: (1) the ethic of consequences, (2) the ethic of rights and responsibilities, (3) the ethic of social justice, and (4) the ethic of care. Often-encountered ethical dilemmas are then discussed, as well as political and mircopolitical considerations that may arise in the conduct of fieldwork.

Chapter 4 describes major qualitative research genres: ethnography, phenomenological studies, and sociolinguistic studies. We also discuss case studies to engage with the confusion that often arises around this research strategy. Chapter 5 presents the complex thinking that goes into *conceptualizing, planning, and designing* a qualitative project. Three considerations are paramount: (1) do-ability (feasibility), (2) want-to-do-ability (interest), and (3) should-do-ability (ethics and politics). The elements of a qualitative research project design are discussed, with examples from our characters showing how they weigh alternatives and make informed decisions.

Chapters 6, 7, 8, and 9 are the heart of the book. They present strategies and considerations when implementing a qualitative study. Chapter 6 discusses *entry and access:* preparing for fieldwork, negotiating with participants, expectations and building relationships, and reciprocity. Chapter 7 provides details on *gathering data* through the primary techniques of talking with people (interviewing); paying attention to actions, activities, and interactions (observing); and collecting artifacts—material culture—to provide insight into the phenomenon of interest. Chapter 8 presents typical issues that frequently arise during data gathering. We illustrate these issues through our characters and examples from our own work and that of our students. Completing this cycle, Chapter 9 presents our characters' data, based on our conviction that seeing real data helps allay anxieties in the beginner.

We then move to data analysis and interpretation. Chapter 10 provides a much-elaborated discussion of the often-opaque processes of *analyzing and interpreting qualitative data*. We present seven phases of generic analysis, discuss these in light of qualitative research genres, and then offer strategies for analyzing interview data, field notes, and material culture. The seven generic phases are (1) organizing the data, (2) becoming deeply familiar with the data, (3) generating categories and themes, (4) coding, (5) interpreting, (6) searching for alternative understandings, and (7) writing the report. These phases mirror elements of the creative process: immersion, incubation, insight, and interpretation. Chapter 11 then presents our characters' analyses with our critical commentary.

In the final chapter (Chapter 12), we discuss various modes for presenting what you have learned in the project. Although we offer ways of organizing and writing a formal report, we encourage the reader to consider alternative modes—for example, social media venues, multimedia presentations, newsletters, and oral presentations. Here we revisit the notion of *voice* as fundamental to representing what you have learned in your research in useful, ethical, and thoughtful ways.

In the three previous editions, we referred to several sources that now have new editions themselves. In most cases, we reference the newer edition because quotes from the first edition may have become outdated. Sometimes, however, the author said it better the first time, so we have retained the older reference. We also still refer to what we consider to be classic sources that we believe stand the test of time and deserve to be recognized.

ONLINE RESOURCES

A companion website at **study.sagepub.com/rossman4e** includes PowerPoint slides, suggested activities, a sample syllabus, video links, and relevant full-text SAGE journal articles for instructors, as well as video resources and SAGE journal articles for students.

Acknowledgments

The fourth edition would not have come to fruition without our many supporters, critical friends, students, and thoughtful reviewers—our *community of practice*. First are the many students we have taught over the years; we have learned much from them. The work of several students appears as examples throughout the text. Some we reference directly; others we do not for confidentiality reasons. We are most appreciative of their critical and constructive comments.

Colleagues also continue to give us important feedback, as did the following reviewers:

Diane Barone, University of Nevada

Gerardo Blanco Ramirez, University of Massachusetts–Boston

Curtis Child, Brigham Young University

Michael Grimes, Louisiana State University

Ane Turner Johnson, Rowan University

Lisa R. Merriweather, University of North Carolina at Charlotte

Lauren Moret, University of Tennessee

Susan L. Wortmann, Nebraska Wesleyan University

This edition would not have been possible without Rachael B. Lawrence, a graduate student in our program. She has provided sustained and thoughtful critique, editing, and searching for new and fresh examples. She is a wizard at locating phrases that are out of date or could be phrased more felicitously. She has been an incredible companion on this journey. Finally, our editor Helen Salmon, has become a great friend and is an outstanding editor. Both Helen and our previous editor, Vicki Knight, have been our "True North" because of their keen insights and willingness to provide tough feedback, all the while holding on to the ultimate goal of the work.

About the Authors

 **Gretchen B. Rossman** is professor of international education and chair of the Department of Educational Policy, Research, and Administration at the College of Education at the University of Massachusetts Amherst. She has served as a visiting professor at Harvard University's Graduate School of Education. Prior to coming to the University of Massachusetts, she was senior research associate at Research for Better Schools in Philadelphia. With an international reputation as a qualitative methodologist, she has expertise in qualitative research design and methods, mixed methods monitoring and evaluation, and inquiry in education. Over the past 30+ years, she has coauthored numerous books, two of which are editions of major qualitative research texts (this fourth edition of *Learning in the Field*, with Sharon Rallis, and *Designing Qualitative Research*, sixth edition, with Catherine Marshall—both widely used guides to qualitative inquiry). She has authored or coauthored more than 45 articles, book chapters, and technical reports focused on methodological issues in qualitative research syntheses, validity in qualitative research, mixed methods evaluation practice, and ethical research practice, as well as the analysis and evaluation of educational reform initiatives both in the United States and internationally. Professor Rossman has served as a principal investigator or co–principal investigator on several international projects in countries such as Azerbaijan, India, Malawi, Palestine, Senegal, Tanzania, and the Gambia, as well as an external evaluator on several domestic projects, including a Department of Education–funded reform initiative, a National Science Foundation–funded middle-grades science initiative, and a number of projects implementing more inclusive practices for students with disabilities. She regularly presents papers at the annual meetings of the American Educational Research Association and the Comparative and International Education Society. She received her PhD in education from the University of Pennsylvania with a specialization in higher education administration.

 **Sharon F. Rallis** is Dwight W. Allen Distinguished Professor of Education Policy and Reform at the University of Massachusetts Amherst. Previously, she was professor of education at the University of Connecticut, lecturer on education at Harvard, and associate professor of educational leadership at Peabody College, Vanderbilt University. Her doctorate is from the Harvard Graduate School of Education. She has coauthored numerous books, including several on leadership: *Principals of Dynamic Schools: Taking*

Charge of Change (with Ellen Goldring), *Dynamic Teachers: Leaders of Change* (with Gretchen Rossman), *Leading Dynamic Schools: How to Create and Implement Ethical Policies* (with Gretchen Rossman and others), and *Leading With Inquiry and Action: How Principals Improve Teaching and Learning* (with Matthew Militello and Ellen Goldring). Her numerous articles, book chapters, edited volumes, and technical reports address issues of research and evaluation methodology, ethical practice in research and evaluation, education policy and leadership, and school reform. A past president of the American Evaluation Association (2005) and current editor of the *American Journal of Evaluation*, Professor Rallis has been involved with education and evaluation for more than 3 decades. She has been a teacher, counselor, principal, researcher, program evaluator, director of a major federal school reform initiative, and an elected school board member. Currently, her teaching includes courses on inquiry, program evaluation, qualitative methodology, and organizational theory. Her research has focused on the local implementation of programs driven by federal, state, or district policies. As external evaluator or principal investigator, she has studied a variety of domestic and international policy and reform efforts, such as alternative professional development for leaders, collaborations between agencies responsible for educating incarcerated or institutionalized youth, initiatives supporting inclusive education for children and youth with disabilities, local school governance and leadership, labor–management relations in school districts, and leadership development. Her work with students on evaluation and qualitative methodology has taken her as far as Afghanistan, Turkey, and Palestine.

Professors Rossman and Rallis have had productive collaborative careers as coauthors, coinstructors, and mentors of graduate students. They have written together on ethical research practice, ethical policy implementation, mixed methods evaluation practice, validity in qualitative inquiry, as well as other methodological issues. They currently teach a course together at the University of Massachusetts Amherst—Introduction to Inquiry—required for all incoming doctoral students. Their work in this course has led to a companion text, *The Research Journey: Introduction to Inquiry* (2012). Mentoring graduate students informs their writing, and they regularly invite graduate students to write with them. They have worked together with graduate students from Afghanistan, Azerbaijan, Bhutan, China, India, Kenya, Kyrgyzstan, Malawi, Pakistan, Palestine, Sierra Leone, Tajikistan, Thailand, Uzbekistan, as well as the United States. This work has taken them around the globe, where they have facilitated workshops and made presentations to practitioners and academic audiences.

1

Qualitative Research as Learning

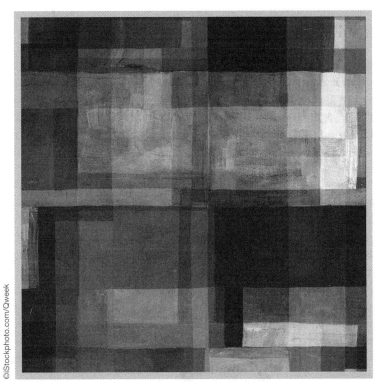

©iStockphoto.com/Qweek

To illustrate the complex and often challenging process of learning about qualitative research and learning through qualitative research, we introduce Marla, Ruth, and Anthony, three students in an introductory qualitative research course who learn as they study and participate in the qualitative research process. They illustrate different perspectives and starting points, but each student experiences the tensions and satisfactions of framing questions, listening, watching, reading, and writing.

DOING QUALITATIVE RESEARCH: TALES OF THREE CHARACTERS

Marla is an experienced health care professional who, early in her career, helped build a clinic in a Central American village. She sees herself as an activist and hopes to improve the U.S. health care system for poor women, so she has enrolled at the university to pursue a master's degree in public health. Although she is not certain about the specific aspect of health care that she wants to address, she is sure that the recipients of the care should take part in posing the questions. Her greatest concern is how the people in her study are affected by it; she envisions involving the study participants in seeking the answers and determining how the answers are used. Her experiences as a Latina in the United States have taught her that collaboration can be effective for changing an existing system, so she is attracted to a form of research that includes small-scale experimentation to change circumstances: action research. The possibility that research can be coupled with action appeals to her proactive nature. She believes that the world can be changed for the better.

Anthony has returned to the university for an advanced degree in public policy. On graduation from college, he volunteered as a community activist in a poor urban area on issues of water quality and housing. When funding for this project was cut, he worked as a legislative intern for a congresswoman representing the District of Columbia. She chaired the joint committee on urban renewal and the arts. His interest in evaluations that compare and contrast various programs to explore their effectiveness springs from these experiences. He learned firsthand, when his project's funding was cut, the effects of policy decisions on community members and their advocates. He hopes that his work can inform the policy-making process, especially for people living in poverty, through the provision of more effective, thoughtful, and detailed information.

The youngest of the three, **Ruth**, is an undergraduate majoring in psychology and is an avid athlete. She has been the point guard for the university basketball team and often works out in the gym early in the morning. For the past several summers, she has worked at a camp for children with disabilities. She enjoys working with children, especially through athletics, and has designed a 3-day wilderness course for deaf children. She volunteers 1 afternoon a week at a local elementary school. Ruth's major requires that she take an introductory research course. She has chosen qualitative research because she believes that it will be a way to explore the lives of the children with whom she works. Ruth's interests draw her to a descriptive study.

The characters learn together in a *community of practice*, "a social group engaged in the sustained pursuit of a shared enterprise" (Pallas, 2001, p. 7; see also Lave & Wenger, 1991; Meyerhof & Strycharz, 2013; Wenger, 1998). They discuss, argue, and commiserate with each other as they conduct their small-scale studies. Together, they learn that "where the circulation of knowledge among peers and near-peers is possible, it spreads exceedingly rapidly and effectively" (Lave & Wenger, 1991, p. 93). At the end of most chapters, we provide learning activities that you can engage in with your community of practice.

The Characters

Marla, a mature social activist committed to improving health care access for poor women

Anthony, dedicated to policy on income and poverty and using information to better lives

Ruth, deeply engaged in working with young people with disabilities

In their first class, Marla, Ruth, and Anthony have just encountered the confusing array of terms that constitute the vocabulary of qualitative research: *systematic inquiry, naturalistic inquiry, instrumental, interpretive, evaluation, enlightenment, transformative,* and *iterative,* to name just a few. The terms represent various processes, uses, and perspectives of qualitative research, as well as specific approaches to gathering, analyzing, interpreting, and writing up data. Many of the terms and differences in approaches are specialized and subtle. Each, however, helps explicate the following central themes of this book:

- Research should be undertaken to generate knowledge.
- The researcher is a learner, continually and consciously making decisions that affect the questions pursued and the direction of the study.
- Research is a process of conceptualizing, designing, conducting, and writing up what is learned.
- Research is recursive, iterative, messy, tedious, challenging, full of ambiguity, and exciting.

themes

We began this chapter by introducing three students whose learning and small-scale studies illustrate the complex (and often confusing) but rewarding world of qualitative research. Next we address the question of what qualitative research is, describing its goals and common features. Then we examine what qualitative researchers actually do in the process. We end the chapter with an overview of the rest of the book.

DEFINING QUALITATIVE RESEARCH

Qualitative research begins with questions; its *ultimate purpose is learning*. To inform the questions, the researcher collects data, the basic units or building blocks of information. Data are images, sounds, words, and numbers. When data are grouped into patterns, they become information. When information is interpreted and put to use or applied, it becomes knowledge (see Figure 1.1).

Learning has occurred. The process is analogous to building a house. Like data, cinder blocks are not particularly useful by themselves, but they can be placed together to make a wall. Like information, the wall can be used to build a house.

Both you, the researcher, and the builder start with questions and end with a product to be used. Research questions are seldom simple, however, and use takes complex forms. Some uses are intended, some are not. We are concerned that expending resources to support research too often results in reports sitting on shelves and articles languishing unread in academic journals. Our position is that research should be conducted with explicit goals for use. Research should have *the goal of contributing to improving the human condition*, whatever form that may take (see, especially, Crano, Brewer, & Lac,

Data are images, sounds, words, and numbers.

FIGURE 1.1   Building Blocks of Knowledge

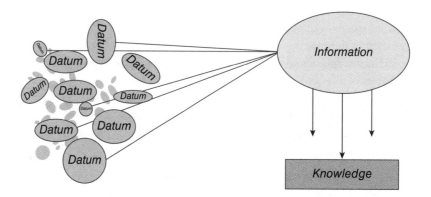

2015; Hostetler, 2005; Organisation for Economic Co-operation and Development, 2013). We take on the issues of multiple use later in this chapter, arguing that the many ways in which knowledge is used are all forms of learning—the central theme of this book.

Qualitative researchers seek answers to their questions in the real world. As you undertake a qualitative project, you will gather data (what you see, hear, and read) from people and places, events, and activities. You will do this in natural settings rather than in a laboratory or through written surveys. We hope that your purpose will be to learn about some aspect of the social world and to generate new understandings that can then be used. Qualitative researchers are central to this process, continually making choices, testing assumptions, and reshaping their questions. As the inquiry process grows from curiosity or wonder to understanding and knowledge building, the researcher may well be transformed. In many cases, the participants change as well. Historically, the individuals who take part in a research study have been referred to as *subjects*, *respondents*, and *informants*. Increasingly, qualitative researchers choose the more inclusive and democratic term *participants*.

Qualitative research has two unique features: (1) *the researcher is the means through which the study is conducted* and (2) *the purpose is to learn about some facet of the social world*. Both of these characteristics are integral to a view of learning that sees the learner as a constructor of knowledge rather than as a receiver. From this perspective, you accumulate data—not reality itself but rather representations of reality. You then transform these data, through analysis and interpretation, into information. When put to practical use—to address recurring social issues—information becomes knowledge.

The transformation of information into knowledge is an *active learning process*. Qualitative researchers are learners, and qualitative inquiry provides the detailed and rich data for this learning process. The learner (the researcher—you) makes choices that shape and are shaped by the emerging processes of inquiry. This notion of the interrelatedness of purpose and process underlies the central themes of this book.

Traditionally, differing purposes distinguish basic research (a term borrowed from the natural sciences) from applied research. *Basic research* aims to generate theory and produce knowledge for its own end, whereas *applied research* aims to inform action and enhance decision making. Basic research is judged by the theoretical explanations it provides; applied research is judged by its effectiveness in helping policymakers, practitioners, and the participants themselves make decisions and act to improve circumstances. Our position is that social scientists rarely engage in basic research, although their findings may, and often do contribute to theory. As a qualitative researcher, you will depict some aspect of the human condition, so your research will be quintessentially applied. The distinction between applied and basic research is neither clear-cut nor precise. For example, scientists may conduct research that leads to some direct practical application, and social scientists may conduct research that contributes to theory.

[handwritten margin note: Basic v. Applied Research]

[handwritten margin note: → qualitative = applied]

Qualitative inquiry is rooted in *empiricism*—that is, the philosophical tradition that posits that knowledge is obtained by direct experience through the physical senses. Perhaps one of the first qualitative researchers was Aristotle, who made sense of the world by watching and listening. He proposed that ideas are concepts derived from experience with actual objects, beings, and events. Aristotle taught that nothing exists in our minds that we have not first perceived with or experienced through our senses. We then use cognitive reasoning to organize and imbue those experiences with meaning—to make sense of the sensory experiences. For example, we group what we have seen or heard into categories based on characteristics of sights and sounds. At the same time, qualitative researchers also are influenced by the Platonic view that knowledge residing a priori within our minds shapes the images we receive. Thus, we argue that qualitative researchers combine their direct experience with their existing understandings, through complex reasoning, to make sense of the worlds they explore. In essence, qualitative researchers are constructivists; they interpret what they see, hear, and read in the worlds around them.

Qualitative research is a broad approach to the study of social phenomena. The approach is *naturalistic* and *interpretive*, and it draws on multiple methods of inquiry (see, e.g., Flick, 2014; Patton, 2015; Silverman, 2010). That is, qualitative research is conducted in natural settings rather than in controlled ones. It assumes that humans use what they see, hear, and feel to make meaning of social phenomena, and it relies on a variety of data-gathering techniques. It is "research that represents human beings as whole persons living in dynamic, complex social arrangements" (Rogers, 2000, p. 51). Historically, qualitative research has been associated with various social science disciplines: cultural or social anthropology, qualitative sociology, history, organizational behavior, and so on. Despite psychology's more recent preference for objectivity and mathematical models, major contributions to that field were discovered through classical qualitative case studies—for example, those conducted by Breuer and Freud (1885/1955), Erikson (1958, 1963), Piaget (1948), Allport (1937), and Lewin (1948). Qualitative research also has clear roots in certain philosophical traditions, notably *phenomenology* (questioning the structure and essence of lived experience) and *hermeneutics* (questioning the conditions that shape interpretations of human acts or products).

These well-established approaches to qualitative research draw on theoretical bodies of knowledge that are traditionally associated with the formal, academic world. Recently, researchers have begun to use approaches to analyzing text that derive from literary criticism and cultural studies. In the latter, *text* refers to more than written words. Construed quite broadly, text embraces all utterances or artifacts of a culture. Writ somewhat smaller, it means the authored words, written and oral, produced in particular social milieu and therefore available for analysis. Yet other researchers conduct studies that espouse explicitly ideological positions, such as feminist, critical theory, postcolonial, or queer studies. These newer approaches challenge the assumption that knowledge is generated exclusively through the traditional academic disciplines. The goal of these researchers is to validate alternative sources of knowledge; they often write about creating opportunities for those previously excluded from formal, academic discourse, such as women, people of color, or gay people, to share their experiences and insights (often critical of the status quo). The qualitative inquiry umbrella covers a continuum from more traditional approaches (often associated with an academic discipline) to cutting-edge experimental approaches.

In subsequent chapters, we more fully describe the various traditions that have shaped qualitative inquiry, and we discuss the assumptions driving these various approaches. For now, we depict what the different members of the qualitative research community have in common. We ask the following questions:

- What are the characteristics of qualitative research?

- What perspectives do qualitative researchers share?

- What stances do qualitative researchers typically take?

- How do they go about their work?

First, to situate the discussion of characteristics, we note that the approaches to research this book presents differ from research approaches that are based on the traditional quantitative *epistemology* (way of knowing the world). Most of us have been socialized to accept a generally positivist view of science that asserts a physical and social reality independent of those who experience it, a reality that can be tested and defined objectively (i.e., free from any distortions brought by observer bias). Positivist views argue that how we learn about reality is by testing hypotheses (predictive statements grounded in a theory or speculation about how two or more variables are related) through experiments, quasi-experiments, or correlations. Researchers using these designs assume that they can control (or seek to control) the various influences affecting the variables by defining the conditions in which an intervention or treatment is applied. They also may compare groups that receive an intervention or treatment with other groups that do not (these are called control groups). Participants (called subjects) are chosen through statistically determined methods. Such research seeks outcomes that are measurable with a number, such as a score, rating, or amount.

In contrast, qualitative research represents a very different, more interpretivist, epistemology that does not test hypotheses or believe that researchers can control aspects of the worlds they are exploring. We elaborate the more common characteristics shared by qualitative researchers next.

COMMON CHARACTERISTICS

Qualitative research (and its practice) typically embodies several common characteristics. In this section, we elaborate several, but we recognize that our list may not be exhaustive. Central to qualitative research is its *orientation toward the natural world*. Qualitative researchers gather data about sensory experience: what people (including researchers themselves) see, feel, hear, taste, and smell. As noted previously, qualitative research shares this focus on the empirical world with quantitative forms of inquiry. Qualitative research, however, stands in stark contrast to experimental laboratory conditions, probabilistic sampling strategies, and quasi-experimental designs that use control groups to compare intervention effects. Qualitative research developed in part as a critique of the artificial settings of the laboratory, searching for ways to systematically understand people's lived experiences. Doing research in the field, rather than in the laboratory or through a mailed questionnaire, became an important, complementary, and legitimate approach to social science.

Qualitative researchers go to the people; they do not extricate people from their everyday worlds. Qualitative researchers work in the field, face-to-face with real people. A second characteristic is that they try to understand people through multiple methods. These methods are interactive and humanistic. Qualitative researchers talk with people, watch and listen as folks go about their everyday tasks, read documents and records, and look at physical space, clothing, tools, and decorations. These are known more formally as the primary techniques of interviewing, observing, gathering documents, and examining material culture, which we will discuss in Chapter 7.

Moreover, qualitative researchers value the messiness of the lived world. They make a sustained focus on context integral to their work and assume that a detailed understanding of human experience is gained by exploring these complexities. Life occurs in context—that is, the natural setting in which the people work, study, play, eat, drink, love—in fact, *live*. Within these contexts, qualitative researchers are interested in individuals, groups, and interactions; they seek depth rather than breadth. A classroom context, for example, includes the students, the teacher, furniture and materials, and maybe the dust on the shelves. Classroom context also has external factors (e.g., the principal, the other classes, students and teachers, resources, and even the weather outside) that have an impact on what teachers and students do inside the room. As well, context is shaped by

What is epistemology?
- What is knowledge?
- How do we know what we know?
- What do we take as evidence?
- What convinces us that something is "true"?

macro forces: federal policies, state regulations, community expectations, global climate change, and so on. Within these nested contexts, however, the individual or groups of individuals are central.

Again, this stance is distinct from experimental conditions in which the messiness of everyday life is controlled through processes of *randomization* (sampling subjects so that each person has an equal chance to be selected) and *standardization* (ensuring that experimental conditions are precisely the same). These processes blur individual uniqueness as they seek generalizations. Qualitative researchers' respect for the individual in context draws them to look at social worlds holistically, as interactive, complex systems rather than as discrete variables that can be measured and manipulated statistically. They describe and interpret rather than measure and predict.

Qualitative researchers try not to impose a rigid, a priori framework on the social world because they want to learn what constitutes important questions from the participants themselves. Qualitative researchers tend to avoid constructing formal hypotheses prior to the study, but they *do* bring a conceptual framework and guiding questions. This conceptual framework, however, can be—and most often is—changed, modified, and refined once the researcher is in the field as other, perhaps more intriguing, questions are discovered. In addition, the specific data-gathering actions can be altered, depending on what makes sense for the setting, the participants, and the researcher's growing knowledge about the project. Another characteristic, then, is the emergent nature of qualitative research.

Qualitative research is fundamentally interpretive; that is, we offer explanations for objects or social actions. In contrast with quantitative approaches that attempt to control and predict, qualitative research focuses on description, analysis, and interpretation with the aim of making sense of the social world. This sense-making reflects a tension between the interpretations given to objects, interactions, and words by participants and the interpretations made by the researcher. The experience is analogous to the *hermeneutic circle* entered when reading (see, e.g., Gallagher, 1992; Rennie, 2012; Walsh, 2008); readers interpret author's presentations of situations through written texts. Similarly, qualitative researchers interactively connect participants, objects of study, and themselves.

The qualitative researcher recognizes that what she is observing, reading, or hearing has a particular meaning to the participants; at the same time, she assumes that understanding (analyzing and interpreting) and representing (interpreting and writing about) what she is learning are filtered through her own personal biography that is situated in a specific sociopolitical, historical moment (context). Through this personal lens, the researcher tries to make sense of what she has learned. She asks "What do I see (her understanding of what is happening)?" "How do participants see this (her understanding of how participants are interpreting what is happening)?" "What does it mean in a larger context?" Her conceptual framework suggests patterns and helps connect her interpretations to other instances. Field notes and snippets of interview transcriptions do not speak for themselves. They must be interpreted in ways that are thoughtful, ethical, and politically astute. The resulting tale of the field (Van Maanen, 1988) is, ultimately, the researcher's story about the stories people have told her (Geertz, 1983).

Historically, qualitative researchers tried to be as objective as possible in studying the lives of people, just like their quantitative counterparts. As the field evolved, however, it became clear that the researcher himself is critically important in conducting the study. Because the researcher enters the world of the participants, he may shape that world in significant ways. Another characteristic of qualitative research, then, is that researchers systematically reflect on how they affect the ongoing flow of everyday life and are affected by it.

However, researchers do more than affect ongoing social life: Their weltanschauung (worldview) shapes the entire project. From early curiosity all the way to writing the final report, your personal biography is the lens through which you see the world. Gender, race and ethnicity, age, sexual orientation, politics, and beliefs all affect any research project. Qualitative researchers recognize the importance of reflecting on who they are and how this shapes their research. Yet another characteristic, then, of qualitative research is an exquisite sensitivity to personal biography. Unlike the allegedly objective social scientist, the qualitative researcher values his unique perspective as a source of understanding rather than as something to be cleansed from the study. We'll see how personal experience and conceptual frameworks work in the process as our three characters develop their projects in this book. Marla, for example, draws on her experiences working with families and health. Anthony recollects working on urban poverty projects that received negative evaluations. Ruth is an avid athlete. These aspects of their biographies alert our characters to personal predispositions and frames of mind that they bring to their studies. This sensitivity is a simultaneous awareness of self and other and of the interplay between the two, captured by the term *reflexivity* (discussed further in Chapter 2).

Qualitative researchers rely on complex reasoning processes. These have traditionally been described as relying exclusively on principles of *inductive* logic—reasoning from the particular to more general statements to theory—rather than also incorporating *deductive* reasoning, which starts with theory and tests its applicability. Our stance is that this characterization of qualitative researchers as inductive rather than deductive oversimplifies and trivializes the complexity of any research, especially qualitative research. Qualitative researchers typically begin a study with a well-thought-out conceptual framework that focuses and shapes their decisions, but this framework is flexible. In fact, qualitative research recognizes that any individual enters a context with a personal perspective that shapes—and is shaped by—perceptions. Recall the discussion of the views of Aristotle and Plato. We argue that all inquiry proceeds through a complex, nonlinear process of induction, deduction, reflection, inspiration, and just plain old hard thinking. This can be conceptualized as *researcher praxis* (see Schön, 1983)—that is, the back-and-forth between theoretical ideas, data, and the researcher's reflection on both. A final feature of qualitative research, then, is a reliance on sophisticated reasoning that is multifaceted and iterative, moving back-and-forth between the parts and the whole (Figure 1.2).

The qualitative researcher . . .

- views the social world holistically.
- systematically reflects on who she is.
- is sensitive to personal biography.
- uses complex reasoning.
- conducts systematic inquiry.

FIGURE 1.2   Deductive and Inductive Reasoning

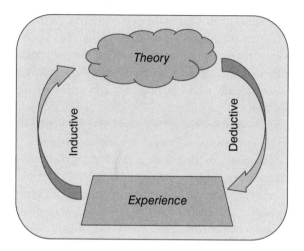

Finally, we claim that good qualitative research is *systematic research* at the same time that it is interpretive, holistic, contextual, and messy. It is systematic because a qualitative researcher follows a deliberate, conscious process of making decisions and explicating those decisions so that others may understand how the study was done, assess its adequacy and trustworthiness, and critique it. Systematic inquiry produces new information. When this information is used to improve the human condition, it becomes knowledge.

To recap, qualitative research is a complex field of inquiry that draws on many diverse assumptions but embraces a few common characteristics and perspectives. A qualitative research project takes place in the field; relies on multiple methods for gathering data; and calls on you to be pragmatic, flexible, politically aware, ethical, and self-reflective. Fundamentally interpretive and emergent, qualitative research is systematic inquiry that is characterized by a stance of openness, curiosity, and respect. On the practical side, qualitative research is labor-intensive, time-consuming, frustrating, and challenging. There are no formulaic rules to follow, only guiding principles gleaned from direct experience, including reading the literature, studying with others, and the actual doing. Moreover, many find it exhilarating and deeply moving, and it can change your worldview.

TYPICAL PURPOSES AND OVERALL APPROACHES

We began this chapter by asserting that qualitative research starts with questions and results in learning. The learning that ultimately occurs, however, is shaped by the questions posed early on and then modified during the research, as appropriate. The guiding questions, in turn, shape the specific research activities. Both elements (research questions and specific research activities) are guided by the researcher's overall purpose in conducting the study. We suggest you ask yourself the following important questions in the early stages of thinking through a research effort:

- What do you hope to accomplish?

- What are your primary goals of the study?

- How will this study contribute to improving the human condition?

Although researchers approach their studies with many and varied purposes, our experience suggests that these can be usefully synthesized into three broad ones:

- Describing

- Comparing and contrasting

- Forecasting

All three purposes can lead to theory building or refinement, improvements in practice, and policy change.

For the first purpose, we claim that there is no such thing as pure description; the very act of describing requires analysis and interpretation. To achieve this purpose, you might want to describe an interesting social initiative in and of itself. This could be a public health clinic in a village in Kenya that serves AIDS-affected children. The researcher's purpose is to describe analytically, fully, and completely, this clinic: its elements, processes, and people. If various initiatives serving AIDS-affected children have already been richly described (by this researcher or others), the researcher might want to compare and contrast two examples in order to understand the differences in juxtaposition. The comparison might involve evaluation or judgment about effectiveness. The researcher might compare an intensive summer program with the activities available at the clinic. Comparing and contrasting these initiatives would clarify features of both, leading to a more informed judgment of merit and worth (Rallis & Rossman, 2001, 2002). Finally, our researcher might want to conduct a small-scale experiment in which he integrated features of the clinic and the summer camp program into a new school-based initiative to raise HIV/AIDS awareness and to serve those affected. His purpose in conducting this experiment would be to learn what works well in order to forecast, or predict, what could be successfully implemented more widely.

Analytic description, comparison, and forecasting are complex, interrelated cognitive activities that are seldom performed singularly or in a linear process. All three activities are related and may be used iteratively. Fundamental is the notion of describing the phenomenon of interest as fully as possible; this stands as the grounding for subsequent comparing or forecasting. Through a similar logic, making comparisons across examples of a program yields rich descriptions and deep understanding that inform judgments. And forecasting under what circumstances a specific program may work well and where it may struggle extends the range of insights into programmatic descriptions.

Analytic descriptive studies . . .

- describe and analyze social phenomena and contribute to understanding about them.

Evaluations or policy studies . . .

- compare with a standard to determine merit and worth and thus inform decision making.

Action research . . .

- takes reasoned action to improve programs or practices and thus to learn and then forecast what works well and what does not.

The accepted wisdom in the research enterprise is that researchers, especially beginners, should not choose methods for data collection and analysis according to a quantitative or qualitative distinction but rather according to what they want to learn and the questions that will lead them toward that learning. Although this wisdom has merit, we have noted that researchers' training and psychological predilections incline them toward particular sorts of questions that demand particular sorts of research methods (see Creswell, 2009). When the most appropriate methods to achieve the purpose of describing, comparing and contrasting, or forecasting require words, sounds, images, and the judicious use of numbers rather than measurements or correlations, and when the phenomenon or case is best observed in its natural context, you should use qualitative methods. Thus, qualitative researchers commonly conduct analytic, descriptive studies of groups or individuals. Their comparative studies often take the form of evaluations or policy studies. Their small-scale experiments are likely to be action research. Our use of the term *action research* is inclusive rather than specialized, stipulating that participatory research, which is explicitly ideological, be included along with other forms of action research.

We argue that these three broad purposes or goals for research map fairly neatly onto three overall approaches: (1) analytic descriptive studies, (2) evaluation or policy studies, and (3) action research. Each overall approach has an embedded purpose: to describe, to compare and contrast to a standard or to past or other similar instances, or to describe and forecast. Within each approach, you may choose to implement the study with a variety of data collection methods that will further the goal for the research. Moreover, as described below, a qualitative research study may draw on more than one approach.

THE CHARACTERS' CHOICES

Our characters offer concrete variations of the three purposes and overall approaches discussed above: Ruth chooses to focus on analytic description for her study. Anthony evaluates a program, using both description and comparison. And Marla's collaborative action research study describes, explores relationships between phenomena, and forecasts potential actions. The questions they pursue are shaped, to a considerable extent, by the overall purpose of their studies.

Descriptive Studies

Ruth wants to understand how to better the lives of children with disabilities. For her, understanding comes through describing their lives, so she chooses to conduct a descriptive study. She soon discovers, however, that description is seldom neutral. Eventually, she develops rich interpretive narratives depicting the children's activities and feelings, as well as those of the people with whom they interact. She explores their struggles, triumphs, courage, and ordinariness. The result is a compelling story about the world she has explored. Descriptive studies depict complex social processes and understandings through detailed analytic description. Their purpose is typically enlightenment, seeking to display deep insights.

Evaluation or Policy Studies

Seeking to inform and influence decision making or planning, **Anthony** chooses an evaluation study. He is hired as a consultant to evaluate the activities of a community arts program. The funding agency wants to know if the program is accomplishing its goals of creating experiences of the arts for a wider, more diverse community audience. To do this, Anthony needs to learn both about the program itself and about the standards for such programs. He might have to read about other community art programs to learn what is possible.

Evaluation research provides formative or summative information that describes and assesses the effectiveness of a program. Formative information is used to improve the program; summative information contributes to a final decision about its value and effectiveness in producing intended changes. Policy studies provide information that helps governmental, institutional, or organizational authorities make policy decisions and develop programs to implement those policies. As in Anthony's case, evaluators or policy researchers are usually contracted by an organization or agency to conduct the study and prepare a report.

Action Research

Marla's questions, which emphasize stakeholder participation and change in practice, lead her to action research. She facilitates a group of women from the clinic's catchment area to identify and describe current problematic conditions; their learning will lead them to advocate for changes in practice. Action research is "the study of a social situation with a view to improving the quality of action within" (Elliot & Keynes, 1991, p. 69). The process involves analysis, reflection, taking action, assessing the effect of those actions, further reflection leading to new action, and so on—in a cyclical manner. Practitioners may study their own practices to improve them. Groups may undertake projects to understand better and improve their environments. In the former, an individual may work alone; in the latter, collective, collaborative, and self-reflective inquiry is undertaken by a group. Their purpose is to promote social change by transforming structures through the influence of the information collected. Marla and the women's group in her project aim to use their results to try to bring changes in access to health care for women living in poor urban settings.

We elaborate their approaches throughout the book as Ruth, Anthony, and Marla design and conduct their studies.

WAYS OF USING RESEARCH

Anthony, Ruth, and Marla embark on qualitative studies because they want to learn something about the social world through close interaction with others. Marla begins with a hunch she wants to explore: She suspects that the health care system does not adequately address women's issues. More specifically, she is puzzled about something she has seen: She noticed that women who visited a clinic where she worked came for initial visits but then seldom returned for follow-up. What might account for this? How could this pattern be changed?

Ruth, in contrast, is simply curious about children with various types of disabilities. She asks, What are their lives like? How do they navigate through a world designed for able-bodied people? How do they feel—included or left out? On the other hand, Anthony wants to know how decision makers use information. He is particularly interested in how they use evaluations to make funding decisions. Each of our characters begins with a question, a curiosity, and an intriguing puzzle. Use is built into the questions both Marla and Anthony ask. Ruth soon recognizes the potential for her descriptions of children to be extraordinarily useful for many audiences.

The ultimate goal of qualitative research is learning—that is, the transformation of data into information that can be used. We argue that use can be considered an ethical mandate, that any study should be designed with potential uses in mind. Usefulness, however, is not a simple unitary concept. We suggest four perspectives for thinking about use: instrumental, enlightenment, symbolic, and transformative. These perspectives serve as lenses to understand how the results of a particular study may be used. Different audiences might use the same written report in different ways—for example, one instrumentally and the other symbolically. You cannot dictate or control the uses that various audiences may make of your study, as Ruth notes in the beginning vignette. You do, however, need to be aware that the study *will* be used, one way or another, and sometimes those uses are different from the ones you intend.

Instrumental Use

People commonly think of use as instrumental—that is, "when a decision or action follows, at least in part [from the research]" (Patton, 2002, p. 332). Specific information is applied to a particular problem. A problem exists or a goal is sought; research is conducted to determine a good solution or approach to reach the goal. For example, a private school hires a research firm to discover why enrollment has dropped, a service agency surveys its community to identify unmet needs, or an international nongovernmental organization wants to know if funds spent to build new schools in Sierra Leone result in higher school attendance rates. The findings of research, then, are developed into knowledge—that is, with plans to implement in practice. Knowledge generation and knowledge utilization are directly linked.

Instrumental use:
- knowledge is applied to specific problems.
- knowledge provides solutions or recommendations.

This perspective on use is linear and assumes a rational decision-making process in which decision makers have clear goals, seek direct attainment of these goals, and have access to relevant research knowledge. As Patton (1997) notes, instrumental use usually requires planning for use before the data are even collected. The researcher works with the intended users to develop relevant questions from which data collection and analysis flow. Evaluation and policy studies, practitioner inquiry, and action research are apt for instrumental use if the researcher and the user work together to produce technical knowledge. For these reasons, Marla's and Anthony's studies are likely to be used instrumentally.

Enlightenment Use

In our experience, the links between knowledge generation and utilization are seldom clear and direct. Research findings often serve to enlighten the user (Weiss, 1998). Knowledge accumulates, contributing to a gradual reorientation of the user's thought and action. Specific information cannot be identified as the basis for a particular decision or action. Moreover, one piece of information may contribute to several decisions. We imagine this model of use as a pool of accumulated knowledge into which the user may dip when making a decision.

From the enlightenment perspective, users base their decisions on knowledge, but the specific information is not important. In her classic work on use, Weiss (1980) describes knowledge as providing a background of working understandings and ideas that "creep" (p. 381) into decision deliberations. Policy actions are not decided in a clear-cut, brisk style with obvious connections among problems, people, and alternative choices. Instead, policy "accretes" (p. 382). Research findings become part of the general culture, incorporated into accepted concepts, beliefs, and values that naturally influence any decision making in that arena.

Detailed findings become generalizations that eventually are accepted as truths and come to shape the ways in which people think. In a classic example, Rein (1970) cites a series of controversial and threatening reports about conditions in a mental hospital. The reports were not used by the hospital staff, perhaps because the staff themselves were criticized. The research findings were initially not compatible with the decision makers' values or goals. The information was, however, picked up by health care advocates to challenge existing beliefs. The result was a gradual change in the operation of mental institutions in general. Rein's point is that, although the information was not used in a directly instrumental sense, it did shape the policy decision arena. The findings worked their way into public consciousness, eventually overturning established values and patterns of thought. Following this logic, Ruth's descriptive study of children with disabilities could serve to enlighten education officials. Similarly, accumulated knowledge can serve to improve practice by enhancing understanding of that practice. If Anthony is able to identify and label particularly effective elements in the program he evaluates, that knowledge is likely to contribute to program improvement.

Symbolic Use

Research findings may also support a variety of symbolic uses (Bolman & Deal, 2013) by reinforcing values and beliefs or by encouraging users to reconfigure old patterns and to see familiar pictures in new lights. Because explanation and understanding are

Enlightenment use . . .

- contributes to general knowledge.
- enhances understanding.
- offers heuristic insight.

important human needs (Maslowe, 1970), we tend to look for patterns and create narratives to make sense of our worlds. Qualitative research can build explanations, making complex, ambiguous experiences and beliefs comprehensible and communicable to others. Creating and disseminating detailed analytic descriptions can evoke deep cultural values and serve to legitimize events or actions within that culture. For example, the conduct and completion of Ruth's study can, in and of itself, serve to foster public acceptance of children with disabilities. Research results also may serve to surface deeply disturbing actions that a culture publicly masks. As well as Rein's research on mental institutions, Tracey Kidder's *Old Friends* (1993) provides an example. His rich descriptions of residents of a nursing home are evocative of aging in America. Similarly, *A Beautiful Mind* (Nasar, 1998) reveals the mysteries of schizophrenia, building the public's understanding and perhaps acceptance.

Furthermore, because qualitative research directly involves the participants, the process in and of itself generates stories. People talk, often underground, about the study and the routines involved in its conduct (see, e.g., Van Maanen's *Tales of the Field*, 1988). This "talk" becomes part of cultural knowledge that offers new and often satisfying interpretations of familiar events. These interpretations become myths—stories that offer explanations and reveal shared understandings. We experienced this effect during a long-term study of cardiopulmonary resuscitation training; we heard stories about our preliminary findings. Participants turned our preliminary findings into stories they retold time and again as explanations for the way things were done in the training and as support for the training's continuance.

As researchers, however, we feel obligated to ensure that the symbolic use does not preclude other uses. Once we evaluated a school restructuring initiative. The goals and objectives of the program were admirable, but little or nothing was happening to implement them. Program staff were talking but not acting. Our formative evaluation reports revealed the problem, but the program manager simply thanked us, checked whether those that required evaluation had been completed, and filed them away. Because we felt that the program had the potential to make a difference for children (and consumed a substantial number of federal dollars), we wanted more than superficial symbolic use in this case. We took steps to end the study. Fortunately, a new manager was coincidentally appointed, and she established with us a strong and productive relationship that facilitated the use of our evaluation information.

Transformative Use

Research also has the potential to change lives. The researchers (and often the participants, as well) hope that the process of inquiry, action, and reflection—and the knowledge it generates—will be transformative, altering some aspect of society. The process and results can become a source of empowerment for participants' immediate daily lives and may affect larger oppressive social relations. The participants are not generating knowledge simply to inform or enlighten an academic community. They are

---

Symbolic use . . .

- provides new ways of expressing phenomena.
- crystallizes beliefs or values.
- reconceptualizes public perceptions.

collaboratively producing knowledge to improve their work and their lives. Participants do the research about their own settings, and the person in the official researcher role facilitates. Transformative use grows out of Paolo Freire's (1970) *Pedagogy of the Oppressed,* the belief that the reflection and action implicit in knowledge can free practice. Freire viewed research as a form of social action. His research in the 1960s and 1970s on Chilean literacy involved members of oppressed communities in identifying issues of vital importance. These collaborative discoveries became a foundation for literacy instruction and for community empowerment. The two purposes of the research were to help participants acquire literacy and to help them improve their lives.

Today, participatory action research and feminist studies offer examples of hoped-for transformative uses. The women who collaborate with Marla in her study become savvy in regularly using clinic services. At the same time, they realize that they avoided the clinic because of sustained and pervasive patterns of subtle discrimination against them due to language, gender, and income levels. Their discoveries encourage them to try to change these patterns for other women. In this light, the research of Marla and her collaborators may well be transformative.

In summary, researchers' questions lead them to collect data. They arrange these data into meaningful patterns. The information becomes knowledge through its instrumental, enlightenment, symbolic, or transformative application—or all of these. The qualitative researcher, then, is in the business of generating knowledge that can serve the society studied, whether through immediate impact on a decision, through shaping people's understandings of a complex topic, through interpreting and reinterpreting the meaning of events, or through actions that can empower the participants.

DISPOSITIONS AND SKILLS

Marla, Ruth, and Anthony are setting out to generate knowledge by learning in the field. They will design studies; collect, analyze, and interpret their data; and present their findings. The process is an active one, and it is not simple. They will face one decision after another for which few prescribed rules exist. Their tasks are not tightly specified, and they have few explicit steps to follow because knowledge creation is not straightforward and linear. *They learn by doing.*

By definition, knowledge is iterative; it builds on itself. Therefore, the research process is *heuristic*—a discovering experience. Heuristic inquiry, from the Greek for "discover," implies personal insight and tacit knowing (Polanyi, 1962). Tacit knowing is deep inner understanding. It is unarticulated knowledge that derives from experience. Out of this knowing come the hunches that drive the questions we articulate. Qualitative research recognizes the heuristic aspect of knowledge creation and works with deeply subjectivist assumptions, as discussed in Chapter 2.

As they learn in the field, Marla, Ruth, and Anthony must be exquisitely conscious of the contexts surrounding their studies. They will come to respect that each interprets

Transformative use . . .

- occurs when participants take actions that empower them to change oppressive structures and practices.

his or her data from a particular perspective, standpoint, and situation. They will learn that each researcher can report only his own discoveries or represent what he believes to be the perspectives of the people he studied. They will not attempt to be "objective" by seeking the one "true" answer. Their processes, then, are *hermeneutic* (or interpretive), leading each to choose from among possible answers.

Ultimately, they will stop asking for a rulebook and learn to trust the process. They will seek meaning in the rich descriptions they create from what they see, hear, and read. They will learn to suspend disbelief and to cope with ambiguity. Their initial questions shape early data collection; this reshapes the questions that, in turn, call for further data. Their decisions cascade, and data form patterns of information that can become knowledge. *They learn by doing.*

Marla, Anthony, and Ruth start with curiosity; the first step in qualitative research is to want to discover something. They will need to be perceptive and to develop competence in certain basic skills: interviewing, observing, analyzing, interpreting, and preparing an engaging presentation of what they have learned. They face, however, a conundrum. They need to know everything about qualitative research to do it, but they can best learn how to do it by doing it! This conundrum was expressed by Anthony in the vignette at the beginning of this chapter. What will help them through this conundrum are certain dispositions in addition to specific skills. The skills are what they learn by doing; the dispositions create the propensity to learn and enact the skills. These dispositions include the following:

- Comfort with ambiguity

- Capacity to make reasoned decisions and to articulate the logic behind those decisions

- Deep interpersonal or emotional sensitivity

- Ethical sensitivity of potential consequences to individuals and groups

- Political sensitivity

- Perseverance and self-discipline

As our characters work in the field, these dispositions and skills become part of their research praxis—intuitive and reasoned actions that make them proficient and ethical qualitative researchers.

In this chapter, we have described qualitative research as an emergent, interpretive, holistic, reflexive, and iterative process that uses interactive and humanistic methods. It is conducted in the real world. Qualitative researchers are learners who are systematic and rigorous while sensitive to the ways in which their own identities and life histories shape their projects. As learners, they generate knowledge that various audiences use instrumentally, to enlighten, symbolically, to transform, or all of these. Qualitative researchers use strategies such as descriptive studies, evaluation and policy studies, and action research. Fundamentally, they develop the dispositions and skills to live and work in this ambiguous and uncertain world.

OVERVIEW OF THE BOOK

The purpose of this book is to introduce you to qualitative research. In this chapter, you have read about the characteristics, use, strategies and overall approaches, and dispositions and skills of good practice.

In Chapter 2, our focus falls on the person doing the research. As a learner, you—the researcher—make assumptions about what you know and what you accept as truth. You will learn about becoming reflexive. This chapter presents you as a constructor of knowledge and explores the worldviews within which researchers operate. Chapter 3 discusses broad standards for judging the credibility, rigor, and worth of qualitative research as well as for ensuring ethical practice. These elements of the trustworthiness of a study are not divorced from the assumptions that undergird your study. This chapter includes a discussion of human subject review and institutional reviews boards.

Chapter 4 presents the different genres of research that shape various methodological strategies. We describe how choices for designs and methods draw from three broad qualitative research traditions and discuss a few others. Chapter 5 examines how an initial curiosity or intriguing problem of practice turns into a conceptual framework for a study. We show how you develop this framework from your ideas and then how you design a study.

Chapters 6 through 10 take you through the process of implementing a study, dealing with entry, data collection, analysis, and interpretation. Texts on qualitative research usually separate data collection into chapters on the two primary techniques: observation and interviewing. Because we find that separation artificial, and because researchers also use other techniques, we create different distinctions. Chapter 6 discusses access and introduction to the research site or participants. Chapter 7 demonstrates how data are collected through looking, asking, listening, and reading. To illustrate the products of data gathering, Chapter 8 offers sets of data collected by our characters with our critical commentary. Chapter 9 discusses several questions that often arise during fieldwork. Chapter 10 then explicates the principles of data analysis and interpretation. In concert with Chapter 8, Chapter 11 presents examples of our characters' analyses.

Finally, if the research is to be used by anyone other than you, the information must be presented so that appropriate audiences can access and understand it. Chapter 12 discusses how you connect with audiences through various ways of reporting the information. At the end of most chapters, we provide learning activities that you may want to use with your community of practice, and we also provide additional suggestions for further reading.

ACTIVITIES FOR YOUR COMMUNITY OF PRACTICE

Study Questions

- What are the distinguishing characteristics of qualitative research?

- In what ways can research findings be used?

- What are the essential strategies of qualitative research?

- How does qualitative research rely on inductive and deductive reasoning processes?

- What topics might you want to study?

Small-Group or Dyad Activities

What Does a Qualitative Researcher Do?

Take 5 to 7 minutes to write down what you imagine yourself doing when you do qualitative research. Introduce yourself to your immediate neighbor and share your thoughts. Report to the whole group.

Describe an Everyday Artifact

We each live in a world that is familiar to us yet may not be familiar to others who enter it. Using a living space that is important to you (e.g., your own room, apartment, or office), choose an everyday object that is a part of your life. Write a detailed description about this object but do not name it. Take 10 minutes. Share this in dyads, comparing and contrasting the focus of the description (e.g., color, texture, function, composition), level of detail, and choice of objects.

Role-Play on Use

Read carefully one of your assigned supplemental readings. Divide into four groups, each representing one of the four uses of research: (1) instrumental, (2) enlightenment, (3) symbolic, and (4) emancipatory. Each group's task is to plan a strategy for the assigned use. For example, how could the study be used instrumentally by policymakers? How could it be used symbolically in a marketing campaign? How could it enlighten consumers? How could it serve to emancipate workers? Discuss and create a role play demonstrating this use (spend about 20 minutes). Present it to the rest of the class.

FURTHER READINGS

Qualitative Research

Corbin, J., & Strauss, A. (2014). *Basics of qualitative research: Techniques and procedures for developing grounded theory* (4th ed.). Thousand Oaks, CA: Sage.

Flick, U. (2014). *An introduction to qualitative research* (5th ed.). Thousand Oaks, CA: Sage.

Given, L. M. (2016). *100 questions (and answers) about qualitative research*. Thousand Oaks, CA: Sage.

Marshall, C., & Rossman, G. B. (2016). *Designing qualitative research* (6th ed.). Thousand Oaks, CA: Sage.

Patton, M. Q. (2015). *Qualitative research & evaluation methods: Integrating theory and practice* (4th ed.). Thousand Oaks, CA: Sage.

Saldaña, J. (2015). *Thinking qualitatively: Methods of mind*. Thousand Oaks, CA: Sage.

Stake, R. E. (2010). *Qualitative research: Studying how things work*. New York, NY: Guildford Press.

Taylor, S. J., Bogdan, R., & Devault, M. (2015). *Introduction to qualitative research methods: A guidebook and resource* (4th ed.). New York, NY: Wiley.

Yin, R. K. (2015). *Qualitative research from start to finish* (2nd ed.). New York, NY: Guilford Press.

Use

Eisner, E. W., & Peshkin, A. (Eds.). (1990). *Qualitative inquiry in education: The continuing debate*. New York, NY: Teachers College Press. (See Part IV, "Uses of Qualitative Inquiry," pp. 301–364.)

Jenkins, M. J. (2014). The use of qualitative methods and practitioners-as-authors in journal publications of police research. *Police Practice & Research, 16*(6), 499–511.

Kline, R. B. (2008). *Becoming a behavioral science researcher: A guide to producing research that matters*. New York, NY: Guilford Press.

Lindblom, C. (1990). *Inquiry and change*. New Haven, CT: Yale University Press.

Lindblom, C. E., & Cohen, D. K. (1979). *Usable knowledge*. New Haven, CT: Yale University Press.

Patton, M. Q. (2008). *Utilization-focused evaluation* (4th ed.). Thousand Oaks, CA: Sage.

Patton, M. Q. (2010). *Developmental evaluation: Applying complexity concepts to enhance innovation and use*. New York, NY: Guilford Press.

Patton, M. Q. (2012). *Essentials of utilization-focused evaluation*. Thousand Oaks, CA: Sage.

Weisner, T. S. (2014). Why qualitative and ethnographic methods are essential for understanding family life. In S. M. McHale, P. Amato, & A. Booth (Eds.), *Emerging methods in family research* (pp. 163–178). New York, NY: Springer International.

Analytic Descriptive Studies

Atkinson, P. A., & Delamont, S. (Eds.). (2008). *Representing ethnography: Reading, writing and rhetoric in qualitative research*. London, England: Sage.

Bogdan, R. C., & Biklen, S. K. (2006). *Qualitative research in education: An introduction to theory and methods* (5th ed.). Boston, MA: Allyn & Bacon.

Crang, M., & Cook, I. (2007). *Doing ethnographies*. Thousand Oaks, CA: Sage.

Emerson, R. M., Fretz, R. I., & Shaw, L. L. (2011). *Writing ethnographic fieldnotes* (2nd ed.). Chicago, IL: University of Chicago Press.

Erickson, F. (1986). Qualitative methods in research on teaching. In M. C. Whittrock (Ed.), *Handbook of research on teaching* (3rd ed., pp. 119–161). New York, NY: Macmillan.

Madden, R. (2012). *Being ethnographic: A guide to the theory and practice of ethnography* (2nd ed.). Thousand Oaks, CA: Sage.

Madison, D. S. (2011). *Critical ethnography: Method, ethics, and performance* (2nd ed.). Thousand Oaks, CA: Sage.

Van Maanen, J. (2011). *Tales of the field: On writing ethnography* (2nd ed.). Chicago, IL: University of Chicago Press.

Ybema, S., Yanow, D., Wels, H., & Kamsteeg, F. (2009). *Organizational ethnography: Studying the complexity of everyday life.* London, England: Sage.

Evaluation and Policy Studies

Chelimsky, E., & Shaddish, W. R. (Eds.). (1997). *Evaluation for the 21st century: A handbook.* Thousand Oaks, CA: Sage.

Goodyear, L., Barela, E., Jewiss, J., & Usinger, J. (2014). *Qualitative inquiry in evaluation: From theory to practice.* San Francisco, CA: Jossey-Bass.

Greene, J. C. (2000). Understanding social programs through evaluation. In N. K. Denzin & Y. S. Lincoln (Eds.), *Handbook of qualitative research* (2nd ed., pp. 981–999). Thousand Oaks, CA: Sage.

Patton, M. Q. (2015). *Qualitative research and evaluation methods* (4th ed.). Thousand Oaks, CA: Sage.

Stone, D. (2011). *Policy paradox: The art of political decision making* (3rd ed.). New York, NY: W. W. Norton.

Weiss, C. H. (1998). *Evaluation: Methods for studying programs and policies.* Upper Saddle River, NJ: Prentice Hall.

Action Research and Participatory Action Research

Greenwood, D. J., & Levin, M. (2007). *Introduction to action research: Social research for social change* (2nd ed.). Thousand Oaks, CA: Sage.

Kemmis, S., & McTaggart, R. (2005). Participatory action research: Communicative action in the public sphere. In N. K. Denzin & Y. S. Lincoln (Eds.), *The SAGE handbook of qualitative research* (3rd ed., pp. 567–605). Thousand Oaks, CA: Sage.

Kincheloe, J. L. (1991). *Teachers as researchers: Qualitative inquiry as a path to empowerment.* New York, NY: Falmer Press.

McIntyre, A. (2008). *Participatory action research.* Thousand Oaks, CA: Sage.

McNiff, J., & Whitehead, J. (2009). *Doing and writing action research.* London, England: Sage.

Reason, P. W., & Bradbury-Huang, H. (2013). *The SAGE handbook of action research: Participative inquiry and practice.* Thousand Oaks, CA: Sage.

Stringer, E. T. (2013). *Action research: A handbook for practitioners* (4th ed.). Thousand Oaks, CA: Sage.

Van der Riet, M. (2008). Participatory research and the philosophy of social science: Beyond the moral imperative. *Qualitative Inquiry, 14*(4), 546–565.

2

The Researcher as Learner

Ruth, Marla, and Anthony have begun to grapple with the many facets of learning about qualitative research. They are considering the questions they want to ask, they are thinking about designs (setting, participants, and ways of gathering data), and they are flirting with their perspectives—the ways they think about research in general and their projects specifically. These are all significant topics to ponder and make decisions about. The challenges they face, at this early stage, are to incorporate new information from class, juxtapose this with assumptions they hold about truth and the social world, and think through their perspectives on their research projects.

All this entails reflecting on their own *personal epistemologies*, the ways in which they understand knowledge and the construction of knowledge. This is, after all, what research is about—the creation of new knowledge or understandings, as discussed in Chapter 1. They undertake these projects because they want to learn more about their topics. As they do their projects, they will construct knowledge. This chapter discusses these important ideas: Researchers are learners who have assumptions, and these assumptions shape how they go about doing their projects.

WHAT IS LEARNING?

Throughout this book, we argue, both explicitly and implicitly, that research should be about learning. All too often, this central idea is lost in discussions of inquiry. But what do we mean by "learning"? How is it useful as a metaphor about research? Since this chapter is about the researcher as learner, it may be useful to spend some time explicating what we mean by this concept.

The *New Shorter Oxford English Dictionary* (1993) defines the noun *learning* as "education, . . . knowledge acquired by systematic study; the possession of such knowledge" (p. 1555) and the verb *learn* is defined as to "acquire knowledge of (a subject) or skill in (an art etc.) as a result of study, experience, or instruction; acquire or develop an ability *to do*" (pp. 1554–1555). Both definitions stipulate that learning is the process of acquiring knowledge. We would like to dicker with these definitions a bit. What is missing is the notion that learning is a constructive process, not merely an acquisitive one. Recent essays and empirical research about learning emphasize that the process is active, that the learner is an agent rather than just a receiver (on agency, see Bandura, 2012; Cleaver, 2012; Luttrell & Quiroz, 2009; on agency and learning, see Caine & Caine, 2013; Caine, Caine, McClintic, & Klimek, 2008; Duckworth, 2006; Vygotsky, 1978). This notion is central to our use of the terms. We see learners as actively engaged in constructing deeper understandings (knowledge) about their topics, the participants, the research process, and themselves as inquirers. Moreover, our researcher-learners learn more than how *to do* something; not all that they learn is instrumental or observable. We hope that they learn to reflect, contemplate, reason, appreciate, and honor.

Central to the social nature of learning is the concept of *community of practice* (Lave & Wenger, 1991; Pallas, 2001), as mentioned in Chapter 1. These are your peers, your colleagues, those with whom you work. In the research field, the community of practice is composed of immediate colleagues with whom you share your work. These could be fellow students, advisors, faculty members, partners, or interested critical friends. Working together and sharing your work strengthens your learning as you move through the research process. You subject your work to scrutiny from this community, testing the clarity of your thinking, eliciting the tough questions, and exploring possible answers that deepen your understanding and make your study robust.   → *colleagues*

The concept of community of practice stands in contrast to a *community of discourse*. Although some authors use the terms interchangeably, we make a distinction. The community of discourse is a group of scholars, policymakers, and practitioners who write and share information about a particular topic. Thus, they collectively develop the discourse about that topic. They may or may not be known to one another (in a face-to-face sense), but they draw on writings by one another to augment and deepen discussions of their research.   — *scholars*

Our characters will draw on writings from the communities of discourse around their topics to develop their conceptual frameworks and literature reviews. Their community of practice, however, is composed of one another, other class members, the instructor, and other interested colleagues. Within this community, they can share their tentative ideas, receive thoughtful feedback and critique, and reflect out loud about their learning. We cannot emphasize enough how a community of practice strengthens both the process and any final written work of research. As we discuss in the next chapter, both your community of practice and the relevant community of discourse are crucial in determining your study's trustworthiness.

THE REFLEXIVITY OF QUALITATIVE RESEARCH

Qualitative methodologists often refer to the researcher as the instrument of the study. We find this an unfortunate metaphor because it evokes an image of an antiseptic enterprise, one in which the researcher is merely a tool. Instead, as we hope we have made clear, we find it useful to frame Marla, Ruth, and Anthony as learners. They will construct understandings of their topics through the questions they ask, the contexts they study, and their personal biographies.

Qualitative research is quintessentially interactive. What does this mean? The researcher is involved, most often face-to-face, with participants in the study. In experiments or surveys, in contrast, participants interact with standardized sets of procedures or written questionnaires; they have little or no direct contact with the researchers. Qualitative studies, as elaborated in Chapter 1, take the researcher into the field, into complex and varied interactions with the participants. This implies that the knowledge constructed during a qualitative study is *interpretive*. The researcher makes meaning of (interprets) what he learns as he goes along. Data are filtered through the researcher's unique ways of seeing the world, his lens or worldview: "What we perceive and interpret about life is greatly influenced and affected by the lenses, filters, and angles—constructs similar to a camera—through which we view the world" (Saldaña, 2015, p. 5). Given this interpretive characteristic, the researcher's personal biography shapes the project in important ways. It is crucial, therefore, that you develop an acute sensitivity to who you are in your work.

These reflexive capacities and their abilities to question and explore will shape our characters' journeys. Also important will be their familiarity with and use of the methodological literature—that is, the learnings of those who have undertaken qualitative research before them and written about it. As they engage with course materials, critique them, and build their own understandings of that literature, they grow to appreciate the traditions and standards for the practice of qualitative research. As they conduct their projects, they develop competence in the skills of seeing, listening, reading, and making sense of their perceptions.

Because you construct the study and because you ask the questions, becoming aware of your perspective—with its built-in interests, biases, opinions, and prejudices—and your assumptions is an ongoing task. We consider *assumptions* to be fundamental propositions that you take for granted. Data do not speak for themselves; they are interpreted through complex cognitive processes. You discover patterns that turn those data into information. Try, therefore, to be exceptionally careful to articulate the framework you use to interpret the data. This framework will include, in part, your assumptions and your perspective. You will develop an "intellectual identity, one that includes a theoretical as well as a methodological orientation" (Lareau, 1989, p. 213). Rather than pretend to be objective, state and make clear who you are and what perspective drives the study. You will need to become clear about your orientation and the approach, boundaries, and limitations of the project. All this depends on some fundamental assumptions that, explicitly or implicitly, shape your study.

Data do not speak for themselves!

PARADIGMS

In the field, talking with people, observing their everyday worlds, and learning about what matters to them is what qualitative researchers do. What undergirds this work? What are the intellectual orientations of qualitative research in general? How does it differ from quantitative research? The perspective of qualitative research is grounded in assumptions about social science and the social world—assumptions about the following:

- What is knowledge?

- What is acceptable as evidence?

- What is the nature of human action?

- What characterizes social structures and processes?

To encourage you to begin to think about these questions, we turn to a discussion of research paradigms and the assumptions that shape them. Getting clear about the assumptions undergirding your work is important for establishing the intellectual traditions to which it connects. Implicit in these assumptions, moreover, are standards for judging your research. Different assumptions imply different standards for what constitutes good research, as we discuss in Chapter 3.

Philosophers and sociologists of science have attempted to understand and describe the complexity of thought that guides definitions of science. They have used the concept of *paradigm* to capture the idea that definitions of science (whether natural or social) are the products of shared understandings of reality—that is, worldviews—complete, complex ways of seeing and sets of assumptions about the world and actions within it. Used this way, the concept has a grand scope, describing whole worlds of thought. Unfortunately, the construct has been overworked, overused, and trivialized. It has proven useful, however, for orienting beginning qualitative researchers toward some deep questions about their work.

The concept may be more easily grasped when thought of in everyday ways as the perspectives that Ruth, Marla, and Anthony—and, by extension, you—bring to research projects. For example, we know that Marla believes that the social world can be improved, Anthony assumes that decisions can be based on data, and Ruth believes that mental health depends on physical well-being.

Burrell and Morgan (1979) developed a typology of paradigms in sociology that has proven useful in provoking thought and reflection about some deep assumptions that underlie approaches to research. We adapt their work as a guide to help you think about where you stand on some basic questions and to begin to situate yourself along two continua of assumptions—one about research and the other about the social world.[2] We recognize that, depending on the context, you may locate yourself at different points on the continua.

> **A paradigm is . . .**
>
> - a worldview.
> - shared understandings of reality.

Interpretivist and Objectivist

At this point in his learning, Anthony asks a rhetorical question about knowing whether participants are telling the truth. Although he may not yet fully realize it, he is asking a fundamental question about assumptions he and his peers make regarding understanding of reality and about knowledge and what knowledge is. What is "social reality" (ontology) and how do we know it (epistemology)? Assumptions that relate to these questions are captured by the *interpretivist and objectivist continuum*. This continuum asks you to think about how you understand social reality and what you believe is truth:

- What do you believe about the nature of reality?

- How do people act in that reality?

- How do you know something is true?

- Does everyone you know agree with what you believe is true?

- How do you trust what someone says to you?

- When you ask a friend or colleague "How do you know that?" what evidence convinces you?

more ?'s to consider

- What is the relationship between the knower and the known or the learner and what is learned?

- What do these beliefs imply for your research methodology?

The continuum appears as follows:

Interpretivist	← ·················· →	Objectivist

Where the characters position themselves depends on answers to important sets of questions. Table 2.1 summarizes the polar extremes of the continuum.

These extreme anchor points represent two fundamentally different conceptions of the work of social science. Although the tendency is toward interpretivist assumptions, qualitative projects can be found at several points along the continuum. Early ethnographic studies, in particular, rested on assumptions that were more objectivist.

The Nature of Reality This facet of the subjectivist–objectivist dimension explores beliefs about reality, which is no small task. This question is important because social science, whatever its methodologic guise, seeks to learn about social phenomena, or reality as people understand it. To help locate yourself on this continuum, ask the following questions:

- Do I believe that reality is of an objective nature?

- Is it "out there," independent of human perception, and therefore something that I can learn about without direct experience?

↑ kinda confused on this

TABLE 2.1 Assumptions About Social Science

Interpretivist Assumptions		Objectivist Assumptions
Contextual dependency	← ·········· →	Generalizing tendency
"Working understandings"	← ·········· →	"Universal verities" or laws
Getting close to the participants	← ·········· →	Systematic protocol and technique
Focus on understanding subjective experience	← ·········· →	Focus on testing hypotheses
Comparative logic	← ·········· →	Logic of probabilities
Case study designs	← ·········· →	Experimental designs
Researcher as "instrument"	← ·········· →	Reliable instrumentation
Interpretive analysis of data	← ·········· →	Statistical analysis of data
Data in the form of words	← ·········· →	Data in the form of numbers

- Does it exist independently of my perception?

- Is reality the product of my individual and social experiences?

- Is reality constructed through my subjective experience and understandings built through interactions with others?

Objectivist assumptions hold that reality exists independent of human cognition and that the work of social science is to discover important facts and processes that constitute that reality. The processes exist out there, waiting to be uncovered. Interpretivist assumptions, in contrast, argue that humans construct understandings of reality through their perceptual and interpretive faculties. Social processes are continually created by human interpretation. They do not constitute reality per se but are concepts that describe it. Another example may help.

In one of their qualitative methods classes, our characters were discussing this point. Ruth asked where chaos theory (Gleick, 1987) would fit along this continuum, asserting that chaos, as a principle of social organization, exists. Almost in one voice, other students dissented, countering that chaos theory is a social construct that helps us better understand reality. They argued that chaos did not exist out there, waiting for Gleick to discover it. Because she claimed that chaos exists, Ruth could be viewed in this instance as holding objectivist assumptions about reality, whereas those disagreeing may well have more interpretivist assumptions.

The Nature of Knowledge and Knowing   What are your assumptions about what constitutes truth and how you know it? Interpretivists tend to hold that the very notion of truth is problematic. They argue that, except for certain principles about the physical world, few truths constitute universal knowledge. Rather, there are multiple perspectives about the world. An objectivist, by contrast, asserts that there is *a Truth* about a particular circumstance that can be determined. Your question, then, follows: In doing research, will you search for Truth (with a capital T) or truths—that is, multiple perspectives?

Questions you can ask yourself:

- How do I learn about something?

- What do I take as "evidence" to support a point?

- Do I tend to accept what I read and hear, or do I examine it based on my own experience?

If Anthony adopted an objectivist position, he might argue that knowledge is tangible and "hard"; that legitimate evidence comes in formal documents, the opinions of experts, clearly argued logic, and, often, numbers. With more interpretivist beliefs, Marla might argue that knowledge comes in multiple forms, many quite personal, including dreams, intuitions, and spiritual and transcendent experiences.

Another question invites you to think about where you believe knowledge can appropriately be produced and who can legitimately engage in that creation.[3] Interpretivist views hold that knowledge about the social world arises from many quarters. Important understandings are evident in novels, the arts, the media, and formal social science reports and articles. A poem or drawing is as legitimate a portrait of life experiences as a research report. An objectivist would see such knowledge as soft, unscientific, and idiosyncratic. By extension, interpretivist assumptions argue that much knowledge production in the social sciences has privileged formal academic knowledge, thereby excluding other ways of knowing. Therefore, many with interpretivist assumptions seek to create spaces in which marginalized voices can be heard. On the one hand are assumptions that objectivity is possible and desirable as the goal of social science inquiry. On the other hand, interpretivist assumptions challenge this notion, asserting that understanding lived experience—the researcher's and those whose lives are studied—is the legitimate project of inquiry.

An example may help clarify this point. Marla, Ruth, and Anthony leave class confused about what qualitative research is and, specifically, are concerned about procedures they do not really understand but will have to follow. Part of their discussion centers on the reality of the class experience and what Professor Kent did or did not say and mean. Debate about what Kent did or did not say, the actual words, would suggest a more objectivist conception of reality: Anthony asks if Kent said that they had to have a plan for dissemination: Did Kent say specifically whether this was required? Ruth's response is an interpretivist stance. She probes for Kent's meaning and searches for a broader interpretation. She responds to Anthony, *"I don't remember Kent actually saying so, but in every class we always talk about use and use and more use. If that's not dissemination, I don't know what is!"* An objectivist stance implies that reality—in this case, what went on in the classroom—is fact based. An interpretivist stance suggests that an understanding (interpretation) of reality is formed through personal experience, interaction, and discussion. Ruth and Anthony's discussion deepens both of their understandings of the classroom reality.

The Nature of Human Agency This facet of the interpretivist–objectivist dimension focuses on assumptions about our relationship with the world in which we live. You might ask yourself the following extreme questions:

- Are our actions conditioned by external circumstances such as social structures and forces?

- Are we creative, exercising free will and agency in shaping our environments and everyday lives?

Objectivists assume that human actions are predictable and, hence, controllable. For this position, the metaphor is a machine where the cogs drive the wheels. Objectivists believe that splicing social phenomena into variables and causal models is not only possible but also desirable. From this perspective, Anthony would assume that if a particular intervention worked with one population, it should work with others. In other words, he would believe that predicting outcomes with a high level of precision is possible. Interpretivists, however, hold that human agency is crucial for shaping everyday lives and larger social patterns. They maintain that unpredictability is the hallmark of human action; the goal here is to describe and interpret how people make sense of and act in their worlds. With this view, Anthony would argue that what works in one setting may or may not work in another. He would be more intrigued with understanding what makes an intervention work in a particular setting.

Methodology   The assumptions made in the previous three categories have implications for the methods you choose to conduct your work. Different assumptions incline you toward different methods. Although none of our characters will do quantitative projects, "pure" objectivist assumptions would incline a researcher toward randomized controlled trials, standardized instrumentation, and quantitative analysis of data. The purpose of research deriving from these assumptions is to generate laws or "universal verities"—to generalize from the research sample to larger populations, making predictions about actions and outcomes.

The kind of project you do likely will be based on the interpretivist assumptions of most qualitative research. This will incline you to focus on individual experiences, small case studies, firsthand knowledge of the social world, and interpretive analyses of data. Research guided by these assumptions moves toward "working understandings" of the subjectively experienced world rather than general predictive laws.

In reflecting on your personal epistemology, you will need to consider another continuum of assumptions about society.

Improvement or Radical Change

The second continuum describes models of society, again encouraging you to probe your beliefs about important theoretical questions. This second dimension posits that, when you investigate social phenomena (when you conduct social research), you do so with some model, theory, or working understandings about society. Often these theories operate at the metacognitive level; your task is to get clearer about where you stand—your theoretical orientation to social research. Think about your political stance toward the social world.

- Do you view society as essentially orderly and predictable?
- Do you view society as characterized by oppression and domination?

On the one hand are researchers who focus on explaining the "underlying unity and cohesiveness" (Burrell & Morgan, 1979, p. 17) of society. On the other hand are those who search for understandings of "deep-seated structural conflict . . . [and] modes of

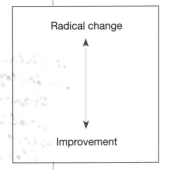

domination" (p. 17). These two perspectives view society in quite different ways. Beware of dichotomizing these views, however. As with the objectivist–interpretivist dimension, think about these two orientations along a continuum that looks like the figure shown here.[4]

The two extremes represent alternative conceptions of society and social processes. A focus on the *improvement*, the predominant model of social science, presumes that society is basically well ordered and functionally coordinated. Researchers espousing this perspective explain why society holds together in predictable ways and, indeed, assume that prediction is possible. They believe that inquiry into social processes holds the potential for improving social and organizational life, that research will help fine-tune social functioning to better meet the needs of the system or the individual. This is the exemplar of instrumental use (see Chapter 1).

In contrast is an orientation about *radical change*, which assumes that social processes are oppressive and deprive individuals and organizations of important satisfactions. Deeply embedded in society are contradictions—structures of domination and oppression—that imprison individuals and organizations in both subtle and explicit ways. Those espousing this perspective strive for the radical transformation of society (recall emancipatory use). Often explicitly political in purpose, radical change researchers tend to be idealistic; they see the possibility of transformation. The contrasts between these two conceptions of society are presented in Table 2.2.

As you learn more about Anthony, Ruth, and Marla, you will see gradations of these orientations about society reflected in their work. Marla falls within the radical change perspective through her drive to involve participants and to do research that has the potential for empowerment. At the start of her study, Ruth is concerned only with the small-scale

TABLE 2.2   Assumptions About Society

The Improvement Orientation		The Radical Change Orientation
Is Concerned With	← ········· →	*Is Concerned With*
The status quo	← ········· →	Radical change
Social order	← ········· →	Structural conflict
Consensus	← ········· →	Modes of domination
Social integration and cohesion	← ········· →	Contradiction
Solidarity	← ········· →	Emancipation
Satisfaction	← ········· →	Deprivation
Actuality	← ········· →	Potentiality

Source: From Burrell and Morgan (1979, p. 18). Copyright 1979. Adapted with permission.

FIGURE 2.1   Four Paradigms

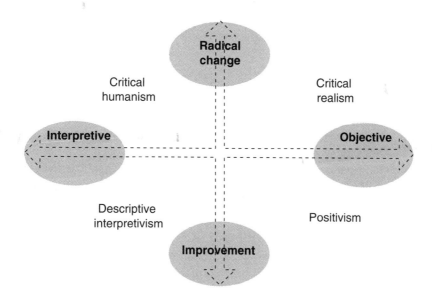

improvement: She thinks she simply will describe the children's lives. In the course of her journey, however, her descriptions take on an explicitly political agenda as she becomes dedicated to the lived experiences of children with physical disabilities. Anthony hopes that his findings will bring about incremental change, situating him above the improvement anchor point. Please note that the discussion above depicts the extremes—our characters illustrate the many possible points along the continua.

Four Paradigms

When the two continua are crossed, the result is four paradigms[5] that capture important sets of assumptions that shape research about the social world. These assumptions often operate at the tacit level. The four paradigms are provided in Figure 2.1. We should note here that others sort social science paradigms somewhat differently. For example, Popkewicz (1984) presents the positivist, interpretive, and critical paradigms, the latter subsuming Burrell and Morgan's (1979) radical humanist and radical structuralist paradigms. Others, notably Bredo and Feinberg (1982), follow a similar pattern. We believe that breaking the critical paradigm into two, one more interpretivist and the other more objectivist, remains a useful distinction.

Each paradigm carries a set of assumptions about social science and about society. We offer a brief description of the four paradigms next. While reading the following sections, consider research that you have read or conducted yourself. Try to analyze the assumptions driving these efforts and situate them within one of the paradigms. Qualitative researchers operate predominantly in the interpretivist paradigm, although their work can operate in the positivist and critical paradigms as well. Keep in mind that researchers within a particular paradigm differ—sometimes considerably—from one another. Our purpose here is to encourage your thinking about orientations toward research in the social world.

Positivism Research conducted within the positivist paradigm has dominated the social sciences. Although there is diversity here, much of the work takes a fundamentally rational view of the social world. Assuming an ordered and predictable social world that is oriented toward the small-scale improvement, the purpose is to explain and improve organizational functioning. Research methodologies represent the application of methods derived from the natural sciences to social phenomena, assuming an objectivist epistemology. Controlled trials and quasi-experimental designs predominate with randomization, the sine qua non of sampling procedures. Researchers operationalize variables that are then measured and analyzed quantitatively. Much research within this paradigm is pragmatic in purpose and instrumental in use. While using primarily qualitative methods, some classical anthropological studies could be categorized as positivist because of their attempts to be objective and to quantify aspects of the social worlds they studied.

Descriptive Interpretivism The descriptive interpretive paradigm holds improvement assumptions about the social world and interpretivist assumptions about epistemology. Interpretive research typically tries to understand the social world as it is (with the possibility of modest improvement) from the perspective of individual experience, hence an interest in subjective worldviews. Prediction is seen as an undesirable goal because with prediction likely comes social control. Rather, the goal is to generate "thick description" (Geertz, 1983) of the actors' worldviews. Humans are viewed as creators of their worlds; thus, agency in shaping the everyday world is fundamental to the paradigm. Research methods are typically humanistic—face-to-face interactions, whether in the form of in-depth interviews or extended observations or some combination.

At the top of the matrix are two other paradigms that make very different assumptions about the social world than either positivism or descriptive interpretivism. Influenced heavily by the writings of Karl Marx, work in both the critical humanist and the critical realist paradigms assume a conflictual society. Society is viewed as composed of oppressive social structures and domination by powerful and hegemonic groups. Work here often tries to liberate or emancipate, either directly or by dissemination, and severely critiques much positivist and descriptive interpretive work.

Critical Humanism Critical humanists view individual consciousness as the means to empower, transform, and liberate groups from dominating and imprisoning social processes. Research and theorizing in this paradigm rely on the notion of "false consciousness," a concept that asserts that human agency is constrained by ideological superstructures (Burrell & Morgan, 1979, p. 32). Radical change occurs at the individual level, transforming social relations locally. Research is typically conducted using the humanistic methods found in the descriptive interpretive paradigm and, clearly, relies on an interpretive epistemology. One significant difference between the descriptive interpretive and the critical humanist paradigms is the researcher's stance. The critical humanist researcher is often explicitly participatory in the research project, sharing the initiation, conduct, analysis, and writing with those studied. The theoretical framework guiding critical-humanist research derives from critical theory and postmodern perspectives.

In their work, Burrell and Morgan (1979) did not anticipate the enormous growth during the past 25 years in the critical perspectives represented by feminist theory, research focusing on race and ethnicity, postcolonial studies, indigenous methodologies, participatory action research from international development work, and current theorizing focusing on sexual orientation. Discussion of these important critical standpoints is largely absent from Burrell and Morgan's work. We argue, however, that much of this current work can be usefully seen as holding interpretivist and radical change assumptions.

Critical Realism   Rather than focusing on individual human consciousness, the critical-realist paradigm analyzes the power relations embedded in political and economic structures. Radical social change is viewed as arising from crises in these basic social systems, leading to more equitable distributions of power and wealth. Although there is diversity within this paradigm, research tends to rely on large-scale data gathering that is often represented quantitatively. One could consider studies focusing on high-stakes testing as serving emancipatory purposes because they seek to highlight inequities across gender and race.

In summary, Burrell and Morgan's (1979) work, although asking questions you might not typically ask of yourself, is useful for understanding the broad sweep of social science research and for beginning to situate various qualitative traditions—as well as our characters' and your own work—along the continua and within the paradigms. However, we introduce a cautionary note here. Given our own interpretivist assumptions, we view the concept of paradigm as just that: a concept. It is not reality out there; it is a heuristic trope that many have found useful in organizing a complex array (a cacophony at times) of research claiming to contribute to understanding the social world. Think of the categories in Figure 2.1 as having mushy and permeable borders. Burrell and Morgan would disagree. They assert that "the four paradigms are mutually exclusive. . . . A synthesis is not possible, since in their purest forms they are contradictory" (p. 25). We disagree and note an internal contradiction in their argument. The notion of continuum assumes infinite points; how could we determine the exact point of leaving interpretivist assumptions, for example, and moving into objectivist ones? Are there no gradations? As they present them, the concepts of paradigm and continuum butt up against one another, leaving some discordance. Perhaps their phrase "purest form" provides the space to resolve this conflict.

Using the previous theoretical discussion, you can begin to understand better where qualitative researchers typically situate themselves, the assumptions they make, the beliefs they hold about what is the important work to do, and the orientations they bring to their work. These considerations, you recall, are important for explicating the theoretical and methodological perspective you take in your work. Because qualitative research is fundamentally subjectivist, interactive, and interpretivist, reflecting on your perspective is crucial. How do you go about doing this besides asking some of the questions posed previously? What do you think about as you begin to conduct a study? What do you construe as your relationship with the participants in your study? What do you bring to the work?

PERSPECTIVE IN PRACTICE

The qualitative researcher needs to be constantly aware of his separateness from the participants in his study. Research is always "a project of someone: a real person, who, in the context of particular individual, social, and historical life circumstances, sets out to make sense of a certain aspect of human existence" (van Manen, 1990, p. 31). Researchers need to know who they are and what they are doing in the setting. This self-awareness allows them to distinguish their sense-making from the sense-making of those from whom they are learning. Anthropologists have labeled the researcher's perspective the *etic*, or outsider, perspective. They refer to the perspective of the participants as the *emic*, or insider, perspective. Because fully representing the subjective experience of the participants (the emic perspective) is an unachievable goal, qualitative researchers strive to represent clearly and richly their understanding of what they have learned (the etic perspective). What they write is interpretations (their own) of participants' understandings of their worlds (the participants' interpretations). The postmodern critique calls us to acknowledge that written work is authored by the author! This seems obvious at first glance, but much traditional research is written in an antiseptic, author-free style. Canons of acceptable practice for writing research reports were built around objectivist assumptions; no author should be visible to the reader. This critique demands that we examine and explicate the ways in which our authorship of text shapes that text. Given this, the notion of representing solely the emic perspective, devoid of our own interpretations (writing), becomes both impossible and irrelevant.

Our characters hope that participants will see themselves in their portrayals, but they recognize that this may not be fully achieved and they take responsibility for the interpretations they put forward. They are scrupulous, therefore, to identify that it is their own understanding, shaped by their perspective, what they have learned, and how they choose to write it up.

The Self at Work: Reflexivity

The personal biography of the researcher and the roles she takes influence the research, both the sense she makes of the setting and how people she is learning from make sense

---

Whose perspective?

- *Emic:* The insider's view and voice
- *Etic:* The outsider's view and voice

Can an outsider capture the emic voice?

of her. Whether the researcher has chosen to participate in the setting, as has Marla, or to be less obtrusive, the very fact of her presence changes the context. Recall the mention in Chapter 1 of the stories we heard about us in our research settings. "There is no way in which we can escape the social world in order to study it. Put simply, a relationship always exists between the researcher and those being researched" (Hammersley & Atkinson, 1983, p. 15). This relationship and the researcher's reflections on it—and her subsequent actions—constitute a phenomenon called *reflexivity* that is central to understanding the practice of qualitative research.

The word *reflexivity* has as its root *reflexive*, which means "capable of turning or bending back" ("Reflexive," 1993). The term has its origins in the Latin word *reflexus*, which means "a bending back," from which we also derive the English use of *reflex* to mean an automatic response produced in reaction to an action or event. When used in the context of social science, reflexive means that a method or theory "takes account of itself or especially of the effect of the personality or presence of the researcher on what is being investigated" ("Reflexive," 1993). As Saldaña (2015) notes, "Reflection . . . is the act of pondering various components of the research project to make sense of and gain personal understanding about their meanings" (p. 8).

Reflexivity in the setting begins with you, the researcher. As you observe or interview, you react to the participants' words and actions. They trigger thoughts, hunches, working hypotheses, and understandings of the setting and the participants. You generate constructs or identify patterns drawn from your theoretical orientation and cultural knowledge to describe and explain the actions you observe or words you hear—you seek to make sense. These constructs or hypotheses begin as unexamined reflexes in reaction to what you see or hear.

Reflexivity, however, also involves the study's participants. The participants react to you; theirs is also an unexamined reflex. By your mere presence, you become a part of their social world, and they modify their actions accordingly. The more you appear to be like the members of this social world or the longer you stay in it, the less your presence may affect everyday routines. In one sense, you become an integral part of the social world, albeit an unusual one. The way participants react to you becomes a part of their repertoire, their recurring actions. As well, how you interpret their actions shapes your *re*-actions. Reflexivity, in this sense, is the package of reciprocal and iterative reactions between the researcher and the participants in the setting.

The root word has another important meaning. It also denotes reflection and introspection. When thinking about research and the writing of a report, *reflexivity* means that an author or text "self-consciously refer[s] to itself or its production" ("Reflexivity," 1993). In qualitative research, reflexivity captures both of these meanings: the reactions that naturally occur because an outsider enters and interacts with the setting and the capacity to reflect on those reactions. Both meanings are crucial. As you reflect on your initial reactions, they grow into an examined and rigorous representation of your complex perspective. In our view, qualitative researchers need to be acutely aware of

Reflexivity

Looking at yourself making sense of how someone else makes sense of her world

FIGURE 2.2   Reflexive Questions: Triangulated Inquiry

Those studied (participants):

How do they know what they know? What shapes and has shaped their worldview? How do they perceive me? Why? How do I know? How do I perceive them?

Reflexive Screens: culture, age, gender, class, social status, education, family, political praxis, language, values

Those who receive the study (audience):

How do they make sense of what I give them? What do they bring to the findings I offer? How do they perceive me? How do I perceive them?

Myself (as qualitative inquirer):

What do I know? How do I know what I know? What shapes and has shaped my perspective? With what voice do I share my perspective? What do I do with what I have found?

Source: From Patton, M. Q. (2015). *Qualitative evaluation and research methods* (4th ed., p.72). Newbury Park, CA: Sage.

both meanings: *reflex*, as in unexamined reaction, and *reflect*, as in the turning back of thoughts. Both words originate from the same Latin root. For a human being, to reflect is to contemplate. We see the researcher's reflection as an essential component of his role. Researchers react, but most important, they contemplate those reactions.

Reflexivity is an interactive and cyclical phenomenon, not a linear one. Both "seeing is believing" and "believing is seeing" are true. The qualitative researcher is open to the interplay of what is considered fact and opinion. He asks "What sense do I make of what is going on or of this person's actions?" This is the etic perspective. At the same time, the researcher asks "What sense do the participants make of what they are doing? What is the individual's sense of his or her own actions?" These questions seek the emic perspective. Although the researcher cannot actually get into the participants' minds, he can search for evidence of their worldviews. Overlaid on these ongoing emic and etic processes is the set of questions about what you are doing (your actions) and how they are perceived.

The objectivist deals with reflexivity by assuming that it can be controlled, hence the scientists' struggle for what they have termed *objectivity*. They admonish the researcher to eliminate all bias, to remain disinterested. Qualitative researchers, however, reject the notion that bias can be eliminated, that anyone can be completely disinterested. Recognizing that reflexivity is present in social interactions, they focus on understanding and explaining the effects of reflexivity. This makes their inquiry systematic and rigorous. Delamont (1992) cautions us to be "constantly self-conscious about [the researcher's] role, interactions, and theoretical and empirical material as it accumulates. As long as qualitative researchers are reflexive, making all their purposes explicit, then issues of reliability and validity are served" (p. 8). The recent concept of *refraction* is relevant here: *refraction*—"deliberately making things problematic or troubling" (Saldaña, 2015, p. 8).

To ensure that data collection is systematic, qualitative researchers begin by being explicit about their purposes and by being themselves. For us, being ourselves means that we have articulated our perspectives or frames of reference toward the topic—that is, we know our beliefs and values, our assumptions and biases relative to that topic. We are clear about our theoretical and methodological orientation, and we consider past experiences that might influence our views. In short, we try to be aware of and vigilant about the many garments (Peshkin, 1988) we wear in any inquiry.

Establishing Perspective

Getting clear about your perspective can be fostered by exploring what others have written about the topic and how you feel about it. First, voracious reading is crucial. You need to know what others have discovered so that you don't reinvent the wheel. Read, think about the reading, and then do more reading.

- Read previous research on the subject.
- Read social science theories about the subject.
- Seek out contrasting viewpoints.
- Identify the issues and critically examine their relevance.

At the same time (and equally important), you should ask yourself how you *feel* about the subject. More often than not, you have an opinion about the worth or value of what you are studying, which may become an abiding interest—possibly a passion. Try not to let this opinion (this interest or passion) prevent you from "seeing" clearly and widely in the settings. Remain open to the views of others. For example, Anthony may not enjoy modern dance, but he still may evaluate the community arts program, which includes modern dance; he is not being asked to critique the performance itself. As long as he remembers that he is tracking the audience's attention and satisfaction, his personal dislike of modern dance does not have to interfere. Drawing on the paradigms discussed previously, as a subjectivist, Anthony recognizes that multiple perspectives (a range of appreciation) are possible. Still, he must be vigilant to ensure that he does not read his lack of enthusiasm into the audience's reactions.

As we discuss in Chapter 5, having a compelling interest is important. For example, Anthony may want to see the community arts program succeed. He will take care to produce thick descriptions that explore all aspects and angles of the program. Because he does not hold objectivist assumptions about an independent reality, he cannot claim to report only hard facts, but he does aim to discover the social construct—the culture—of the program.

Perhaps most important, Anthony—and you—will need to be sensitive to the subtle differences between compelling interest in a subject, advocacy, and out-and-out bias. Qualitative researchers are careful to check their feelings for bias or prejudice. If they encounter a study about which they feel so strongly that they cannot avoid passing judgment, they often consider and clarify their motivations. They may decide not to become involved in the study. Once we refused to do an evaluation of an early childhood program that claimed to teach 3-year-olds to read because we felt our goal would be to debunk the program. In another example, should Ruth find she has no patience for children whose physical disabilities preclude being athletic, her clear bias would prevent her from discovering the realities of these children's lives.

Your perspective is related to your role, as well. Depending on the strategy (evaluation or policy study, action research, or analytic descriptive study), the design calls for particular actions and seeking information in particular forms. Marla's role allows her to participate in the work of the clinic because she has chosen action research. Because she is working in the setting, she has direct access to an emic perspective. As an evaluator, Anthony's role is to provide information to program policymakers and funders who will make decisions about program directions, services to be offered, and resource allocations. He seeks data that can inform decisions, and he is guided by program theory, audience needs, and program impact. His role in evaluating the community arts program is not to critique the displays but to gather data on the community's use of facilities and events: Who attends what activities and who does not? When and why do they attend or not? What do they think of displays and performances? Do folks appreciate certain aspects more than others? What problems are encountered? What are the unexpected costs? His role is also to communicate the resulting information to the decision makers so that they may use it. In each case, qualitative researchers have the responsibility to make clear for study participants what role they intend to take.

Finally, because the qualitative researcher is learning and constructing, and because she is *reflectively reflexive* while doing so, her inquiry is interpretive. It is not, however, unsystematic (systematic inquiry is discussed in Chapter 1). The researcher is meticulous about documentation and recording, both what she sees and what processes she uses. The researcher's process should be deliberate and conscious; decisions and actions should be explicated and displayed so that others may understand the choices she has made and the reasoning behind those choices. In doing so, she makes it possible for others to assess the trustworthiness of the process. Just as researchers collect and display their data, they collect and display data about their own research decisions and actions and their development. Consider the following questions:

- What assumptions do you make?

- What are your opinions about and interest in the study?

- What preconceptions and prejudices do you bring?

- What do you feel about the setting and the participants?

- How do you define your terms?

- What are the parameters of the study?

- What decisions do you make?

- What do you do and why?

- What problems do you encounter?

log of the process

It is better to err on the side of sharing too many details about research design and implementation than giving too few. *Keep a log* of the process. The log can take any form that works for you to keep track of what happens and your reactions to and interpretations of events, interactions, and observations. It is helpful to allocate time shortly after any data collection for processing the observation or interview or for record review, even if it means that you sit in the car or stand on a street corner noting the day's events. One of our students became a regular at the local coffee shop where he stopped at the end of a day of data gathering. In our work, we appreciate fieldwork done as a team so that we can drive together; the ride offers a time to review and elaborate on the field notes and to critique the experience collaboratively.

Documenting your intellectual and methodological journey is crucial for establishing the soundness of the study. Remember, you are engaging in a process of systematic inquiry. Getting clear about your perspective helps establish the intellectual integrity of the project. It places boundaries, describes assumptions, and details the process. All these go far in establishing the trustworthiness of the project, to which we turn next.

DISPOSITIONS AND SKILLS

Fundamental to the qualitative enterprise is the willingness and courage to reflect on the self as learner and knower. This reflection, however, does not occur narcissistically. First, reflection is directly related to the research topic. Second, the reflection embraces the "other" as well as the self *and* the relationship between the two. Marla, Ruth, and Anthony are beginning this reflection process as they face the central challenge of this chapter: understanding how they know what they know and what they accept as evidence for knowledge.

As learners and knowers, they pose questions they want to explore in the studies they will conduct for this introductory class. They understand that they have embarked on a process of discovery. Although they are uncomfortable with not knowing exactly where they will end up, they understand that a certain level of ambiguity is inherent in the inquiry process because discovery involves lots of back-and-forth and because it involves going deeply into the lives of others. Therefore, sensitivity to interpersonal dynamics will be highly important to their learning and knowing.

Learning about and knowing the self, the other, and the relationship challenge qualitative researchers to confront and articulate the assumptions they bring to their work.

- How do I know what I know?
- How do I think about reality?
- Do I believe that my actions are predetermined, or am I free to choose?
- Do I believe society is essentially orderly or dynamic?

How they answer these questions reveals researchers' orientations to interpretivism, objectivism, and social change. These orientations determine how they will go about doing their research. Their decisions are shaped by these personal epistemologies. The challenge, however, is to articulate these sufficiently to explain and justify actions taken in the field.

In this chapter, we have seen the three students begin to explore their capacities for the dispositions and skills that will build their competence in good qualitative research practice. They locate themselves on the subjectivity–objectivity continuum. They take a position—which may move—on social change. Through this process of sustained and systematic reflection, our characters construct their research questions and consider their approaches. This process of acting and reflecting, reflecting and acting, helps them develop competence. Knowing themselves and their ways of knowing, Marla, Ruth, and Anthony are getting ready to design their studies. They are engaging with the following:

- Comfort with ambiguity
- Capacity to make reasoned decisions and to articulate the logic behind those decisions
- Deep interpersonal or emotional sensitivity
- Ethical sensitivity of potential consequences to individuals and groups
- Political sensitivity
- Perseverance and self-discipline

ACTIVITIES FOR YOUR COMMUNITY OF PRACTICE

Study Questions

- What epistemologic assumptions about subjectivity and objectivity underlie major inquiry paradigms?
- How do these paradigms view change in social systems?
- How might these paradigms shape your inquiry?

- What is your role as a researcher?

- How will your personal biography and interactions with participants likely shape your study?

Small-Group or Dyad Activities

Where Is the Author?

Read articles from different paradigmatic stances on the same topic. In small groups, discuss the following:

- Where is the author's voice?

- Where does the author fall in the four paradigms?

- How does the author use data to create knowledge?

- What more would you like to know about this author?

Back to Your Artifact

Take out the notes you wrote previously describing an everyday object. In dyads, let your partner read what you wrote and tell you what inferences he makes about you, based on your description. Caution: Be thoughtful and sensitive in what you say! Questions to consider include the following: What sensory mode does this person seem to prefer? What might you infer about your partner's lifestyle? Is your partner detail oriented? Does she focus on the aesthetic or the practical?

Reflexivity Exercise

Choose an object with which you and the people in your community are familiar (e.g., a bottle of water). Hand the object to one person and ask her to describe it in any way she chooses. She passes it to another, who adds to the description in any way he chooses. Continue this process through four or five more people or until the responses become strained. In dyads, discuss how the descriptions have developed in relation to each other. Having heard others' descriptions, in what ways do you see the bottle differently? How have individual descriptions changed your understanding of the bottle?

Discussion on Role, Subjectivity, and Personal Biography

Read selected articles on subjectivity, role, and personal biography. In groups of three or four, discuss and respond to the questions below (in addition to others that you generate).

- What is the author's position on subjectivity? What argument (evidence) does the author present to support this position?

- Does the author use metaphors to capture the subtleties and complexities of the researcher's role? How are metaphors used? Are other concepts central to the author's argument?

(Continued)

(Continued)

- What salience does the author give to personal feelings and reactions? In what ways?

- What strategies does the author propose for thinking about subjectivity and the relationship between researcher and participants in the study?

- What issues about or insights into the tensions of doing qualitative research have arisen for you? How will these shape your own small-scale study?

When all groups are finished (about 45 minutes), report out what your group discussed.

Writing Activity

Personal Reflections

Write a short memo on who you are in relationship to your research project. Use the memo to reflect on what you bring to the study: your background, experiences, values, and feelings. What prior connection do you have to the topic, people, or setting you are studying? How do you think and feel about these? What assumptions have you been making about the topic, setting, or people? How might these be affecting your conduct of the study?

The purpose of this memo is to provide you with an opportunity to think about how who you are relates to how you approach your study and what you bring to the research in terms of expectations, assumptions, and concerns. The rationale for this memo is that many beginners—even many experienced researchers—make a sharp separation between their research and the rest of their lives. This has a couple of major drawbacks. First, it creates the illusion that research exists in a sterile, antiseptic, "objective" environment, subject only to rational and impersonal constraints. This mystifies the actual motives, assumptions, and agendas of researchers and leaves unexamined the influence of these on the research process and conclusions. Second, it cuts off the researcher from a major source of insights, emerging hypotheses, and assessments of the validity of the data and the conclusions.

In this memo, you have an opportunity to reflect on and critique your motives and assumptions and to discover what resources and "blinders" your experiences may provide. Please do not write a general account of your background (we do not need to hear your whole life story). Try to be more concrete and precise about personal experiences and beliefs that affect your study.

NOTES

1. We draw on the work of Burrell and Morgan throughout this section. To avoid redundancy, we do not reference each point unless we quote directly from their work.

2. In their 1979 work, Burrell and Morgan do not address this question specifically. The current critique of "normal" social science, however, invites consideration of this issue.

3. Burrell and Morgan (1979) describe the status quo point as the "sociology of regulation." We prefer using the term *improvement* to capture assumptions within this domain.

4. Burrell and Morgan's (1979) terms for the four paradigms are *functionalist, interpretivist, radical humanist*, and *radical structuralist*. We have modified three of these terms to *positivist, critical humanist*, and *critical realist*, leaving *interpretivist* as in the original.

FURTHER READINGS

Learning

Brown, M. N., & Keeley, S. M. (2014). *Asking the right questions: A guide to critical thinking* (11th ed.). Upper Saddle River, NJ: Pearson.

Caine, R. N., & Caine, G. (1997). *Education on the edge of possibility*. Alexandria, VA: Association for Supervision and Curriculum Development.

Caine, R. N., Caine, G., McClintic, C., & Klimek, K. (2009). *The 12 brain/mind principles in action: Developing executive functions in the human brain* (2nd ed.). Thousand Oaks, CA: Corwin Press.

Duckworth, E. R. (2006). *"The having of wonderful ideas" and other essays on teaching and learning* (3rd ed.). New York, NY: Teachers College Press.

Haraway, D. (2001). Situated knowledges: The science question in feminism and the privilege of partial perspective. In M. Lederman & I. Bartsch (Eds.), *The gender and science reader* (pp. 169–188). New York, NY: Routledge.

Kahneman, D. (2011). *Thinking, fast and slow*. New York, NY: Farrar, Straus & Giroux.

Lave, J., & Wenger, E. (1991). *Situated learning: Legitimate peripheral participation*. Cambridge, England: Cambridge University Press.

O'Sullivan, E. (1999). *Transformative learning: Educational vision for the 21st century*. New York, NY: Zed Books.

Swimme, B. (1984). *The universe is a green dragon: A cosmic creation story*. Rochester, VT: Bear.

Communities of Practice

Amin, A., & Roberts, J. (2008). Knowing in action: Beyond communities of practice. *Research Policy, 37*(2), 353–369.

Friedman, V. J. (2008). *Action science: Creating communities of inquiry in communities of practice*. Thousand Oaks, CA: Sage.

Pallas, A. M. (2001). Preparing education doctoral students for epistemological diversity. *Educational Researcher, 30*(5), 6–11.

Piantanida, M., & Garman, N. B. (1999). *The qualitative dissertation*. Thousand Oaks, CA: Corwin Press.

Paradigms

Burrell, G., & Morgan, G. (1979). *Sociological paradigms and organizational analysis*. London, England: Heinemann.

Creswell, J. W. (2012). *Qualitative inquiry and research design: Choosing among five approaches*. Thousand Oaks, CA: Sage.

Gage, N. L. (1989). The paradigm wars and their aftermath: A "historical" sketch of research on teaching since 1989. *Educational Researcher, 18*(7), 4–10.

Goertz, G., & Mahoney, J. (2012). *A tale of two cultures: Qualitative and quantitative research in the social sciences*. Princeton, NJ: Princeton University Press.

Guba, E. G. (Ed.). (1990). *The paradigm dialogue*. Newbury Park, CA: Sage.

Lincoln, Y. S., & Guba, E. G. (1985). *Naturalistic inquiry*. Beverly Hills, CA: Sage.

Newman, I. (1998). *Qualitative-quantitative research methodology: Exploring the interactive continuum*. Carbondale, IL: Southern Illinois University Press.

Popkewicz, T. S. (1984). *Paradigm and ideology in educational research: The social functions of the intellectual*. London, England: Falmer Press.

Punch, K. F. (2013). *Introduction to social research: Quantitative and qualitative approaches*. Thousand Oaks, CA: Sage.

Rallis, S. F., & Rossman, G. B. (2012). *The research journey: Introduction to inquiry*. New York, NY: Guilford Press.

Reichardt, C. S., & Rallis, S. F. (Eds.). (1994). The qualitative–quantitative debate: New perspectives. *New Directions for Program Evaluation, 61,* 1–98.

Reflexivity, Subjectivity, and Objectivity

Alvesson, M., & Sköldberg, K. (2009). *Reflexive methodology: New vistas for qualitative research*. Thousand Oaks, CA: Sage.

Berger, R. (2013). Now I see it, now I don't: Researcher's position and reflexivity in qualitative research. *Qualitative Research, 15*(2), 219–234.

Brizuela, B. M., Stewart, J. P., Carrillo, R. G., & Berger, J. G. (Eds.). (2000). *Acts of inquiry in qualitative research*. Cambridge, MA: Harvard Educational Review.

Chase, S. E. (1996). Personal vulnerability and interpretive authority in narrative research. In R. Josselin (Ed.), *Ethics and process in the narrative study of lives* (pp. 45–59). Thousand Oaks, CA: Sage.

Copp, M. A. (2008). Emotions in qualitative research. In L. M. Given (Ed.), *The SAGE encyclopedia of qualitative research methods* (2nd ed., pp. 133–155). Thousand Oaks, CA: Sage.

Foster, M. (1994). The power to know one thing is never the power to know all things: Methodological notes on two studies of black American teachers. In A. Gitlin (Ed.), *Power and method: Political activism and educational research* (pp. 129–146). London, England: Routledge.

Heshuius, L. (1994). Freeing ourselves from objectivity: Managing subjectivity or turning toward a participatory mode of consciousness. *Educational Researcher, 23*(3), 15–22.

Jones, S. R., Torres, V., & Arminio, J. (2013). *Negotiating the complexities of qualitative research in higher education: Fundamental elements and issues*. New York, NY: Routledge.

Lincoln, Y. S., Lynham, S. A., & Guba, E. G. (2011). Paradigmatic controversies, contradictions, and emerging confluences, revisited. In N. K. Denzin & Y. S. Lincoln (Eds.), *The SAGE handbook of qualitative research* (4th ed., pp. 97–128). Thousand Oaks, CA: Sage.

deMarrais, K. B. (Ed.). (1998). *Inside stories: Qualitative research reflections*. Mahwah, NJ: Lawrence Erlbaum.

Milner, H. R., IV. (2007). Race, culture, and researcher positionality: Working through dangers seen, unseen, and unforeseen. *Educational Researcher, 36*(7), 388–400.

Olesen, V. (2011). Feminist qualitative research in the millennium's first decade. In N. K. Denzin & Y. S. Lincoln (Eds.), *The SAGE handbook of qualitative research* (4th ed., pp. 129–146). Thousand Oaks, CA: Sage.

Peshkin, A. (1988). In search of subjectivity: One's own. *Educational Researcher, 17*(7), 17–21.

Phillips, D. C. (1990). Subjectivity and objectivity: An objective inquiry. In E. W. Eisner & A. Peshkin (Eds.), *Qualitative inquiry in education: The continuing debate* (pp. 19–37). New York, NY: Teachers College Press.

Rager, K. B. (2005). Self-care and the qualitative researcher: When collecting data can break your heart. *Educational Researcher, 34*(4), 23–27.

Rallis, S. F., & Rossman, G. B. (2010). Caring reflexivity. *International Journal of Qualitative Studies in Education, 23*(4), 495–499.

Toma, J. D. (2011). Approaching rigor in applied qualitative research. In C. F. Conrad &

R. C. Serlin (Eds.), *The SAGE handbook for research in education: Pursuing ideas as the keystone of exemplary inquiry* (2nd ed., pp. 263–280). Thousand Oaks, CA: Sage.

Tufford, L., & Newman, P. (2012). Bracketing in qualitative research. *Qualitative Social Work, 11*(1), 80–96.

Wagle, T., & Cantaffa, D. T. (2008). Working our hyphens: Exploring identity relations in qualitative research. *Qualitative Inquiry, 14*(1), 135–159.

Weis, L., & Fine, M. (2000). *Speed bumps: A student-friendly guide to qualitative research.* New York, NY: Teachers College Press.

3

The Researcher as Competent and Ethical

Marla, Ruth, and Anthony are at the point in their learning when they question the processes they might use in their studies. They aim to be competent researchers—that is, to use the necessary knowledge, skills, and abilities to conduct studies that produce meaningful findings that are trustworthy and useful. But they are confused by what makes a study trustworthy and useful. They are wondering how the setting will influence what they do and in turn how their research will affect the setting and the participants. They have read about standards for practice established by various groups (institutional review boards [IRBs]; the National Research Council [NRC]; and various professional groups such as the American Educational Research Association, the American Psychological Association, and the American Evaluation Association), but they are becoming aware that applying these standards to real people in real settings may be challenging. Although it seems daunting at this point, Ruth, Marla, and Anthony begin to consider the worth of their projects: How can they evaluate the quality of their work? How can they ensure that their projects will be viewed as legitimate/scientific? Can they, at the same time, honor the particularity of a setting and the individuality of the participants? In short, they are concerned that they might have to balance accepted/ normative procedures with building ethical relationships with participants.

Any research setting is complex, unique, full of politics, and ever changing. As James Watson (1968) writes in his book on the discovery of deoxyribonucleic acid (DNA), "Science seldom proceeds in the straightforward logical manner imagined by outsiders. Instead, its steps forward (and sometimes backward) are often very human events in which personalities and cultural traditions play major roles" (p. ix). Specifically, qualitative research settings are natural environments in which participants live, play, and work. As researchers, Marla, Ruth, and Anthony will be entering these participants' worlds, interacting with them in their daily lives. The relationships they establish in their study settings shape the quality of the data they will collect. Thus, for their research to be trustworthy, they must follow standards for practice that are both scientific and ethical. But what does that mean for what they should do as they implement their studies. And they ask, Who decides?

Feminist research theorizing and methodology, as well as critical perspectives in many disciplines, have brought to the forefront of qualitative research thinking that *all research is political*. By this is meant that research takes a position on social change, either explicitly seeking social change or not. We agree with this position, arguing that politics are ubiquitous in social life; research is no different. By politics, we mean the powers of government, universities, thesis or dissertation committees, and social science disciplines to set research agendas and determine appropriate methodologies. We also include as politics the undercurrents of power that shape organizational life and social interactions. These are often called micropolitics. Anthony, Marla, and Ruth will find that they need to consider what constraints surround their studies and who has placed them there. Who are the key powerful actors, whether individuals or agencies, and how might they influence the study?

Research as a process to produce knowledge is a Western concept. As such, the process often fails to recognize as legitimate and to honor non-Western and indigenous conceptualizations of knowledge and knowledge production. Many of the newer or alternative forms of research, such as those with a critical perspective or the more inclusive action research, can be adapted to collaboratively generate knowledge that respects and honors indigenous and non-Western participants. Furthermore, with the purpose of protecting human subjects, IRBs often establish procedures that may not be workable in non-Western cultures (as well as in many domestic U.S. cultural settings). To produce trustworthy knowledge, qualitative researchers are challenged to build relationships that authentically protect their participants and their knowledge while maintaining the systematic inquiry standards expected by their various communities of practice (see Denzin, Lincoln, & Smith, 2008).

In this chapter, we explore the many factors that contribute to conducting a trustworthy study: scientific principles, credibility and rigor, human subjects ethics, and moral principles. Throughout, each are woven political considerations about power dynamics: who sets agendas, defines appropriate methods, determines what is important, and controls access. We claim that competent practice (in terms of design and methods) by itself is not sufficient; the study also must be reasoned through ethical and political sensitivities. Thus, judgments about ethical and politically thoughtful practice also must be central to judgments about the trustworthiness and credibility of *any* study.

WHY DOES TRUSTWORTHINESS MATTER?

As described in Chapter 1, we believe that the ultimate aim for a study should be its *use*; that is, the conduct of the study and its findings are sufficiently believable that others will use those findings to take action to improve social circumstances. All research aims to produce findings that are "worth paying attention to, worth taking account of" (Lincoln & Guba, 1985, p. 290)—findings that are trustworthy. For a study to be useful, then, readers—potential users—must believe and trust in its integrity. It must be credible to potential users, whether these are other researchers, policymakers, practitioners, or the participants themselves. However, as Patton (2015) notes, each group assesses the study's integrity and value using different criteria. Researchers—the community of discourse—judge the conceptual framework and rigorous use of methodology. Policymakers ask if the study addresses important policy concerns and how the results help them make policy and program decisions. Practitioners think about ways the results shape their everyday work. Participants judge how ethically and sensitively their words and perspectives are portrayed. Each group, to varying extents, considers whether the study was well conceptualized, implemented in sound ways, and written up with care and rigor.

Standards for judging the value of research projects were once considered clear and uncontested. Reliability, validity, generalizability, and objectivity were the historic criteria and are still used in judging many research studies. If the instruments were reliable, the study was valid in its conclusions, which were then generalizable to a defined population. If the study met all these conditions and was conducted objectively, it was judged to be scientifically well done. However, as qualitative inquiry has matured, a substantial body of discourse has developed that both critiques the historic standards and offers alternatives. Thus, canons for trustworthiness for *any* study are no longer quite so clear and uncontested. In the next section, we discuss guidelines often used in making judgments about the worth of qualitative studies. We then offer strategies that you can implement during the conduct of a study to help ensure that it will meet those guidelines.

WHAT MAKES A TRUSTWORTHY STUDY?

To produce a trustworthy study—that is, one that is credible and usable—researchers need more than simple competence. In addition to the knowledge, skills, and abilities they gain in their training, they engage in ongoing rigorous reasoning regarding decisions. To qualify as systematic inquiry, a research study entails "a continual process of *rigorous reasoning* [italics added] supported by a dynamic interplay among methods, theories, and findings" (Shavelson & Towne, 2002, p. 2). The process is deliberate, intentional, transparent, mindful, and ethically conducted and adheres to norms of practice determined by the relevant professional community. Our position is that the trustworthiness of a qualitative research project is evaluated by two interrelated sets of standards. First, was the study conducted according to norms for acceptable and systematic research practice? Second, did the study follow the procedures for human subjects research? These standards are applied through rigorous reasoning—that is, through a process that is *meticulous, conscientious, careful, diligent, attentive, scrupulous, exact, precise, accurate, thorough, sensitive,* and *particular.* What rationale drove each decision? Was the study conducted in ways that honor participants? What moral principles were in play? Which power relationships influenced the researcher? Which affected the participants? Was the researcher sensitive to the politics of the topic and setting?

The standards and reasoning are interrelated because it is our stance that a study can meet accepted standards for practice but, if not conducted ethically and with political sensitivity, fall short in integrity. Put simply, an unethical study is not a trustworthy study. "Bad science makes for bad ethics" (Rosenthal, 1994, p. 128), and bad ethics makes for bad science. We add: Bad science makes for bad politics, and bad politics makes for bad science. We have observed that widely used texts on qualitative methods separate out ethics and power dynamics from discussions of reliability and validity. Our position is that these cannot be separated. For a study to be trustworthy, it must be more than reliable and valid. It must be ethically conducted with sensitivity to power dynamics.

Attention to methodological matters (e.g., sampling, design, and methods), ethical issues, and political dynamics should be consistently addressed throughout a project and be evident in the final product. This determines the integrity of the project—its wholeness and coherence. Integrity, however, also implies *soundness of moral principle,* the ethical dimension that constitutes the second element of trustworthiness. Recent advances in theoretical perspectives, moreover, have made power dynamics (politics) a central consideration in matters affecting public life. Thus, explicating the theoretical and methodological orientations, the moral principles, and considerations of power dynamics that have guided your project is crucial. You must convey these to the reader of any written report. In what follows, we first discuss standards for competent methodological practice and then turn to the sometimes thorny ethical and political considerations involved in doing qualitative research.

SYSTEMATIC PRACTICE

"Advances in scientific knowledge are achieved by the *self-regulating norms of the scientific community* [italics added] over time, not, as sometimes believed, by the mechanistic application of a particular method to a static set of questions" (Shavelson & Towne, 2002, p. 2). To help frame the standard for systematic practice, we draw on the well-known report by the NRC's *Scientific Research in Education* (Shavelson & Towne, 2002). This document lists six principles that should, the authors argue, guide the design and conduct of any study for it to be scientific. Research should

1. Pose significant questions that can be investigated empirically;
2. Link research to relevant theory;
3. Use methods that permit direct investigation of the question;
4. Provide a coherent and explicit chain of reasoning;
5. Replicate and generalize across studies; and
6. Disclose research to encourage professional scrutiny and critique. (pp. 3–5)

These principles provide some guidance in thinking about what constitutes a *trustworthy study*, the term that we prefer to use. In their narrative, Shavelson and Towne (2002) integrate the principles as follows:

> To be scientific, the design must allow direct, empirical investigation of an important question, account for the context in which the study is carried out, align with a conceptual framework, reflect careful and thorough reasoning, and disclose results to encourage debate in the scientific community. (p. 6)

As a form of systematic inquiry that is deliberate, intentional, and transparent, qualitative research meets these standards. All research, no matter what its paradigmatic roots, should respond to legitimate questions that readers (potential users) pose. These questions focus on the accuracy of what is reported (its *truth value*), the methods used to generate the findings (its *rigor*), and the usefulness of the study (its *generalizability* and *significance*). We will discuss each in turn.

What Is the Truth Value of This Work?

As a qualitative researcher, you seek multiple perspectives about some phenomenon; you search for truths, not Truth. You typically assume that reality is an interpretive phenomenon and that meaning is constructed by participants as they go about their everyday lives. Your task is to render an account of participants' worldviews as honestly and fully as possible. This rendition of what has been learned, however, is also an interpretation—the researcher's (i.e., yours). In judging the truth value of a project, readers depend on how adequately multiple understandings (including the researcher's) are presented and whether they "ring true" (have face validity).

What Can the Researcher Do? Several strategies help establish the truth claims of qualitative research. One is to design the study so that data are gathered over time or intensively rather than in a one-shot manner. A second is sharing your interpretations of the emergent findings with the participants. A third strategy is designing the study as participatory or action research from beginning to end, thereby ensuring that the truth value of what you discover and report is intimately linked to participants' understandings. A fourth is to triangulate—that is, draw from several data sources, methods, investigators, or theories to inform the same question or issue. Using a colleague or peer as a critical friend also strengthens the value of what you conclude and report. Judicious and modest writing about your perspective (your personal biography with your interests, potential biases, strengths, and unique insights) helps the reader explore how and in what ways you as the researcher have shaped the project and the findings you report. Finally, a stance of humility in the claims you make establishes that you understand the conditional and approximate nature of knowledge about complex social phenomena. Contextualizing your findings to the specific setting and participants also tells the readers that your conclusions are bounded by time and space.

How Rigorously Was the Study Conducted?

Another criterion readers use for judging research is whether it has been rigorously conducted. Many of the principles for scientific research focus on considerations of rigor, such as posing significant questions, linking to theory, using methods for direct empirical investigation, and providing a coherent chain of reasoning. From an objectivist perspective, this has meant that results are replicable because the instrumentation used for data gathering is reliable: If the study is repeated, will the results be the same? From interpretivist assumptions, however, this notion of replicability becomes difficult. The purpose of qualitative research is not to immaculately replicate what has gone before. In fact, such replication is impossible, given the dynamic nature of the social world and given that the researcher is not *an instrument* in the experimental sense. As Merriam and Tisdell (2015) note,

> Because what is being studied [in qualitative research] is assumed to be in flux, multifaceted, and highly contextual, because information gathered is a function of who gives it and how skilled the researcher is at getting it, and because the emergent design of a qualitative study precludes a priori controls, achieving reliability in the traditional sense is not only fanciful but impossible. (p. 251)

Is the study credible?

- Does the research derive from participants' views?
- Does the researcher reflect on her role?
- Can another researcher follow the internal logic in developing conclusions?

Instead, for qualitative studies, this historic concern shifts to a consideration of how thoughtfully and dependably the researcher conducted the study—it focuses directly on implementation. Was the study well conceived and well conducted? Are decisions clear? Was sufficient evidence gathered and presented? Was the researcher rigorous in searching for alternative explanations for what was learned? Are differing interpretations put forward and assessed? Is the researcher's chain of reasoning explicit?

Rather than judging whether replication would yield the same results, this standard for practice assesses the extent to which an outsider can scrutinize the logic of the study that has led to the results, given the data collected and displayed. Can someone else understand the logic and assumptions of the study and see the reasoning that resulted in the interpretations put forward? Are these interpretations sound and grounded in the data? Is the process of analysis clear and coherent?

What Can the Researcher Do? One strategy to help ensure that your qualitative study is rigorously conducted is to make your position clear, a demand we stress throughout this book. Another is to rely on multiple methods for gathering data, thereby enhancing the complexity of what you learn in the field. A third is to document assiduously the process of gathering, analyzing, and interpreting the data. Establishing your perspective and making your process transparent for others maps neatly onto the NRC's fourth principle, listed above. Erickson (1986) refers to this as the natural history of the inquiry. Keep a log or journal. Write interim analytic memos. These serve to document the intellectual odyssey of your study and help you establish its rigor to readers and potential users.

How Is the Study Useful for Other Situations?

Another concern is whether the study will have applicability to other situations. This parallels the requirement for generalizability in positivist research. Strict, probabilistic generalizing, however, can be done only to the population from which a sample was (randomly) drawn. What about other, similar populations? Even in quantitative research, generalizing from one population to another must be done through the reasoning of comparison and contrast, or analogic logic, rather than through probabilistic logic. Let us explicate this a bit more.

We would like our research findings to be useful in other settings or for subsequent studies. There are two primary pathways for helping make this possible: (1) generalizing the findings from a sample to a population and (2) arguing that a new situation is sufficiently similar for the original findings to be applicable. In the former, generalization is based on the logic of probabilities and relies on the power of mathematics to argue that findings from a randomly selected sample can be applied (generalized) to the population from which the sample was drawn (within certain confidence parameters). In the latter, an argument is put forward that the new instance is sufficiently similar to the original that application can be made. We like to think of these as a strict, probability-based definition of "generalization" and a broader definition that captures the human tendency to look for similarities and differences between instances of a phenomenon.

What is often missing in the discourse about generalizing is the recognition that strict, probabilistic generalizing can only be done to a population from which a sample was randomly drawn. To apply findings to those outside the carefully defined research population, one must rely on the logic of comparison and contrast—reasoning by analogy.

While it is important to be aware of these distinctions in building a case for how your study might be useful to others, remember that qualitative research is not searching for "abstract universals" but rather "concrete universals" (Erickson, 1986, p. 130), working hypotheses (Cronbach, 1975), or working understandings. The standard of generalizability is not typically part of the qualitative research vocabulary, but what is learned in one study can still be *useful* for other settings. As we have discussed thus far, usefulness is an important consideration in any research.

What Can the Researcher Do? To establish the usefulness of a study, provide thorough descriptions of your theoretical and methodological orientation and the research process. Also, provide a thick, rich description of what you have learned. This description should include as much detail about the context as is feasible. Potential users can then determine for themselves whether your results will be of use in a new but similar setting. They can compare and contrast the specifics of your study with their own settings and consider whether the two are sufficiently similar for your findings to be insightful. This logic is different from generalizing probabilistically; it is the same, however, as applying findings about one population to another. The reasoning requires careful assessment about the similarities and differences of the instances.

General Strategies for Ensuring Credibility and Rigor

You can rely on several strategies that help enhance the credibility and rigorousness with which you conduct a qualitative study. These include the following:

- *Triangulation:* Multiple sources of data, multiple points in time, or a variety of methods are used to build the picture that you are investigating. This helps ensure that you have not studied only a fraction of the complexity that you seek to understand.[1]

- *Being there:* Also known as *prolonged engagement*, being present for a long period in the setting or spending a substantial amount of time with participants helps ensure that you have more than a snapshot view of the phenomenon.

- *Participant validation:* Also known as *member checks*, you take emerging findings back to the participants for them to elaborate, correct, extend, or argue about. This can be done with interview transcripts as a method for eliciting further information and with emerging analyses.

Is the study useful to others?

- Is there sufficient description to determine similarity and difference?
- Does the community of practice see the logic in the interpretations?

- *Using a critical friend:* Also known as a *peer debriefer*, this person serves as an intellectual watchdog for you as you modify design decisions, develop possible analytic categories, and build an explanation for the phenomenon of interest.

- *Using the community of practice:* You engage in critical and sustained discussion with valued colleagues in a setting of sufficient trust so that emerging ideas, tentative hypotheses, and half-baked ideas can be shared.

These standards for practice and for judging the integrity and value of qualitative studies (truth value, rigor, and usefulness) are important considerations when designing and conducting a study. Our characters are learning about these as they read and discuss the many writings about the theory and practice of doing qualitative inquiry. Also, they will learn even more as they implement their own studies and experience the complexity of the decision processes involved. They will be mindful of what constitutes good practice.

Our Characters' Strategies **Ruth** has decided to explore the experiences of children and youth in wheelchairs who play basketball at a local after-school care center. In discussions with her classmates, she has created a new term—*bodied-ness*—to capture the contradictions inherent in playing sports while using a wheelchair. She came to this through watching the Special Winter Olympics at Salt Lake City and was enthralled with the slalom skiers who were paraplegics.

Because she volunteers at the school where the care center meets, she expects to observe and interview the children regularly over the semester. She anticipates that this frequent and easy participation with the children will bring a depth of knowledge about their perspectives on bodied-ness. One of her strategies is, therefore, *being there.* Her observations and interviews will contribute to *triangulation*, another strategy.

Anthony has accepted the challenge to evaluate a community arts program. His design calls for using multiple methods to gather data, which include observing programmatic activities, observing and talking to people in the center, and interviewing artists and community members. Thus, he will use *triangulation* as a primary strategy. In addition, he plans to share his preliminary findings with a selected group of key center members for *participant validation.*

Marla and her team use a variety of strategies. Because she is working with a team of women who use the clinic, *participant validation* is built into her study. Also built in is the strategy of *being there* because Marla volunteers on a regular basis. The team will observe and conduct interviews, thereby relying on *triangulation* as well.

Anthony, Marla, and Ruth use each other as *critical friends*, and as members of Professor Kent's class, they have a *community of practice.* Overall, the six principles of the NRC can serve to guide their work to be systematic and competent.

Beyond Systematicity

We have argued, however, that our characters also must demonstrate rigorous reasoning that leads them to act in ways that honor the participants—to be ethical practitioners.

The NRC principles, while important, do not go far enough to ensure a credible, trustworthy study. They do not explicitly address either the ethics of conducting research or the political nuances of the research world and the context of the study (although context is mentioned by the NRC in its summary of scientific research we quoted earlier). When examined closely, however, some of the principles suggest considerations of ethics and politics.

Principle 1: *Asking important questions* clearly has ethical and political elements and captures the "should-do-ability" notion (which we discuss in Chapter 5). Thus, judging whether a question is significant should entail judgments about whether it would be ethical to pursue this question and whether pursuing the questions would redress previous power imbalances in society. Applying this principle brings to mind a doctoral student who proposed to ask whether school boards tended to hire the more physically attractive candidates in pools of principal applicants. We questioned not only whether such a study would contribute any important knowledge but also whether the question itself was ethically offensive with its implied disrespect for individual differences.

Furthermore, what is considered important is shaped by multiple influences. First, as researcher, your personal biography guides your preferences and interests. At the same time, the institutions and environments in which you live and work contribute to setting research agendas and determining appropriate methodologies. Funding agencies put forth requests for proposals on specific topics, thereby signaling what they consider important. If you want funding from that agency, you will have to conform to its interests. Similarly, university departments, research committees, and individual faculty members (your advisor, perhaps) establish what they consider to be legitimate research questions to pursue. All of these influence your project in important ways. An illustrative example is the way the more than a decadelong emphasis the U.S. federal government placed on randomized controlled trials (RCTs) as the gold standard for research and evaluation has shaped the choices of research questions posed in proposals for funding. The postmodern critique (discussed in Chapter 4) challenges this hegemony of the policy world over inquiry and calls on us to push at the borders of what is considered legitimate work and who deems it so. Doing so has some risks, however, especially for the beginner.

Principle 2: *Linking to relevant theory* also draws one into considerations of the ethical and political. As we show in Chapter 5, the conceptual framework (the relevant theory in which the study is embedded) should recognize the political situation of the context for the study. The conceptual framework also articulates the researcher's stance, or intellectual orientation, and signals for whom or for which groups the question is worthy and important to pursue (back to Principle 1). This framework also grounds the specific study in larger considerations or issues, inviting the ethical question of purpose and beneficence—Is the burden of participating in this research worth the benefits? Should energy be expended to pursue this question?

[handwritten margin note: Asking important ?'s]

[handwritten margin note: Link to relevant theory]

using methods for direct investigation

Principle 3: *Using methods for direct investigation* has clear ethical and political considerations, because the use of particular methods with specific participants entails, as we argue below, ethical sensitivities throughout the conduct of the study. Moreover, particular methods may well be politically unsavory or inappropriate, disrupting hierarchies in dangerous ways. For example, Marla's choice to collect her data through participant involvement may reflect both political and ethical concerns. The choice of method for direct investigation may carry additional limitations in international settings; for example, which settings may be culturally inappropriate to observe? Or when might gender influence who can interview whom and where? One doctoral student studying women's health in Afghanistan found that she could not speak privately with the adolescent girls whose knowledge of personal health she wished to understand.

Just as institutions and actors shape appropriate research questions, they determine what method is "best." Despite a long and respected history in anthropology (see Chapter 4), qualitative researchers struggled long and hard to create legitimacy for their work in applied fields such as urban policy, management, education, nursing, and social work. One still finds departments engaged in the sometimes vicious qualitative–quantitative "paradigm wars" (Gage, 1989). As the postmodern perspective has moved out of literary criticism and into the social sciences, just what constitutes good qualitative research has become contested. For example, some academic departments do not allow the use of the pronoun *I* in the final dissertation, thus hampering a qualitative researcher's effort to establish his voice. These politics are often paramount and hold hostage the student who is trying to learn and understand research methods.

Principle 4: *Providing a coherent chain of reasoning* must, in our view, include reasoning about ethical issues and dilemmas that arose during the conduct of a study, as well as discussing the political dynamics that emerged. Recall reflexivity (discussed in Chapter 2), which we consider to be an ongoing activity of reasoning through moral principles that is integral to any competent and trustworthy study.

Principle 5: *Replicating and generalizing across studies* lends itself to considerations of ethics and politics as one might argue that using any study for further purposes should be evaluated through an ethical lens. Can findings from one context be applied directly to another with equity, fairness, and probity?

Principle 6: *Disclosing research to professional scrutiny* should include, as mentioned above, discussions of the ethics and politics encountered, in order for the community of discourse to make a fully informed judgment about the merit and worth of the study.

While the principles can be argued to have ethical and political dimensions, we believe that this was not the intent of the NRC document. Thus, we are more comfortable considering the above principles as guidelines for competent research practice but argue that ethics and politics must be highlighted (brought into the foreground) and seriously considered for a study to be truly trustworthy. Our definition, thus, goes beyond the principles articulated above. A second standard to help establish trustworthiness is that the study be conducted in an ethical manner, with sensitivity to the complex interpersonal situations that being in the field embraces.

ETHICAL PRACTICE

Qualitative research begins with questions. As we claim at the outset, informing these questions should have a goal of learning to improve some social circumstance, and so the questions themselves thus establish a moral position. In qualitative research, you, the researcher, are the means through which the questions are explored and informed. You continually and consciously make decisions about conceptualizing, designing, conducting, interpreting, and writing up findings. As an ethical researcher, you draw on your moral principles to guide this decision making. Your interpretations construct the knowledge, so you systematically document your decisions and reflect on what you are learning, how you are learning it, what role you play in the interpretations, and what the learning might mean to participants and other audiences. You use complex moral reasoning that is both multifaceted and iterative, moving back and forth between the specifics and the whole, between yourself (the knower) and what you claim to know. You are, in short, ethically reflexive, reasoning and acting according to a code or standard for conduct that is based on moral principles. Simultaneously, you attend to the procedures required for human subjects research. We begin with ethical reasoning, move to procedural standards, and then present challenges you may face.

Ethical Reasoning

In practice, qualitative researchers encounter ethics in every decision they make, every action they take. Yet, while we talk a lot about ethics, the word is seldom defined or explicated. The word *ethics* originates from the Greek *ethos*, meaning "character." Your moral principles—what you consider to be *good* or *bad*, *right* or *wrong*—define your ethics and, thus, your character, which guides your actions. In other words, moral principles provide the rules that tell you how to act in any given situation.

Not everyone agrees, however, on a common set of moral principles. Philosophers and ethical theorists have described and delineated numerous different moral theories to analyze or direct ethical behavior according to the criteria each uses to decide which behaviors are right or wrong: *consequences*, *rights and responsibilities*, *social justice*, or *care*.

Most ethical theories can be grouped into two broad categories: consequentialist and nonconsequentialist. The moral principles derived from *consequentialist ethical theories focus on outcomes.* Any particular action is not intrinsically good or bad; rather, it is good or bad because of its results in a particular context—its consequences. When determining

outcomes

the rightness or wrongness of an action, the consequentialist asks "What happens as a result of this action?" and "What are the probable consequences to whom and under what circumstances?" This ethic is most clearly illustrated by *utilitarianism*, "the doctrine that the greatest good of the greatest number should be the guiding principle of conduct" ("Utilitarianism," 1993). Explicated by late 18th- and early 19th-century philosophers such as A. O. Hume and John Stuart Mill, this doctrine declares "that actions are right if they are useful or for the benefit of a majority" ("Utilitarianism," 1993). Among themselves, utilitarian philosophers debate "What is good?" and "Whose good?" The basic idea underlying utilitarianism, the *ethic of consequences*, is a valuable and worthwhile facet of sound ethical reasoning.

Nonconsequentialist ethical theories, on the other hand, recognize universal standards to guide all behavior regardless of the consequences in a specific context. If an action is wrong in one setting, it must be wrong in all possible contexts. Two nonconsequentialist theories with which qualitative researchers operate are the *ethic of individual rights and responsibilities* and *the ethic of justice*. The first upholds the unconditional worth of and equal respect to which all human beings are entitled and the corresponding obligations (or responsibilities) that individuals have to protect those rights. All people are endowed with fundamental rights that may not be denied, even for the greatest good for the greatest number. The philosopher Kant (1788/1956) recognized the unconditional value of the human being: Each person must be treated as an end in herself, not as a means to an end. Kant's ideas direct us to act as we would want everyone else to act. Examples of fundamental rights include the right of free consent, of privacy, of freedom of conscience, of free speech, and of due process. These statements of fundamental rights are notably Western ideas, but they are encoded in United Nations' documents.

Another nonconsequentialist theory is the *ethic of justice*, which goes beyond individual rights to espouse the redistribution of resources and opportunities to achieve equity above equality, especially in circumstances of social and economic disadvantage. Relying on principles of fairness and equity to evaluate which actions are right or wrong, this doctrine aims to ensure that everyone is better off. While some redistribution may be unequal, the result is equitable. According to Rawls (1971), the benefit or welfare of the least advantaged, not that of the majority or average, must drive any decision. Such apparently unequal treatment is justified because, according to the ethic of justice reasoning, benefitting the least benefits the whole. These nonconsequentialist perspectives consider questions of power and representation, asking, Who defines what is right in a given setting? They encourage researchers to pay extra attention to previously silenced voices.

These two categories of ethical theories offer guidance for relationships between researchers and participants, but their underlying principles are generated externally to be applied to the particular relationship. Other perspectives situate the morality within the relationship or context itself. The *ethic of communitarianism* (MacIntyre, 1981) acknowledges that communities differ on what is morally good or right. Thus, as a researcher, you may find that not all in your research study share fundamental values—and that these values may even conflict with your own. A postmodern or critical view would remind you that power and dominance shape the research relationships and thus the research (Foucault, 1977).

Still, because they are theories, none of the above perspectives may be practically helpful to get you through the ethically important moments (Guillemin & Gillam, 2004) you will encounter. A more powerful and practical way to conceptualize the moral and ethical aspects of qualitative research might spotlight the relationships within the study through an *ethic of care*. This ethic emphasizes concrete circumstances over abstract principles. You ask, What does *this* participant need in *this* moment? Care theory emphasizes the moral interdependence of people: "Our goodness and our growth are inextricably bound to that of others we encounter. As researchers, we are as dependent on our [participants] as they are on us" (Noddings, 1995, p. 196).

> Ethical decisions must be made in caring interactions with those affected by the discussion. Indeed, it is exactly in the most difficult situations that principles fail us. Thus, instead of turning to a principle for guidance, a carer returns to the cared-for. What does he or she need? Will filling this need harm others in the network of care? Am I competent to fill this need? Will I sacrifice too much of myself? Is the expressed need really in the best interest of the cared-for? (Noddings, 1995, p. 187)

Your aim is to build the mutual respect necessary for a caring research relationship to be possible; reciprocity is key. "One must meet the other in caring. From this requirement there is no escape for one who would be moral" (Noddings, 1984, p. 201). Mutual care and respect can bridge the gap between the purposes and needs of both members in the relationship.

> Research involving human participants starts from a position of ethical tension. In the great majority of cases, research involving humans is a process of asking people to take part in, or undergo, procedures that they have not actively sought out or requested, and that are not intended solely or even primarily for their direct benefit, although participants may indirectly benefit from the process . . . [note violation of Kantian maxim that people should never be used as a means to someone else's end] this tension can be resolved, however, if the subjects of the research take up the goals of the research as their own; they are not then being used as a mere means or tools by the researchers. (Guillemin & Gillam, 2004, p. 271)

As you see, different ethics exist and can be used to guide your decision making. We believe that they all direct us to act as we would want others to act in any given situation, in ways that treat humanity as ends as well as means. Put simply, one person should never exploit others to his own advantage. Because people have the capacity to make moral choices, qualitative researchers must weigh sometimes competing ethical principles. However, we are quite firm in our belief that the ethical researcher does not exploit any

don't exploit people -- obviously

person in any circumstances regardless of differences in status, race, gender, language, and other social identity considerations. We also believe that care theory, with its emphasis on relationships, can connect principles and context, providing a practical guide for making moral decisions.

Procedural Ethics: Institutional Review Boards

Because research has not always honored the balance between the need to produce knowledge and the obligation to protect the humans studied,[2] federal law has entered the research scene. The National Research Act, Public Law 93-348, mandates the establishment of a Human Subjects Committee—an IRB—in every university and organization that receives federal funding and conducts research involving human subjects. The IRB reviews all proposals for research before the research can be conducted to ensure that no humans or animals are put at risk and that each proposal includes necessary protections. If organizations do not comply, they risk losing federal funding. The general criteria for IRB approval are as follows:

- Risks are minimized.
- Risk/benefit ratio is reasonable.
- Subject selection is equitable.
- Informed consent is obtained and documented.
- Data are monitored and secured.
- Privacy and confidentiality are protected.

Additional protections are required for subjects vulnerable to coercion or undue influence. The Office for Human Research Protections of the U.S. Department of Health and Human Services also states, "Informed consent is not a single event or just a form to be signed—rather, it is an educational process that takes place between the investigator and the prospective subject" (Yoder, 2009, slide 35). We strongly agree—in fact, we could not have said it better.

The protections are based on three basic principles, described in the Belmont Report (U.S. Department of Health and Human Services, 1979), generally accepted in Western cultural tradition as particularly relevant to the ethics of research involving human subjects: the principles of respect of persons, beneficence, and justice.

- The principle of respect for persons incorporates two ethical convictions: first, that individuals should be treated as autonomous agents and, second, that persons with diminished autonomy are entitled to protection.
- The principle of beneficence reflects the moral obligation to (a) do no harm and (b) maximize possible benefits and minimize possible harms.

- The principle of justice is more complicated. It addresses the questions concerning *fairness in distribution* or *what is deserved*: Who ought to receive the benefits of research and who shall bear its burdens? An injustice occurs when some benefit to which a person is entitled is denied without good reason or when some burden is imposed unduly. Another aspect of justice is equality and equity; different criteria may be used (paraphrased from the Belmont Report cited above): (a) to each person an equal share, (b) to each person according to individual need, (c) to each person according to individual effort, (d) to each person according to societal contribution, and (e) to each person according to merit.

Each IRB has codified its rules for applying these principles and criteria according to the federal regulations. Please note that these rules vary widely by institution, with some requiring extensive details in informed consent forms including, for example, type of equipment used (video cameras, still photography, or audiotape) and contact information for not only the student but also the professor supervising the research. But in general, these rules seek to ensure that individual privacy is respected and that the risk to participants is minimal. *Minimal risk* usually means the potential that the proposed research might harm participants is no greater than the risks in daily life. The rules specifying proper procedure, however, can be quite stringent and, in some cases, seem to operate with little appreciation for the interactive and humanistic methods of qualitative inquiry.

Most IRBs have a procedure for exemption from full review for research. Conditions may include the following:

- Normal education practices in established educational settings

- Interviews or observation procedures of public behavior unless the participants are under age 18, the individual can be identified, or disclosure would place the participant at risk

- Projects designed to study public benefit or service programs

 Research involving children (under age 18) is never exempt, and in all cases, it *must* include informed consent of parents or guardians. Some recommend that the child's informed consent form be written in a language appropriate to the child's age and notation be included if the form is to be read to the child.

The IRBs of each institution are empowered to make decisions to approve or disapprove research proposals. Knowledge of your institution's or organization's procedures is crucial as you begin to design your study. As a regulatory body, the IRB is a political force, historically grounded in positivist assumptions, that can limit your choices but at the same time ignore the full scope of ethical decisions you will face. We encourage you to recognize that your reasoning may at times involve a balancing act between procedural requirements and what you consider to be right based on your moral principles. For example, in Rallis, Rossman, and Gadja (2007), we discuss the challenges qualitative researchers face, both domestically and internationally, in obtaining signatures indicating informed consent.

Challenges in Ethical Practice

Within the research relationship, then, practical tensions are present: harm and burden versus respect and benefit. Avoiding harm (physical, emotional, or social) is basic (Guillemin & Gillam, 2004), and bearing undue burden may be harmful (see Hemmings, 2006). However, in qualitative research, potentials for harm "are often quite subtle and stem from the nature of the interaction between researcher and participant" (Guillemin & Gillam, 2004, p. 272). Professional groups and social science disciplines have established formal codes of ethics to guide their fields' research relationships and activities. So, too, have the United States and other national governments. Deceptive and downright harmful research conducted earlier in this century led to the development of ethical codes. They are intended to serve as guidelines for practice to ensure that participants in research projects are protected from harm and are not deceived. We argue that each researcher develops his own standards for ethical practice as he encounters situations that demand complex moral reasoning. These personal guidelines, however, cannot be wildly idiosyncratic. They must be cognizant of the formal codes that exist in the discipline or profession and of the writings of qualitative researchers about the ethical dilemmas and issues with which they have grappled in their own practice. Some ethical considerations are generic, others are study specific. We discuss three generic ones and give some specific examples.

> Ethical situations are not solvable. They are dilemmas that the researcher must reason his way through based on intuition, personal values, standards within the profession, and moral principles.

Keep in mind that *ethical dilemmas are not solvable* but are reasoned through moral principles. You must be able to explain your reasoning, although it may not agree with the prevailing dominant principle. For example, undercover investigators for a news network who sought to expose conscious mishandling of food in a supermarket chain lied on their applications for work in the stores. The supermarket chain sued for damages resulting from the exposure of information gathered through the deception. The investigators justified the lie as being for the greater good of society (utilitarian principles). The courts made the news network pay damages and fines because, they reasoned, lying violated a preeminent principle.

The following issues are generic to qualitative research. They suggest dilemmas that the researcher must reason through with thoughtfulness and sensitivity to the uniqueness of the setting. Relevant ethical principles may conflict; hence they are called dilemmas. The dilemma lies in how you choose to apply the principles.

Privacy and Confidentiality   Qualitative research takes place in the field, with real people who live and work in the setting. They are not anonymous to the researcher, and if she is not diligent in protecting their identities, they may not be anonymous to anyone.

CONFIDENTIALITY

Thus, if researchers promise confidentiality to the participants, they must be sure that they can deliver confidentiality. This challenge has two elements: (1) protecting the privacy of participants (identities, names, and specific roles) and (2) holding in confidence what they share with you (not sharing it with others using their names). A current counterargument is that making people anonymous deprives them of agency in the work of the study. Those holding this position argue that the participants themselves should decide whether they want to be named in a written report or whether the organization or setting should be named. We acknowledge the persuasive politics of this argument but urge caution, particularly for the beginner. The ways in which written reports can be used go well beyond the control of either researcher or participants. Through reading and experience, the researcher may well have a more subtle view of potential hazards if an organization or individuals are specifically identified. We urge that the default position should be to mask specific identities unless a compelling reason not to is put forward.

We remember studies we conducted as beginners when we unwittingly came close to breaking our promise of confidentiality. Participants sometimes ask what others have said to us in their interviews. In the spirit of conversational give and take, our reflex then was to begin to answer. Fortunately, we realized that the promise of confidentiality was to all participants. Our response was similar to the following: "We said we wouldn't share what you tell us with others, so we can't tell you what anyone has said, either."

Over time and with experience, the response to protect becomes the reflex, rather than the urge to tell. A cautionary note, however: It is also important to remind participants that you will use their words in direct quotes in a written report. Although you will do all you can to protect their identities, an organizational sleuth might be able to figure out who said what. Sharing this conditional aspect of confidentiality is a more ethical (and accurate) stance than pretending that you can be omniscient and powerful and can protect their identities no matter what.

INFORMED CONSENT

Deception and Consent Gaining the *informed consent* of participants is crucial for the ethical conduct of research. In fact, university human subject review committees (often called IRBs, discussed more fully below) require a sample informed consent form with each dissertation and research proposal that is conducted under the university's auspices. Although often codified in a standardized form, the ethical principles underlying informed consent are as follows:

- Participants are as fully informed as possible about the study's purpose and audience.

- They understand what their agreement to participate entails.

- They give that consent willingly.

- They understand that they may withdraw from the study at any time without prejudice.

they know what's up

This means that the participants are not deceived about the study and that their participation is voluntary.

Informed consent, however, also serves to protect the identities and privacy of participants (see above). Thus, participants are aware that their names and identifying information, such as specific roles, will not be used in any discussions or written documents about the research. IRBs require informed consent for research involving human beings (and, increasingly, for similar assurances about protection from harm for research with animals). This has evolved because of deeply disturbing research with human subjects in previous decades in which participants were explicitly deceived, leading (in some cases) to psychological damage.

We are often asked how to manage informed consent with participants who do not speak English as their first language, who are not literate, or for whom such an act is considered highly inappropriate (because of history or cultural norms). The first condition can be easily met by translating the form into a participant's first language. The second can be addressed by explaining orally the intent of informed consent and then asking the participant to make his mark on the form. This may need the facilitation of a cultural liaison or translator. The third, however, is a bit more tricky. In some cultural contexts, having to sign one's name or put one's mark on a piece of paper is highly suspect. If previous colonial powers or current authoritarian regimes required such action and then used it against citizens, the threat or fear is quite clear. How does the ethical researcher conform to the (quite appropriate) demands of an IRB but still respect the cultural values (equally appropriate) of participants? Our advice has been that students *must* observe the ethical intent of informed consent. They can, quite naturally, explain the assurances of informed consent and obtain agreement orally. This has often worked. Figure 3.1 is an example of an informed consent letter.

All this seems quite clear. On closer examination, however, the precise implementation of informed consent and its considerations of privacy and honesty get a bit murky. *Some* deception may be involved in much research: Just how much can we fully tell participants about our conceptual framework (how much do they care)? Do we deceive them when we briefly summarize it? If we take on a role, as Marla does as a volunteer, are we masking our full identities? What if the purpose of the study shifts? Do we inform everyone we have interviewed already? Can participants fully understand what their words will look like in a written report before the report is written? Your task is to be as open and honest *as you possibly can be* as you move through a study and build relationships with members of the setting. The key is that the researcher must take every possible precaution to ensure that no harm will come to the participants as a result of their participating in the study.

Another aspect of deception needs mention. At times, in some circumstances, the potential benefits of a study may outweigh the demand to be open and forthright (utilitarian principles). Studies of classroom interaction patterns, for example, have

FIGURE 3.1   Sample Informed Consent Letter

STUDY OF TEACHER

EXPERIENCE AND ATTITUDES WITH EDUCATING STUDENTS WITH PHYSICAL DISABILITIES

CONSENT FOR VOLUNTARY PARTICIPATION

I agree to volunteer to participate in this qualitative study and understand that I will be interviewed by using a guided interview format. The questions I will be answering address my views on issues related to my experiences and beliefs about educating students with physical disabilities in my school. The primary purpose of this research is to understand what the beliefs and assumptions held by teachers are regarding students with physical disabilities. The interview will be tape recorded to facilitate analysis of the data. I understand that tape recordings will be stored on a password-protected computer and destroyed after transcription.

My name will not be used, nor will I be identified personally, in any way or at any time. The researchers will work to protect my identity by using pseudonyms when necessary. I may withdraw from part or all of this study at any time. I understand that results from this research may be included in Mary Trucie's classwork and may be used in manuscripts submitted to professional journals for publication. I am free to participate or not to participate without prejudice. Because of the small number of participants, approximately four, I understand that there is some risk that I may be identified as a participant of this study.

If you have questions or comments regarding this study, please feel free to contact Mary Trucie. Mary's phone number is 555-555-5656 and e-mail address is mtrucie16@flagshipstate.edu. You may also contact Mary's professor, Dr. Rallman, at 555-555-5757 or rallman@flagshipstate.edu or the Associate Dean for Academic Affairs, Dr. Lindstrom, lindstrom@flagshipstate.edu.

Researcher's Signature	**Date**	**Participant's Signature**	**Date**

shown the persistent, subtle, and complex ways in which otherwise well-intentioned teachers privilege boys and white children (Sadker & Sadker, 1994). Those researchers might not have learned about this inequitable treatment of students in such detail if the teachers studied had known that sexist and racist actions were the focus. In these studies, the researchers simply told the teachers that they would be observing teacher–student interactions. Was this really deception? If so, was the deception worth it? Punch (1994) comments on this as follows:

> One need not always be brutally honest, direct, and explicit about one's research purpose, but one should not normally engage in disguise. One should not steal documents. One should not directly lie to people. And, although one may disguise identity to a certain extent, one should not break promises made to people. (p. 91)

Would you deceive?

If so, under what circumstances?

Punch (1994) takes a pragmatic position that some dissimulation is intrinsic to social life and therefore also to fieldwork (p. 91), but he cautions that care must be exercised so that participants come to no harm. This is a delicate balance.

Trust and Betrayal Qualitative research involves building and sustaining relationships with people. The long, in-depth interview can be quite intimate and disclosing; people often tell more than they know they are telling, and the researcher often learns more than she wishes. Ethnographic fieldwork entails becoming part of the fabric of the participants' social world, a true albeit unusual member of the community. When the research is over, what happens? The researcher ends the interviews, leaves the field, and writes up the study. One could argue that the very role of researcher involves some deception; you are deeply interested in people's stories, but that interest is conditional and bounded. Siskin (1994) calls this the *seduction and abandonment* inherent in much qualitative research. The image is that you seduce the participants into disclosing their worldviews and then abandon them when you have gotten what you want—data. Punch (1994) reasons that this may be particularly painful for those who seek "solidarity in the field" but then must "depart and start writing up their experiences for academic consumption" (p. 94). This self-interested view of qualitative research is challenged directly by some feminist and postmodern researchers who argue for participatory, shared, and purposeful (other than research purposes) engagement with participants.

Betrayal may come in other guises. Recall the previous quote from Punch (1994) in which he says that you should not break promises made to people. For example, you promise confidentiality to a student but learn, in the course of several in-depth interviews, that the student may be the victim of child abuse. If you are a *mandated reporter* (one with a legally defined role relative to children—that is, a teacher or counselor), you must report this information to appropriate authorities. In so doing, do you put the child at risk for further abuse? Do you violate your promise to protect her from harm and to respect her privacy? In a less dramatic example, suppose you observe an unethical or illegal practice. Do you report this to authorities and, in so doing, break your promise of confidentiality to the participants? You will have to reason through the potential consequences to the actors in the setting, yourself, the profession and consider the larger social concerns of whatever action you take. Your personal ethical code determines the decisions you reach and the actions you take. Be aware that your code may not fully align with a prevailing code. Think of industrial whistle-blowers. Your actions might cause you to lose your job or take you into court.

Coping With Micropolitics As discussed above, power dynamics operate in all social settings. Some involve the power of personality or position; others involve the politics of race and gender. These are often the most salient and yet difficult predicaments for the qualitative researcher. We have met program funders who demand particular results, whether to ensure the program's continuance or its demise. Gatekeepers, those in positions of power in organizations, can support or quash a project (discussed in Chapter 6). Influential actors on the scene can ease access or make it difficult even to schedule interviews. Also, issues of race and gender may play out throughout the entire project. Political dynamics among groups in a setting can torpedo the best intentions of a beginner. Becoming aware of micropolitics in general and those specific to your site will stand you in good stead as you navigate the sometimes turbulent waters of a qualitative project.

Ethical dilemmas you may encounter in the field have no easy solutions. No template or moral calculus can help you weigh the risks and benefits for the many actors and groups that surround your research. Ethical issues are not solved. We are suspicious of beginning researchers who identify thorny and troublesome ethical situations and tell us they have solved them. Solutions are ephemeral; someone else might argue for a radically different course of action. Instead, we look for sensitivity to the generic and specific ethics in a study and complex and subtle moral reasoning that identifies a range of risks and benefits for those involved. Such subtle argumentation stands you in good stead for justifying decisions made in the field. Given our increasingly litigious society, knowing your own code of ethics and moral principles becomes especially important should you ever be called on (e.g., in a court of law) to articulate your thinking and justify your actions.

What Can the Researcher Do? Although no template for reasoning through ethical issues or resolving dilemmas exists, we do believe that people move through generic levels of thinking about the ethical decisions they make. (These levels are adapted from an excellent and thorough discussion of ethical decision making in Newman & Brown, 1996.) These levels are as follows:

- Intuition
- Rules, standards, or codes
- Principles or theories
- Personal values

Intuition guides the first level. We have an intuitive response to a situation: What's wrong here? Why am I uneasy? I'm not sure how to act in this situation. I feel very uncomfortable. This level of thinking is *intuitive* because it is not necessarily rational or logical; it is more about feelings the researcher has in a situation. The result of this thinking is either to proceed as planned or to decide that a potential ethical dilemma exists and, therefore, to stop and conduct further analysis.

The next two levels of thinking explore existing resources for decision making. What *rules, standards, or codes* might apply to this situation? Does the rule, standard, or code fit this dilemma? Or do I recognize that a broader principle is involved? The result of this thinking is either a decision to apply a relevant rule or code and take the corresponding action or a decision to consider *ethical principles or theories* underlying the dilemma. At this next level, we deliberate on criteria (consequence/rights and responsibilities/social

[handwritten margin note: → no solutions to ethical issues]

justice/care) that the theories suggest should be used to determine action. In determining when to apply which principle, we ask the following:

- What are the possible consequences to individuals and groups?

- What rights must be protected? What are my responsibilities to protect these rights?

- Are participants' needs and interests considered equitably? Am I aware of the needs and interests of the less powerful participants?

- How might the participants perceive our relationship?

- What unique needs, interests, rights, or consequences play into this specific setting?

- How will actions affect the relationships among the people in the setting?

The final level of ethical consideration relies on our own *personal values* to mediate our decision for action. This is the point where we ask ourselves "What kind of person am I?" and "What is important to me as a researcher?" We explore the alternatives, assessing the risks and rewards of each. We have reasoned through rules, principles, and values to reach a decision we believe we can live with. We take action accordingly. Ethical action often demands courage.

Our Characters' Dilemmas and Challenges As **Ruth** develops a relationship with Sebastian, one of the teenage boys in her study, she learns more than she would like to know about his family dynamics. Sebastian hints at events and patterns that deeply trouble Ruth. She ponders what her role should be, given questionable behaviors by Sebastian's mother. Should she tell someone the vague innuendoes? Who? Will this betray Sebastian's trust? In addition, she questions whether these data are relevant to her study about Sebastian's sense of bodied-ness. Should she include them? How? At what risk to her relationship with Sebastian?

Later, Ruth has a facedown with her institution's IRB. It initially refused approval for her small-scale study, citing that she needed the approval of the children's primary care physicians to conduct this study. The IRB even questioned her right to ask students in wheelchairs how they felt about their bodies.

One of **Anthony**'s informants, Nick the metal sculptor, is particularly critical of the center's use of photographs of his work. The media director has used several shots in promotional materials without appropriate credit. Nick tells Anthony about other artists who have had similar experiences over the years. He reminds Anthony not to reveal his identity because it would compromise the low studio rental that he gets at the center. How can Anthony use this information without betraying Nick's trust? Even if he uses a quote from Nick without identifying the source, Anthony worries that someone at the center will know—or assume—it was Nick. Also, Anthony confronts politics directly after an informal meeting with the director of the agency funding the evaluation. Anthony, perhaps unwisely but nonetheless honestly, shared some data that were quite negative about a major activity in the arts program. The director said, "We think this is a good program and want to keep funding it. Your results should help us out here. Understand?"

One afternoon while **Marla** is filing health records in the main office at the clinic, she overhears a conversation between a physician and a nurse. The nurse pleads with the physician to review the record of Felicia Montenegro, who has symptoms that the physician attributes to alcohol abuse but the nurse believes may be the result of the physician's overprescribing her blood pressure medicine. Marla does not know what to do. Marla's action research study is fraught with micropolitics. The poor women, the physician's assistants, the physicians, and the nurses all interact in ways that sustain the traditional hierarchy of the medical profession. The women feel increasingly dismissed as they learn in more depth about the subtle ways in which power and dominance are enacted in the clinic. Should she report her concerns to the committee that oversees the clinic? Would that jeopardize Felicia's continued care? How might this come to harm her? Since Marla feels this conversation is data that informs the action research project, she also wonders whether she should write up detailed field notes.

DISPOSITIONS AND SKILLS

Learning to be competent and ethical researchers challenges Marla, Ruth, and Anthony to consider their relationships with and obligations to people, both the people they will study and the people who will read and use their work. As the process unfolds, they recognize those decisions over which they have control, as well as those in the hands of others. Sensitivity to interpersonal dynamics, politics, and ethics will be highly important to their learning and knowing. They articulate their ethical principles and work their way through ethical dilemmas. They begin to figure out how to meet the demands of multiple groups that have some relationship to their proposed studies.

As we have noted, our characters form a community of practice. They explore possibilities, testing out with each other their understandings and proposals—that is, they share, critique, question, and suggest. Their mutual support helps them move forward in their thinking about implementing their studies. Together they are learning what it means to be competent and ethical researchers and building the following dispositions and skills:

- Comfort with ambiguity
- Capacity to make reasoned decisions and to articulate the logic behind those decisions
- Deep interpersonal or emotional sensitivity
- Ethical sensitivity to potential consequences to individuals and groups
- Political sensitivity
- Perseverance and self-discipline

ACTIVITIES FOR YOUR COMMUNITY OF PRACTICE

Study Questions for Students

- Why are standards for research practice important?

- What ethical and political issues do you need to consider in fieldwork?

- What makes a study trustworthy?

- How can you ensure the trustworthiness of your study?

- What are your institution's IRB guidelines? How might you apply them?

Small-Group or Dyad Activities

Assessing Trustworthiness

This activity is intended to encourage in-depth reading and judgment of how authors address issues of trustworthiness in published work. Select three articles that report qualitative studies and are in well-respected research journals. Each dyad or small group reads one article and attempts to determine how trustworthy the article is and explains why. Identify your criteria, and give specific examples of how the article does or does not meet those criteria. Each small group is responsible for sharing its individual analyses and developing the supporting evidence. Then each group presents its analysis to the larger group.

Debate on Van Maanen's Choice

This activity is designed to have you argue either for or against John Van Maanen's ethical choice as presented in "The Moral Fix: On the Ethics of Field Work" (1983). To refresh your memories, in the situation he discusses in the article, he decided not to intervene in events that could be argued to involve police brutality. His reasoning in this decision centered on what he considered an ethical obligation to the police with whom he had been working, based on norms of reciprocity and trust. Recall that, in the Western context in which Van Maanen lives and works, ethical decisions involve the balancing of often conflicting sets of obligations to various people or ideas: to the participants, to the profession, to society, to knowledge, to a funding agent, and to oneself as researcher and human being.

For this activity, divide into groups of three or four. Each group then takes a position: One group will be asked to take the position that Van Maanen's decision was sound. This group should argue in favor of the decision using the moral principles or ethical concerns presented in this chapter. The other group will take the position that his decision was unethical and present an argument that supports an alternative choice.

Take 15 to 20 minutes to develop your logic, and then present it to the other group. The group arguing in favor of his decision should go first, taking about 10 minutes to present its case. Conduct this like a debate, following procedural rules that allow one group to present its position, then the other, then each having a chance to rebut.

The strength of this activity lies in your arguing cogently and passionately for the position you have been assigned. At first glance, many might disagree with Van Maanen's decision, but if you consider carefully the circumstances of the police and the expectations he had created for rendering support, your assessment of his decision may be more subtle.

Critiquing Your Institution's IRB Forms

Find your institution's IRB website and print out the application forms for research with human subjects. Review the types of questions to which you must respond and the procedures for obtaining approval. Critique the forms and procedures for their relevance for qualitative research. With your community of practice, discuss how you might meet particularly challenging requirements.

Writing Activity

Reflections on Ethical Issues

Woven throughout this book is careful consideration of the ethical issues inherent in the conduct of any inquiry. Some of these issues are generic—that is, they are frequently encountered in studies; others are more specific to your own particular study. Supplemental readings (indicated at the end of the chapter) provide some discussion of those issues that are generic; you will identify many that are specific. Although we understand that all qualitative studies are context specific, some issues recur.

In a reflections paper, consider the issues that have arisen in the conduct of your study. First, briefly describe your study to orient the reader. Next, focus on the generic issues that you have had to deal with. These might include learning personal information that is not directly relevant to your research questions or observing harmful or discriminatory behaviors in the setting. Another could be how you discussed and reached agreement on the extent and ways in which the participants would collaborate with you. A third might be about the political nature of their organization and participants' concerns should information be shared in insensitive ways. Include commentary from the methodological readings in your discussion.

Next, comment on the issues that seem specific to your study. This distinction may become arbitrary; if so, do not force it. Again, include the methodological readings for guidance as relevant. Remember, the demand in considering ethical and political issues is not that you show how cleanly and tidily you resolved them. Rather, it is to demonstrate that you are developing the sensitivities associated with ethically and competently conducted research.

NOTES

1. Classical discussions of triangulation also include using multiple theoretical perspectives and multiple researchers as strategies to enhance credibility. We do not discuss these here because they are rarely implemented by the beginner.

2. Most notable is the Tuskegee Syphilis Study begun in 1932 and continued until 1972, during which time treatment was withheld from the poor African American men recruited as lifetime subjects.

FURTHER READINGS

Trustworthiness

Bloomberg, L. D., & Volpe, M. (2012). *Completing your qualitative dissertation: A road map from beginning to end*. Thousand Oaks, CA: Sage. (See chap. 10)

Dillon, D. (1989). A microethnography of the social organization of a secondary low-track English-reading classroom. *American Educational Research Journal, 26*(2), 227–259.

Koro-Ljungberg, M. (2008). Validity and validation in the making in the context of qualitative research. *Qualitative Health Research, 18*(7), 983–989.

Lather, P. (1986). Issues of validity in openly ideological research: Between a rock and a soft place. *Interchange, 17*(4), 63–84.

Lincoln, Y. S., & Guba, E. G. (1985). *Naturalistic inquiry*. Beverly Hills, CA: Sage. (See chap. 11)

Loh, J. (2013). Inquiry into issues of trustworthiness and quality in narrative studies: A perspective. *Qualitative Report, 18*(33), 1–15.

Patton, M. Q. (2015). *Qualitative evaluation and research methods* (4th ed.). Thousand Oaks, CA: Sage. (See chap. 9)

Rallis, S. F., & Rossman, G. B. (2001). Communicating quality and quantities: The role of the evaluator as critical friend. In A. P. Benson, D. M. Hinn, & C. Lloyd (Eds.), *Visions of quality: How evaluators define, understand, and represent program quality* (Advances in Program Evaluation) (pp. 107–120). Oxford, England: JAI Press.

Rossman, G. B., Rallis, S. F., & Kuntz, A. M. (2010). Validity: Mapping diverse perspectives. In E. Baker, B. McGaw, & P. Peterson (Eds.), *The international encyclopedia of education* (3rd ed., pp. 505–513). Oxford, England: Elsevier.

Smith, J. K., & Deemer, D. K. (2000). The problem of criteria in the age of relativism. In N. K. Denzin & Y. S. Lincoln (Eds.), *Handbook of qualitative research* (2nd ed., pp. 877–896). Thousand Oaks, CA: Sage.

Whiting, M., & Sines, D. (2012). Mind maps: Establishing "trustworthiness" in qualitative research. *Nurse Researcher, 20*(1), 21–27.

Ethics

Battiste, M. (2008). Research ethics for producing indigenous knowledge and heritage: Institutional and researcher responsibilities. In N. K. Denzin, Y. S. Lincoln, & L. T. Smith (Eds.), *Handbook of critical and indigenous methodologies* (pp. 497–509). Thousand Oaks, CA: Sage.

Blee, K. M., & Currier, A. (2011). Ethics beyond the IRB: An introductory essay. *Qualitative Sociology, 34*(3), 401–413.

Cannella, G., & Lincoln, Y. (2011). Ethics, research regulations, and critical social science. In N. K. Denzin & Y. S. Lincoln (Eds.), *The SAGE handbook of qualitative research* (4th ed., pp. 81–90). Thousand Oaks, CA: Sage.

Christians, C. G. (2000). Ethics and politics in qualitative research. In N. K. Denzin & Y. S. Lincoln (Eds.), *Handbook of qualitative research* (2nd ed., pp. 133–155). Thousand Oaks, CA: Sage.

Denzin, N. K., & Giardina, M. D. (2007). *Ethical futures in qualitative research: Decolonizing the politics of knowledge.* Walnut Creek, CA: Left Coast Press.

Eisner, E. W. (1991). *The enlightened eye: Qualitative inquiry and the enhancement of educational practice.* New York, NY: Macmillan. (See chap. 10)

Etherington, K. (2007). Ethical research in reflexive relationships. *Qualitative Inquiry, 13*(5), 599–616.

Fisher, P. (2012). Ethics in qualitative research: "Vulnerability," citizenship and human rights. *Ethics & Social Welfare, 6*(1), 2–17.

Flinders, D. J. (1992). In search of ethical guidance: Constructing a basis for dialogue. *Qualitative Studies in Education, 5*(2), 101–115.

Guillemin, M., & Gillam, L. (2004). Ethics, reflexivity, and "ethically important moments" in research. *Qualitative Inquiry, 10*(2), 261–280.

Hammersley, M., & Traianou, A. (2012). *Ethics in qualitative research: Controversies and contexts.* Thousand Oaks, CA: Sage.

Hemmings, A. (2006). Great ethical divides: Bridging the gap between institutional review boards and researchers. *Educational Researcher, 35*(4), 12–18.

Josselson, R. (Ed.). (1996). *Ethics and process in the narrative study of lives.* Thousand Oaks, CA: Sage.

MacLeod, J. (2004). *Ain't no makin' it.* Boulder, CO: Westview Press.

Miller, T., Birch, M., Mauthner, M., & Jessop, J. (Eds.). (2012). *Ethics in qualitative research.* Thousand Oaks, CA: Sage.

Newman, D. L., & Brown, R. D. (1996). *Applied ethics for program evaluation.* Thousand Oaks, CA: Sage.

Punch, M. (1994). Politics and ethics in qualitative research. In N. K. Denzin & Y. S. Lincoln (Eds.), *Handbook of qualitative research* (1st ed., pp. 83–97). Thousand Oaks, CA: Sage.

Rallis, S. F. (2010). "That is NOT what's happening at Horizon!" Ethics and misrepresenting knowledge in text. *International Journal of Qualitative Studies in Education, 23*(4), 435–448.

Rallis, S. F, Rossman, G. B., & Gajda, R. (2007). Trustworthiness in evaluation practice: An emphasis on the relational. *Evaluation and Program Planning, 30,* 404–409.

Rossman, G. B., & Rallis, S. F. (2010). Everyday ethics: Reflections on practice. *International Journal of Qualitative Studies in Education, 23*(4), 379–391.

Rupp, L. J., & Taylor, V. (2011). Going back and giving back: The ethics of staying in the field. *Qualitative Sociology, 34*(3), 483–496.

Sieber, J. E. (1992). *Planning ethically responsible research: A guide for students and internal review boards.* Thousand Oaks, CA: Sage.

Soltis, J. F. (1990). The ethics of qualitative research. In E. W. Eisner & A. Peshkin (Eds.), *Qualitative inquiry in education: The continuing debate* (pp. 247–257). New York, NY: Teachers College Press.

Politics

Barone, T. (2000). *Aesthetics, politics, and educational inquiry.* New York, NY: Peter Lang.

Bhavnani, K. (1993). Tracing the contours: Feminist research and feminist objectivity. *Women's Studies International Forum, 16*(2), 95–104.

Blase, J. (1991). *The politics of life in schools: Power, conflict, and cooperation.* Newbury Park, CA: Sage.

Cameron, J., & Gibson, K. (2005). Participatory action research in a poststructuralist vein. *Geoforum, 36*(3), 315–331.

Conti, J. A., & O'Neil, M. (2007). Studying power: Qualitative methods and the global elite. *Qualitative Research, 7*(1), 163–182.

Denzin, N. K. (2009). The elephant in the living room: Or extending the conversation about the politics of evidence. *Qualitative Research, 9*(2), 139–160.

Morse, J. M. (2006). The politics of evidence. *Qualitative Health Research, 16*(3), 395–404.

Torrance, H. (2011). Qualitative research, science and government: Evidence, criteria, policy and politics. In N. K. Denzin & Y. S. Lincoln (Eds.), *The SAGE handbook of qualitative research* (4th ed., pp. 569–580). Thousand Oaks, CA: Sage.

Walford, G. (1991). *Doing educational research.* London, England: Routledge.

4

Major Qualitative Research Genres

By now, Anthony, Ruth, and Marla are forming a better sense of their purposes and possible questions. As these elements of qualitative research take shape, their task is to think more concretely about where they want to focus their data collection and analysis. This will help them and, in turn, refine their research questions so that their projects become manageable. As noted in the above vignette, all too often, beginners want to learn everything about their topics—Marla soon will find herself overwhelmed if she does not focus her study to one layer of complexity. This is very common as beginners explore the many facets of the social world that interest them. Soon, however, they must focus. As they discuss their topics further and learn more about the major genres of qualitative research, our characters begin to settle on a particular locus of action. Historically, this is called the *unit of analysis.* The concept draws attention to the level or layer of some social phenomenon that is of compelling interest to the researcher. Is it the individual and his experiences and perspectives? Is it a group—an organization or a program—and its structures and processes? Is it the language people use to construct and share meaning? Decisions about locus will shape subsequent data-gathering decisions.

The developing research questions and interests direct our characters to different loci of action. One useful example is the classification by type of phenomena investigated offered by Gall, Gall, and Borg (2007). Their three groupings are as follows:

- **The Individual and Her Experiences and Perceptions**
  - What is she thinking or experiencing?

- **The Group and Its Culture**
  - What are the participants doing, and what does it mean to them?
  - How do they share meaning?

- **Language and Communication Patterns**
  - What do the participants speak about?
  - How do they communicate those meanings?
  - What do symbols and signs mean to participants?

Seldom are studies so tidy that researchers can limit their focus to just one locus of interest, but they do make choices that are based on the direction in which their questions lead them. At this point, the most common qualitative research genres offer frameworks and tools for refining the focus and questions and for strategies to collect and analyze data. Other methodologists offer differing typologies (see, e.g., Creswell, 2013; Patton, 2015).

CHOOSING THE LOCUS OF INTEREST

Qualitative approaches to inquiry represent a lively and flourishing community of traditions. Scholars of qualitative research suggest numerous typologies, drawing from academic disciplines like sociology, psychology, and anthropology, as well as philosophical traditions such as phenomenology, symbolic interactionism, constructivism, and feminism, to name a few. The various approaches are related, although sometimes the resemblance is hard to detect; they often bicker among themselves, seeking to distinguish themselves along subtle dimensions.

Since the publication of the third edition of this book, interdisciplinarity has become quite salient in the social sciences and applied fields. These creative efforts blur the boundaries that historically demarcated the traditional social science disciplines, which no longer hold when considering various "genres" of qualitative inquiry. The separate social sciences do not have clear identities; so conventions of interpretation must be rebuilt to accommodate the fluidity, plurality, decenteredness, and untidiness of real situations (Geertz, 1983). In this edition, we suggest that "genres" are categories that serve to organize a complex field. The term *genres* works well, especially when encountering a new area of study, because "genres resonate with people because of the familiarity, the shorthand communication, as well as the tendency of genres to shift with public mores" (Genre, n.d.). Mindful of these developments, we find it useful to group the various approaches into three broad genres frequently found in the literature. We use these terms broadly and inclusively:

1. *The ethnographic genre:* classical ethnography, autoethnography, and critical ethnography

2. *The phenomenological genre:* classical phenomenological studies, and life histories, oral histories

3. *The sociolinguistic genre:* classical linguistic studies, discourse analysis, and critical discourse analysis

The categories in this typology are shaped by the locus of interest implied by the questions typically found in each approach: Ethnographies look at social groups or culture and at actions and interactions of individuals and groups. Phenomenological studies look at the person, seeking to understand individual lived experience and seeking to learn about the individual's perspectives and worldview. Sociolinguistic studies examine closely how people talk and express themselves, both verbally and nonverbally; the gaze is on communicative expression. To these canonical three, we add case studies as a conceptually separable genre. Case studies are a useful heuristic that capture a focus on a "unit," as our characters mention in the vignette that opens this chapter. But a case study can be of an individual (more phenomenological), a group or project (more ethnographic), or specific speech patterns (more sociolinguistic). In practice, researchers may blur these boundaries, as noted above, and draw on the tools of more than one genre.

Each genre, with its various subgenres, can be framed by traditional interpretivist assumptions or by more critical and postmodern assumptions—recall the discussion in Chapter 2 on assumptions about inquiry and society. What we call traditional qualitative research typically holds interpretivist assumptions: Knowledge is viewed as subjective, the researcher should engage directly with participants to understand their worldviews, and society is generally viewed as orderly.

More critical, postmodern, and postcolonial assumptions also view knowledge as subjective but, in contrast, view society as essentially conflictual and oppressive.

(We recognize that, by lumping together these quite different worldviews, we are over-simplifying both. Postmodern ideas actually call into question many of the assumptions held by critical theorists. When viewed through Burrell & Morgan's [1979] paradigms, however, they both fall into the upper two quadrants.) These assumptions critique historic knowledge production (i.e., research) because it privileges social science knowledge rather than practical knowledge. Inquiry is viewed as leading to radical change or to transforming oppressive social structures.

Here is a very brief history of these critical perspectives. As the 20th century drew to a close, traditional social science came under increasing scrutiny and attack as those espousing more critical perspectives challenged objectivist assumptions and traditional norms for the conduct of research. This critical tradition has burgeoned over the past 15 years. Postmodernists tend to reject the notion that knowledge is definite and univocal. Central to this critique are four interrelated assertions:

1. Research fundamentally involves issues of power.

2. The research report is not transparent, but rather it is authored by a raced, gendered, classed, and politically oriented individual.

3. Race, class, and gender (the canonical triumvirate to which we would add sexual orientation, able-bodied-ness, and first language, among others) are crucial for understanding experience.

4. Historically, traditional research has silenced members of oppressed and marginalized groups.

One implication of this critique is that we, the community of qualitative researchers, can no longer assume that we can write up our research in an antiseptic, distanced way. Reflexivity has become central to the qualitative project, demanding that we examine the complex interplay of our own personal biography, power and status, interactions with participants, and the written word. We examined this concept closely in Chapter 2; for now, it is important to remember that the critique assumes that all inquiry is embedded in power relationships and privileged knowledge. The project of the more critical perspectives is to interrupt the traditional conduct of research and report writing and to place at the center considerations of how we (the researchers) represent the other (the participants) in the inquiry. We argue that these postmodern notions can shape inquiry in any of the three major genres. Although we fear that displaying the genres in a table may appear to be an oversimplification, we also suspect that some graphic representation might help (see Table 4.1).

We acknowledge that qualitative research texts sometimes include grounded theory in their typologies (notably Creswell, 2013). Initially articulated by Glaser and Strauss (1967), grounded theory is viewed as an approach to data collection, analysis, and theorizing. In its constructivist form (developed primarily by Charmaz, 1995, 2002, 2005), grounded

Ethnographies focus on culture.

TABLE 4.1   Major Genres of Qualitative Research

Genre	Purpose	Mode and Method	Traditional Questions	Critical Questions
Ethnographic	Seek to understand the culture of people or settings	Long-term, sustained engagement; multiple, flexible methods	How do people's beliefs and values guide their actions and their understanding of those actions?	How do the actions of one group affect the beliefs and actions of other, often marginalized, groups?
Phenomenological	Seek to understand the lived experiences of a small number of people	In-depth, exploratory, and prolonged engagement; iterative interviews	What has this person experienced? What meaning does the person make of these? How does the person understand his or her experience?	What do the stories people narrate about their lives mean? How does the articulation of their stories empower them?
Sociolinguistic	Look for meaning in words, gestures, and signs	Tape- and video-recording of speech events; analysis of sign and symbol systems	What words, gestures, and signs do people draw on to communicate? What meanings are conveyed?	How do communicative systems marginalize groups and maintain power inequalities?
Case studies	Seek to understand a larger phenomenon through intensive study of one specific instance	Descriptive, heuristic, and inductive; multiple, flexible methods	What is going on in this case? What are the actors doing? How are they doing it? What are the outcomes?	How do the patterns of action and interaction in this case affect power relationships? Do they reproduce existing inequalities? How?

theory espouses the following principles: "(a) multiple realities exist, (b) data reflect the researcher's and the research participants' mutual constructions, and (c) the researcher, however, incompletely, enters and is affected by participants' worlds" (Charmaz, 2002, p. 678). What distinguishes grounded theory from other approaches is the perspective that (a) the researcher enters the study with few preconceived ideas about what matters to the participants in the setting and (b) analysis and the search for theoretical understandings of the phenomena begin very early in the process and continue throughout. We note here that the overarching purpose of grounded theory is to *theorize*—that is, to construct robust explanations of actions and interactions; we do not include grounded theory in our typology of genres because we view it, arguably, as more of an analytic approach than an overall approach to qualitative inquiry. We suggest that any one of our genres could be approached from a grounded theory perspective.

Several new approaches may represent emerging genres that are appearing in qualitative studies. They include—but are not limited to—arts-based or arts-informed research (Barone & Eisner, 2006; Leavy, 2015; Pink, 2012), multimodal research (Dicks, 2013; Pink 2011; Price, Jewitt, & Brown, 2013), and indigenous approaches (Bishop, 2011; Li, 2012; Pe-Pua, 1994). These approaches do not neatly fit into the genres we describe but may be found within the genres described above, may cross genres, and may even cross paradigms. These approaches may inform the various stages of research, from data collection to analysis and presentation of findings.

ETHNOGRAPHIC GENRES

Ethnographies are the hallmark of qualitative research, derived from the disciplines of cultural anthropology and qualitative sociology. Central to ethnographic work is the concept of *culture,* a vague and complex term that describes the way things are and prescribes the ways people should act. It thus determines what is *good* and *true* (Rossman, Corbett, & Firestone, 1988). Culture captures the beliefs and values shared by members of a group that guide their actions and their understandings of those actions. Ethnographers often focus closely on the face-to-face interactions of members of a cultural group. They are interested in how interactions shape meaning in particular organizational settings. They ask the following questions:

- What social actions take place in this particular setting?
- What do these actions mean to the actors involved at the moment the action took place?
- How are the actions organized in social patterns?
- What norms apply?
- How do these patterns relate to patterns in other dimensions of the setting and in other settings? (See Erickson, 1986)

Ethnographers study cultural groups or communities through ethnographic observation (the hallmark methodology). This work entails long-term immersion, called *participant observation,* in an intact cultural group. Because historically ethnographies required a major time commitment, many researchers conduct *compressed ethnographies* utilizing the questions and techniques of ethnography (see below). Data-gathering techniques are multiple and flexible, typically relying on observations, formal and informal interviews, interpretation of artifacts, and the researcher's own experience of events and processes.

insider=emic [handwritten]

The ethnographer seeks to understand insiders' views of their lives (*the emic view*) and render an account of that cultural worldview. This, however, is interpreted through the researcher's worldview. An analytic framework can be applied that derives from social science theory and the researcher's experience; this is called *the etic view*. Analysis tends to be emergent, guided by detailed or "thick" (Geertz, 1973) description of patterns and interactions.

me/researcher: *etic* [handwritten]

Sociologists also use ethnographic methods with specific emphasis on rules, roles, and relationships within groups, organizations, or social movements. Long-term immersion in the setting is also necessary for the researcher to discover and interpret the patterned meaning of organizational or collective life. Qualitative sociologists link their work to recurring sociological topics that include political processes and institutions, urban and community studies, stages of life, criminology, organizations and occupations, and medical sociology.

Many subgenres of ethnographic work have emerged, including Internet ethnography, autoethnography, compressed ethnography, and critical ethnography. While there are others, we discuss these four briefly.

Internet Ethnographies — *self explanatory online culture* [handwritten]

Internet ethnography, cyberethnography, netnography, or virtual ethnography has emerged from the basic principles of ethnography but takes up sites on the Internet as its focus (Markham, 2013; Markham & Baym, 2009) with the purpose of "understanding and analyzing the medium as a central feature of contemporary social life" (Marshall & Rossman, 2016, p. 31). Reasoning that the cyberspace is a socially constructed virtual world (Hine, 2000), researchers seek to understand identity (through the use of avatars) in an identity-free space. Often, researchers are full participants in these virtual worlds (see, e.g., Gatson & Zwerink's [2004] study of a website devoted to discussions of the popular television series *Buffy the Vampire Slayer*), describing themselves as true participants—"natives"—on the sites. The ethics of research practice for this emerging virtual world is uncertain, raising questions about how fully informed participants are, whether it is ethical to "lurk" online to identify participants without their knowledge, and whether the research can ethically use text on blogs without the bloggers' consent (Mann & Stewart, 2004). *haha* [handwritten]

Autoethnographies — *analyzing self* [handwritten]

This subgenre takes up the self as the focus for inquiry. Using ethnographic methods, the researcher critically describes and analyzes her own experiences. Autoethnography exemplifies the hybridity and flux of typologies, as this approach can be viewed as aligned with personal narrative inquiry (hence the link to sociolinguistic studies and phenomenology). The focus is on the self, the personal experience that warrants narration. In one use of the term *autoethnography*, the researcher references his own actions (*researcher as doer*); in another, the researcher's subjects reference their own actions, which are then studied by the researcher (*participant as doer*) (see Butz & Besio, 2004). Common across all forms of autoethnography is the central positioning of the author in relation to the social, cultural, or political (Reed-Danahay, 1997), with the assumption that the narrator–researcher's experience is illustrative of the wider phenomena. Autoethnography often has a radical, disruptive stance, a "radical democratic politics—a politics committed to creating space for dialogue and debate that instigates and shapes social change" (Holman Jones, 2005, p. 763). Diverse rhetorical devices are often incorporated into autoethnographies: personal reflections, poems, and private journal writing. These may then be linked to larger social forces or circumstances that shape the narrator's worldview and that she, in turn, shapes.

Compressed Ethnographies   ~smaller scale, shorter time

Compressed ethnographies have gained recognition in light of the limitations and demands that traditional ethnographies present in terms of time and resources. Compressed ethnographies follow the same principles of ethnographic research but require three conditions: (1) familiarity with the local setting and language, (2) focus on one particular aspect of the culture to be studied, and (3) collaboration with local experts (LeCompte & Schensul, 2010). Compressed ethnographies are particularly valuable when conducting small-scale research (Knight, 2002) because this type of research involves one or few researchers, limited or no funding, and limited time in the field. For these reasons, compressed ethnographies may be appealing to development practitioners conducting research and/or evaluations, to graduate students conducting dissertation or thesis work, and to faculty members continuing lines of scholarly inquiry in limited time.   *me*

Critical Ethnographies ~power & oppression

Grounded in critical and postcritical assumptions, critical ethnographies take a radical perspective, explicitly examining issues of power and oppression in social settings. They pursue emancipatory uses and the radical change of oppressive social structures. The theoretical framework for critical ethnography is critical theory, drawing on Marxist and neo-Marxist thought, whereas the methodology used is conventional ethnographic research. This perspective assumes a conflict model of society, one in which the powerful groups oppress and dominate those less powerful. Critical ethnographers object to the notion of a value-free science and see a dialectic relationship between inquiry and action or theory and practice.

Although differing strands can be identified, most critical ethnography considers research to be a process of examining the dynamic interplay of culture, knowledge, and action. Critical ethnographers link key findings to issues of social power and control. Key concepts are reproduction and resistance. Institutions and relationships are structured to reproduce the unequal distribution of power based on income, race, and gender; less powerful social actors unwittingly participate in or resist the reproduction of class-, race-, and gender-based hierarchies. The researcher's narrative attempts to empower by privileging the voices of the less powerful and through advocacy for a particular group. Direct action is not necessarily taken by the researcher. Methodologically, critical ethnographers gather data in ways similar to their less critically oriented colleagues; the lens for analysis, however, is distinctly different.

Our Characters' Choices **Anthony** decides to design a compressed ethnographic evaluation (compressed, because, as you recall, the study is to be completed during one semester) that takes an in-depth look at the culture of the community arts program. He will explore the subtle, taken-for-granted values and beliefs about participation, aesthetic standards, and artistic expression. He chooses long-term observation in the center as his primary way of gathering data. He will focus on the culture of the arts program: the patterned ways of determining activities, soliciting community input, and encouraging participation. Anthony also could ally himself with the critical ethnographic approach should he become committed to community activism in the arts and to promoting substantial change in access to artistic expression.

Marla considers ethnography but decides not to focus on cultural beliefs about serving poor women because such a design would be too labor-intensive to accomplish during a single semester, given the complexities of her topic, the context, and her commitment to participation. At this point, she is more interested in the experiences of individual women and their understanding of the clinic. She decides to consider some other qualitative genre. She and her team, however, use ethnographic tools such as observation, cultural interviews, and document review and analysis.

Ruth's interest in children with physical disabilities could be conceptualized and designed as an ethnography. Asking questions about the subtle beliefs and values surrounding disability and children with disabilities would suggest a focus on their culture. In-depth and long-term participant observation in schools or day care centers could result in a rich ethnographic description. As Ruth's interests evolve, however, she finds herself more captured by the stories of the children themselves. Although she considers an ethnography, her interests in the individual children and their lived experiences suggest some other tradition.

PHENOMENOLOGICAL GENRES — lived experiences

A second genre that our characters might consider is phenomenological, through which the *lived experience* of a small number of people is investigated. Extensive and prolonged engagement with individuals typifies this work, often through a series of in-depth, intensive, and iterative interviews. The researcher seeks to understand the deep meaning of a person's experiences and how he articulates these experiences.

Phenomenology is a tradition in German philosophy with a focus on the essence of lived experience. Those engaged in phenomenological research focus in depth on the meaning of a particular aspect of experience, assuming that through dialogue and

> Phenomenology explores the meaning of individual lived experience.

reflection, the quintessential meaning of the experience will be revealed. Language is viewed as the primary symbol system through which meaning is both constructed and conveyed (Holstein & Gubrium, 1994). The purposes of phenomenological inquiry are description, interpretation, and critical self-reflection into the "world as world" (van Manen, 1990, p. 5). Central are the notions of intentionality and caring. Throughout, the researcher engages in critical self-reflection about the topic and the process.

Phenomenological in-depth interviewing has received increasing attention as a qualitative genre. Seidman (2006) advocates a series of three long, iterative interviews, each with a specific purpose:

1. The first interview inquires into the interviewee's history and life story.

2. The second orients both the researcher and the interviewee to the specific experience of interest.

3. The third then draws these together in a reflective dialogue about the meaning of the interviewee's experience in light of her history.

Subsumed under this broad category focusing on the individual's lived experience is *life history research.* Deriving from several academic disciplines (e.g., literature, psychology, and gender and race studies), life history research also focuses on a person's experience of her lifeworld and how she constructs meaning for her experiences. Life history research may be called a biography, an oral history, or a case study (discussed later in this chapter). Methods for gathering data include reviewing and interpreting personal correspondence (diaries, letters, and journals), direct interviewing of the participants, and perhaps observing them as they go about their everyday lives. The assumption in life history research is that the individual represents a more widely shared pattern of life experience. Thus, one could do life history research on a veteran teacher whose professional life spanned several decades of educational reform. One also could study a young woman who was born into poverty and succeeded in the business world, despite odds against such success. In each instance, the individual is selected because she is an example of the experience of interest.

Increasingly important in the social sciences is *narrative inquiry,* or narrative analysis. This tradition focuses on people's storytelling, reasoning that telling stories is an important means for representing and explaining personal and social experience. The tradition of narrative research has several branches, some more aligned with phenomenological studies (e.g., oral histories, life histories), whereas others are more sociolinguistic (discourse analysis—see the next section). All focus, however, is on speech and the meanings that inhere in oral expression. Oral histories, folktales, parables, sayings, and even plays, novels, and films depict collective and individual experiences. These verbal forms of communication often contain prescriptions for proper behavior, lending an instructional component to the message. Narrative research is interdisciplinary in nature and covers a wide range of specific approaches, including life histories, biographies and autobiographies, autoethnographies (mentioned above), oral histories, and personal narratives. The link to phenomenological studies is obvious. All hold in common the assumption that storytelling is integral to the understanding of our lives and that it is ubiquitous. This, in and of itself, makes narratives worthy of inquiry.

Narrative research focuses on the structure and content of stories people tell that help them make sense of their experiences. Some approaches are quite technical, searching for the sociolinguistic devices that the narrator uses. Others focus on the flow of life events and their meaning, as constructed by the narrator. Methodologically, narrative research entails long, extended interviews with the individual(s) of interest. In the case of life histories and biographies, other sources of data may be introduced into the written report. Some approaches are collaborative, with researcher and narrator co-constructing the final document. In others, the researcher acts traditionally, deriving data from the interviews and writing the final report. When framed by feminist or critical theory, the purpose may become transformative. For example, one of our doctoral students (who came from Tajikistan) sought to tell the unique stories of girls who were completing secondary school in Afghanistan; since circumstances only allowed her to meet with the girls in a group, the process of capturing their narratives took on multiple meanings.

Our Characters' Choices **Ruth's** choice of a phenomenological study leads her to explore the meaning of bodied-ness and participation in sports for children in wheelchairs. She frames her study as evolving over time to capture the lived experience of disability, the meaning sports take on for the children, and how this shapes their understanding of themselves. She will use phenomenological, in-depth, iterative interviewing with three children who use wheelchairs. She also will observe them participating in sports.

If **Marla** were working within the phenomenological genre, she would have explored the deeply private experience of being a poor woman trying to access sustained health care. She would have interviewed three or four women over several months following the three-interview format. Her purpose would have been to understand the experience of maintaining health while living in poverty and how each woman's personal history shaped the meaning she brings to that experience. Questions would have focused on the meaning of health, disease, poverty, and interactions with health care professionals.

SOCIOLINGUISTIC GENRES — language

Similar to ethnographies, sociolinguistic studies explore the meaning participants make of social interactions and settings, but the locus of interest is *communicative behavior,* messages sent and received, and the ways that signs and symbols convey meaning. These studies focus on "the study of language as it functions in society and the study of the interaction between linguistic and social variables" ("Sociolinguistics," 2015). Sociolinguistic researchers study modes of communication, especially language, in specific social contexts, but they differ from many ethnographic researchers in that they often turn their focus onto fine-grained interactions, speech acts, signs, and various texts produced by a society. Questions include the following:

- What words and actions do people use to communicate in different social groups and settings and for different purposes?
- In what ways do they use these words and actions?
- What is the communicative meaning of other signs within the setting?
- What is the meaning of texts?

Under this broad category are those researchers who view communication as a system of signs, one of which is language. Other signs might include the decorations on a school's bulletin board, paralinguistic behaviors (winks, hand gestures, and body position), or dress (see Roth, 2001). From this perspective, "anything in the social environment is a 'text' that can be read and interpreted" (Gall, Borg, & Gall, 1996, p. 629).

Language and communication research is grounded in the sociolinguistic and semiotic traditions. Sociolinguists (sometimes also referred to as discourse analysts) posit that a person's identity is intrinsically related to the way he speaks; identity is expressed outwardly in the choice of words and the interactions associated with this choice. Thus, sociolinguists look at how social characteristics (e.g., age, ethnicity, gender, and socioeconomic status) shape language use and communication behaviors. With critical assumptions, critical discourse analysis seeks to identify how oppressive structures and processes are reproduced in talk and text. As another subgenre, semiotics is the study of human communication through sign systems. The signs may be words or objects, but the semioticist seeks to understand what they symbolize and how they convey that meaning. The words or objects themselves are less important than when and where we use them and the meanings we attach to them.

- What meaning does the participant intend?
- What meanings do other participants assign to the words or objects?
- What is the process by which meaning is transmitted?

In both the sociolinguistic and semiotic views, meaning is a social construction.

Sociolinguistic research requires the microanalysis of naturally occurring speech events and interactions within their context. By naturally occurring, we mean those events and interactions that have not been created by the researcher, as in an interview. These researchers often videotape or audiotape events and analyze sections of the transcription for patterns in discourse (speech acts), proxemics (use of space), and kinesics (body motion). Two studies illustrate discourse analysis: (1) one of our students analyzed math classrooms for patterns of univocal versus dialogic discourse to understand the use of authority by teachers and students and (2) one of us explored the effects of an alternative professional development initiative for school superintendents by documenting and analyzing their conversations during debrief sessions to track changes in content and interactions (Rallis & Militello, 2009).

Semioticists study conformity to and deviance from the intended meaning of signs; they often combine fieldwork with analysis of the sign system of interest. As another example, one of us conducted a study of high school culture in which the prevailing sign system was about "good behavior" rather than academic achievement. Several signifiers for this sign were identified, including language use in daily communications, speeches at the graduation ceremony, and behavior that was labeled deviant and therefore required punishment (Rossman, Corbett, & Firestone, 1988). The study conducted by one of our doctoral students for his dissertation offers another example. For his critical discourse analysis of Jamaican education policy and policy making, he examined newspaper articles, transcripts, and interactions of parliament members regarding the development of legislation related to K–12 policy in Jamaica (Brissett, 2011).

Our Characters' Choices As one source of data about the clinic, **Marla** decides to examine the discourse between certain female patients and a male physician's assistant. She and her team videotape selected interactions. Their microanalyses of the speech acts and behaviors reveal persistent patterns of degradation of the women's views and opinions—interruptions of the women, distraction (not making eye contact when the women spoke), infantilization of word choice, and a hurried demeanor characterized these encounters.

Within **Anthony's** ethnography of the community arts program, he might explore the symbolic meaning of artwork produced in various classes. What do these works of art signify about the beliefs and values of the people in the community? What is the shared meaning about these artistic productions? How is this meaning transmitted?

Ruth might choose to use a sociolinguistic approach, recording speech and interaction events and analyzing them to learn how the boys' and girls' communication expresses their identities. From a semiotic approach, she might consider the meanings of jokes the children share or the teasing in which they engage.

Our characters' choices about the loci of interest for their studies help them make decisions about the specific level or layer of complexity on which to focus. The various qualitative research genres tend to focus on a specific level within a social environment. Phenomenological studies focus on individuals; ethnographies focus on groups or cultures; and sociolinguistic studies focus on either communicative acts or sign systems. Thus, identifying a genre in which Marla, Ruth, and Anthony feel comfortable and that holds promise for yielding data to respond to the developing research questions is helpful. This focusing assists decisions about the "unit of analysis," introduced at the beginning of this chapter. This concept and its related question, "What is the unit of analysis for your study?" helps our characters further delimit their studies.

In this process, Ruth will have to ponder whether she is interested in the individual children in wheelchairs who participate in sports or in the particular group of children that attend the after-care facility. Anthony will consider whether his best strategy for the evaluation will be to focus on individual artists and their contributions to the arts center or on the relationship (partnership) between the arts center and the community.

One of our students, for example, wanted to understand whether partnerships formed between schools and faith-based organizations could improve student achievement. He could have chosen principals and the leaders of the organizations as the unit of analysis; interviewing would be the primary data collection technique. However, because his interest truly focused on the phenomenon of *the partnership* and he wanted to understand how it operates in practice, he decided to conduct a case study of a specific partnership between an urban school and a nearby parish church. As a result, he used multiple techniques and immersed himself in that particular case of the phenomenon.

CASE STUDIES

As discussed above, the three major genres of qualitative research help our characters focus on their studies and identify the unit of analysis in which they are most interested. Complicating their decision making, however, is the *case study approach* to research. Kent discussed it in class one day, but the students are still confused. Their conversation highlights the reasons for their puzzlement.

Marla: What is a case study, anyway? It seems to me that everything is a case study. I just don't know how to tell what is and what isn't.

[*She rubs her forehead.*]

Ruth: Yeah. Like, are we all doing case studies of one form or another? Kent said case studies can be of people, groups, events, organizations. Whew! Isn't that everything?

Anthony: Yup, it's confusing all right! But I've done some reading from that Merriam book and the Yin one that Kent mentioned—I guess a case study is when you look at something as a case of something else.

Ruth: So . . . what does that mean?

Anthony: The case is "a single instance or example of a problem, issue, or hypothesis." Like that study we read that looked at one class in a school that included special education students in regular classes—to illustrate what an inclusive class can be.

Marla: *Entonces*, the specific context makes the case important?

Anthony: Yes. And another thing I learned that's important—case studies rely on lots of different data sources about that one case. Case studies also may use quantitative tools—they are not necessarily only qualitative research. That's a big point of confusion all around.

Ruth: What do you mean? I thought case studies are qualitative! That's what my roommate who's taking stats says.

Anthony: Well, she's wrong! Lots of case studies use a mix of methods.

Marla: I'm still not sure what all this means. Am I doing a case study of a particular health clinic or case studies of particular women who use urban clinics? Or am I just studying how women interact with urban clinics? What's a case study and what's not?

We introduce this confusion about case studies as an approach that draws on the major genres because our experience is that many students (and researchers as well) find the concept of case studies difficult to place boundaries around. Many assume that case studies must use only qualitative methods; others assume that case studies are only of organizations or intact groups. Both positions are wrong. We discuss case study research with an eye to helping the beginner understand what case study research is and what it is not. With a better understanding of the boundaries around the concept, our characters— and you—should be able to use the approach fruitfully and as appropriate.

Case studies are generally considered an overall strategy rather than a genre of research (Stake, 2000). Case studies are in-depth and detailed explorations of single examples (an event, process, organization, group, or individual) that are "an instance drawn from a class" of similar phenomena (Adelman, Jenkins, & Kemmis, 1983, p. 3). They seek to understand the larger phenomenon through close examination of a specific case and therefore focus on the particular. Case studies are *descriptive, holistic, heuristic,* and *inductive*. Case studies do not, however, necessarily link to cultural anthropology or qualitative sociology, as do ethnographies. Ethnographies can be argued as special instances of case studies. Their roots in anthropology, a defining characteristic of ethnographies, make them specialized case studies.

Some case studies are organizational studies; others, with psychological roots, focus on individuals. Program evaluations often are conducted as case studies to produce rich illustrations of what is happening in the program, to provide plausible explanations, and to "extrapolate *lessons learned*" (Patton, 2002, p. 500).

Case studies are complex and multilayered. They are particularly useful for their rich description and heuristic value. Most case studies are descriptive or explanatory; that is, they depict events, processes, and perspectives as they unfold—the "real-life context" (Yin, 1994, p. 25)—and often build an explanation for those events or outcomes. Description illustrates the complexities of a situation, depicts how the passage of time has shaped events, provides vivid material, and presents differing perspectives

> Case studies seek to understand a larger phenomenon through intensive examination of one specific instance.

or opinions. By providing detail and complexity, case studies illuminate the reader's understanding, thereby extending comprehension of some complex set of events or circumstances. When more than one case is studied, the researcher can conduct cross-case analyses (Miles & Huberman, 1994) for comparison purposes. These analyses respect the integrity of each case and then seek commonalities across cases as well as differences. Because of their particularistic focus, case studies are "an especially good design for practical problems—for questions, situations, or puzzling occurrences arising from everyday practice" (Merriam, 1998, p. 11).

Despite our characters' assumption that case studies rely primarily on qualitative methods for gathering data, such is not the case. (But see Gall et al., 1996, who assert, "In our view, then, case study research is one of several approaches to qualitative inquiry" [p. 544].)

Case studies typically rely on a variety of techniques for data gathering and are conducted over time. Case studies may use questionnaires, archival records, or psychological testing in addition to interviewing, observing, and analyzing documents. Just as with ethnographies, case studies are methodologically eclectic. Whatever his choice of techniques, the researcher immerses himself in the case setting or individual of interest. As Stake (2000) notes, "Case study is not a methodological choice but a choice of what is to be studied. By whatever methods, we choose to study *the case* [italics added]" (p. 435).

Because case studies focus on the particularities of the specific case, they are context dependent. As such, what we learn from a case study cannot be generalized, in the probabilistic sense (recall the paradigm discussion in Chapter 2). Using the logic of probabilities, conclusions from a case cannot be applied directly to another case because no two cases are identical. However, another logic—that of *reasoning by analogy*—allows the application of lessons learned in one case to another population or set of circumstances "believed or assumed to be sufficiently similar to the study sample that findings apply there as well" (Kennedy, 1979, p. 665). Also described as assertorial logic, this form of argumentation asserts or affirms that something is so and draws on supportive evidence to convince the reader that conditions in the new circumstances are sufficiently similar to the original research conditions for generalization to be appropriate.

The strength of case studies is their detail, their complexity, and their use of multiple sources to obtain multiple perspectives. The result is the thickness of description that allows the reader to interpret and decide the applicability of case learnings to other settings. With a well-written case study, the reader is empowered to make judgments about the applicability of the learnings. Thus, one case study may, by analogy, shed light on or offer insights about similar cases.

Critical case studies are grounded in a critique of existing social structures and patterns. They assume theoretically that oppression and domination characterize the setting and seek to uncover how patterns of action perpetuate the status quo.

Our Characters' Choices Because he is seeking to understand the culture and outcomes of a specific program, **Anthony**'s evaluation of the community arts program is a case study. He relies primarily on the ethnographic tools of observation, one-on-one interviews in context, document analyses, and documentation of material culture such as pieces of artwork. He studies intensely the different components of this particular program and considers how these components contribute to its effectiveness. His report describing the processes, interactions, and relationships will increase understanding of the community and the impact of the arts program on this community. Because it defines and describes the components that contribute to program success, his evaluation also can offer insights into other similar community arts programs.

Marla and her participants consider their inquiry to be self-reflective case studies of the women's use of health services. The questions they pose include the following: What are our health needs? How do we seek care? How do we interact with the health care system? How do we view doctors and nurses? Are there other sources of health care to which we turn? Do the people in the system understand our rights and responsibilities? They use a collage of tools, including sociolinguistic tools of discourse analysis, ethnographic observations and interviews, and document review and analysis. The team adopts a critical perspective, specifically a feminist one. This perspective leads the women to explore the ways in which the health care system is structured patriarchically, ways in which they feel devalued and depersonalized, and how they might participate in sustaining these structures. Marla, as one member of the team, adopts a class-based perspective, seeking to understand how poverty shapes these women's use of health care.

Ruth could do a case study of a day care center that includes two or three children who use wheelchairs. This is, in fact, where she begins her design thinking: locate a center, identify key actors, gather data, and write about this instance of an inclusive program. Had she continued with a case study, she might have framed it as an organizational study and defined the parameters of the program; mapped participation, administrative structures, and activities; and surveyed and interviewed a sample of staff, children, and families. Ruth is, however, much more interested in the life stories of the children than she is in the organization or the program, so she frames her work as a phenomenological study.

Our characters' thinking and understanding of qualitative research is growing. They have increasingly specific notions of the shape of their projects and the genres to which their studies best link. In reality, their studies may well draw from all three genres, using tools and techniques from each to collect and analyze their data. They have considered alternatives and thought about the feasibility, ethics, and politics of their projects. Now, if needed, they could develop full research proposals, although Kent, their professor, does not require this. If, however, they were pursuing funding from an agency or writing theses or dissertations, they would have to elaborate their thinking in a formal proposal. The major elements of such a proposal are presented in Chapter 5.

DISPOSITIONS AND SKILLS

Marla, Ruth, and Anthony could be overwhelmed with the available options for exploring their topics. They see that qualitative research does not have a set of prescribed procedures or rules, that the genres are blurred (see Geertz, 1983), and that several different approaches could be used to make sense of the worlds they choose to explore. They will shape their work not by a single genre according to what ought to be done but according to what works in the field. As they become comfortable with the ambiguity inherent in designing and conducting qualitative research, they also are building respect for the reasoning behind the decisions and the politics of practicing research. They see that there are almost endless choices, and it is their responsibility to decide among them—as long as they document and explain their decisions so that their community of practice understands and accepts. And so, with increased awareness of their choices and their empowerment to choose, Marla, Ruth, and Anthony are finally ready to design their studies.

ACTIVITIES FOR YOUR COMMUNITY OF PRACTICE

Study Questions

- What are the major genres of qualitative research? How do these differ from one another?

- What questions might each genre address?

- What modes (traditional or critical) exist within each genre?

- How can these genres help you refine your study? How might your research question change in a different genre?

- What is a case study, and when is it used?

Small-Group and Dyad Activities

Exploring Qualitative Genres

Read three articles representing different genres. In a small group, identify the predominant genre, goals, and methods used in one article and whether the study is traditional or critical. If the study is traditional, how could it become critical or postmodern? If it is postmodern or critical, what would a similar traditional study look like? With a larger group, compare and contrast differences across genres in the studies.

Writing Activity

A Short Prospectus

Consider writing a short (one or two pages) description of what you could do for a small-scale qualitative research study. In the prospectus, address three topics. First, describe the focus of the proposed study. This necessarily will be brief but should include the tentative research questions, puzzles, or curiosities that have captured your interest and that you wish to pursue systematically. This section should be a paragraph or two.

Second, describe the setting where you might conduct the study. Discuss this setting in modest detail, indicating how access to the site and people could be obtained. Even at an early stage, discuss your ideas with an official in the setting to gain initial approval for the study. This should be one paragraph.

Third, stipulate how you plan to gather data: in what ways, with whom, how often, and under what circumstances. Overall, the prospectus should be no longer than two pages, although one page would be even better. It should demonstrate that you have thought about the research project you want to undertake and have some sense that it is doable.

FURTHER READINGS

Critical and Postmodern Assumptions

Cannella, G. S., Salazar Perez, M., & Pasque, P. A. (Eds.). (2015). *Critical qualitative inquiry: Foundations and futures.* Walnut Creek, CA: Left Coast Press.

Denzin, N. K., & Lincoln, Y. S. (2011). *The SAGE handbook of qualitative research* (4th ed.). Thousand Oaks, CA: Sage.

Kincheloe, J. L., McLaren, P., & Steinberg, S. (2011). Critical pedagogy, and qualitative research: Moving to the bricolage. In N. K. Denzin & Y. S. Lincoln (Eds.), *The SAGE handbook of qualitative research* (4th ed., pp. 163–178). Thousand Oaks, CA: Sage.

Lincoln, Y. S., Lynham, S. A., & Guba, E. G. (2011). Paradigmatic controversies, contradictions, and emerging confluences, revisted. In N. K. Denzin & Y. S. Lincoln (Eds.), *The SAGE handbook of qualitative research* (4th ed., pp. 97–128). Thousand Oaks, CA: Sage.

Morrow, R. A. (with Brown, D. D.). (1994). *Critical theory and methodology.* Thousand Oaks, CA: Sage.

Olesen, V. (2009). Do whatever you can: Temporality and critical, interpretive methods in an age of despair. *Cultural Studies-Critical Methodologies, 9*(1), 52–55.

Rosenau, P. M. (1992). *Post-modernism and the social sciences: Insights, inroads, and intrusions.* Princeton, NJ: Princeton University Press.

Phenomenological Studies

Castro-Klaren, S., & Beverly, J. (2008). Testimonio, subalternity, and narrative authority. In *A companion to Latin American literature and culture* (pp. 571–583). Chichester, England: Wiley. doi:10.1002/9780470696446.ch33

Holstein, J. A., & Gubrium, J. F. (2011). The constructionist analytics of interpretive practice. In N. K. Denzin & Y. S. Lincoln (Eds.), *The SAGE handbook of qualitative research* (4th ed., pp. 341–357). Thousand Oaks, CA: Sage.

Josselson, R., & Lieblich, A. (Eds.). (1993). *The narrative study of lives.* Newbury Park, CA: Sage.

Kvale, S., & Brinkmann, S. (2015). *Interviews: Learning the craft of qualitative research interviewing* (3rd ed.). Thousand Oaks, CA: Sage.

van Manen, M. (1990). *Researching lived experience: Human science for an action sensitive pedagogy*. Albany: State University of New York Press.

van Manen, M. (2002). *Writing in the dark: Phenomenological studies in interpretive inquiry*. London, ON: University of Western Ontario Press.

Riessman, C. K. (2008). *Narrative methods for the human sciences*. Thousand Oaks, CA: Sage.

Seidman, I. E. (2012). *Interviewing as qualitative research: A guide for researchers in education and the social sciences* (4th ed.). New York, NY: Teachers College Press.

Tierney, W. G. (2000). Undaunted courage: Life history and the postmodern challenge. In N. K. Denzin & Y. S. Lincoln (Eds.), *Handbook of qualitative research* (2nd ed., pp. 537–553). Thousand Oaks, CA: Sage.

Ethnographies

Atkinson, P. A., & Delamont, S. (Eds.). (2008). *Representing ethnography: Reading, writing and rhetoric in qualitative research*. London, England: Sage.

Atkinson, P. A., Delamont, S., Coffey, A., Lofland, J., & Lofland, L. (Eds.). (2007). *Handbook of ethnography*. London, England: Sage.

Behar, R. (1996). *The vulnerable observer: Anthropology that breaks your heart*. Boston, MA: Beacon.

Crang, M., & Cook, I. (2007). *Doing ethnographies*. London, England: Sage.

Delamont, S. (2016). *Fieldwork in educational settings: Methods, pitfalls, and perspectives* (3rd ed.). London, England: Routledge.

Fetterman, D. (2010). *Ethnography: Step-by-step* (3rd ed.). Thousand Oaks, CA: Sage.

Gobo, G. (2008). *Doing ethnography*. London, England: Sage.

Tedlock, B. (2011). Braiding narrative ethnography with memoir and creative nonfiction. In N. K. Denzin & Y. S. Lincoln (Eds.), *The SAGE handbook of qualitative research* (4th ed., pp. 331–340). Thousand Oaks, CA: Sage.

Van Maanen, J. (Ed.). (1995). *Representation in ethnography*. Thousand Oaks, CA: Sage.

Wolcott, H. F. (2004). *The art of fieldwork* (2nd ed.). Walnut Creek, CA: AltaMira Press.

Autoethnography, Internet, Compressed, and Critical Ethnographies

Carspecken, P. F. (1996). *Critical ethnography in educational research: A theoretical and practical guide*. New York, NY: Routledge & Kegan Paul.

Chee, F. M. (2015). Online games and digital ethnography. *The International Encyclopedia of Digital Communication and Society*. doi: 10.1002/9781118767771

DeVault, M. (2013). Institutional ethnography a feminist sociology of institutional power. *Contemporary Sociology: A Journal of Reviews, 42*(3), 332–340.

Dillon, D. R. (1989). Showing them that I want them to learn and that I care about who they are: A microethnography of the social organization of a secondary low-track English-reading classroom.

American Educational Research Journal, 26(2), 227–259.

Evans, L. (2010). *Authenticity online: Using webnography to address phenomenological concerns*. Retrieved from https://www.inter-disciplinary.net/wp-content/uploads/2010/02/evanspaper.pdf

Hine, C. (2000). *Virtual ethnography*. London, England: Sage.

Kozinets, R. (2009). *Netnography: Doing ethnographic research online*. Thousand Oaks, CA: Sage.

LeCompte, M. D., & Schensul, J. J. (2010). *Designing and conducting ethnographic research: An introduction*. Lanham, MD: AltaMira Press.

Lee, B. K., & Gregory, D. (2008). Not alone in the field: Distance collaboration via the Internet is a focused ethnography. *International Journal of Qualitative Methods, 7*(3), 31–46.

Madison, D. S. (2012). *Critical ethnography: Method, ethics, and performance* (2nd ed.). Thousand Oaks, CA: Sage.

Markham, A. N. (2004). Internet communication as a tool for qualitative research. In D. Silverman (Ed.), *Qualitative research: Theory, method, and practice* (2nd ed., pp. 95–124). London, England: Sage.

McCarty, T. L. (Ed.). (2014). *Ethnography and language policy.* New York, NY: Routledge.

Noblit, G. W., Flores, S. Y., & Murillo, E. G., Jr. (Eds.). (2005). *Postcritical ethnography: Reinscribing critique.* Cresskill, NJ: Hampton Press.

Smith, D. E. (Ed.). (2006). *Institutional ethnography as practice.* Lanham, MD: Rowman & Littlefield.

Steinmetz, K. F. (2012). Message received: Virtual ethnography in online message boards. *International Journal of Qualitative Methods, 11*(1), 26–39.

Vittadini, N., & Pasquali, F. (2013). Virtual shadowing, online ethnographies and social networking studies. In G. Patriarche, H. Bilandzic, J. Linaa Jensen, & J. Jurisic (Eds.), *Audience research methodologies: Between innovation and consolidation* (Vol. 2, pp. 160–173). New York, NY: Routledge.

Ward, K. J. (1999). Cyber-ethnography and the emergence of the virtually new community. *Journal of Information Technology, 14*(1), 95–105.

Williams, M. (2007). Avatar watching: Participant observation in graphical online environments. *Qualitative Researcher, 7*(1), 5–24.

Ybema, S., Yanow, D., Wels, H., & Kamsteeg, F. (2009). *Organizational ethnography: Studying the complexity of everyday life.* London, England: Sage.

Sociolinguistic Studies

Cazden, C. B. (2001). *Classroom discourse: The language of teaching and learning* (2nd ed.). Portsmouth, NH: Heinemann.

Chase, S. E. (2011). Narrative inquiry: Still a field in the making. In N. K. Denzin & Y. S. Lincoln (Eds.), *The SAGE handbook of qualitative research* (4th ed., pp. 421–434). Thousand Oaks, CA: Sage.

Cheek, J. (2004). At the margins? Discourse analysis and qualitative research. *Qualitative Health Research, 14*(8), 1140–1150.

Connelly, F. M., & Clandinin, D. J. (1990). Stories of experience and narrative inquiry. *Educational Researcher, 19*(5), 2–14.

Fairclough, N. (2003). *Analysing discourse: Textual analysis for social research.* New York, NY: Routledge.

Gee, J. P. (2010). *An introduction to discourse analysis: Theory and method* (3rd ed.). New York, NY: Routledge.

Knight, P. (2002). *Small-scale research: Pragmatic inquiry in social science and the caring professions.* London, England: Sage.

Locke, T. (2004). *Critical discourse analysis.* New York, NY: Continuum.

Philips, L., & Jørgensen, M. (2002). *Discourse analysis as theory and method.* Thousand Oaks, CA: Sage.

Riessman, C. K. (2007). *Narrative analysis: Methods for the human sciences.* Thousand Oaks, CA: Sage.

Rogers, R. (Ed.). (2011). *An introduction to critical discourse analysis in education* (2nd ed.). Routledge.

Roth, W.-M. (2001). Gestures: Their role in teaching and learning. *Review of Educational Research, 71*(3), 365–392.

Schiffrin, D., Tannen, D., & Hamilton, H. (Eds.). (2001). *Handbook of discourse analysis.* Oxford, England: Blackwell.

Silverman, D. (2011). *Interpreting qualitative data: Methods for analyzing talk, text, and interaction* (4th ed.). Thousand Oaks, CA: Sage.

Wodak, R., Johnstone, B., & Kerswill, P. E. (2010). *The SAGE handbook of sociolinguistics.* Thousand Oaks, CA: Sage.

Case Studies

Farquhar, J. D. (2012). *Case study research for business*. Thousand Oaks, CA: Sage.

Flyvbjerg, B. (2011). Case study. In N. K. Denzin & Y. S. Lincoln (Eds.), *The SAGE handbook of qualitative research* (4th ed., pp. 301–316). Thousand Oaks, CA: Sage.

Merriam, S. B. (1988). *Qualitative research and case study applications in education* (Rev. ed.). San Francisco, CA: Jossey-Bass.

Merriam, S. B., & Tisdell, E. J. (2015). *Qualitative research: A guide to design and implementation* (4th ed.). San Francisco, CA: Jossey-Bass.

Remenyi, D. (2013). *Case study research: The quick guide series*. Reading, England: Academic Conferences.

Repko, A. F., Newell, W. H., & Szostak, R. (2012). *Case studies in interdisciplinary research*. Thousand Oaks, CA: Sage.

Stake, R. E. (2000). Case studies. In N. K. Denzin & Y. S. Lincoln (Eds.), *Handbook of qualitative research* (2nd ed., pp. 435–454). Thousand Oaks, CA: Sage.

Stake, R. E. (2006). *Multiple case study analysis*. New York, NY: Guilford Press.

Swanborn, P. (2010). *Case study research: What, why and how?* Thousand Oaks, CA: Sage.

Unluer, S. (2012). Being an insider researcher while conducting case study research. *Qualitative Report, 17*(29), 1–14.

Yin, R. K. (2008). *Case study research: Design and methods* (4th ed.). Thousand Oaks, CA: Sage.

Yin, R. K. (2011). *Applications of case study research* (3rd ed.). Thousand Oaks, CA: Sage.

Arts-Based and Arts-Informed Research

Barone, T., & Eisner, E. (2006). Arts-based educational research. In J. L. Green, G. Camilli, & P. B. Elmore (Eds.), *Handbook of complementary methods in education* (3rd ed., pp. 95–108). New York, NY: Routledge.

Butler-Kisber, L. (2010). *Qualitative inquiry: Thematic, narrative and arts-informed perspectives*. Thousand Oaks, CA: Sage.

Butler-Kisber, L., & Poldma, T. (2011). The power of visual approaches in qualitative inquiry: The use of collage making and concept mapping in experiential research. *Journal of Research Practice, 6*(2), M18.

Chilton, G., & Leavy, P. (2014). Arts-based research practice: Merging social research and the creative arts. *Oxford handbook of qualitative research* (pp. 403–422). New York, NY: Oxford University Press.

Eisner, E. W. (1991). *The enlightened eye: Qualitative inquiry and the enhancement of educational practice*. New York, NY: Macmillan.

Knowles, J. G., & Cole, A. L. (Eds.). (2008). *The handbook of the arts in qualitative research: Perspectives, methodologies, examples, and issues*. Thousand Oaks, CA: Sage.

Leavy, P. (2015). *Method meets art: Arts-based research practice*. New York, NY: Guilford Press.

Margolis, E., & Pauwels, L. (Eds.). (2011). *The SAGE handbook of visual research methods*. London, England: Sage.

Pink, S. (2012). *Situating everyday life*. London, England: Sage.

Rose, G. (2012). *Visual methodologies: An introduction to researching with visual methods* (3rd ed.). London, England: Sage.

Shannon-Baker, P. (2015). "But I wanted to appear happy": How using arts-based and mixed methods approaches complicate qualitatively driven research. *International Journal of Qualitative Methods, 14*(2), 34–52.

Sullivan, G. (2010). *Art practice as research: Inquiry in visual arts*. Thousand Oaks, CA: Sage.

Multimodal Inquiry

Bezemer, J., & Mavers, D. (2011). Multimodal transcription as academic practice: A social semiotic perspective. *International Journal of Social Research Methodology, 14*(3), 191–206.

Dicks, B. (2013). Action, experience, communication: Three methodological paradigms for researching multimodal and multisensory settings. *Qualitative Research, 14*(6), 656–674. doi:10.1177/1468794113501687

Dicks, B., Mason, B., Coffey, A., & Atkinson, P. (2005). *Qualitative research and hypermedia: Ethnography for the digital age.* London, England: Sage.

Hurdley, R., & Dicks, B. (2011). In-between practice: working in the "thirdspace" of sensory and multimodal methodology. *Qualitative Research, 11*(3), 277–292.

Jewitt, C. (Ed.). (2009). *The Routledge handbook of multimodal analysis.* London, England: Routledge.

O'Halloran, K. L., & Smith, B. A. (Eds.). (2011). *Multimodal studies: Exploring issues and domains.* New York, NY: Routledge.

Pink, S. (2011). Multimodality, multisensoriality and ethnographic knowing: Social semiotics and the phenomenology of perception. *Qualitative Research, 11*(3), 261–276.

Price, S., Jewitt, C., & Brown, B. (Eds.). (2013). *The SAGE handbook of digital technology research.* Thousand Oaks, CA: Sage.

Indigenous Approaches

Bishop, R. (2011). Freeing ourselves from neocolonial domination in research. In *Transgressions: Cultural studies and education* (Vol. 66, pp. 1–30). Rotterdam, Netherlands: Sense.

Castleden, H., Morgan, V. S., & Lamb, C. (2012). "I spent the first year drinking tea": Exploring Canadian university researchers' perspectives on community-based participatory research involving Indigenous peoples. *The Canadian Geographer/Le Géographe Canadien, 56*(2), 160–179.

Denzin, N. K., Lincoln, Y. S., & Smith, L. T. (2008). *The handbook of critical and indigenous methodologies.* Thousand Oaks, CA: Sage.

Evans, M., Miller, A., Hutchinson, P., & Dingwall, C. (2014). Decolonizing research practice: Indigenous methodologies, aboriginal methods, and knowledge/knowing. *The Oxford handbook of qualitative research* (p. 179). New York, NY: Oxford University Press.

Li, P. P. (2012). Toward an integrative framework of indigenous research: The geocentric implications of Yin-Yang Balance. *Asia Pacific Journal of Management, 29*(4), 849–872.

Pe-Pua, R. (1994). Advances in the development of indigenous social research methods. *DLSU Dialogue: An Interdisciplinary Journal for Cultural Studies, 27*(2).

5

Conceptualizing and Planning the Research

©iStockphoto.com/Qweek

Ruth, Anthony, and Marla are challenged by Professor Kent's assignment to come to the next class with a *prospectus*—that is, a one- or two-page description of what they hope to do for their small-scale studies. The past few weeks have been enlightening and helpful because they have read excerpts from a couple of qualitative studies. They feel somewhat daunted, however, by the task of conceptualizing and designing their actual qualitative research studies—no matter how "small scale." Kent underscored how writing a prospectus is similar to writing a proposal for a larger, more comprehensive study but on a smaller scale and with certain considerations relaxed.

PRACTICAL CONSIDERATIONS

Our three characters have embarked on the complex process of designing qualitative research projects. It is confusing, exciting, and just plain old hard work. Many considerations go into the preliminary decisions that are represented in a written proposal. Marla, Ruth, and Anthony will consider three such considerations: (1) the feasibility of the project (the *do-ability*), (2) their own personal interests (the *want-to-do-ability*), and, (3) the significance and ethics of the study (the *should-do-ability*) (Marshall & Rossman, 2016). Think of these considerations as points on a triangle or as circles in a Venn diagram (Figure 5.1). For some studies, feasibility becomes a paramount constraint; for others, it is the ethical issues that may arise. The goal is to find some balance in these considerations so that you can proceed with a manageable project that is sensitive to the ethics and politics of the situation and is sustained by sufficient interest. Interest in the research questions is critical. Even a small-scale project can become tedious. Unless you have a deep concern for the topic, the project likely will flounder. Similarly, designing a project without sufficient resources to implement it leads to frustration; it, too, may never be completed. Also, the politics or ethical issues you confront may put up barriers. Although you cannot predict all the messy politics or subtle ethical dilemmas that may arise, thinking and talking about them while designing a project can help surface potential thorny issues.

Can you do the study? Is it feasible?

Do you want to do the study? Are you passionate about it?

Should you do the study? Is it worth doing? Is it ethical?

FIGURE 5.1   Practical Considerations

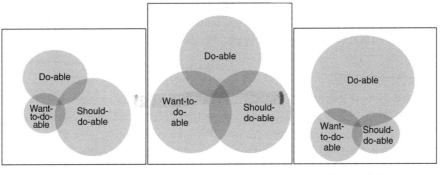

Common balance   *Ideal* balance   *Common* balance

Do-Ability

Research projects are implemented in the real world of organizational gatekeepers, participants' schedules, available time (yours and theirs), sufficient resources to buy things such as tape recorders and photocopying, and your knowledge and skills. Considering all these in designing a study reaps important benefits. Ruth knows children with disabilities from her work at summer camp, but they all attend the school for the deaf. She will need to find children with physical disabilities who are willing to talk with her. Access is not an issue for Marla, although she will have to think about the officials in the health clinic and their procedures for approving a study, even a small-scale one. Agencies that provide health services often have complex procedures for approving research projects. One of our students spent the better part of a semester working through the various committees in a hospital before she could proceed with her project.

Anthony's evaluation project is funded by an outside agency, so his worries about do-ability should focus on gaining access to the community members who participate in the arts program and to the artists. All three characters have yet to think about details of the costs (time and money) of their projects. Access and resources are often linked, especially if the site you want to study is far away. A student from Kenya wanted to study the challenges facing children who had become heads of household when their parents died of AIDS. Despite the support of village elders for the study, she could not find the time or funding to travel to Africa. A less dramatic example is the student whose limited resources (time and money) forced him to reduce the number of sites he could visit to understand how welfare policies were implemented across different urban cities.

As beginners, Ruth, Marla, and Anthony have concerns about whether they have the knowledge and skills necessary to conduct the research. As they read the methodological literature, practice new skills, and learn as they go along, however, their competence grows. This competence will serve as a foundation for future projects.

Finally, our characters will have to think carefully about the design for implementing their projects. Elaborate designs (with extensive data-gathering efforts) demand heavy allocations of time and, sometimes, money. Their most pressing resource concern will focus on their time commitments to the projects. As they learn about the time involved in gaining access, scheduling observations and interviews, writing field notes, and analyzing data, they can build realistic designs for projects that are manageable and do-able.

Want-to-Do-Ability

You need to have a sustaining interest in the topic. Period. All research goes through phases of intense effort and exhilaration coupled with periods of tedium and frustration. Getting through the difficult times requires discipline and commitment. That commitment comes from a deep desire to learn more about the topic and to answer the questions you have posed. Picking a topic just because it seems easy likely will lead to uninspired work. As Murray and Overton (2003) note, "The student should choose a topic that rings

Can you do this
study?

bells and sets off fireworks in the mind. Being very interested in the matter you are going to invest a significant part of your life in is a bare minimum" (p. 24).

Your interest, often derived from personal experience, is what sustains the work. In essence, you are making a claim or putting forth an argument about the topic you are interested in. Our characters already show how they care about their projects: Their experiences and concerns are reflected in their choices. Ruth is fascinated with how children with physical handicaps deal with sports; she believes that participation can build self-confidence. Marla's lifework focuses on women's health issues; she has long felt that poor women have limited access. Anthony believes that the lives of poor people can be enhanced through participation in the creative and expressive arts. He is interested in policies that support community involvement but concerned that only a few segments of any community take part in the activities and decision making.

Inquiry is shaped by our personal interests and interpreted through our values and politics. When does interest become bias? What about objectivity? All three characters face the challenge of acknowledging their interests and sorting through where their passions for their topics become bias. Ethical and trustworthy researchers (see Chapter 3) address this issue explicitly. They build in strategies to put their perspectives and assumptions up front and for surfacing potential bias by closely and diligently examining alternative interpretations. They interrogate emerging findings, asking "What else might explain this?" They try to hold no truths too closely, respecting the notion that all knowledge is conditional and approximate. Also, they are humble in their claims.

Do you really *want* to do this study?

Should-Do-Ability

Given a feasible design and sufficient interest, ask yourself if the study *should* be conducted. Does it have the potential to contribute? Is the topic significant? To whom? Could the participants (or you) come to harm? What about the politics in the setting, as well as your own personal politics? Ethics, politics, and importance should be considered at three levels: (1) the personal, (2) the setting and the participants, and (3) social policy.

Marla knows that access to continuous health care is a pressing social problem, especially for women living in poverty. Therefore, it is a significant social policy issue. Her personal political beliefs, moreover, demand that she conduct a study that focuses on women and that is participatory and involving rather than detached. Her ethical concerns may well focus on the subtle undercurrents of power and prejudice that shape the culture of health care for women. Anthony will have to think about the potential backlash of conducting a mandated evaluation. The politics of the funding agency will have to be balanced against participants' interests. At a personal level, he will have to ask himself if he feels he ought to conduct this project and can do so in an ethical manner. Ruth has a commitment to children with special needs. She is acutely aware of the prejudice and suspicion surrounding physical disabilities. The political and economic issues of access and equity in schools sit high on public policy agendas.

Should the study be conducted?

These are the kinds of considerations that need to be addressed in thinking about a research project. One difficulty is that potential "should" issues cannot be forecast with perfect clarity, nor can all the costs associated with a project be predicted. Think about them and talk about them with your community of practice. Consider alternatives. Holding these considerations in mind as you conceptualize and design a study is crucial.

WHAT IS A RESEARCH PROPOSAL?

Think of a proposal as an initial plan to guide your actions as you conduct the project. The conceptual portion keeps you grounded in specific questions; the design and methods focus your actions in the field. Keep in mind, however, that qualitative research is uniquely suited to discovery and exploration. If you think of inquiry as a journey, the proposal is your itinerary. You know the general destination, but the precise route you take may change. Retaining flexibility in the proposal, and as you implement the study, fosters the responsiveness that is fundamental to qualitative research.

A research proposal consists of two major sections: (1) *what* the researcher wants to learn more about (the study's conceptual framework) and (2) *how* the researcher will learn about this issue or question (its design and methods). (Many people call this section "methodology"; however, the strict definition of *methodology* is "the study of methods." For the purposes of this chapter, we prefer to use the term *methods*.) These sections need to be well integrated and congruent in their epistemological assumptions (see Chapter 2). Imagine the conceptual framework as a funnel; the large end describes the general phenomenon—the topic—and articulates the theoretical perspective; the smaller end describes the specific project proposed. The design and methods section, then, stipulates how the study will be implemented: where and what you will do and how you will do it. Proposals for qualitative research typically have the sections listed in Figure 5.2. Keep in mind that your study may follow a different order, but all elements must be there.

The conceptual portion describes the topic and how it is framed, the research problem or issue to be investigated, the relevant related literature including any foundational theories, the general and specific questions, and the potential significance of the study. In this section, you place boundaries around the study (delimitations). Here, you also describe relevant aspects of your personal biography and your stance toward research (your epistemologic assumptions) and the topic. Throughout, you define important concepts and terms, relying on relevant literature to support points, show gaps in that literature, and establish the importance of the topic. The particular literatures establish the framework that grounds the study.

The proposal's design and methods section stipulates how you will gather data to address the research questions. This section details the overall approach to the study (also called the design); processes for site and population selection and sampling people, events, and processes; gaining access; gathering and analyzing data; ensuring trustworthiness; and involving participants, if relevant, along the way. As you should throughout

FIGURE 5.2 Research Proposal Outline

Introduction
   Overview of conceptual framework and design and methods

Conceptual Framework (the what)
   Topic and statement of the problem
   Purpose and significance
   Background for the study (literature review)
   Overview questions and subquestions
   Personal biography of the researcher
   Limitations

Design and Methods (the how)
   Overall approach and rationale
   Site or population selection and sampling strategies
   Data-gathering procedures
   Analytic framework and preliminary data-analysis procedures
   Trustworthiness and methodological limitations
   Ethical considerations

Appendixes
   Informed consent forms
   Draft interview guide
   Draft observation protocol

subject to change!

the proposal, here also you retain flexibility because you may alter the specifics of data gathering once the project is under way. Making sound *field decisions* is integral to learning how to do qualitative research; therefore, the proposal stipulates solid, albeit tentative, plans for implementing the study.

Note that a proposal represents decisions—or choices—so that a particular theoretical framework and design and methods will help generate data appropriate for responding to your research questions. These decisions are based on complex reasoning and consideration of a variety of research questions, possible frameworks, alternative designs and methodologies, as well as the do-ability, want-to-do-ability, and should-do-ability of the proposal. Considering all these captures the complex, iterative process of designing a qualitative study—weaving back and forth between possible research questions, frameworks, approaches, methods, and related considerations. As you consider alternative designs and methods (e.g., in-depth interviews or participant observation), the research questions shift. As you refine the research questions, fruitful and appropriate designs become more obvious. All this should be bounded by thinking through issues of feasibility, resources, interest, ethics, and politics. Your job is to decide what will work well, given the unfolding questions to be pursued and the potential constraints.

Building the proposal requires that you hold possible choices for all elements in your mind at the same time. This early conceptualization and design work is by far the most challenging

Becoming a
good qualitative
researcher means
becoming a good
decision maker.

and rigorous of the entire process of proposal development. It is nonlinear and difficult. It is hard work and will stretch you in important ways. As you consider alternatives, you may find guidance in some of the qualitative research traditions you learned about in Chapter 4. These approaches and designs have been used by qualitative researchers over the years.

CONCEPTUAL FRAMEWORK

The first major chunk of a research proposal is the conceptual framework. Here, you establish the *what* and *why* of the study.

- What do you want to learn about?
- Why are you interested?
- What are your feelings about this topic?
- What is already known about this topic? — *lit review*
- What questions remain unanswered?
- What assumptions are you making when you ask these questions?
- Why is studying this topic important?

the what & why

The conceptual framework is your working understanding of the topic, setting, and situation you are interested in. You are not coming to the research as a blank slate, an empty vessel. You are choosing this study for a reason, and the reason needs to be fully explicated. Through your conceptual framework, you connect your own individual experience and views with a larger concept or research or theory, and you do this with critical scrutiny, with fresh openness to ideas that are not congruent with your own. As you build this working understanding of your topic, you begin to articulate your own perspective.

Throughout, relevant literature is woven into the discussion to recognize what is already known, suggest theoretical frameworks, provide substantiation for points, clarify logic, define concepts, and justify decisions. We believe that conceptualizing your study is the most important step in your research process. It directs the kind of data you will collect and where and how, and it guides your analysis. Without a clear and detailed conceptual framework, you—and the audience for your study—will have trouble making sense of the data you gather. The conceptual framework explains the way in which you are thinking about your topic; through it, you reveal your perspective (recall the discussion of subjectivity in Chapter 2), the angle at which you approach the topic. The conceptual framework presents *your theory of the world you will be studying.* In essence, you are making an argument. And finally, your conceptual framework conveys "how and why your ideas matter relative to some larger body of ideas embodied in the research, writings, and experiences of others" (Schram, 2006, p. 58), and it establishes the significance of your study.

establishes significance

A conceptual framework is a structure that organizes the currents of thought that provide focus and direction to an inquiry project. It is the organization of ideas—the central concepts from theory, key findings from research, policy statements, professional wisdom—that will guide the project. Framework stands for organization or structure, and conceptual stands for concerning thoughts, ideas, perceptions, or theories.

The conceptual framework is grounded in your own experience, existing research, and, often, an existing theoretical base. These three foundations of the conceptual framework underscore the interaction between the inductive and deductive processes of research described in Chapter 1. We recognize that "theory is implicit in any human action" (Schratz & Walker, 1995, p. 105). As we noted in Chapter 4, even grounded theory acknowledges the researcher's perspective and construction of reality. Theories inform our experiences; they guide what we look at and listen for and how we make sense of what we see and hear. In turn, what we see and hear re-informs our theories. We modify and possibly reject theories when they contradict or do not apply to what we have seen or heard in the field. Thus, practice, research, and theory all contribute to this worldview you form.

Thus, the conceptual framework provides the basis for a coherent study. It connects the *what* with the *how* of the inquiry. In short, you conceptualize the *what* by embedding your ideas and questions in a larger pool of ideas and questions: What experiences have you had with the question or problem? What are its related concepts? What have others already learned about the issues? What research has already been conducted? What Theories (with a capital *T*—more on this in a moment) might inform the ideas? You are making an argument and positioning it on the terrain of your journey. The framework also links to the design for the study, ensuring that the approach and methods are coherent and flow logically from the framework, and it provides a preliminary map for analyzing the data (as depicted in Figure 5.3).

First, your own experience in practice informs your conceptualization. What do you know about the topic from your own experience? Because you, as the learner, are integral to the conceptual framework, the aspects of your personal biography that are relevant to the topic and help explain your perspective are important. For example, Ruth would want to describe herself as an athlete and note that she has worked with children who have disabilities. Similarly, Marla would reveal her training and work as a health care professional. She also might relate an experience working with immigrant women who did not feel empowered to use a neighborhood clinic where she worked. Anthony might tell of his work among policymakers and in community building. In each case, the personal experiences of our characters shape their interest and their perspectives. Establishing this subjectivity is imperative so that the audiences for the research understand their choices.

Second, what other people have discovered about the topic is foundational. You do not need to rediscover knowledge that already applies to your topic—metaphorically, we say that you do not need to reinvent the wheel. So you ask "What other questions have been explored that relate to mine?" and "What previous research exists for me to build on?" The more you know of the existing research, the easier it is to see the gaps and, thus, the better able you are to narrow and focus the questions guiding your research.

Finally, the conceptual framework has a *theoretical base*. At this point, we want to differentiate between *Theories* and *theories*. Theories (with a capital *T*) are propositions that

The conceptual framework—your theory of the world you want to study.

The conceptual framework keeps you on track; refer to it often.

FIGURE 5.3 Conceptual and Analytic Framework

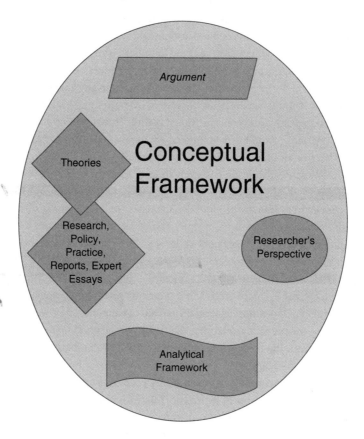

(handwritten marginal note) capital T = Piaget + Gardner

t = lowercase t = personal ideas

are grounded in extensive research: They have been tested and are accepted as explanations for particular phenomena. For example, Piaget's Theory explains human development and Howard Gardner's Theory explains multiple intelligences. The other use of the word *theory* (with a lowercase *t*) refers to personal theories in use that guide our work (see Argyris & Schön, 1974). We hope, we have clarified how theories inform conceptual frameworks. The researcher cannot, however, ignore theories. You need to ask what assumptions underlie your questions. What theories help explain your assumptions? For example, Ruth is assuming that wheelchair athletes see their skills as special; she might use Gardner's Multiple Intelligence Theory to understand their experiences with sports. Anthony assumes that an arts center in a community can support the creation and use of other resources in the community, so he draws on various Theories of Community Development to identify criteria by which to judge the success of the community arts program. Because Marla is interested in individual empowerment, she might find Paolo Freire's Theories on Literacy helpful as she tries to make sense of how the women use the neighborhood clinic.

In summary, the conceptual framework of a study is a traditional part of the theoretical machinery of the inquirer. This crucial section

- aids in describing and explaining the phenomenon, diagnosing the situation, and proposing plans of action;
- constructs an argument that establishes perspective;
- provides insight into the basic character of the phenomenon;
- provides categories for analysis;
- sharpens the focus;
- serves as a source of question or hypothesis generation; and
- links the inquirer's questions to larger theoretical constructs and policy discussions.

The conceptual framework serves yet another crucial function: as the keystone of a study's trustworthiness. As we described earlier, qualitative research is systematic inquiry—that is, a process of making explicit decisions about data (their gathering, their analysis, and their reporting). Systematic inquiry requires clarity of documentation and explication of the process so that others may see and understand the research decisions and assess their adequacy and trustworthiness. All your decisions are grounded in the conceptual framework, so it must be clear. If your framework is clear and the design decisions flow logically, the audience for your study will understand the process and see how you reached conclusions. Your audience may disagree with your choice of conceptual framework, but readers cannot disagree that what you discovered emerges from the data, given your perspective and process.

Conceptualizing a research study entails reading, reflecting, engaging in dialogue with a community of practice when possible, and finally writing. What follows are guidelines for writing sections of the conceptual framework of the prospectus or proposal. Keep in mind that you need not label each section; some may be integrated into others; some may be short, with only a paragraph or two. Different *requests for proposals* and academic committees have their own specified subsections, so you should alter the sections presented below to meet particular proposal requirements. We list the sections separately to be sure that you consider each topic, and we call on our characters to provide examples where useful. First, however, we comment on the various uses of related literature in a proposal.

Use of the Literature

Previous research and theoretical writings ground your study in an *ongoing conversation* about the topic. Here, you enter into a community of discourse. This discourse also contributes to the particular framework that guides your understanding of the topic.

In discussing the literature, you share with the reader the results of previous studies that are related to yours. You identify and discuss major theoretical and empirical literatures and use them to place important boundaries around the study. (The term *empirical* has come to be associated with quantitative research, when, in fact, it means "originating in or based on observation or experience" and "capable of being verified or disproved by observation or experiment"; Empirical, n.d.). Also, you show gaps in that literature to which your study can contribute. Where do you discuss all this? It depends.

Traditionally, reviews of the literature are presented in a separate section of the proposal. Sadly, these reviews are often lifeless and read as dull, intellectual exercises. A more lively presentation weaves the literature throughout a proposal, drawing on previous research or theoretical concepts to establish what your study is about and how it is likely to contribute to the ongoing discourse. Weave this discussion into the sections of the proposal that present the topic and the research problem or issue, and establish the study's significance. Through this discussion, you build a framework that guides your work.

Some qualitative researchers argue that the literature should not be extensively reviewed at the proposal stage; it might contaminate the inductive, open-ended nature of qualitative inquiry. We hold a different view. Discussing the literature helps articulate your perspective and establish your credibility as a researcher, indicating that you are familiar with the conversation in your topic area. Although extensive reviews are not necessary, some discussion is crucial for framing the study. Try for a creative, inductive use of previous research and theory to build a case for your study. Use that literature throughout the conceptual portion of the proposal.

Introduction

The introduction to a qualitative research proposal does just that; it introduces the study to the reader and the reader to the study. This section discusses the larger topic to which the study relates and the problem or issue that it will attempt to address. It sets the context or domain of the study. It describes the focus of the proposed research and briefly forecasts the design and methods. This section also identifies an audience for the document by articulating who might find the study of interest or value. Finally, the introduction provides a transition to the more detailed discussions that follow. This section may be no more than a few paragraphs.

But why are introductions important? Quite simply, if you don't engage your readers' attention right away, you lose them. If a reader is obligated to read your work (e.g., your professor), this may not be as important as when you write a policy brief, a scholarly journal article, a grant proposal, or even a short piece for a newspaper. Engaging your reader *right away* means that this person may actually continue on and read your entire piece. If the reader is not engaged, the introduction may be all that he or she reads. Given our commitment to use, this seems like a waste of your—and your reader's—time.

The introduction establishes the credibility of the project and should evoke the reader's interest. Write it with *hooks* that capture the reader's attention. Begin with a sentence that stimulates interest and conveys an issue that is intriguing. For example, Ruth might write "Children in wheelchairs can jump." Marla could begin with "Women living in poverty have limited access to sustained health care." Anthony might begin his introduction with "A community can bring the arts to everyone." Beginning this way provides a succinct statement of the larger topic or issue that the study will address and engages a broad readership.

Some find it easier to write this section last. Sometimes, it is difficult to know just where the document will wind up (because writing, itself, is a process of inquiry). Beginning at the very beginning can be daunting. If you choose to write it early on, be prepared to revise it substantially once the other sections are written.

This is also where you establish your *voice,* or authorial point of view. Different disciplines (audiences) have different norms governing what voice is appropriate for scholarly writing. The choice of voice depends on the focus of action. The first person (*I* and *we*) places agency directly with the author(s). Although we cannot document this empirically, it is our impression that disciplines amenable to qualitative studies encourage the more literary style of the first person. In this case, the writer takes the stand, tells the story, and has a direct relationship with the action. The danger of writing in the first person is that the author's story may dominate the text. Using the second person (*you*) engages the reader directly with the text. The third-person voice (*he*, *she*, and *they*) is a general construction and shifts the attention to the topic of inquiry. The third person also can be distancing, as when the term *the researcher* or *the investigator* is used. When talking about yourself and your actions, we suggest using *I*. Aim for the active rather than passive voice. Use verbs to connote agency and action. We use all three voices throughout this text for specific purposes. When writing about ourselves (our work and our position), we use *we*. When directly addressing the reader, we use *you*, either implied or expressed. When discussing researchers more generally or our characters, we use the third person.

Having offered the reader an overview of the study and established voice, you are ready to move into the body of the conceptual framework. Recall that a discussion of the general topic, issue or problem of the study, research questions, and significance are all interrelated. Although we discuss these in separate sections, you will need to establish the organization in ways that suit your writing style and the development of the overall logic of the study.

The Topic

Topics are what interest us. In the case of our characters, these are women's access to health care, children with disabilities, and community arts programs. Topics may come from personal interests or from theory, research, social and political circumstances, and situations of practice. In the beginning, it can be useful simply to name your topic. Ask yourself to describe your interest by filling in the blank in the following sentence (adapted from Booth, Colomb, & Williams, 2008, pp. 40–48):

I want to learn about _____.

Next, narrow down the topic by questioning it. Ask the following:

- What are the component parts of the topic?
- How do these parts relate to one another?
- How does the topic relate to a larger domain?

Anthony asks about the organizational elements of the arts program—how these interact with one another, how the program operates, and how it fits into the larger community structures.

You might also interrogate the topic by viewing it as dynamic and changing.

- What is the history here?
- What were its beginnings, and where is it now?

Marla could ask about the history of access to health care in satellite clinics in poor areas: When and where were they first established? Who was involved? What were the early political obstacles?

Further refine the topic by asking about its categories and characteristics.

- How does it vary? Along what dimensions?
- How are cases of it different from and similar to one another?

Anthony could ask how typical this arts program is, what defines it as unique, and how it is like other community-oriented programs.

With a more complex and elaborated understanding of the topic, you can review the literature to establish what is known, what the unanswered questions are, and what the recurring issues are that research could address. By questioning the topic, you have generated a raft of leads to pursue. Your own interests will narrow these as a guide for reading the literature. This reading establishes a research problem or issue, one that you can address through a qualitative study.

Statement of the Research Problem or Issue

Beginning researchers often confuse a general topic in which they are interested with a research problem or issue. Research problems derive from general topics but focus on questions in the literature or recurring issues of practice. This section of the conceptual framework identifies and describes some problem situation or issue that a study can address. Problem or issue statements often focus on what is not yet known or understood well. Embed the problem in the ongoing dialogue in the literature, as we have suggested.

This sets your study within a tradition of inquiry and a context of related studies and serves the following five purposes:

1. Establishes the *theoretical framework* that guides your study

2. Demonstrates that you are *knowledgeable* about the topic and the intellectual traditions that surround and support the study

3. Reveals *gaps* in that literature that your study can begin to address

4. Leads toward the general *research questions* that your study will pursue, and

5. Articulates a *sound rationale* or need to conduct the study

At this point, you might move to a more precise description of the problem or issue by elaborating the topic question with an indirect question (adapted from Booth et al., 2008, pp. 40–48):

> I want to learn about women's health care to find out who/what/when/where/whether/why/how _____.

Marla might write several of these statements, giving her a range of questions to pursue. She would read the related literature with these questions in mind to decide which have the potential for study and which really interest her.

Next, try to put forward a rationale for your study (adapted from Booth et al., 2008, pp. 40–48):

> I want to learn about women's health care to find out what the perspectives of poor women are in order to understand/contribute to how/why/what _____.

By disciplining yourself to describe what you want to understand more fully and how you want the study to contribute, you are establishing a rationale for its conduct.

Our Characters' Choices **Marla**'s sentence reads as follows:

> *I want to learn about women's health care to find out what the perspectives of poor women are in order to improve their access to sustained care.*

Anthony's reads as follows:

> *I want to judge the effectiveness of a community arts program in increasing the participation of community members in the arts in order to inform decision making by program staff and the funding agent.*

Ruth's statement is as follows:

*I want to learn about the lived experiences of children with physical disabilities, partic-
ularly the essence of their understanding of their bodies in relation to sports, in order
to enhance society's understanding and appreciation.*

Purpose

A statement of purpose captures, in a sentence or paragraph, the essence of the study. It
should describe the intent of the study, ground it in a specific qualitative genre, discuss the
central concept or idea, provide a general definition of that concept, and stipulate the unit
of analysis (Creswell, 2013). Traditionally, methodologists have noted four possible purposes for research: (1) to explore, (2) to explain, (3) to describe, or (4) to predict. In Chapter
1, we synthesized these into describing, comparing and contrasting, and forecasting. To
these three, we would add some synonyms such as to understand, to develop, or to discover.
Notable in its absence, however, is a reference to empowerment or emancipation—those
purposes consistent with critical assumptions. To stipulate empowerment as the purpose
of a study, however, creates some tricky cognitive dissonance. A researcher cannot mandate or stipulate empowerment per se; he can, however, discuss the purpose of a study
as creating an environment or a set of circumstances in which participants may become
empowered. The difference in language is subtle but important. An ethical critical paradigm researcher knows the boundaries of empowerment. Although empowerment may be
a goal and the ultimate use of the project, its achievement is serendipitous.

A discussion of the study's purpose should convey the emergent nature of qualitative
inquiry, thereby preserving the right to make field decisions. The purpose also should
capture participants' experiences as the central focus of the study. This strategy reminds
the reader that the study is quintessentially qualitative and seeks to describe (explore,
explain, and understand) the emic perspective. Here, too, mention what is called the *unit
of analysis*—this is the level of action on which you have decided to focus. Ask yourself
what you want to be able to talk about at the end of the study, for example, individuals,
a group, a process, or an organization. This focus stipulates where the data-gathering
efforts will go.

Creswell (2009) offers a useful script to help you develop a purpose statement (we have
adapted his original script):

- The purpose of this study is to _____ (describe? compare and contrast? forecast?) the _____ (central concept being studied) for _____ (the unit of analysis: person? group? discursive practices?) using a _____ (method of inquiry:
  ethnographic design? phenomenological design? sociolinguistic design? case
  study design?).

- The result will be in a _____ (descriptive portrait? discussion of themes and patterns?
  analysis of talk and/or text?).

- At this stage in the research, the _____ (central concept being studied) will be defined generally as _____ (provide a general definition of the central concept).

Although we might critique these long and unwieldy sentences on literary grounds, practice using the script to get clear about the purpose of your study, its central concept, and overall approach.

Our Characters' Choices **Anthony**'s statement follows:

The purpose of this study is to describe and evaluate the effectiveness of bringing arts to community members, using a compressed ethnographic design. The study will result in an evaluation report to inform decision makers and funders. Bringing arts to the community means providing actual, usable opportunities for people who live in the neighborhood to both appreciate and create various forms of art.

Ruth's purpose statement is as follows:

The purpose of this study is to uncover the deep inner meaning of bodied-ness for children in wheelchairs using a phenomenological design. The study will result in portraits and stories of these children's relationships with sports. The central concept of bodied-ness will be explicated through the children's words.

Marla develops this purpose statement:

The purpose of this study is to describe the experiences of poor women in accessing health care, using an action research case study design. The study will result in proposed actions to improve health care in the community. At this stage in the research, health care is defined as preventive health maintenance; access is defined as the tone and climate in a clinic that signal welcome or dismissal.

Significance

In discussing the topic, research problem or issue, and the purpose of the study, you are implicitly or explicitly stating why doing this particular study is important and how it may contribute. The topic discussion establishes that this is a worthy area for investigation, as does the problem statement. Formal proposals, however, typically include a section in which the potential significance of the study is more fully detailed. When space is limited, however, this section is often incorporated into another.

Reasoning that the study is significant and should be conducted entails building an argument that your work will contribute to one or more of the following domains: (a) scholarly research and literature, (b) recurring social policy issues, (c) concerns of practice, and (d) interests of the participants. Your challenge is to situate your study as addressing a particular, important problem. How you define the research topic and problem shapes the study's significance.

The conceptual discussion emphasizes the contributions to the relevant domains. For example, a study of the integration of children with disabilities into the regular classroom could be significant for both policy and practice. Framing the study as a policy study requires that the problem be situated in national and state education policy on special education. Alternatively, framing the study as most significant for practice would necessitate a problem definition focused on restructuring schools to be more inclusive or on classroom practice to support more diverse students. Either frame is legitimate and defensible; the researcher identifies where the study is likely to contribute the most.

If you are preparing a proposal for a funding agency, you should be sure that statements about the project's significance match the agency's needs and priorities. The foundation that takes pride in funding action projects will want to see how the proposed research will directly help people or change a problematic situation. If you are seeking funds from an agency with goals of expanding knowledge and theory (e.g., the National Science Foundation), however, you would want to emphasize undeveloped or unsolved theoretical puzzles to demonstrate the significance of the research.

In summary, the significance section responds to the following questions:

- Who has an interest in this domain of inquiry?

- How will this new research add to theory, policy, and practice in this area?

- How might it be of benefit to the participants and therefore of significance to them?

Overview Questions and Subquestions

Research questions are critically important for guiding your work. Recall that the entire conceptual framework keeps you grounded as you gather data. Stipulating general overview (grand tour) questions and related subquestions is especially useful for delimiting the study. The process of doing qualitative research often raises more questions than it answers; the road you take has many intersections, each more intriguing with possibility than the last. Pursuing the inviting back road (exploring the unknown) is what qualitative research is all about, but taking each and every turn can paralyze the project. Reminding yourself of the questions driving the study helps keep you on track; thus, creating questions with clear focus is important.

The locus of interest you have chosen situates you in a genre that can guide you as you frame the questions. If you want to understand an individual's experiences, your questions will ask about perceptions and explanations: *How do first generation college students represent their experiences?* If you want to learn about a group and its culture, your questions may focus on actions: *How did the teachers use what they learned in the training?* If your interest lies in language and communication, you might frame the questions around the use of words and possible meanings: *What words do the members of the group use to express their pleasure, their anger, to welcome outsiders? What patterns do these communications take?*

We suggest you frame the study as responding to only one or two general questions to be followed with a reasonable number (e.g., three to five) of subquestions to refine the general ones. Perhaps the most important thing to keep in mind is your purpose. Often, when first posing research questions, beginners ask quantitative questions masquerading as qualitative ones. You are not measuring something or looking to establish cause and effect. Beware of the question that asks about influence, impact, or amount (e.g., "How much does whole-language instruction influence student reading achievement? Or to what degree did the teachers use the strategies covered in the professional development session on student-centered learning?"). Overall, you want to understand; you want to learn.

More specifically, whether you plan to conduct an analytical or descriptive study, an evaluation or policy study, or action research, you want to explore, discover, explain, inform, identify, and forecast. Thus, you will want to phrase your questions to allow that openness by beginning your questions with *words* such as "What . . . ? How . . . ? What happened . . . ? Why . . . ? In what ways . . . ?" Be sure your questions remind the reader (and yourself) that you are focusing on perceptions, beliefs, actions, and symbol systems. For example, ask "What benefits do teachers perceive in the use of instructional technology?" instead of "What are the benefits of instructional technology?" Avoid wording your questions in ways that solicit yes or no answers. *Questions should be nondirectional.*

Finally, expect that your questions will evolve as the project unfolds. Because qualitative research refines and redefines as it emerges, you should expect change. Keep the questions open ended to foster exploration and discovery. Table 5.1 provides some preliminary questions to stimulate your thinking.

Our Characters' Choices As **Marla** and the women in her study work on the conceptual framework, their general questions and refining subquestions are the following:

- Why do women from the local community use this clinic?

- How does it meet their needs? How not?

- What alternative sources do they use?

- What are the dynamics of the clinic?

- How do the women perceive that they are treated?

- How do the women interact with the physician's assistants?

- What are conversations like between the women and the health care personnel?

- What happens in the waiting room?

TABLE 5.1   Generating Research Questions by Genre and Strategy

	Ethnographic Study	Phenomenological Study	Sociolinguistic Study	Case Study
Evaluation or policy study	What is the culture of the program? How do participants or stakeholders define success or effectiveness? Are these definitions congruent with effective or exemplary programs?	What meaning do participants in the program make of their experiences? How do these contribute to the functioning of the program?	How has the discourse of policymakers shifted in recent years? What does this reflect about national values? How does the discourse contribute to its effectiveness?	What are the different components of the program? How do they contribute to its effectiveness? What is this program an instance of?
Descriptive study	What do participants believe? What are their values? What is tacit in the setting? How do these beliefs and values shape their understandings and actions?	What is the lived experience of the individual or group? What is the essence of that experience?	What words, actions, and signs do people use to communicate meaning? How do they differ across groups and settings? How are the meanings transmitted?	What are the different meaning perspectives of participants in the program? How do these interact with one another? What values and beliefs are apparent in the actions and interactions?
Action research	What deeply held values and beliefs guide actions, interactions, and activities? What difference does changing actions, activities, or interactions make to the group or the individual?	What is the meaning of actions, activities, or interactions for the group or the individual? What does changing actions and activities mean?	What is the meaning of discourse in the setting? What effect does changing the discourse have? How does this shift power dynamics?	What are the recurring cycles of action and reflection in this case? How do these cycles bring about change?

Anthony's questions are the following:

- How effective is this program in bringing arts to people living in the neighborhood?
- Who attends events at the arts center?
- How do they respond to the various activities?

- Who participates in the creative workshops?

- What are the outcomes of the workshops?

- How do the artists perceive their roles? How do the participants see the artists' roles?

Ruth's general question is as follows:

What deep meaning do children in wheelchairs make of their bodied-ness and athleticism?

Because Ruth's study is so closely linked to what she learns, she is reluctant to specify subquestions before talking with the children. Her reliance on the grand tour question is greater than that of her colleagues.

Limitations

Limitations set some conditions that acknowledge the partial and tentative nature of any research. You have delimited the study throughout the conceptual discussion by describing what the study is and how it is framed; *delimitations imply what the study is not.* Limitations, however, derive from the design and methods and help contextualize the study. Limitations stipulate the weaknesses of this study, thereby encouraging the reader to judge it with these limitations in mind. Limitations arise from, among others, small sample size, reliance on one technique for gathering data, and selection procedures. We urge you not to elaborate these in too much detail. Rather, this discussion serves to remind you, as well as the reader, that no studies are perfect, that findings are tentative and conditional, that knowledge is elusive and approximate, and that our claims should be humble, given the extraordinary complexity of the social world we want to learn more about.

DESIGN AND METHODS

The design and methods section of the proposal serves three major purposes. First, it presents a *plan—the road map*—for conducting the study. Second, it demonstrates to the reader that you are *capable* of conducting the study. Third, it preserves the design *flexibility* that is a hallmark of qualitative methods. Achieving this latter purpose is often the most challenging.

Typically, six topics constitute this section:

1. Overall genre and rationale

2. Site or population selection and sampling strategies

3. Data collection procedures, including sampling people, events, processes, and interactions

4. Preliminary data analysis strategy

5. Trustworthiness, including limitations

6. Ethical considerations

Woven into the discussion of these topics are the twin challenges of presenting a clear, do-able plan balanced by the necessity of maintaining flexibility (see Figure 5.4). Several of these topics we have discussed already: personal biography of the researcher (reflexivity) in Chapter 2 and trustworthiness and ethical considerations in Chapter 3. Other topics are detailed in subsequent chapters: Data collection is described in detail in Chapters 6, 7, 8, and 9 and data analysis in Chapters 10 and 11. In the remainder of this chapter, we discuss overall genre and site or population selection. We also briefly discuss data management and analysis.

Overall Genre and Rationale

Although general acceptance of qualitative inquiry is currently widespread, we recommend that you provide a rationale for the specific genre guiding your study. The most compelling argument is to stress the unique strengths of interpretive research in general and the specific genre to which your study links. Readers who are unfamiliar with qualitative research need explications of the purposes and assumptions of this paradigm. This is especially important for studies that are exploratory or descriptive, that assume the value of context and setting, that search for a deeper understanding of the participants' lived experiences, or that do all the three. Explicating the logical and compelling connections (the epistemological integrity) between the research questions, the genre, and the methods can be quite convincing. Although the range of possible qualitative genres is quite large, we have focused on three. As our characters depict, linking your study to one of these approaches depends on the focus for the research, the problem or issue to be

FIGURE 5.4   The Balancing Act

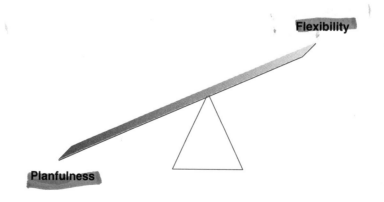

addressed, the research questions, the locus of interest, and considerations of do-ability. Remember to explicitly reserve the right to modify aspects of the research design as the study unfolds. If you are framing your research as a case study, you will need to explain what this means and why it is an appropriate decision given your purposes.

Site or Population Selection and Sampling Strategies

Once the overall genre and a supporting rationale have been presented, the proposal outlines the setting or population of interest and plans for the selection of people, places, and events. There are two waves of decision: The first identifies the setting or population of interest and the second details how you will sample within the setting or population, for example, those individuals you intend to interview or those events you intend to observe. Here, you provide the reader with a sense of the scope of your study and whether the intensity and amount of data you can generate will help you fully respond to the research questions. And remember, since qualitative research relies on detail and thick descriptions, you are aiming for depth over breadth in your choices.

You cannot gather data intensively and in depth about all possible participants, events, or places. You make choices. The first and most global decision—choosing the setting, population, or phenomenon of interest—is fundamental to the entire study. This early significant decision shapes all your subsequent ones and should be described and justified clearly. → in HS art classroom

Some research is site specific. Anthony's decision to focus on a specific setting (e.g., the community-based arts program in Portland, Oregon) is a fairly constrained choice; the study is defined by and intimately linked to that place. If he chose to study a particular population (participants in community-based arts programs), the study would have been somewhat less constrained. It could be conducted in several locations. A decision to study the phenomenon of community involvement in the arts is even less constrained by either place or population. If your study is of a specific program, organization, place, or region, your reader needs some detail regarding the setting. Also, you should provide a rationale that outlines why this specific setting is more appropriate than others.

The ideal site is one where

- entry is possible.

- there is a rich mix of the processes, people, programs, interactions, structures of interest, or all of these.

- you likely can build strong relations with the participants.

- ethical and political considerations are not overwhelming, at least initially.

Although this ideal is seldom attained, your proposal should describe what makes the selection of this particular site especially sound. A site may be well suited for its representativeness, interest, and the range of examples of the phenomenon under study, but if you cannot get beyond the front desk, your study will be thin. Similarly, if you feel very uncomfortable or endangered in a site, or if you believe the participants may be particularly uncomfortable or come to harm, reconsider doing the study.

The second decision wave identifies the specific participants. When studying a specific site or program, as Anthony does, you must stipulate how many individuals and why those individuals, what and how many events and why, and which examples of material culture and why you intend to include them in data gathering. When the focus of the study is on a particular population, as in Marla's case with poor women and the health care system and Ruth's on children with disabilities, you should present a strategy for selecting individuals from that population as well. You also need to provide assurances that your selection process is likely to be successful and indicate why these particular individuals are of interest. For example, in a dissertation study of forced terminations of psychotherapy, Kahn's (1992) strategy was to post notices in local communities asking for participants. Her dissertation committee had lively discussions at her proposal hearing about the feasibility of this strategy. When we were given assurances that this had worked in the past as a way of soliciting participants, we agreed; the strategy was ultimately successful.

In qualitative research, these sampling strategies are called *purposeful*. This is in contrast to random sampling in quantitative studies. As its name suggests, you have reasons (purposes) for selecting specific participants, events, or processes. Typical strategies for purposeful selection of cases and individuals, events, or processes include the following (adapted from Patton, 2015, pp. 266–272):

- Typical case sampling
- Critical case sampling
- Snowball or chain sampling
- Criterion sampling
- Extreme or deviant case sampling
- Maximum variation sampling
- Stratified purposeful sampling
- Homogeneous sampling
- Theory-based sampling
- Politically important cases sampling
- Convenience sampling

Within these broad sampling strategies, you must make decisions about how many to choose. We are often asked *how many is enough?* And we always respond *it depends*. It depends on the conceptual framework, research questions, genre, data-gathering methods, and time and resources. For example, given feasibility constraints, if you are doing a phenomenological study with three very long interviews with each participant, it would be unwise to have a sample of more than three to five people. Let us take you through the arithmetic. If each interview is 1½ hours long, each is likely to yield more than 30 pages of typewritten transcription. Multiply this by three iterative sessions and you have close to 100 pages for each participant. This is a lot of data. In addition, the rough time estimate for transcribing tape-recorded interviews is 5:1 to 6:1—that is, 5 to 6 hours of transcribing for each hour of interviewing. If you have 4½ hours (three interview sessions lasting 1½ hours each) of taped interview, you could spend more than 25 hours transcribing. Remember, this is just one participant. But this genre yields rich, in-depth details about lived experience. Also, the purpose of this genre is to honor the individual's life experience—something difficult to do in a brief, one-time interview.

On the other hand, as with Anthony, you may want some data from a range of participants and events. This suggests a sampling strategy that is broader than that above. Your interviews may be shorter and more numerous; you probably will use informal conversations collected during observations as well. This strategy generates information about a wide range of perceptions and experiences.

Data-Gathering Procedures

Once you have made the initial decision to focus on a specific site, population, or phenomenon, waves of subsequent decisions cascade. The proposal describes the plan that will guide decisions in the field. As mentioned above, decisions about selecting people (to interview) or events (to observe) develop concurrently with decisions about the specific data collection methods you will use. You should think these through in advance. These plans, however, are often changed given the realities of field research, but at the proposal stage, they demonstrate that you have thought through some of the complexities of the setting and have made some initial judgments about how to deploy your time. Such plans also indicate that you have considered the resource demands of specific decisions, as well as the ethical and political considerations in the setting.

As Chapters 7 and 8 detail, the primary ways of gathering qualitative data are through interviewing, observing, and reviewing material culture (documents, artifacts, records, decorations, etc.). Ethnographies and case studies rely on multiple ways of gathering data, whereas phenomenological studies typically use a series of in-depth interviews. Sociolinguistic studies often rely on recordings of communicative acts or events or on existing texts and other media. Your decisions about what techniques to use and with how many people, from what role groups, for how long, and how many times are crucial design and resource decisions.

Consider Anthony's study. The elements of a community-based program are many and complex. Because Anthony interrogated his topic and problem, as described previously, he decides to focus on specific elements of the program: participation at center events, staff and participant attitudes toward the activities, and views of non-participating community members about the program. He will document participation

How many participants are enough?

Well . . . it depends.

Data come from . . .

- interviewing.
- participating and observing.
- analyzing cultural artifacts.

through observation and logs kept by staff members. Attitudes toward the program will be obtained through two techniques: (1) in-depth interviews and (2) a brief survey. Anthony now needs to decide how many participants and nonparticipants to interview and survey. He decides, given the resources available, to survey participants as they attend activities and to invite active participants to be interviewed. He further decides that short and focused interviews with 8 to 10 "actives" will give him an in-depth portrait of their involvement and views about the program.

Interviewing and surveying nonparticipating community members will be more difficult. He decides to survey households within five blocks of the arts center. To do so, he will walk the neighborhood on Saturday mornings, leaving surveys, and, when possible, invite household members to sit for a brief interview. He is not sure how many of these nonparticipating member interviews he can do, but he will stop after he has completed approximately 10 interviews.

Data Management and Preliminary Analysis Procedures

Analyzing qualitative data is time-consuming. It can be tedious but also exhilarating. The specific analysis strategy you adopt depends on the genre of your qualitative study and is guided by the theoretical bases of your conceptual framework. At the proposal stage, you will need to provide some preliminary guidelines for managing data, and you will be expected to outline your analytic framework (which is informed by your conceptual framework; e.g., what theories might help you make sense of the data?). These points are elaborated in Chapter 10.

For now, consider that the interpretive act remains mysterious in both qualitative and quantitative data analysis. It is a process of making sense of your data that is necessary whether you speak of means and standard deviations or offer rich descriptions of everyday events. The interpretive act brings meaning to what you have learned (your data) and presents that meaning to the reader through the report. We discuss the processes of analysis and interpretation in Chapter 10, while Chapter 11 provides examples from our characters. Chapter 12 discusses writing the report or presenting the findings through alternative media.

The remaining sections of the proposal—trustworthiness and ethical considerations—draw on the ideas presented in Chapter 3. Here, your task is to outline how you will try to ensure the strength and sensitivity of your study.

DISPOSITIONS AND SKILLS

Our characters have encountered the multiple decisions involved in designing a qualitative research project. The central tension here is to be "planful" while being flexible and open to change. They have focused their research questions and placed boundaries around what they will explore in detail. They begin to realize that there are no prescriptions for how to proceed and no templates they can implement magically. As they actively design their studies, the concept of ambiguity becomes more real. As they see the possibilities for multiple avenues to truths, they have to consider alternatives and make decisions. They must be able to explain and justify these decisions. Again, they employ their developing understanding of the principles of good practice. As Anthony realizes, plans are necessary, but his plans may well have to change once he is in the field. He is building the skills he will need to conduct a thoughtful small-scale study.

This chapter has discussed the complex thinking and decision making that goes into developing a research proposal. Our characters are not required to elaborate their work in such detail; they do, however, have to consider each element as they move from design to implementation, the topic of the subsequent chapters.

ACTIVITIES FOR YOUR COMMUNITY OF PRACTICE

Study Questions

- What is a research proposal? What are its major elements?

- What is the purpose of your study? How does it fit into the qualitative research genres?

- What literatures inform your topic?

- What research strategy will help you answer your questions fully? How might a different strategy change the questions?

- How will you select your site or population?

- What data-gathering procedures will be most useful?

Small-Group and Dyad Activities

Scripting Your Study

Complete a purpose statement script that describes the purpose you see for your study.

In dyads, share your scripts and generate alternative ideas for the script.

Concept Mapping

In this activity, you will develop a picture that depicts possible relationships between the ideas that come to mind as you think about your research. In dyads, discuss briefly the phenomenon in which you are interested. Individually, brainstorm a list of terms that you associate with this phenomenon.

(Continued)

(Continued)

Now, take the available art materials (crepe paper, Magic Markers, glue sticks, Post-it notes, yarn, etc.) and build a collage that reflects how you see the key terms relating to one another.

When everyone is finished, group members share orally what they have depicted, explaining their assumptions and the linkages they see. Others ask the *why* questions and suggest gaps or additional directions, helping the presenter develop a deeper understanding of the phenomenon.

As a final activity, write a brief narrative explaining what your collage says about the phenomenon and your perspective on the phenomenon. What unanswered questions remain? What leads does this give you about further conceptualizing your study?

Developing a Proposal

Following the proposal outline in the chapter and starting with your purpose statement script, write a sentence or two for as many of the sections as you can. Meet with your dyad partner and explain and justify what you are planning.

FURTHER READINGS

Proposal Development and Research Design

Biklen, S. K., & Casella, R. (2007). *A practical guide to the qualitative dissertation.* New York, NY: Teachers College Press.

Bowen, G. A. (2006). Grounded theory and sensitizing concepts. *International Journal of Qualitative Methods, 5*(3), 1–9.

Creswell, J. W. (2013). *Qualitative inquiry and research design: Choosing among five approaches* (3rd ed.). Thousand Oaks, CA: Sage.

Creswell, J. W. (2014). *Research design: Qualitative, quantitative, and mixed methods approaches* (4th ed.). Thousand Oaks, CA: Sage.

Herr, K., & Anderson, G. L. (2015). *The action research dissertation: A guide for students and faculty* (2nd ed.). Thousand Oaks, CA: Sage.

Marshall, C., & Rossman, G. B. (2015). *Designing qualitative research* (6th ed.). Thousand Oaks, CA: Sage.

Maxwell, J. A. (2013). *Qualitative research design: An interactive approach* (3rd ed.). Thousand Oaks, CA: Sage.

Merriam, S. B. (2009). *Qualitative research: A guide to design and implementation.* San Francisco, CA: Jossey-Bass.

Munhall, P. L., & Chenail, R. J. (2008). *Qualitative research proposals and reports* (3rd ed.). Sudbury, MA: Jones & Bartlett.

Piatinida, M., & Garman, N. B. (2009). *The qualitative dissertation: A guide for students and faculty* (2nd ed.). Thousand Oaks, CA: Sage.

Rallis, S. F. & Rossman, G. B. (2012). *The research journey: Introduction to inquiry.* New York, NY: Guilford Press. (See, especially, chaps 5 and 6)

Schram, T. H. (2006). *Conceptualizing and proposing qualitative research* (2nd ed.). Upper Saddle River, NJ: Prentice Hall.

6

Entering the Field

©iStockphoto.com/Qweek

Marla, Ruth, and Anthony have designed their studies and made some preliminary decisions about their settings and participants. They are ready to begin collecting data, but
first, they must get into the sites or connect with the individuals, whom they will interview. Access is more than physical entry or obtaining official permission to collect data.
As you can see, they are facing the following crucial questions:

- How do they introduce themselves to the participants?

- Who in the setting needs to know what information?

- What position or role will each play in the sites?

- What relationships will be established?

- What promises will be made?

As qualitative researchers enter a setting, their objectives are to ensure freedom and integrity for both the researchers and the participants in their studies. This relationship will vary depending on how collaborative the research is intended to be. Schatzman and Strauss (1973) express a traditional perspective:

> For the researcher, this means his own relative freedom to move about, to look and listen, also, to think in his own terms, and to communicate his thoughts to his own intellectual community. For the host, it means freedom for him and his group to pursue their own work unencumbered and unafraid. (p. 29)

The ethical researcher—one whose conduct is guided by a set of moral principles— achieves this balance of freedom and integrity with the participants through a process of presenting her purpose and negotiating acceptance. The entry process may appear to happen quickly in some instances or may seem to take forever in others, but access is a continuous process of building relationships in the setting and taking care not to disturb the "delicate interaction rituals" (Hammersley & Atkinson, 2007, p. 43) of the field.

Qualitative researchers develop a repertoire of strategies to gain access to sites. They draw on all their interpersonal dispositions and skills, as well as their theoretical understanding of social relationships and organizations. Ball (1993) likens the process to going on a blind date; the researcher "must charm the respondents into cooperation" (p. 32). Their choice of particular entry strategies may be idiosyncratic, but the objective is the same as that of their colleagues: to gain acceptance. Like Anthony, who is sponsored by the program funder, you may find that even with official or formal permission to begin the study, participants still decide how much and in what ways they will share information. One of our students, for example, wanted to study the superintendent's council in a large urban district. The superintendent agreed and invited him to attend council meetings. The student soon noticed that, although he could observe the meetings, the principals and department chairs who made up the council rarely spoke to him directly and seemed reluctant to answer his questions. He realized that they were limiting his access to the full processes of council deliberations. More nuanced access to subtle meanings and operations would require building relationships with the key actors. This chapter details the delicate and subtle processes of preparing for and making initial contact with participants at the site.

Access is a continuous process, not an event.

PREPARATION

Preparation facilitates access. Preparation entails reading, choosing an approach, meeting the gatekeepers, identifying potential obstacles, and negotiating some reciprocity (Jorgensen, 1989) that would be of mutual benefit for all parties. Most important, the researcher tries to allow time for the entry process. He seeks an opening or a door through which he can discover the players and the operations of the world within. Once the researcher has established initial entry, he can build on the relationship, using his skills to renegotiate arrangements as necessary.

A clearly articulated *conceptual framework* is important for entry. The framework helps clarify your focus and purpose and provides a rationale for research decisions. While you may decide to alter this framework over the course of the fieldwork, you start with the questions that emerge from this initial orienting. For example, Marla knows that she and her team will clarify her questions as she spends time in the clinic, but she begins with a framework of poor women's health issues. Anthony's reading has offered him images of a state-of-the-art community arts programs, but he will need to refine and delineate those characteristics that are relevant to his setting. Drawing from her understanding of sports psychology and human development, Ruth brings a conceptualization of "bodied-ness" and athleticism. This conceptualization will change as she learns from the children.

The conceptual framework defines your purpose and strategy. Consider the following questions:

- Are you evaluating a program or a service?

- Will program administrators use your results to inform their decisions?

- Will funders use your findings to continue or withdraw support?

- Will policymakers or legislators use the information to shape policies?

- Do you intend to contribute to theory from your discoveries?

- Will your descriptions change the way in which people see their world and encourage them to act differently?

Your strategy (whether it is to evaluate or inform policy, to analytically describe an individual or setting, or to change practice) shapes your purposes and thereby your actions.

Articulating strategy and purpose is especially important for entry because it affects the participants and influences the way in which they will perceive the researcher. Recall the discussions of reciprocity in Chapter 3. Qualitative researchers notice that folks in field sites receive them differently depending on what the participants see as your research purpose. Evaluators may seem to be given red carpet treatment, but doors often remain closed; university researchers are either ignored or collared by those who

Preparation

- Know why you are there
- Be able to explain why you are there
- Be able to articulate your strategy
- Be aware of the key actors

have a particular interest in the topic; and action researchers are expected to move in and "go native." Just as in all social interaction, qualitative researchers learn to use their interpersonal dispositions and skills—within their ethical principles—to understand the way in which participants see them and their purposes.

As a qualitative researcher, you try to know a great deal about the site before attempting entry. Read and talk to informed people about the setting. Maybe spend some time hanging out at the site. Have a pretty clear idea of why you are entering this particular setting. Then draw on your accumulated knowledge to approach and present yourself to the participants.

INTENDED INVOLVEMENT

In every study you do, you will find that your roles and interactions with the participants differ. Sometimes you get to know the people really well and spend a long time with them. Sometimes you become a part of the setting. Sometimes you feel that you have "taken the data and run." The context of your setting, the strategy, and the genre of research all shape your role. In a preliminary way, however, you can think about two aspects of your involvement: (1) how involved you want to be in the setting or with the participants and (2) how you will portray this intended involvement to them. The following questions may help:

- Will you participate in the activities of the setting being studied, or will you simply be a spectator?

- If you will participate, do you plan to immerse yourself fully in the setting or to join selectively in activities?

- Do you intend your involvement to be coparticipation, wherein you and members of the setting will share equally in the responsibility of designing and conducting the study?

- Whatever your involvement maybe, how will others see your role?

Given our acceptance of reflexivity, we believe that all researchers are, to varying extents, participants in their settings. Thus, we do not spend time considering whether to be a participant-observer or a nonparticipant-observer. Instead, we consider the level and type of our participation and how that participation is portrayed to members of the setting.

Degree of Involvement

Participation can be illustrated as a continuum that ranges from coparticipation to immersion as a participant to isolation as an onlooker (see Figure 6.1). The latter is not overtly involved in the processes of the setting. We have not seen the term *coparticipation* used before in the literature on involvement. We believe that it captures the radical and critical stance of participatory action researchers.

FIGURE 6.1   Degrees of Involvement

Coparticipation ◄------ Immersion ------- Limited participation ------► Spectator

Still, we believe that even the spectator is active and fully engaged in experiencing what is happening around her. The difference is similar to that between the football player on the field and the avid spectator in the stands. Moreover, your position on the continuum can change over the course of the study. Marla, Ruth, and Anthony again provide examples of different degrees of participation, including Marla's choice to coparticipate in the inquiry into women's health care services and Anthony's choice to be a spectator at some of the arts events.

The degree of a researcher's participation is usually shaped by design decisions and by what is possible or appropriate (ethically, politically, or just plain naturally) in the setting (see Chapters 3, 4, and 5). Different *degrees of participation* can either facilitate or hinder data collection. An observer can sometimes learn the most by playing the game, joining in the discussion, or making and serving the soup. At other times, such involvement would be awkward or would actually prevent data collection. Recording children's responses in a reading group is difficult if you are responsible for leading the lesson or awkward if you are pretending to be one of the children.

Immersion and coparticipation enable the researcher to learn the specialized language and norms of the setting and are more likely to yield a deep emic understanding than simply standing around and watching people. Full participation in the activities of the culture, however, is often limited by how similar to members you appear in background, race, and ethnic identification as much as by the nature of your specific actions. Often, the more you stand out, the harder you have to work to become a member of the group. Sometimes researchers may sacrifice possible data they could be collecting because they must engage in what may seem to be complicated, eccentric, and perhaps unnecessary entry effort.

Design also shapes involvement by the amount of time that has been allocated to spend in the field. More involvement requires more time. Time may range from a single observation or interview of a limited duration (e.g., 1 hour) to long-term and multiple observations and interviews over months or even years. Coparticipation, in particular, is extraordinarily time intensive. The more the time spent in the field and the more involved a researcher can be in day-to-day activities at a site, the less likely it is that members of the setting will react to his presence and will change their behavior as a result. The less the researcher is a curiosity, the less people take notice. Usually, the more familiar the participants are with the researcher, the more they trust him and are willing to share their feelings and knowledge. In rare instances, however, the opposite happens; people become suspicious over time. Thus, each researcher makes decisions about participation and duration according to the special circumstances of each study. The same holds true while working with individual participants.

The experience of a graduate student who conducted a study in Manus, Papua New Guinea (the site of Margaret Mead's research), provides an interesting and unexpected example of acceptance in a foreign culture (see Demerath, 1996). He and his wife had little difficulty gaining full acceptance because the role of anthropologist has been given an accepted and legitimate place in that community. In fact, the persons with whom they stayed are known as "those who take care of the anthropologists." In this case, the researcher's participation in the community was already defined based on the community's previous history with researchers (this may be the most extreme illustration of reflexivity we can imagine).

Portrayal of Involvement

Qualitative researchers also decide how to present themselves to the participants in the setting. Here are some questions to ask yourself:

- Will you make your presence as a researcher known and be explicit about your purposes?

- Will you quietly blend into the setting, hiding your purposes and persona as a researcher?

- Will you simply be "truthful but vague" (Taylor & Bogdan, 1984, p. 25) about your role?

Even a coparticipator, such as Marla, will portray herself in a particular way. Again, how a researcher chooses to portray her role and purpose to the participants in the study settings is best illustrated by continua (see Figures 6.2 and 6.3).

In most studies we have conducted, our participation was overt; people knew who we were and why we were there. Sometimes they formed a vague idea of our purposes and cared

FIGURE 6.2   Portrayal of Researcher Role

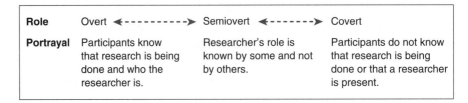

Role	Overt ◄----------►	Semiovert ◄-------►	Covert
Portrayal	Participants know that research is being done and who the researcher is.	Researcher's role is known by some and not by others.	Participants do not know that research is being done or that a researcher is present.

Source: From *Qualitative Evaluation and Research Methods* (2nd ed., p. 217), by M. Q. Patton, 1990, Newbury Park, CA: Sage. Copyright 1990 by Sage Publications. Adapted with permission.

FIGURE 6.3   Portrayal of Purpose

Explanation	Full ◄------►	Partial ◄-----►	Covert ◄-----►	False
Portrayal	All participants know about the study's purpose; participants are fully informed.	Participants know something about the study's purpose; participants have limited understanding of the study.	No explanation is given; participants do not know about the study.	False explanations are given; participants are deceived.

Source: Patton, M. Q. (1990). *Qualitative evaluation and research methods* (2nd ed.). Newbury Park, CA: Sage.

Note: From *Qualitative Evaluation and Research Methods* (2nd ed., p. 217), by M. Q. Patton, 1990, Newbury Park, CA: Sage. Copyright 1990 by Sage Publications. Adapted with permission.

to know no more. Other times, they questioned us and talked with us about what we were doing. Sometimes they were integral to data collection and analysis. Whether the setting was a classroom, a community meeting, or a cardiopulmonary resuscitation training session, we came with a defined role. Our involvement in the activities was negotiated. Ruth portrays herself fully and openly to the children and their parents. Anthony's portrayal is clear and overt to some (staff and some community members) and more ambiguous to others. He may find no need to explain himself to the people who come to the gallery opening or to the modern dance exhibition. Marla will be explicit and overt about her role and purposes as she and the participants in the action research define and implement the study collaboratively.

Research activities can be piggybacked onto other activities. For example, Marla will facilitate the study at the same time she is serving as a volunteer in the clinic. Although most people at the clinic see her primary role as a volunteer, she does not intend to hide from her coworkers that she is a student facilitating action research. Quite likely, many of the workers will forget about her project, whereas others, including workers and clients, may never be aware of her dual roles. Of course, the women working with her in the action research will see her dual roles.

At times, we have collected data while performing other jobs. Such research is overt because we inform participants of our intent to collect the corollary data; we negotiate informed consent at that time. For example, we collected data on the progress of our students during an action research seminar we led for teams of schoolteachers. We were teaching them how to conduct action research studies, but we also documented, with their permission, their learning and activities to study the impact of action research on teacher practice.

We also have collected data that we then used for another, unanticipated purpose. We used such data in writing *Dynamic Teachers* (Rallis & Rossman, 1995). We had reams of notes from years of observations of teachers in various school settings from our roles as director and evaluator of a professional development and school improvement initiative. We used the actual data and knowledge gained in conceptualizing and describing dynamic teachers. Another illustration is the chapter that Kaye and Rallis (1989) wrote on advanced cardiac life support training, which was based on their extensive observations of advanced cardiac life support training during various studies about this type of training. In both cases, the original data collection was overt, but the participants in these instances could not have known about the future uses because we did not know about them ourselves.

The qualitative researcher may choose not to fully disclose her specific focus when she believes that awareness of the details might make participants particularly self-conscious. For example, we have supported students who describe their studies as focusing on classroom interactions in general without revealing their interest in gender or race. In such cases, the researchers felt that if the participants were aware of the specific focus, they might monitor and alter their actions. As another example, if Marla was using a traditional approach to study clinic services for poor women, she might fear that revealing her specific focus on poor women would draw unusual attention to them. Thus, she might say simply that she is studying health services at the clinic.

If Marla told no one in the clinic setting that she was collecting data for a study, however, she would be violating our code of ethics. Covert research is not acceptable. Similarly, if Anthony were to tell the program director only that he was interested in community arts without revealing his role as evaluator, his research would be covert and unethical.

APPROACH AND NEGOTIATIONS

Negotiating entry is a process and seldom happens quickly and smoothly. The process is one of allocating time for negotiating the terms of the introduction or invitation and for securing written permission.

Time

Qualitative researchers learn to anticipate the time involved in gaining access. In fact, the process of negotiating entry can be as insightful about the people or setting as subsequent observations and interviews themselves. Researchers tend to be wary of any entry that seems to progress flawlessly. They have learned that this may be a "front," and barriers will pop up later. Moreover, key personnel change jobs, programs move location, and weather and other natural events can interfere with scheduling. Most often, the contact people with whom researchers make the arrangements are pleasant and cooperative, but the site visits are seldom high on their priority lists. The researcher, therefore, must adapt to the schedules and routines of the site and participants.

We recall an entry negotiation that became an odyssey. The study was on high school change (Rossman et al., 1988), and we had selected three schools in different districts. We obtained the superintendent's approval in each district without a hitch. Each superintendent referred us to the respective high school principal. At one high school, we began with letters and a phone call to set up an initial meeting with the principal. One month passed before that first meeting. The principal supported the study but said that we needed to meet with his vice principal before any official fieldwork could begin. The vice principal suggested that we meet with the teachers' union, so we scheduled yet another meeting. The union representatives asked us to meet with the department heads to explain the study. The department heads were impressed, so we returned to the principal for official sanction. At this point, however, the principal decided that he wanted the entire faculty to vote their approval or disapproval. At a full faculty meeting, the teachers voted and approved our entry. Finally, we were in—but 6 months had passed.

Each step served as a legitimate screening device for the organization, but precious time had elapsed since the original inquiry. Symbolically, we had been negotiating with the organization rather than with an individual. Having passed the organization's protective mechanisms, we were allowed to enter. Because the entire organization had been involved in the decision to let us in, we found we had access to many levels, and we believe that most members were forthcoming. The results were worth the time.

The same holds true with individuals whom the researcher would like to invite to participate. Quite appropriately, from their perspective, they may resist, ignore, or even sabotage the invitation. As the researcher, you may discover that you need to use extraordinary measures that consume considerable time to engage the desired individuals in the project. At some point, you must decide whether obtaining interviews with these persons is worth the time it takes.

Introduction and Invitation

Unless the site is entirely open and public, you generally need to obtain a formal invitation before entering the field. Whether visiting a classroom, a therapy session, a community activist gathering, or a performance, you need permission for or some acceptance of your presence. Even if observing in a public setting, as did Whyte in *Street Corner Society* (1943/1981), you need the acceptance of the inhabitants or regulars to "see" anything. Getting permission or an invitation is not usually as difficult as it is time-consuming. We note that many of the examples we provide focus on access to settings, organizations, events, or groups. However, some studies are concerned with individuals. For example, Ruth is interested in children and their experiences. Most of the suggestions or principles we offer are intended to apply to both the settings and the individuals.

Initial contact may be made by phone or letter, via e-mail, in person, or through an introduction. Having more than one method of introduction eases the process. For example, if we do not know people in the setting and have no one to introduce us, we write before calling. Cold calls can catch the recipient off guard. If we are seen as strangers, the recipient can be leery of our intent. Often, the person we need to contact for entry is busy and important and would be unlikely to accept an unexpected call from someone he or she did not know. An e-mail or letter allows that person time to prepare a response (or toss it away).

Gaining Access Takes Time
- Making contact
- Negotiating with gatekeepers
- Obtaining an invitation
- Getting formal permission
- Building relationships

Usually, we try to have someone familiar with our project make an introduction, or we use existing relationships to establish contact. For example, when looking for sites to study teacher-researchers, we sought the support of the director of the innovation division of a national teachers' association. She helped us choose the schools and placed calls to the principals as an introduction. When we were conducting the evaluation of a district's inclusion initiative, we knew that support of the principals would be important. We asked the superintendent to call a meeting of the principals at which we could introduce ourselves and describe the study. In both cases, we first considered how the principals would react to the individuals we were asking to introduce us. Do they respect those persons? Might they resent an apparent power play? Might the persons misrepresent us? Because the answers satisfied us, we proceeded with the introductions.

If you are seeking to interview people rather than survey a setting, you might need to try some additional strategies to make contact. We had one student who posted flyers in a coin-operated laundry. A religious woman who was our doctoral student wanted to interview women in other religious orders about their definitions of social justice, so she attended functions at a nearby center for equity and justice to meet women who fit her criteria. Another student found his interviewees by following up respondents to a questionnaire relevant to his topic that a public agency had distributed. Yet another student told her physician about her dissertation topic. The doctor remarked that she had some other patients who might be interested in the topic and offered to pass on the student's number to patients who would be willing to be interviewed.

Making initial contact in person is useful if the setting is relatively public or if you know little about it. Approaching a site in person with no introduction is also a good idea if you suspect that a formal introduction by someone highly placed in the organization might prejudice participants against you. In these settings, you may simply want to go and hang around, getting your feet wet to find out what you want to focus on, who are the important contacts, and how you might get accepted. For example, if you wanted to observe sports programs at private schools but had no contacts, you might begin by attending games to discover who the players are and what informal rules govern interactions off the field. Similarly, Anthony might initially simply hang around the arts center.

Obtaining Permission

Part of the entry negotiations is obtaining permission—sometimes written and sometimes oral (see Chapter 3)—from participants. Some people are willing to give permission under certain conditions and not others. For example, some will not allow their interviews to be audiotaped, but they will allow you to take notes. You should try to accommodate your interview partner whenever possible. In some instances, written permission is covered by the formal permission you received in getting access to the institution, as long as you confine your interview questions to the topics on which you agreed. For example, we did not need permissions from every person in the schools when we did the inclusion study because we had been contracted by the district office and our questions fell within the purview of the participants' work. Whatever the situation, all participants need to be informed and give their consent, either in writing or orally. Be aware, however, that sometimes the mere mention of informed consent changes the tone of the conversation. This can feel quite awkward; however, it is the researcher's responsibility to find an ethical way to communicate purpose and expectations and to be reasonably sure that the participants understand and voluntarily agree.

Whenever the research is piggybacked on other work, such as using data that were collected for one purpose and were used for another unanticipated purpose, the researcher must ensure the following:

- The data originally were collected systematically and ethically.

- The data do not qualitatively change when analyzed for purposes other than the original.

- No one in the original setting objects to, or no rights are violated by, the new use of the data.

EXPECTATIONS AND RELATIONSHIPS

Unlike in the blind date situation to which the entry process has been compared, the parties in a research study are not likely to either hit it off or "strike out" with the first encounter; it is not usually that dramatic. Thus, negotiations are ongoing. The terms or conditions set during entry establish what will be expected of all parties in a preliminary way. Although these expectations can be—and likely will be—adjusted as the fieldwork progresses, they set the tone for the relationship that develops. Ultimately, this relationship has implications for how trustworthy the data are considered. In his classic work, Johnson (1975) noted,

> The conditions under which an initial entree is negotiated may have important consequences for how the research is socially defined by the members of that setting. These social definitions will have a bearing on the extent to which the members trust a social researcher. (p. 51)

Trusting relations between a researcher and the members of a setting are likely to yield a trustworthy report, "one which retains the integrity of the actor's perspective and its social context" (Johnson, 1975, p. 51).

Entry requires time because usually more than one group of participants need to negotiate agreement on terms and conditions. An experienced qualitative researcher recognizes that several parties may be interested in or affected by the research. The several parties were obvious when we performed a court-ordered evaluation in a school system. The court identified "interested parties" as the plaintiff (i.e., the advocacy group representing the parents who had brought the suit), the school system, the parents' advisory group, and the court monitor. We discovered that additional parties fell within the boundaries of the school system: the principals, the teachers, and the department heads, as well as the central office. Even these groups could be broken down by special interests, such as itinerant teachers. Despite the legitimate interests of many groups, we saw that the logistics of including everyone in the negotiations would be impossible. We singled out the key parties to agree on the terms of the evaluation before we proceeded.

Expectations to be discussed include (a) permissions; (b) how data will be recorded; (c) the roles of various actors, materials, and documents that the participants will need to find and collate; (d) the amount of time the researcher will spend at the site; (e) what areas are open or closed to the researcher; (f) where the researcher can set up a work space if necessary; and (g) the amount of time or other resources the participants will devote. Negotiations also must cover the more political or symbolic issues, such as reciprocity and gatekeeping.

Reciprocity

Reciprocity recognizes the need for *mutual benefit in human interaction*. Norms of reciprocity operate in all social life, and fieldwork is no exception. Research is a two-way street. The researcher wants something: to enter the site freely and to collect data unhindered. The site participants also want something: not to be seriously disturbed in their work or lives and to gain from participating in the study. At times, they participate to take action on some aspect of their lives through a collaborative inquiry process. They expect some change for the better. Sometimes participants are satisfied with an intellectual gain; other times, they want more. The qualitative researcher needs to establish expectations for reciprocity at the start to avoid misunderstanding and resentments later, as well as to ensure that all participants (including the researcher) are treated fairly. Although these early negotiations set the tone, remember that your relationship is being constantly renegotiated.

Clarifying the relationship, difficult as it may be, is especially important because research is quite unlike any other social interaction and is often misunderstood. As depicted in the modern university, research is presented as a Western, masculine, and joyless enterprise that many cultures and people find alien and off putting. Unequal power relationships between the *researcher* and the *researched* give the *researcher* all the authority. She defines the boundaries and the disposition of outcomes. The *researched* is made to feel ignorant, impotent, and easy to forget. In addition, the qualitative research process has the potential to seduce the researched with promises and desert her when the study is over (Siskin, 1994).

Teachers in schools near large research universities often feel seduced and abandoned. These schools serve as research sites, and teachers and students are labeled "subjects." We have heard discussions in which teachers said they felt that they had been "raped" by the university people, who vaguely or implicitly promised pleasure and intimacy greatness,

the fuck?

Building Relationships

- How does entry define the research?
- What are the mutual benefits?
- Who owns the data?
- How do gatekeepers receive you?

Reciprocity

"This has helped me out a lot; I hope you found it useful, too."

and new understanding but seldom ever returned to share their results. This inequity between the researcher and researched need not be the norm and is becoming increasingly unacceptable ethically. A mutually beneficial relation is preferable.

Under *norms of reciprocity*, the researcher obtains data, while the participants "find something that makes their cooperation worthwhile, whether that something is a feeling of importance from being [studied], pleasure from interactions with the [researcher], or assistance in some task" (Patton, 2002, p. 312), or actual changes in life circumstances from action research. Again, truthfulness, on both sides, is the byword for establishing reciprocity. The researcher states what she wants and what she intends to do: to move about the setting, to watch, to ask questions, to take notes, and to read documents and other written materials. The site participants also clarify any limitations they deem necessary: A reasonable exclusion may be certain private personnel meetings.

In addition to setting boundaries, participants also make requests and express the expectations they have. These may include reassurances of confidentiality and anonymity and also may involve questions about what will be done with the results. Unless the project is collaborative, most participants are not interested in the details of the study. They do, however, want to know about any findings related to their work or activities. The principals of the schools in the inclusion study asked that we personally share the findings about their schools with them, so we decided to create school feedback sheets for each one. Some of the school-specific information on these feedback sheets never appeared in the final report because it was important only to the principals.

Usually, people in the settings we have studied had no trouble identifying the benefits they could gain from the research. A physician whom we interviewed numerous times during a yearlong study on in-hospital training and organizational change called us his "administrative *yentas*." He viewed interview sessions as therapeutic. The director of an intervention program we studied disseminated our analyses in a monthly newsletter; she reported that the public relations value was extraordinary. We were pleased that she found such a use for the work. The teachers and principals in the proposed teacher–researcher sites view the study as holding a potential for communication between the schools. They have asked that we help them seek funds for Internet connections and technology training so that they can use computers to collaborate on projects that they will propose together.

Not all participants are as sophisticated or savvy as those we just described. Consider the following thorny problems:

- What if participants, quite legitimately, find Western notions of research anathema and hence know little about the process and its possibilities for harm or benefit?

- What if participants are unaware of their rights to privacy?

For example, the women Marla tries to involve in her action research may have no experience to comprehend what she is asking of them. They may feel that they have little authority to ask questions and seek answers as she proposes they do, nor will they assume the authority to disagree with her. Marla's challenge is to facilitate their empowerment to generate questions and methods that are practical for them rather than for herself as the researcher. As all other qualitative researchers, she will have to be especially sensitive to imbalances of power and authority. She will need to make the potential benefits apparent to the participants.

Reciprocity discussions also might include the question of who owns the data and who can review and edit a written report. Some key players in the setting may want to see the results before they are made public. Some may insist that they read all the field notes and interpretations, and some may even demand editing rights or veto power. Some want coauthorship. We believe that each case must be decided individually. For example, in collaborative action research, participants are appropriately coauthors because they are involved in data collection, analysis, and interpretation. An evaluation such as Anthony's does not warrant participants' veto or coauthorship because the researcher is presenting his view—his interpretation and judgment of the program. The researcher's obligation is to make explicit that it is his voice that is being presented and not necessarily the voices of the participants. Lightfoot (1983) describes how she shared her portraits of good high schools with their principals. She relates how she decided to hold on to her interpretations even when they differed from what the principals saw. To the extent possible, issues such as these should be considered during entry negotiations to avoid misunderstandings that could ultimately limit what use is made of the data. A cautionary note: All these issues cannot be finalized; they often surface unexpectedly. Be aware and remember that negotiations are continuous.

The following painful example illustrates the importance of raising issues of benefit and ownership before the research begins and keeping the discussion open as the research unfolds. We knew a doctoral student who spent a year interviewing and shadowing a handful of successful women leaders for her dissertation. The women were willing to share their thoughts and lives with her because, in part, they felt that their stories were important. They were gratified with the deeper understanding of their own lives that they had gained from their conversations with the student. She neglected, however, to negotiate ownership and confidentiality with the women. In fact, several wanted their real names to be used. When the researcher published the results using pseudonyms, the women leaders were furious. "Those are not her stories! They are ours! How dare she steal them to make money?" said one of the women, expressing the anger of the group. Because the doctoral student had not negotiated this aspect of the study, she may have hurt the credibility of researchers in general. If Marla believes that the stories of the women in her collaborative study are worth publishing, to be ethical and respectful, she must discuss these possibilities with the women:

- Should the stories be published?
- Who should author them?

- Who would receive any royalties from publishing the stories?

- What alternatives to traditional publishing might be appealing?

Organizational Gatekeepers

Recall the discussion of micropolitics and specifically of gatekeepers in Chapter 3. In the discussion at the beginning of this chapter, Marla hopes that because she is volunteering in the clinic, she will not be excluded from routines that will yield valuable information. Anthony is concerned that awareness of his sponsorship by the foundation to do an evaluation might cause program folk to give him an artificial welcome or to close doors precipitously. Ruth knows that she must make contacts that will bring her close to children in wheelchairs. All three realize that no matter how righteous their questions, how sound their methodologies, or how prepared they are, the people in the setting will help them or hinder them and will open up or block off paths to information. Sponsors, gatekeepers, and key sources of information determine, in part, the quality and quantity of data. (Sources of information have traditionally been called *informants*. We are not comfortable with the sinister connotations of that word. Clearly, we do not see key sources of information and insight as spies or turncoats. We invite suggestions for a new term for this role.)

Most bureaucracies have policies or regulations defining who can or cannot have access to what. The individuals who implement or enforce these regulations or policies are typically called *gatekeepers*: the people in settings who control "avenues of opportunity" (Hammersley & Atkinson, 1983, p. 38). Some gatekeepers hold formal positions with legitimate authority to grant or withhold permission. Others possess informal authority and may not be obvious initially. They use their positions to reveal or protect what an outsider may see of themselves, their colleagues, and their organizations. Often, those who hold the keys to revealing information are those who appear unlikely—perhaps the nonprofessionals, the backup crew, or the quiet ones. In schools, for example, we have found that custodians or bus drivers may know more about a particular event than the principal or teacher simply because they can see and hear more sides of the story.

Anyone in an organization can act as a gatekeeper. What makes one person more or less important is the degree to which he can lead you to valuable information, send you off in an irrelevant direction, or block your inquiry at the start. As you enter the setting, ask yourself who holds what information and what routines or strategies these people are likely to use in disseminating their knowledge. Secretaries, for example, are often the first and the best gatekeepers. They hold the keys to their employers and often to the entire organization. When we make initial contact with a director or administrator, we have learned to ask the secretary for her name, and we make sure she knows ours. This way, in future contacts, we can ask for her personally and build on our previous conversations. This simple personal attention makes us familiar; thus, the secretary as

> Gatekeepers can make or break your study. Handle them gently.

gatekeeper is more willing to facilitate our access to relevant information and people. Otherwise, secretaries can put up formidable barriers.

Sponsors can be gatekeepers, and gatekeepers can choose to become key sources of information. The line between the roles is not a clear one. In the inclusion study, our "sponsor" was a central office contact, a highly placed administrator. Technically, her role was to ease our access to the schools. At one level, she filled that role by providing necessary print material and demographics to help us choose sites and by writing official letters of introduction to the principals. She became a gatekeeper, however, because she was inordinately slow in posting the letters of introduction and failed to obtain some of the legal permissions we needed (eventually, we called the district's general counsel ourselves).

As she developed respect for us, however, she became a key source of information. She offered suggestions as to which schools were appropriate and told us details about effective programs in each site. The challenge is to turn a resistant gatekeeper into an active, possibly even collaborating, source of information. A strategy that can facilitate this transformation is establishing what is termed as *comembership*. That is, the researcher finds some common bond on which to build a sense of shared understanding. For example, Marla, whose primary language is Spanish, will have little trouble establishing kinship with the Spanish-speaking women in the clinic.

We use comembership regularly in our research. Our histories as principal and teacher ease our entry into schools. One tense situation occurred when an angry principal sat us down to tell us "what is *really* happening here." For 15 minutes, she shouted about lack of resources to meet the children's extreme needs. Finally, we asked her a question we could only have known to ask from direct experience in a similar situation. From that point on, the interview became a valuable and mutual conversation. Subsequently, she cleared the way for further meaningful observation and conversation throughout the school. Our ability to demonstrate that we shared "membership" with her made the difference.

Qualitative researchers may build this bond through some minor or seemingly irrelevant similarity, as long as they are honest and the correspondence is true. For example, Anthony may refer to his cousin, the puppeteer, to indicate that he has some familiarity with the challenges facing these artists. A female student who chose to study adolescents at a private boys' school found that if she mentioned her teenaged brother early in her interviews, the boys became less nervous and reticent. In the cardiopulmonary resuscitation studies, we drew on personal affinities with the training director (each of us had protested the Vietnam War and each of us likes classical music). The grounds for comembership are less important than that they are genuine.

DISPOSITIONS AND SKILLS

Qualitative researchers make scores of decisions in the course of a project; many concern entry to the setting. The challenge here is negotiating a relationship that is ethical, sensitive, and as natural as possible, given its temporary and artificial nature. As we stated earlier, the research process is a heuristic, discovering experience. This is highly salient during entry. Each setting—even those with which the researcher believes he is familiar—exists to be discovered, and each researcher has a unique way of discovering. As Marla, Ruth, and Anthony make contact and negotiate entry, their growing understanding of the principles of good practice facilitates their discoveries. Our students who choose international sites for their research often assert that difficulties of approach and negotiation are intensified by distance and cultural differences. We suggest that even studying your own backyard can present surprises and still requires sensitivity to the possible benefits and burdens and demands respect for participants.

The challenge of balancing their needs as researchers with those of the people they will be observing and interviewing is both daunting and exciting. Ruth must protect the privacy of the children and families she interviews, and she also hopes they will feel free to disclose very private experiences and feelings. Marla wants the women with whom she will collaborate to look closely at possible injustices they may experience, but she cannot promise them that the study will yield improvements. Anthony wants to cover areas where the community arts program can improve, but he does not want the foundation to use the program's weaknesses as a reason to withdraw funding.

Because Anthony, Ruth, and Marla are dealing with fellow human beings, they learn to recognize that every entry will be unique and most likely unpredictable. As they build relationships with participants, they will try to be exquisitely sensitive to the participants' feelings, worldviews, and interests. They work with their subjectivist assumptions (see Chapter 2) to build relationships that enact reciprocity; they present the studies and benefits as they see them; and they are careful that they make only promises they are sure they can keep. They create conversations and engage in dialogue more than they expect neat, tidy answers. Above all, they try to be honest and truthful in their relations with folks in the field. They realize that their entries are fluid, changing processes. As they negotiate and renegotiate their entries, they apply the principles of good practice.

Now, they have access to their sites; they have entered the field. In Chapter 7, we join them as they begin to collect data and practice the following key dispositions and skills:

- Comfort with ambiguity
- Capacity to make reasoned decisions and to articulate the logic behind those decisions
- Deep interpersonal or emotional sensitivity
- Ethical sensitivity of potential consequences to individuals and groups
- Political sensitivity
- Perseverance and self-discipline

ACTIVITIES FOR YOUR COMMUNITY OF PRACTICE

Study Questions

- How will you prepare to enter the field?

- What is the nature of your relationship with the study participants or the site?

- With whom do you negotiate access? What about formal consent?

- How do you establish your expectations and learn about those that the participants have?

Small-Group and Dyad Activities

Issues of Access

In small groups, dyads, or triads, discuss possible gatekeepers and potential barriers to access in your study. Help your colleagues propose strategies for negotiating with these gatekeepers and overcoming barriers.

Portrayal of Involvement Role Play

Using Figures 6.2 and 6.3, which portray involvement, locate your proposed design for study on the continua and create a role play in which you introduce and explain your study and intended involvement. Your dyad partner plays the part of a difficult, challenging gatekeeper.

Writing Activity

Access

Gaining access to a particular setting and working out an understanding of your study entails negotiation with participants. This often takes much more time than a beginning qualitative researcher anticipates. Moreover, it may provide interesting insight into the prevailing, taken-for-granted assumptions of those in the setting.

Write a memo that documents this process. First, describe chronologically the events that led up to receiving formal permission to do a study. Second, comment on the deeply held assumptions you may have encountered in that process. And third, describe your reactions as you negotiated for access.

FURTHER READINGS

Bogdan, R. C., & Biklen, S. K. (2006). *Qualitative research for education: An introduction to theory and methods* (5th ed.). Boston, MA: Allyn & Bacon.

Delamont, S. (2001). *Fieldwork in educational settings: Methods, pitfalls, and perspectives* (2nd ed.). London, England: Falmer Press.

Dewing, J. (2002). From ritual to relationship: A person-centered approach to consent in qualitative research with older people who have dementia. *Dementia, 1*(2), 157–171.

Feldman, M. S., Bell, J., & Berger, M. T. (Eds.). (2003). *Gaining access: A practical and theoretical guide for qualitative researchers*. Walnut Creek, CA: AltaMira Press.

deMarrais, K. B. (Ed.). (1998). *Inside stories: Qualitative research reflections*. Mahwah, NJ: Lawrence Erlbaum.

Patton, M. Q. (2015). *Qualitative research and evaluation methods* (4th ed.). Thousand Oaks, CA: Sage. (See Chapter 2)

Symonette, H. (2008). Cultivating self as responsive instrument: Working the boundaries and borderlands for ethical border crossings. In D. M. Mertens & P. E. Ginsberg (Eds.), *The handbook of social research ethics* (pp. 279–294). Thousand Oaks, CA: Sage.

Weis, L., & Fine, M. (Eds.). (2000). *Speed bumps: A student-friendly guide to qualitative research*. Albany: State University of New York Press.

7

Gathering Data in the Field

©iStockphoto.com/Qweek

Gathering data is a discovery process. Ruth, Marla, and Anthony talk with people, observe actions and interactions, and pay attention to physical surroundings to learn about aspects of the social world they want to understand better. Interviewing, observing, and studying material culture are the primary ways to discover and learn in the field. *Interviewing* includes talking with participants both formally (when an interview is set up beforehand) and informally (when the researcher is present in the setting for other activities). Interviewing also can take place on the Internet using Skype or some other application. *Observing* includes a formal, structured noting of events, activities, and speech (e.g., when the researcher observes a classroom or a meeting) and participant observation (an overall strategy where the researcher is present in the setting experiencing and noting events). And, as noted in Chapter 4, observing may take place on an Internet site, as in Internet ethnography. Gathering aspects of *material culture* includes artifacts and written material that may be available in or about the setting or about individuals. These may include documents, minutes of meetings, most e-mails, newspaper articles, clothing, diaries, personal objects, and decorations—anything relevant that may reveal information about the person, setting, or event. Material culture also is found on websites and blogs that contain photos, videos, stories, and poems, to name a few potential sources of data.

These ways of learning about the phenomenon and setting are often referred to as methods or techniques. We prefer the term *technique* because it captures the notion of "the manner and ability with which an artist, writer, dancer, athlete, or the like employs the technical skills of a particular art or field of endeavor" (Technique, 2015). When used to describe the work of artists and craftspeople, *technique* implies learnable knowledge and skills. The expression of the technique, however, is unique to each artist. Dancers trained in classical ballet master formal aspects of the dance by learning and practicing certain movements. A weaver learns the techniques of warping a loom and throwing the shuttle with skill and grace. When performing, however, each dancer brings a unique artistic understanding and expression to the act, and each weaver creates a unique piece of fabric. Just as with dance or weaving, qualitative researchers engage in common actions (formal details of the work), but the specific way one qualitative researcher does the work (performing it) is unique to that individual and the project.

The primary techniques of qualitative research provide ways of discovering and interpreting aspects of realities; they are formal ways of gathering information. Through observing, interviewing, and documenting and analyzing material culture, qualitative researchers capture and represent the richness, texture, and depth of what they study. Data gathering is accomplished (performed) by practicing the techniques. Though composed of elements, it is a seamless enterprise. The techniques provide structure, and the resulting complex tapestry (the final report or other medium for sharing what has been learned) is a unique expression woven by the researcher.

> Interviewing requires good observing skills— they go hand in hand.

Textbooks on qualitative research typically treat the skills of observing, interviewing, and studying material culture separately, but this is a bit artificial. As integrated facets of a qualitative study, skill in one tends to relate to skill in another. Our experience suggests that a good interviewer is also a good observer, just as a good observer tends to be a good interviewer. Conducting a rich, informative interview requires strong questioning and listening skills, as well as finely honed observation skills. Marla, Ruth, and Anthony are observing while they drive to interviews, enter offices, and wait for appointments. They notice the body movements and dress of their participants during interviews, based on the assumption that nonverbal cues are central to people's perceptions (see Knapp & Daly, 2011, chap. 8; Manusov & Patterson, 2006).

Participants' emotions, attention and interest, authenticity, and fatigue are observable and inform an interview. These cues suggest avenues to explore and when to redirect questions. In short, observations are intertwined with interviews, suggesting questions the researcher had not anticipated and suggesting topics to explore. Ideas exchanged during interviews suggest other places to observe and potential sources of material culture. Aspects of material culture, in turn, may well provide impressions to pursue through observing and interviewing. Findings from one technique may confirm hunches or suggest new directions. While in the field, Anthony, Ruth, and Marla find that they are continuously observing, interviewing, and studying material culture, although at any given point, their energies focus more on one particular technique.

Observation, interviewing, and studying material culture are not passive states, and the researcher is much more than a sponge that simply absorbs data. A qualitative researcher's mind is trained to be alert and to work actively. With experience, qualitative researchers become extraordinarily sensitive in perceiving relevant data from numerous sources. Their techniques vary as they reflect on newly generated data; they develop preliminary analyses and tentative interpretations as data are gathered. Discovery and learning are integral to these processes. This chapter describes how qualitative researchers discover and learn through observing, asking questions of participants and themselves, and exploring aspects of the material world.

> **Collecting data is not passive.**

DECISIONS ABOUT GATHERING DATA

The processes of gathering data may seem simple at the beginning, but they entail complex and intertwined decisions and actions. Your choice of technique at any point in the project depends on the strategy adopted (see Chapter 1), views on the social world and epistemology (see Chapter 2), the specific qualitative genre to which your work links (see Chapter 4), and how these preliminary choices interact with participants in the setting. Ask yourself the following questions:

- Is the project an evaluation, an action research, or a descriptive study?
- What are my assumptions as a researcher about reality and knowledge claims?
- Are you interested in a group and their interactions, individual lived experience, or talk and text?
- How do actions and reactions of participants (and my interactions with them) shape what is possible, desirable, and ethical?
- What are your research questions?
- What techniques will best inform these questions?

Decisions in these areas may be forecast in the research design but, because flexibility and responsiveness are integral to qualitative research, you repeatedly revisit those initial decisions and modify them in light of the unfolding project. Thus, what you do at any given moment is influenced as much by what you encounter and what evolves in the field as by what you anticipated in the research design.

Given choices about strategy, epistemology, and genre, three major considerations influence your decision making about data-gathering techniques: how deeply or broadly you will apply them, how prefigured or open ended you would like them to be, and what the ebb and flow among techniques will be. Think of these decision arenas as continua, just as in Chapter 2. You may stipulate a position along the continua in designing your project but may find it necessary to adjust and reconsider as your project evolves.

Depth or Breadth

Qualitative researchers decide how deeply or broadly to employ data-gathering techniques. However, the researcher's initial decisions are always negotiated with participants (often tacitly) and always mediated by the context for the research. Where you position yourself along this continuum involves trade-offs. Given the triangle of do-ability, want-to-do-ability, and should-do-ability (see Figure 5.1), it's not possible to gather data both broadly and in depth. You must make choices for a study to be doable. The questions you pose guide your choice: Do you want to know a little from many or a lot from few? Gathering data from a large number of participants yields information from many perspectives, which gives the study breadth—but few researchers can also explore the nuances of individual perceptions and experiences from a large pool of participants. Focusing on a few participants, in contrast, encourages an in-depth understanding not possible with a larger sample. Qualitative studies tend to value depth over breadth.

Ruth gathers data from a few participants, consistent with her strategy of a descriptive study and the phenomenological genre framing her methodology. Her study is essentially *in depth*.

Marla and her action research team decide that they want to gather data from the community served by the health clinic. They observe in the clinic for a few weeks, gathering data broadly about the setting. The team decides to interview women and seek a *balance between breadth and depth* by briefly interviewing 15 to 20 women once and then focusing with further interviews on three women whose stories are particularly compelling. Because Marla is working with a team, she may capture both broader perspectives and in-depth portraits of the women's lives.

Given the demands of Anthony's evaluation, he must gather data broadly to satisfy the decision makers' needs. He begins by observing a variety of events. He supplements this with surveys and short interviews. To elaborate these broad findings, he decides to conduct in-depth interviews with a few users and nonusers. He, too, seeks a *balance between breadth and depth*.

Prefigured or Open Ended

Planning interviews or observations entails thinking about how tightly you want to control questions or topics—that is, whether the techniques will be structured in advance or more open ended. Prefigured techniques carefully specify interview questions or closely structure observations. Anthony prefigures most of the techniques he uses. He relies on checklists in observing arts activities. He has developed forms with categories for noting actions and interactions and for judging audience reactions to events. He has determined the important focuses for his attention based on his reading of the literature about arts programs and his own experiences with the arts. His interviews, similarly, consist of a set of questions that he asks of users and nonusers. He modifies the questions as he moves through his project, but they remain essentially as he anticipated.

Open-ended techniques, in contrast, are designed to encourage the important observation or interviewing categories to emerge as the project unfolds. Ruth's and Marla's projects take a more open-ended approach. Ruth's decision to approach her study in an open-ended way, consistent with the phenomenological genre, means that her observations and interviews are more holistic and exploratory than Anthony's. She chooses to do some preliminary observation in the after-school center, so she goes there several days in a row, letting impressions (sights, sounds, and scents) shape her impressions about what is important. Her subsequent interviews with children and their families are guided by a small number of topics that she wishes to explore. Moreover, she carefully listens for what matters to the children. She developed the topics from some reading of the literature on it but assumes that she will learn considerably more as the project evolves. Marla and her research team also develop a more open-ended approach. They identify four or five broad, open-ended questions to start their conversations with the women they interview. Both Ruth's and Marla's studies are consistent with a grounded theory approach to analysis and theorizing, especially Ruth's.

Our characters' stances relative to this continuum are shaped by the specific qualitative strategies they employ and the genres to which their studies link. Evaluations and policy studies are focused and instrumental. As Anthony noted in the opening vignette, evaluations are typically more constrained, offering fewer opportunities for open-ended exploration. Although all qualitative research is open ended, to a greater or lesser extent, evaluations tend to be more tightly focused by the researcher from the outset. Descriptive studies, however, are designed to be more emergent than evaluations. Of the three strategies, action research is the most open ended, because participants and researcher collectively determine what is important to inquire about and how tightly they will structure their techniques.

Ebb and Flow

The mix of techniques is another important consideration in planning qualitative research. This mix, too, is forecast in the study's design and may change over the course of the research. In some projects, observing takes the lead and is complemented by interviews and analyses of material culture. In others, interviews and observations proceed hand in hand. For still others, interviews may be the primary technique used, supplemented by limited observations.

As noted previously, Marla decides to do some preliminary holistic observation in the clinic to gain a sense of interactions and issues to be explored. As her action research team gels, it conducts structured interviews of several women. These are then complemented with in-depth, more phenomenological interviews with three women. The team members work together to design the study, determining their focus and priorities for data collection. Anthony designs his evaluation to include observations, interviews, and a survey of community members—both users and nonusers of the program. From the outset of the project, he implements all three techniques. Although what he learns through one technique informs his use of another, they proceed as parallel streams. Ruth begins with holistic observing. As she builds relations with children and their parents, she relies exclusively on iterative, in-depth interviews. Thus, like our participants, which technique takes center stage in your project at any particular moment depends on your preliminary design, what is learned during implementation of your study, and your unique interest in emerging ideas or insights.

SYSTEMATIC INQUIRY

The skills involved in gathering data (asking questions, listening, looking, and reading) are skills used in everyday life. Human beings use all four skills in daily life to establish, maintain, negotiate, verify, and participate in everyday events (Blumer, 1969). These activities are a "part of the psychology of perception, and, as such, they are a tacit part of the everyday functioning of individuals as they negotiate the events of daily life" (Evertson & Green, 1986, p. 163). People observe, ask questions, listen, and read more deliberately, systematically, and instrumentally when learning something new. A child learning a new game may observe until she discerns the rules, or she may read a book that covers the rules. The child might ask questions of players to discover the nuances of the game. On the surface, the skills used in data gathering are everyday actions that are sometimes consciously and other times unconsciously used.

As naturally occurring sets of activities, inquiry cycles involve a trigger → questions → immersion (research) → incubation (letting it cook) → insight (ah-ha!) → communicating and testing the information → using it as knowledge. While the process appears on paper to be linear and sequential, in practice, it is iterative and cyclical, one activity building on another with a lot of recycling back.

Observing, interviewing, and studying material culture as systematic inquiry, however, are different from simply watching actions or events, talking to people, or reading about a topic. When employed in a research project, these sense-making activities are used more diligently and systematically. As inquiry techniques, they are differentiated

People see, hear, smell, taste, and touch in everyday life.

Purpose and discipline turn these activities into systematic inquiry.

from their everyday counterparts by purpose and discipline. Qualitative researchers use these techniques to capture actions, words, and artifacts—data—so that they may scrutinize these data to learn about social phenomena.

Data That Inform the Research Questions

As researchers, Marla, Ruth, and Anthony learn to record data systematically so that they and others may examine and reflect on those data. The data are more than just ideas or images floating around in the observer's head; they are images and ideas documented as completely and accurately as possible to form a record of what has been learned. Once recorded, data become tangible to both the researcher and the researcher's potential audience, as well as available to share with a community of practice for critical feedback. They can be examined and reflected on. Recall Ruth saying that gathering data is like a loop: record, reflect, record, and reflect again. Multiple analytic reflections transform the data into information that can be used to build knowledge.

(margin note: record / reflect)

During data gathering, the researcher's challenge is to sufficiently gather convincing evidence for the findings or conclusions that will be drawn. Recall the discussion in Chapter 2 about knowledge claims. If you claim to know something as a result of your research, data must exist to support those claims. Vague, impressionistic assertions will not do. Observation notes (field notes) describe settings, activities, people, and their interactions. Interview records may be either direct transcripts of tape-recorded conversations or detailed, handwritten notes of the dialogue. Records about material culture might include photographs, descriptions of objects, printouts of Internet sites, public e-mail exchanges, or documents. Notes added to interview transcripts and field notes include your comments about methods choices, difficulties or surprises encountered, impressions, and analytic and interpretive possibilities. All these records constitute the corpus of data from which your assertions should logically flow.

Data About the Process and Yourself

Just as you gather and record data from observations, interviews, and material culture, you record data about your own research activities and their development. Consider these questions:

(margin note: personal reflections)

- What do you observe and why?

- What questions do you ask and why?

- What changes in the preliminary design do you make and why?

- What preconceptions and prejudices are shaping your project?

- What problems do you encounter?

- How does your membership in particular social groups (race, gender, primary language, and age) shape the research?

As noted previously, err on the side of telling more about the natural history of the project than too little.

Because qualitative inquiry happens in a natural environment, the discipline to document findings and procedures systematically and thoroughly is more essential than in a laboratory or experiment in which conditions are controlled. Occurrences in the setting—such as people's moods and health, weather, crises and accidents, political events, and births and deaths—all affect data gathering. For example, one of our doctoral students was preparing to conduct research in the West Bank of Palestine when access to the research sites was disrupted by an increase in attacks and counterattacks. She could neither travel on the roads, nor could she visit schools. Her research had to be postponed. As another example, a doctoral student proposed a study in Sierra Leone on teacher coaches. Central to her framing of this work was a deep acknowledgment that in mid-2015 Sierra Leone was emerging from a devastating Ebola epidemic. She had to put forward a plan for how she could access schools in remote areas and, if this were unsafe, what an alternative plan would be.

Anthony develops prefigured, standardized instruments (observation protocols, interview guides, and questionnaires) to capture participant responses so they can be easily compared. He finds that these instruments limit what people say and how he records what people do. He cannot always use the same instruments in the same way. He finds this too constraining for the complexity of the arts program and participants' views. Using the same instruments at every art event, every time he observes at the center, or with every person he interviews, moreover, does not yield standardized data. Part of his craft knowledge is knowing when to modify the design and instruments. Fully and accurately documenting what he sees, hears, and reads as data requires skill. He builds systems to record how, where, and under what conditions he gathered these data.

Data gathering, then, is a deliberate, conscious, systematic process that details both the products (the data) and the processes of the research activities so that others may understand how the study was performed and can judge its adequacy, strength, and ethics. Recording what is learned takes persistence and effort, but as a researcher, you undertake this discipline so that you may analyze the data and others may decide whether they are convinced that the processes, evidence, and conclusions are sound. The data are not unexamined impressions that speak for themselves but are strong, complete, detailed documentation that includes the interpretive material of the researcher's perspectives and values. Data gathering entails diligently recording and reflecting—that is, recording those reflections and reflecting on those recordings—the loop again.

Practicing systematic qualitative inquiry is both simple and complex, at least as simple and complex as the world you study. Your decisions are driven by your goal: to describe sensitively and accurately the focus of your study. The techniques you use help you do that. Blumer (1969) notes,

> *Methods are mere instruments* [italics added] designed to identify and analyze the obdurate character of the empirical world, and as such, their value exists only in their suitability in enabling this task to be done. The choices made in each part of the act of scientific inquiry should and must be assessed in terms of whether they respect the nature of the empirical world under study. (pp. 27–28)

Blumer, H. *Symbolic Interactionism*, © 1969, pp. 27-28. Pearson Education, Inc., Upper Saddle River, New Jersey.

As qualitative researchers gather data, they strive to make decisions that respect the specific empirical worlds they study. Unfortunately, as no social world is simple, the decisions in designing and carrying out research are not simple either. In the next sections, we describe the three primary ways of gathering data using examples from our characters and our own work.

GENERIC IN-DEPTH INTERVIEWING

In-depth interviewing is the hallmark of qualitative research. How does interviewing for research differ from everyday conversation or the interviews we commonly hear in the media? Some argue that U.S. society has become an "interview society" (Gubrium & Holstein, 2003; Holstein & Gubrium, 2003; Silverman, 2000) with the ubiquity of television talk shows and interviewing as part and parcel of social fabric. Within qualitative inquiry, "talk" is generally viewed as essential for understanding how participants view their worlds. Often, deeper understandings develop through the dialogue of long, in-depth interviews, as interviewer and participant "co-construct" meaning. Interviewing takes you into participants' worlds, at least as far as they can (or choose to) verbally relate what is in their minds. However, it is important to keep in mind that an interview is, in a sense, an artificial event and can be distinguished from naturally occurring talk. We comment on "naturally occurring data" below in the Interviewing and Sociolinguistic Genres section.

As you design a research project, consider the following rationales for interviewing:

- To understand individual perspectives

- To deepen understanding of events and experiences

- To generate rich, descriptive data

- To gather insights into participants' thinking

- To learn more about the context

Note that the skillful interviewer asks for elaboration and concrete examples, which can elicit the detailed narratives that make qualitative inquiry rich. Often, an interview begins with a "grand tour" question—that is, literally, inviting the interview partner to take you on a tour of whatever aspect of her social world you are interested in. Such a question can set a direction for future, more focused questions. This section details processes and considerations in generic in-depth interviewing; the following section discusses specialized forms.

Types of Interviews

Described as "a conversation with a purpose" (Burgess, 1984, p. 102), "a conversational partnership" (Rubin & Rubin, 1995, p. 11), and a social "encounter" (Gubrium & Holstein, 2002, p. 3), in-depth interviewing may be an overall approach to a study (as Ruth's becomes) or one of several techniques (as with Anthony's and Marla's studies). Interviewing varies in how prefigured it is, how broadly applied it is, and when it takes center stage in a study. Patton (2015) categorizes interviews into three types: (1) informal conversational interviews, (2) the interview guide approach, and (3) standardized open-ended interviews. To these we add the dialogic interview. *Informal interviews* are serendipitous, occurring while you hang around a setting or as you are entering a home to conduct a more formal interview. These are casual conversations, incidental to social interactions. Beginners often wonder if these produce "real" data. These informal conversations are recorded in field notes as part of the ongoing flow of social life and may well be an exciting and valuable way to gather data. Described as "mobile interviewing" that occurs "while on the move (walking and/or driving)" (Brown & Durrheim, 2009, p. 911), informal conversations often provide intriguing insights.

The *interview guide approach* is typically used in qualitative studies. The purpose of guided interviews is to elicit the participant's worldview. The researcher develops categories or topics to explore but remains open to pursuing topics that the participant brings up. The researcher identifies a few broad topics (perhaps framed as questions) to help uncover the participant's meaning or perspective but otherwise respects how the participant frames and structures responses. The balance of talk, then, is in favor of the participant. The researcher poses open-ended questions followed by requests for elaboration; the participant responds with long narratives. This approach to interviewing exemplifies an assumption of qualitative research—that is, the participant's perspective on the phenomenon of interest should unfold as the participant views it and not as the researcher views it. The researcher's role is to capture that unfolding. The typical phases in these types of interviews are depicted in Figure 7.1.

Standardized open-ended interviews are tightly prefigured, having fixed questions that are asked in a particular order of all participants. Because of the nature of the questions, however, participants respond freely. A degree of standardization in questions may be necessary in, for example, a multisite case study or when many participants are interviewed. The most important aspect of the interviewer's approach concerns conveying an attitude of acceptance and respect, establishing that the participant's views are valuable and useful.

Dialogic interviews are true conversations in which the researcher and the participant together develop a more complex understanding of the topic. Instead of being guided by a

FIGURE 7.1   Typical Phases of a Guided Interview

- Introduction

   Overview and Purpose

   Informed Consent

   Tape Recording

   Ownership of Content

- Body of the Interview

   Themes or Topics

   Elaborations

   Transitions and Summaries

- Summary and Closure

   Thanks

   Keeping the Door Open

   Review Process for Sharing Transcript

   Next Steps

script or protocol, the interviewer scaffolds questions on the interview partner's answers. Distinctions between the "roles" of the interviewer and the interviewee become blurred. These interviews entail authentic give and take (a mutual exchange of perspectives, understandings, insights), and "talk time" is more balanced between the researcher and the participant than in the interview guide approach. We are reminded of our research on principals as leaders. While we were guided by a conceptual framework that drew on current leadership theory, the interviews became conversations about how these school leaders acted in their daily practice. We derived the questions from their stories; the interviews were dialogic. Several specialized forms of dialogic interviews exist (we discuss these in the next section). Qualitative researchers commonly rely on either the interview guide approach or dialogic interviews. Each can be implemented in various settings and by using various media, including the Internet.

Strengths and Limitations of Interviewing

Interviewing is a generative way to get rich, detailed data about how people view their worlds. The technique, however, has limitations. Interviews involve personal interaction, whether face-to-face or virtually, so willing engagement of the participant and strong interpersonal skills of the interviewer are essential. Quite appropriately, interviewees may be unwilling or uncomfortable sharing all that the interviewer hopes to explore. They may choose to tell you what they believe you want to hear. They also may be unaware of recurring patterns in their lives. Sometimes you may be unable to ask questions that evoke rich responses, either because of limited expertise in or familiarity with the local language or because of lack of skill. By the same token, the meaning intended by the participant may be difficult for the interviewer to understand; thus, building in time for clarification is often necessary. Sometimes, participants may have good reason for not being truthful (see Douglas, 1976, for a classic discussion on participant deception in research).

Strong interviewers are superb listeners and deeply interested in other people. They are skilled in interpersonal interaction, question framing, and gentle probing for elaboration. An interviewer may obtain volumes of data, but the data are time-consuming to analyze—no shortcuts exist, even with computer applications (discussed in Chapter 10). The choice of interviews as the sole technique should be consistent with the conceptual framework, epistemology, strategy, and genre of the study. In Ruth's case, she argues that the subjective view is what matters; observing would not generate the kind of data she seeks. Studies looking for a broader view triangulate interview data with data gathered through other techniques.

Whether formal or informal, an interview is a conversation with a purpose, as this section began. As in any meaningful conversation, both parties have a genuine, although perhaps temporary, interest in the subject. You ask questions for which you truly want answers, and you listen responsively to those answers. A flow develops between question, responses, and the next question, all guided by the topic. Although we often start an interview with an opener such as "Tell me about your work with single mothers," we attempt to keep the conversation related to that work. A completely unbounded and unorganized conversation usually ends up telling no story at all.

Seen as conversation, the interview yields a narrative. Unless the study design is authentically and collaboratively participatory, the narrative is your interpretation of the participants' words. Although you may enter an interview with a structure and sequence of questions, the negotiated flow and organization depend on the subtle interactions between you and the participant. Narratives can be organized in many forms, for example, around time, chronologically or episodically; around place or space; or around themes or messages to be conveyed. The interview may follow inductive lines, starting with details and then elaborating the big picture, or it may proceed deductively, moving from the gestalt to specifics. Differences in values, beliefs, or purposes between the interviewer and the participant can either foster understanding or create barriers. Membership in social groups as well as personal style influences the patterns and power relationships that develop when interviewing. Because social group identities affect interpersonal relationships so deeply, we briefly discuss that issue next.

Social Group Identities

Qualitative research takes you into participants' worlds. The dynamics that evolve in interviews are influenced by multiple nuanced beliefs, expectations, and stereotypes (both yours and the participants'). Social group identities within the interview either ease conversation or make it tricky. Furthermore, interview relationships are fraught

Tips to Maintain Good Relations

- Select participants purposively— those who are knowledgeable.
- Build rapport.
- Acknowledge social differences.
- Share common experiences.
- Avoid taking sides on issues.
- Be yourself!

with issues of power (see Milner, 2007; Ryen, 2003; Subedi & Rhee, 2008), many of which reflect the power structures in the larger society. Race, gender, class, religion, primary language, age, sexual orientation, and able-bodiedness all can shape the interview context. How you negotiate these subtle undercurrents within the interview experience depends on how sensitive you are to these issues in your own life and those of other people, in this case, the participants.

Does this mean that a white interviewer should not interview an African American, that only gay men should interview other gay men, or that a middle-aged interviewer will be less effective interviewing adolescents than someone in his 20s? It depends—sometimes the answer is yes, and sometimes it is no. The circumstances of the interview, the topic, and the personal styles of both the interviewer and the participant all help accomplish the interview. How social group identities play out in creating an open, equitable flow is complex. A middle-aged interviewer may elicit detailed responses from an adolescent because the younger person sees the interviewer as a parental figure or someone easy to talk with who will not judge her (unlike her peers). If the adolescent has had difficult parental relationships, however, a different scenario might ensue. A gay man interviewing his peers may assume much. The interview might unfold with a great deal of tacit sharing, such as when a participant responds with "Oh, you know what I mean," and the interviewer says "Sure" assuming that he understands exactly what the participant means. Such tacit understanding, although reflective of shared social identities, precludes eliciting and recording rich, detailed data. A straight person might probe for more elaboration because he does not have a full understanding of the experience. The comfort people feel with others they think are like them, however, can be powerful in setting a tone for open communication. The task is to be acutely sensitive to these issues, reflect on them, and assess how they play out in the interview experience.

For example, cultural differences affected interviews that an Anglo student conducted in a Hispanic community in the southwestern United States in tangible ways during her project. The researcher sought to establish a chronology of events in the participants' lives through her interview questions. She asked, "After you came to this country, then what happened?" expecting the narrative to follow a then-to-now sequence reflective of her Western, Anglo worldview. The participants, however, understood their lives episodically, linked by feelings, rather than as a linear progression of events. The interview stalled because the researcher asked for elaboration about sequence rather than episode. The researcher struggled to understand the participants' responses because of this deep cultural difference in how each interpreted and communicated about time.

We recall long conversations with an African American colleague who studied institutional racism at a predominantly white university. She was intrigued with African American students' experiences of racism. We talked and argued about whether a white researcher could do the study as successfully as she. Would black students feel comfortable talking with a white researcher? What about tacit understandings? Could a white researcher elicit detailed narratives? Could a white researcher even get students to participate in the study? The answers were not clear-cut. A white researcher would bring some unique and important perspectives to the study; our African American colleague brought others. In sum, as an interviewer, it is important to be sensitive to ways that various social group identities affect the interaction, while being open to alternative worldviews.

These issues are tricky and subtle. Given interpersonal sensitivities and skill in eliciting narratives (the ultimate purpose in interviews), we argue that sharing social group identity can be powerful. For example, as women, we are particularly sensitive to the history of research about women done by men and how impoverished that research is. It is crucial, however, that the researcher be skilled interpersonally and sensitive to subtle cultural cues. No level of comembership will overcome a thoughtless, rude, and ungracious interviewing style (these qualities, of course, are culturally defined). When you interview, be aware of and work with issues of social group identity and the particular way the participant organizes her experience. As data collection is your primary agenda, however, you cannot ignore your research needs in structuring the interview. Seek an equitable balance between your needs and your participant's that matches your questions and the participant's responses, listening for the questions implicit in her answers.

Follow-Up Questions

Interviews involve follow-up questions to elicit elaborations and clarifications. You ask for more detail, hoping to discover deeper meanings or more concrete examples. Inviting the participant to elaborate indicates that you are truly interested in more than superficial accounts. Follow-up questions take the interview to "a deeper level by asking for more detail" and "are a natural part of any conversation" (Ulin, Robinson, Tolley, & McNeill, 2002, p. 86). The ability to ask skillful follow-up questions comes from "knowing what to look for in the interview, listening carefully to what is said and what is not said, and being sensitive to the feedback needs of the person being interviewed" (Patton, 2002, p. 374). Both verbal and nonverbal cues are important: nodding the head, facial gestures, saying "uh huh," and even silence can signal to the participant that you understand or that you would like more detail. Follow-up questions can help the participant explore new ideas about the topic. Asking for further detail invites the participant to understand the experience more fully, as the participant provides you with the detail you seek.

Consider the following excerpt from an interview conducted early in Ruth's study. This interview was with an 11-year-old boy who is one of only three or four students who use wheelchairs in a middle school. In this example, there are several places where Ruth could have asked the student to elaborate. We indicate these in italicized, bracketed comments.

> The quality of an interview rests on the relevance of the questions and on your skill in asking follow-up questions.

Ruth:	How do you feel about how you're treated by others in the school?
Student:	Not so great. . . . In fact, it sucks. I've told my parents I want to get out of there. I don't like it.
	[*Tell me about what was so terrible. What was one of the specific things?*]

Ruth:	If you decide you really want to get out, what might keep you there?
Student:	It doesn't matter because my parents won't let me get out anyway. They like it too much because it's close to the house.

[*Is that a big source of conflict with them? Or tell me about the talks you've had with them about this.*]

Ruth:	Do you think this makes you work less hard in the classroom?
Student:	Not really. I know that wherever I am, I'm still going to get good grades.

[*Tell me what grades mean to you. What makes you want to get good grades?*]

Student:	But it makes it a real drag that my parents won't let me go to East Overbrook. That doesn't mean I'm going to try to flunk out.

[*What's so attractive about East Overbrook? Why would you rather be there? Trying to flunk out would be pretty drastic. Have you ever thought about it? Or it seems that it's been pretty difficult for you. What specifically has been so tough?*]

The student's responses about what made school "terrible" could lead to important insights into the actions that contributed to his feeling different and marginalized. His answers could lead Ruth to understand that another school might be more supportive of and thoughtful about students with various disabilities. She might have uncovered much more data on the student's values and beliefs as well as on his specific experiences, including his successes at school. His responses throughout this excerpt needed immediate, thoughtful follow-up questions. As Ruth becomes more skilled in asking follow-up questions, she will obtain more useful data through interviews. Follow-up questions are often challenging for beginning researchers because they are *not actively listening* to participants. Instead, beginning researchers are often thinking about their next planned question. With practice, the interview becomes more like a conversation, and follow-up questions become part of the natural flow. Table 7.1 provides examples of requests for more detail and elaboration.

Generally, we find that if we are sincerely interested in the topic, participants appreciate requests for elaboration because they facilitate reflection and self-discovery. In one case, a program director thanked us for the opportunity to articulate reasons why he felt especially pleased with some aspects of his program but not with others. He told us that, because of participating in the interview, he felt that he better understood his management style and future options. A genuine interest in the topic makes asking for elaboration easier.

Some of our most challenging interviews, however, have been with believers in or ideological advocates for a particular topic—those whose passion leads them to want to

TABLE 7.1   Follow-Up Questions

Open-Ended Elaborations	Purpose
Would you tell me more about that?	More detail
That's helpful. I'd appreciate it if you'd give me more detail.	More detail
I'm intrigued by what you're telling me, but I'm not sure I get the whole picture yet.	More detail

Open-Ended Clarifications	Purpose
I want to be sure I understand. Could you go over that again?	Rephrasing
I think I see what you mean, but I'm not sure I understand fully.	Implying that more detail will help

Detailed Elaborations	Purpose
Who else was there?	Others present
When did all this happen?	Timing of events
Describe the room.	Physical environment
How were you involved? What was your role?	Interactions and roles
Where did this happen?	Location

convince *you* to share their beliefs. These people are often unwilling to consider that their ideas or projects might have any other (even negative) aspects. Digging beneath the surface without appearing rude to these conversational partners is not easy. We take care not to intrude or violate their senses of privacy, but we do want elaboration. We once interviewed a leader of a school reform program. His program was philosophically sound, but we had heard that implementation was not proceeding smoothly. When we asked about what was actually going on with the program, his response was a predictable description of how many schools were in the network, generalities about what teachers were doing, and how excited they were. We pushed for specific evidence of schools' activities but got nowhere. We had to take a different tack, so we asked, "What if a school in the program is not meeting the first goal after 2 years?" This hypothetical question enabled him to launch into several examples of problems that schools were encountering.

Interview conversations can take many forms, depending on the decisions about questions, strategy, epistemology, and genre. In addition to generic in-depth interviewing, specialized forms include ethnographic, phenomenological, elite, and focus group interviewing. Each is described briefly in the next two sections.

SPECIALIZED IN-DEPTH INTERVIEWING

Each of the qualitative research genres claims to use specialized forms of interviews. Ethnographic researchers interview participants about their cultural worlds, phenomenological researchers search to understand lived experiences, whereas researchers working within sociolinguistic genres tend to work with "naturally occurring" data—that is, data that they have not elicited through an interview. In turn, case study researchers seek multiple perspectives on the phenomenon of interest. Two other specialized forms that might be used in any strategy or genre are elite and group interviewing. With any of these, children may be the participants. Special consideration toward participants who are children is important and is discussed below.

Interviewing Within Ethnographic Genres

Grounded in the disciplines of cultural ethnography and qualitative sociology, much ethnographic interviewing is thematic or topical in structure. The researcher identifies domains of experience of interest and develops questions or topical statements to elicit the participants' understanding of those domains. As Roulston (2010) notes, "The focus of ethnographic interviews is on generating participants' descriptions of key aspects related to the cultural world of which he or she is a part—that is space, time, events, people, activities, and objects" (p. 19). Since the researcher seeks to capture participants' own views on their cultural worlds, being open to their questions and avoiding a kind of cultural imperialism by allowing preconceived topics or themes to dominate is important. This form of ethnographic interviewing is similar to generic interviewing, but with a specific focus on aspects of a cultural world. More specialized forms, however, derive from the subdiscipline of cognitive anthropology and seek to elicit the cognitive structures guiding participants' worldviews. Described as "a particular kind of speech event" (Spradley, 1979, p. 18), ethnographic questions are used to gather cultural data from a cognitive perspective.

Representing this form, Spradley (1979) identifies three main types of questions: (1) descriptive, (2) structural, and (3) contrast. Descriptive questions allow the researcher to gather information about the participants' perspectives on "their experiences, their daily activities, and the objects and people in their lives" (Westby, Burda, & Mehta, 2003). Structural questions discover the basic units in that cultural knowledge, whereas contrast questions elaborate the meaning of various terms that participants use. The success of this technique, as in all interviewing, is highly dependent on the skills of the researcher.

Anthony might use ethnographic interviewing to uncover the domains of understanding about the arts and ways of participating in arts events. He could structure interviews to understand the terms people use to describe the arts program and ways of participating in arts events. For example, "dancing in the streets" is a way of participating in the arts.

Interviewing Within Phenomenological Genres

This form of interviewing is a specific type of in-depth interviewing grounded in the theoretical genre of phenomenology. As noted in Chapter 4, phenomenology is the study of participants' lived experiences and worldviews. Phenomenology assumes that shared experiences have an effable structure and essence. Interviewing elicits people's stories about their lives. van Manen (1990) notes that the phenomenological interview serves two primary purposes:

> (1) it may be used as a means for exploring and gathering experiential narrative material that may serve as a resource for developing a richer and deeper understanding of a human phenomenon, and (2) the interview may be used as a vehicle to develop a conversational relation with a partner (interviewee) about the meaning of an experience. (p. 66)

For phenomenological interviews to be successful, the researcher must identify "participants who have both experienced, and are able to talk about the particular lived experience under examination" (Roulston, 2010, p. 17). Seidman (2013) calls for three iterative interviews for the phenomenological data-gathering process:

- Interview 1: Focused Life History
- Interview 2: Details of Experience
- Interview 3: Reflection on the Meaning

The first interview asks participants to narrate their personal life histories relative to the topic, with the focus on past experiences up to the present. An example of beginning a first interview follows:

> "Think of a time when you experienced _____ and describe that in as much detail as possible.
>
> Possible follow-up questions include:
>
> You mentioned _____ tell me what that was like for you.
>
> You mentioned _____ describe that in more detail for me." (Roulston, 2010, pp. 16–17)

The second brings the narrative into the present, with a focus on specific details of participants' experiences of the topic. The third asks participants to reflect on the meaning of their experiences, "The intellectual and emotional connections between the participants' work and life" (Seidman, 1998, p. 12). Questions in the third interview ask the participant to integrate the two previous interviews. For example, the researcher might ask "Given what you have said about your life before you became a mentor teacher and given what you have said about your work now, how do you understand mentoring in your life? What sense does it make to you?" (Seidman, 2013, p. 22).

During the process, the researcher tries to bracket the presuppositions she brings to the study to identify the phenomenon in its "pure form, uncontaminated by extraneous intrusions" (Patton, 2002, p. 485). The data are clustered around themes that are expressed in the interview texts. The final product articulates the deep structures of the participants' lived experience of the phenomenon. A variant of this type of interviewing is "voice-centered interviewing" (Brown & Gilligan, 1990), which seeks to uncover the enmeshed, contrapuntal voices that speak through a dialogic interview text.

We note that qualitative interviewing in general has been heavily influenced by the field of phenomenology (see Brinkman & Kvale, 2015). You may find that you want to incorporate aspects of phenomenological techniques even if your study is more ethnographic or is a case study.

Ruth relies on phenomenological interviewing as her primary technique. She identifies a few children who use wheelchairs and invites them and their families to participate in three iterative interviews about the lived experience of using a wheelchair. Her focus is on the experience of this phenomenon, how the children and their families understand it, and what it means for their everyday lives. The previous excerpt was from Ruth's second interview with the first student in her study, in which she was trying to understand his current experiences of using a wheelchair.

Narrative Inquiry Interviewing

As noted in Chapter 4, narrative inquiry embraces several strands, including oral histories and life histories, among others. All have in common the desire to understand an individual's "story," based on the assumption that we all have stories to tell. Stories are typically elicited through in-depth interviews. Oral histories and life histories are similar: "Oral history involves the collection of oral narratives from ordinary people in order to chronicle peoples' lives and past events" (Roulston, 2010, p. 23), while "life history research typically involves small numbers of participants over a lengthy period of time" (Roulston, 2010, p. 25). *Oral history interviews* typically gather many interviews on a particular event and have become quite salient in the United States. For example, current oral history projects include The Oral History Project of the Vietnam Archive (http://www.vietnam.ttu.edu/oralhistory/), the Voices of Feminism Oral History Project (https://www.smith.edu/library/libs/ssc/vof/vof-intro.html), and the September 11, 2001, Oral History Projects (http://library.columbia.edu/locations/ccoh/digital/9-11.html). Oral history scholars and practitioners now have an association that stresses ethical practice, specifically the protection of participants (Oral history Association, at http://www.oralhistory.org/about/principles-and-practices/).

Life histories, in some contrast, tend to focus on "ordinary" people, seeking to uncover their lives as they have unfolded. The goal is to describe this individual's life, focusing on what it is like to be this person. As storytelling has become ubiquitous in U.S. popular culture, life history interviews are witnessing a resurgence of interest. As one website notes,

> A life interview is a powerful way to connect individuals and generations. It's a chance to travel through time. In the present moment, the best gift you can give someone is to listen to them. You'll find out about the past as you hear about real-life experiences. And along the way, you may discover some timeless insights to help guide you through your own future. (Legacy, 2015)

Questions may range across childhood, youth, early adulthood, and so on to capture the individual's unique life story.

Narrative inquiry researchers tend to view the interview as an exploration and discovery of the participants' experiences and perspectives. Interviews are open ended, based on the assumption that it is more humanistic to encourage the participant to narrate his world as he uniquely defines it and to raise important issues that the researcher may not have been aware of. This stance further assumes that a fixed sequence of questions, as in the standardized open-ended interview format, is inappropriate for capturing subtle and nuanced perspectives articulated by the participant.

Marla and her team conduct oral history interviews to elaborate on the preliminary analyses they have performed on records of interactions between physician's assistants and patients at the clinic. The preliminary analyses identified patterns of inattention on the part of the physician's assistants. The in-depth oral history interviews elicit detailed perspectives of the women's experiences of the clinic.

Interviewing and Sociolinguistic Genres

Much of sociolinguistic research focuses on "naturally occurring" data, as forecast above. Typical studies might tape record a series of interactions among participants as they go about their everyday activities (e.g., children in a classroom, professionals at work). These interactions have not been prompted by the researcher; rather, they have occurred naturally—in vivo, if you will. An example of this type of work comes from Deborah Tannen (1986, 1990) whose analyses of "talk" between men and women led her to theorize about the gendered differences in speech patterns. Tannen was trained as a linguist and is a distinguished faculty member; her research represents this genre quite well.

Discourse analysts, critical discourse analysts, and semioticists draw on data that are also naturally occurring. Policy documents, text books, movie scripts, films and videos, advertisements, posts on Facebook, and so on could all be data for the focus of their analyses. As an example, consider the wave of responses to the U.S. Supreme Court's decision on gay marriages. The image of the gay pride multicolored flag became overwhelmingly present on social media platforms. At about the same time, the controversy surrounding the Confederate flag also brought this iconic image to social media. Such examples are the sorts of images that are ripe for analysis within sociolinguistic genres.

However, note that these approaches rely on data that are present in social life, rather than eliciting them through interviews.

SPECIAL CONSIDERATIONS

With the above in mind, there are several additional considerations about interview partners or ways of interviewing that deserve special consideration. These include interviewing "elites" (as the literature tends to refer to them) or experts; focus group interviewing; interviewing children; interviewing using computer applications and the Internet, including digital storytelling; and issues around translation and transcription. We consider each briefly below.

Interviewing Elites or Experts

Special considerations arise when interviewing elites or experts. These are individuals considered to be influential, prominent, well informed, or all three, in an organization or community and are selected on the basis of their expertise in areas relevant to the research. Valuable information can be gained from these participants because of their positions in social, political, financial, or administrative realms. Think about various kinds of elites: philanthropic elites, political elites, ultra-elites (e.g., Nobel laureates or Olympic athletes), and organizational elites (see Delaney, 2007). Access to elite individuals is often difficult because they are usually busy people operating under demanding time constraints. The researcher may have to adapt the planned-for flow of the interview based on the wishes and predilections of the person interviewed. Although this is true with all in-depth interviewing, the elite individual is typically quite savvy and may resent the restrictions of narrow or ill-phrased questions. An active interplay with the interviewer may be desired. Elites respond well to inquiries about broad topics and to intelligent, provocative, open-ended questions that allow them the freedom to use their knowledge and imagination. In working with elites, great demands are placed on the ability of the interviewer, who must establish competence by displaying a thorough knowledge of the topic or, lacking such knowledge, by projecting an accurate conceptualization of the problem through shrewd questioning.

   Anthony interviews elite individuals as part of his evaluation: the program director and community leaders. These individuals are quite skilled in "managing" interviews because they are often called by newspaper reporters to comment on local events. His challenge, then, is to find time to meet with these people and then to ask crisp, focused questions that provoke thought and reflection but do not take too much of the participants' time.

Focus Group Interviewing

The technique of interviewing participants in focus groups comes largely from market research. Groups are generally composed of 7 to 10 people (although they can be as small as 4 and as large as 12) who are not well-known to one another and have been selected because they share certain characteristics. The interviewer creates an open environment, asking questions that focus closely on one topic (hence its name) to encourage discussion and the expression of varying opinions and viewpoints. The interaction among the participants is the critical characteristic of this type of interviewing. The goal is for the group to generate new understandings or explanations as individuals react to and interact with others. This approach assumes that an individual's attitudes and beliefs do not form in a vacuum. People often need to listen to others' opinions and understandings to clarify their own. Often, the questions in a focus group setting are deceptively simple. The objective is to promote interactive talk through the creation of a supportive environment. Anthony's focus group brings together nonusers of the arts center on one Saturday morning. Seven people discuss how they spend their free time and react to the possibilities that are available at the center (see Krueger & Casey, 2015, for details).

Interviewing Children

Whatever the approach to interviewing, children may be your participants. Interviewing children is fun and frustrating. Young children are often lively and active; it is unrealistic to expect them to sit face-to-face and engage in a long dialogue with a researcher. Talks can occur, however, during other activities. For example, join them at lunch or snack time, invite them to work on a puzzle with you, or sit with them as they play with blocks or Legos. Fascinating perspectives often emerge during these activities. We have interviewed young children (8-year-olds) in a focus group. At snack time, we invited them to join us around a large, round table. Six of them came. Much talk ensued about the tape recorder. They played with it, recording their own voices, and playing those segments back, accompanied by shrieks and laughter. Then we settled down to business—snacks! As we munched, we talked with them about Katie, a classmate with multiple sclerosis. What was it like having her in their class? What did they have to do differently? One particularly articulate girl described how she knew Katie better than the others because they had been in class together the past year too. She elaborated about Katie's needs for extra time and how she spilled her crayon box all the time, but that it was OK because "that's just how Katie is. No big deal." The data gathered were eloquent in depicting a truly inclusive classroom in which meeting Katie's needs were part and parcel of everyday life.

Interviewing young adults is also fascinating. Some adolescents prefer the intimacy of a one-on-one interview, whereas others find a focus group setting more conducive to talking about their lives. In a study of early graduation from high school, the researcher found that students preferred talking with her privately. So much anguish colored their decisions to leave high school early that the students felt uncomfortable talking about them with other people around. The researcher was trained as a counselor, so she was skilled in asking probing questions with delicacy and tact. In another study, we found that talking with high school students about the curriculum and graduation requirements worked well in small groups. Ideas flowed and "popped" as one student shared his experiences, triggering recollections and insights in the others. Given this variability, it makes sense to vary your interviewing strategies when working with young adults or to be prepared to modify the strategy if it is not working well.

Ruth interviews children who use wheelchairs. With the younger ones, she engages them in play activities through which they can talk about their lives—the joys and challenges in navigating a world designed for people who can walk. She joins them for lunch or recess to defuse the focus on straight face-to-face talk. With older students, she tries one-on-one interviewing. With some, it works; others appear to feel too shy or reticent for much talk to ensue.

Interviewing Using Computer Applications and the Internet

Increasingly, the Internet is used as a space for conducting interviews through the use of various applications that permit talking with participants in real time (synchronous) and chat messaging with participants in either synchronous or asynchronous time, recording these chats either orally or transcribed into text, using e-mail or social network applications for interviewing, using survey software for qualitative interviewing (e.g., SurveyMonkey, Google Forms), and so on. The explosion in the applications for and use of computer technology and the Internet has revolutionized qualitative data gathering and analysis and has called into question our historic conceptions of what an interview is.

When thinking about conducting interviews using the Internet, consider the following:

- Ease and strength of access to the Internet for you and your participants
- Both parties' comfort with the medium
- Loss of paralinguistic cues
- True protection of participant identity

However, we encourage you to experiment with using computer applications. As with any data-gathering technique, the rationale for this choice should be firmly grounded in your conceptual framework.

Digital Storytelling An emerging form of narrating stories is digital storytelling. Using video-editing computer applications (e.g., iMovie for Macs or MovieMaker for PCs), the narrator constructs a story and then enhances it with video clips, images, sound clips, and other materials to develop the story. Widely used in community development and education, digital storytelling is a user-friendly mode for those comfortable with computer applications. It can, however, be intimidating to those not as familiar with such applications. Bear in mind, however, that these stories may be selective presentations of your participants that reflect a preferred perspective or edited view of an event through their perspective.

Digital storytelling is increasingly used in public health, community development projects, and educational settings. Younger people are quite savvy about using the technologies, as many are "digital natives." However, some find the open-ended nature of this highly creative process intimidating, and the costs of equipment may be prohibitive. Several universities and community-based organizations offer workshops on digital storytelling, creating a community of practice to support experimentation and learning. The final product—the digital story—is often quite short, typically between 4 and 8 minutes long, with all the advantages of pictures and stories for enhancing attention to the report.

Transcribing and Translating

Many texts on qualitative inquiry treat transcribing interview tapes as unproblematic. Even less consideration is given to translating interviews from one language into another. Our position is that neither is a merely technical task—something to deal with when the time comes. Language is crucial for expressing and conveying deeply held cultural beliefs and values. In fact, qualitative inquiry typically presents words and interpretations of words as the primary data. Given this, how you respect and render your participants' words is central to an ethical study. Helpfully, the methodological literature is beginning to address these issues. For example, the Research Consortium on Educational Outcomes and Poverty website notes that "all social research involves translation, if only from the 'language of the streets' into formal academic prose" ("Translating and Transcribing Data," 2008, sec. 2). Keep this in mind when both transcribing and translating.

Transcribing tape-recorded interviews is not simple, and it involves judgment. As Marshall and Rossman (2016) note, "We do not speak in logical, organized paragraphs, nor do we signal punctuation as we speak" (p. 208). Therefore, important judgments are made in how the stream of words is rendered into text. The act of transcribing involves interpretation, as the insightful study by Temple and Young (2004) illustrates.

Rendering your interview partners' words into text becomes even more problematic when the interview is conducted in one language but then must be translated into a second one. Since languages do not translate perfectly, we suggest that you strive to create a reasonable text that captures your interview partners' meaning and intent, to the extent possible. We often recommend to our students that they include words (and symbol systems, as appropriate) in the language of the interview to signal to the reader of the report or article that the interviews were not conducted in the language of the report. These issues are discussed further in Chapter 9.

In our experience, transcribing always takes longer than we anticipate. Some researchers say to allow 3 hours for every hour of tape. Depending on your skill in transcribing and on the complexity of the interview, you may need more time. It helps to keep in mind that the act of transcribing is also analysis and interpretations—you make sense of the data as you turn the sounds into written words. For this reason, we encourage you to do as much transcription as you can yourself (rather than hire a professional transcriber); by the time you have the transcript of an interview, you are well on your way with analyses and interpretations.

As with many aspects of research, transcribing interview tapes can be assisted through software. Using a digital tape recorder while conducting an interview can ease transcribing, as software such as Express Scribe™ and Olympus Digital Wave Player™ are useful. Several other applications can be found through an Internet search. Voice recognition software has also become popular, although it takes a long time to "train" the software to recognize your voice. Dragon Naturally Speaking™ and e-Speaking™ are solid examples. Be prepared to spend a good deal of time learning and training this software so you become adept at using it.

Another primary way of gathering data is through observation. Observation generates field notes as the running record of what you notice in a setting. Like other data-gathering techniques, it may focus broadly or in depth, and it may be open ended or particularistic.

OBSERVING PEOPLE, ACTIONS, AND EVENTS

As noted at the beginning of the chapter, observation is fundamental to all qualitative inquiry. Even in in-depth interview studies, observation plays an important role as the researcher notes body language and affect in addition to the participant's words. Observation takes you inside the setting, and it helps you discover complexity in social settings by being there.

Consider the following reasons to include observation as part of your qualitative study:

- To understand the context
- To develop thick descriptions of settings and activities
- To see tacit patterns
- To see patterns people may not see themselves
- To see patterns people may not want to discuss
- To provide direct personal experience and knowledge
- To move beyond the selective perceptions of both yourself and the participants

Observing entails the systematic noting and recording of events, actions, and interactions. Within the sociolinguistic genres, observing may entail videotaping events and interactions to create a permanent record for subsequent analysis. The challenge is to identify the "big picture" while noting huge amounts of detail in multiple and complex actions. Figure 7.2 provides some possibilities for focusing your observations.

For studies relying exclusively on observation, the researcher makes no special effort to have a particular role. To be tolerated as an unobtrusive observer might be all that one can hope for. Classroom observational studies are one example often found in education. Through observation, the researcher sees actions and infers the meanings those actions have for participants. This technique assumes that actions are purposeful and expressive

FIGURE 7.2   What to Observe?

- The Social System

  Formal or Informal

  Patterns of Interaction

  Ways People Organize Themselves

  Tacit Rules in Operation

  Recurring Events and Meanings

  Down Time

- Activities and Actions

  Full Sequence of Events

  Time Sampling

  Rituals and Ceremonies

  Crises

  Unplanned Activities

of deeper values and beliefs. We caution you, however, to note that what you are observing can be viewed from multiple perspectives: yours as researcher, the actors in the site, or audiences who read your notes, to name a few.

Observation can be tightly prefigured—using structured, detailed notations of behavior guided by checklists—or it may be a more holistic description of events and activities. Again, these observations are often videotaped. Recall Erickson's (1986) questions that we introduced in Chapter 4; these may help you structure your notes to move from immediate-actions observed (What is happening in this particular setting?) to the bigger picture of patterns (How are the actions organized in patterns of social organization?) and beyond the setting itself (How are these patterns related to what is happening in surrounding settings such as the building or the community?).

In the early stages of a study, qualitative researchers often enter the setting with broad areas of interest but without predetermined categories or strict observational checklists, as do Ruth and Marla. The researcher thus can discover the recurring patterns of events and relationships. After such patterns are identified and described through early analysis of field notes, checklists or protocols become more appropriate and context sensitive. Focused observation may then be used at later stages of the study.

Taking Field Notes

You need to turn what you see and hear (or, perhaps, smell and taste) into data. Even if you are videotaping events in the setting or studying an Internet site, you will need to

Tips on Taking Field Notes

- Write descriptively, not evaluatively
- Capture specific and concrete details
- Use action verbs
- Use adjectives

Note

- Who was there; who was not
- What happened
- When it happened
- Where it happened
- Why it (may have) happened

systematically record your impressions, insights, and emerging hypotheses. You do this by writing field notes, the written record of your perceptions in the field. Field notes have two major components: (1) the descriptive data of what you observe and (2) your comments on those data or on the project itself. The former are called *the running record*, and they are exactly that: You capture as much detail as possible about the physical environment and the activities and interactions among the people in that environment. If you are conducting an Internet ethnography, the images from the site can be stored electronically.

The second component, your commentary on that running record, is typically referred to as *observer comments*. These may include your emotional reactions to events, analytic insights, questions about meaning, and thoughts for modifying your design. The running record is the data about the research; the observer comments are the data about the process and yourself. Such observational field notes also are added to interview transcripts to augment and interpret the exact words of the interview.

The particular form that raw field notes take is idiosyncratic. You need to find what works for you, but it is crucial to have as much detail as possible. Raw field notes are typically taken by hand in the setting. In some settings, you might be able to use a laptop computer, but be careful that the technology is not distracting or obtrusive. In rare instances when taking notes would be totally inappropriate, you need to find a way to remove yourself to a quiet place to write notes that you will elaborate later. The bathroom can be used for this purpose!

Making Raw Field Notes Usable

As soon as possible after fieldwork, it is critical to write up the raw notes. Writing up involves transcribing handwritten notes into the computer, elaborating skimpy data, and adding commentary. Try to organize the notes while doing so, thus doing some preliminary analysis. Ideally, these write-ups occur the same day or the day after. This is a good time to catch vague statements and clarify unfounded assumptions that appear in the data. For example, if our notes say "All students were expected to have partially filled out a similar chart from the day before," "She looked nervous," or "The cases at the clinic this week were more difficult than last," we try to add why we knew what was expected of the students, what actions led us to believe the woman was nervous, or what cases we observed this week and why we saw them as more difficult than the previous week's. Usually, if the fieldwork was done quite recently, what we have said in our notes sparks our memories for details. If our memories are blank, we recognize a hole and try to seek further information later.

This is the stage when you write *thick descriptions* (see Geertz, 1973). Thick descriptions present details, emotions, and textures of social relationships. Denzin (1994) notes that "an event or process can be neither interpreted nor understood until it has been well described" (p. 505). Thick descriptions are necessary for "thick interpretation" (Denzin, 1989, p. 83). In an early attempt at field notes, Anthony writes, "Fifty people from the neighborhood attended the dance exhibition. Several ethnic groups and both genders were there. Everyone enjoyed themselves." Later, he writes,

Eavesdropping on a cluster (three women, one man; black, white, Hispanic) near the sculpture of "City Girl," I heard conversation about how the artist has done the girl's hair. One asked, "How could she get the cornrows so realistic?" Another begins to describe the method she heard about in her ceramics workshop. Conversation turns to how (can?) artists make a living. One leaves to refill her glass; she returns with a tray of finger foods.

From time to time, you may need an assist to remind you of your focus in writing field notes. Creating or adapting existing instruments can be helpful in recording data. Tables, checklists, diagrams, blueprints, and sketches that chart spatial relationships, classify or quantify interactions or verbal content, map work flow or workstations, or illustrate social relationships serve to make data out of what you see and hear. Because your task is to record what you see and hear, for it to become data, use whatever instruments will facilitate that process.

STUDYING MATERIAL CULTURE

Qualitative researchers often supplement observing and interviewing with studying aspects of material culture produced in the course of everyday events. These might include objects, such as children's schoolwork or photographs from a staff picnic, but they are typically documents—the written record of a person's life or an organization's functioning. Journals, diaries, minutes of meetings, policy statements, letters, and announcements are all examples of material culture that researchers gather and analyze to better understand the social worlds they study. Sociolinguistic researchers tend to focus on talk and text produced as people go about their lives; semioticists tend to focus exclusively on productions of material culture, gathering and analyzing the icons expressive of a culture. Gathering documents and other aspects of material culture is relatively *unobtrusive* and potentially rich in portraying the values and beliefs in a setting or social domain.

Archival data are another example of material culture. These are the routinely gathered records of a society, community, or organization; for example, attendance records, test scores, and birth and death records. Marital patterns among a group of native Mexicans, discovered through fieldwork in a community, could be tested through marriage records found in the offices of the county seat or state capitol. Descriptions of articulated funding priorities by policymakers could be corroborated (or not) through an analysis of budgetary allocations. For an evaluation of a policy that rewarded teachers' professional development activity, we sought evidence that salaries increased and that highly qualified teachers were attracted to the district. To that end, we needed to analyze changes in salary and hiring since the new policy took effect. First, we sought and obtained permission to review personnel records, but the available archives went back only a few years because the district initiated a new format for storing its data. Unwilling to give up, because these files were essential to the evaluation, we contacted the state department of education and found older records.

While these required some effort to analyze according to the newer format, we were able to track changes and discover effects that could be attributed to the new policy.

The analysis of documents often entails a specialized approach called content analysis. Best thought of as an overall approach, a method, and an analytic strategy, content analysis entails the systematic examination of forms of communication to objectively document patterns. A more objectivist approach than other qualitative methods, traditional content analysis allows the researcher to obtain a quantitative description. The raw material of content analysis may be any form of communication—usually written materials (textbooks, novels, newspapers, and electronic mail). However, other forms of communication, such as music, pictures, or political speeches, also may be included.

Discourse, critical discourse, and semiotic analysts might assume that all products of a society are text. Movies, plays, or advertisements, for example, could form the basis for such analyses. The strategy here is to analyze critically what is portrayed and symbolized in such textual representations and what is absent or silenced. A semiotic researcher might analyze billboard advertisements for his or her depiction of women or study posters in an urban area for evidence of a social awareness campaign about HIV/AIDS. Anthony, for example, could examine the "text" of an arts event from a socioeconomic perspective, searching for evidence of middle-class values and oppression of working-class ones.

Further examples may help. When we are in an office of a principal who tells us "All children in *my* school learn," we look for evidence of children's work. One principal described how she assisted teachers to implement inquiry-based, student-centered learning by revising their lesson plans to meet state requirements. She was pleased to open her files and illustrate the before and after plans. Seeing these materials clarified for us her efforts as well as her purposes. In another case, neither interviews with the teacher nor observations in the classroom were as powerful as the booklets and newsletters the class had produced or the videotape a parent had made of the class during the entire year.

Material culture, importantly, can offer data that contradict words and even observations. A counselor may declare a deep interest in every one of his adolescent clients, but a daily schedule jam-packed with an impressive number of clients in short sessions with no time for reflection may lead us to doubt his sincerity. Letters to the editor of the local newspaper complaining of the glaring graffiti on the walls and the debris around the community center can belie the director's contention that her board and the neighborhood are having success in cleaning up the area. The zoo's program director promises new hands-on activities for members, and the glossy brochures advertise "new ways to see the animals." The schedule, however, lists traditional sit-and-watch-the-animals-perform events. The absence of any current textbooks and relevant curricula in the newly constructed classrooms of a developing country raises questions to counter the government's claim that teachers are using modern materials and instructional methods. All of these schedules, booklets, advertisements, plans, and letters are objects that may become data and can enrich understanding of the phenomena studied.

Is everything "text"?

Innovative ways to collect data appear regularly; we cannot cover them all. One that is being used in the field of community development, public health, and education draws on all three techniques—observing, interviewing, and studying material culture—and includes participant involvement. Commonly referred to as *photovoice*, the practice combines photography with social action. Participants are asked to represent their experiences or perspectives by taking photographs, discussing them together, and developing narratives to accompany the photos, with a goal of developing action steps. As the process is relatively complex and so many variations exist, and because it is considered to be more a community development tool than a research technique, we do not discuss photovoice in detail here. If innovation in tools for data collection is of interest to you, it is important to keep abreast of developments in the field through involvement in interest groups within professional associations (e.g., the Special Interest Groups of American Education Research Association or Topical Interest Groups of the American Evaluation Association) or via academic journals.

DISPOSITIONS AND SKILLS

The challenge that Ruth raises in the vignette that begins this chapter is how to develop the skills to recognize what can become relevant data and to render these sights, sounds, words, images, and artifacts into data. Like Ruth, the beginning qualitative researcher can be overwhelmed by the plethora of potential data. Other beginners wonder where the data are, thinking "Nothing's happening." Again, becoming competent in the general dispositions and skills of qualitative inquiry is crucial. These skills open your eyes and ears to what is going on and sensitize you to what is important, and they provide the structure for creating interesting, useful, and accurate data. It is in this creative process (constructing field notes, interview transcriptions, and memos) that diligence and perseverance is rewarded. As our characters gather data in the field, questions arise. We turn to these in Chapter 9, relying on our own work and that of our students for answers.

ACTIVITIES FOR YOUR COMMUNITY OF PRACTICE

Study Questions About Data Gathering Generally

- What are the areas of decisions researchers make about gathering data?

- How do researchers generate data?

- What are the primary techniques for gathering qualitative data?

- How do Marla, Ruth, and Anthony justify their choices of techniques?

(Continued)

(Continued)

Study Questions About Observing and Reviewing Material Culture

- What are fruitful sites for observation?

- What do researchers look at or for while observing?

- How do they know how and when to focus their observations?

- What aspects of material culture are relevant? How do researchers decide?

Study Questions About Generic Interviewing

- What are the purposes of interviewing?

- What strategies can researchers use to accomplish these purposes in their interviews?

- What are the generic types of interviews? What are the benefits and challenges of each type?

- What are natural ways to follow up an interview question?

- How can interviews elicit narratives? What strategies are most effective?

- How can the interviewer deal with issues of difference? Does difference make a difference?

Study Questions About Special Topics in Interviewing

- How does the interviewer deal with special populations, such as children, peers, elites, and people whose first language is not the same as the interviewer's?

- What are focus groups? When are they an effective interviewing strategy? When are focus groups inappropriate?

Small-Group and Dyad Activities

Generating Data

With your dyad partner, watch a short (10–15 minutes) film clip of an activity of interest to you. Record as much of the actions and interactions you can in field notes. Share your notes, comparing and critiquing the data you have each generated.

What Do We See This Time?

With your dyad partner, watch the same film clip as you did in the activity above, but 1 week later. This time, look for specific actions, interactions, or features of the setting. Comment to one another on what you saw this week that you did not the previous week, how today's notes differ from the previous week's, and what you would look for if you watched the film a third time.

Role-Play Interviews

With volunteer colleagues, role-play the following scenarios for the whole group:

- Anthony interviews Carlos, a 6-year-old child currently enrolled in the mixed-media class.

- Ruth interviews a focus group of seven teachers and aides at the Culverton After Care Center.

- Marla interviews the Director of Public Health for the entire metropolitan area.

Peer Interviewing

This activity is designed as an opportunity for you to practice interviewing skills in a setting that is less risky than when interviewing for your project. Spend some time brainstorming possible questions to ask one another about a general topic (e.g., "adult students returning to graduate school"). Questions could focus on decisions to return to graduate school, experiences in courses and with advising, support for adult students, and balancing school commitments and other commitments (work, families, partners, and organizations).

Remember that you want to learn about the persons you interview, so questions should be designed to help them feel comfortable talking about their experiences. To that end, questions should be open ended, seeking descriptive narratives about one another's experiences.

Break into groups of three (be sure these are people you do not already know well), and spend the next hour or so doing the following: (a) conducting a short interview (about 15–20 minutes), (b) observing an interview, and (c) being interviewed. At the end of each interview, take 5 to 10 minutes to give one another feedback about the process. The person being interviewed should comment on what it felt like and what questions "worked" and then make suggestions for alternative approaches to the interview. The other two should do the same. By the end of the exercise, you will have played all three roles—the interviewer, the participant in the interview, and the observer of an interview. These are the three perspectives on which you can reflect. Each perspective is quite different.

Writing Activity

The First Interview

The purpose of qualitative in-depth interviewing is to learn from the person you are interviewing. This entails a stance of interest, respect, and focus. Your first interview will probably not go as smoothly as you would like. This activity asks you, however, to summarize the interview (both content and process) and reflect on what went smoothly and what felt uncomfortable for you.

First, set the scene. Briefly describe the purpose of your project and the purpose of this interview. Reflect on what you hoped you would learn, and describe what you told the interviewee when you asked for her participation. What questions did the person have? How did you respond?

(Continued)

(Continued)

Discuss the preparation you made for the interview. Then describe where, with whom (without personally identifying the participant), and when the interview took place.

Next, summarize the content of the interview. In this section, develop a theme or idea that emerged in the interview. Discuss the theme as it relates to your project. Use quotes from the interview to support your points. Then summarize the process. Interviews typically have a beginning (introductions, getting started) and some form of closure (summary of what the person talked about, thank-yous, and follow-ups). In the middle of this, the interview can flow smoothly, hit "sore spots," pause, and so on. Think about what the pacing and tone of the interview felt like to you and describe it. You also can ask the person interviewed to reflect on this and incorporate those reactions and thoughts.

In the final section, reflect on the experience. This is an opportunity for you to be gently critical as well as supportive of your own "performance." As you listen to the tape, analyze your questioning strategy and specific questions for their effectiveness in eliciting "talk" from the person. How well did you make transitions? Use prefatory remarks? When did you talk too much? Use specific examples from the interview transcription and discuss how you would modify your questioning in subsequent interviews.

FURTHER READINGS

In-Depth Interviewing

Atkinson, R. (1998). *The life story interview.* Thousand Oaks, CA: Sage.

Brinkmann, S., & Kvale, S. (2015). *InterViews: Learning the craft of qualitative research interviewing.* Thousand Oaks, CA: Sage.

Center for Digital Storytelling [website]. Retrieved from http://www.storycenter.org

Clandinin, D. J., & Connelly, F. M. (2000). *Narrative inquiry: Experience and story in qualitative research.* San Francisco, CA: Jossey-Bass.

Digital Storytelling [website]. Retrieved from http://electronicportfolios.com/digistory/

Digital storytelling: Using technology to tell stories [website]. Retrieved from http://www.umass.edu/wmwp/DigitalStorytelling/Digital%20Storytelling%20Main%20Page.htm

Fontana, A., & Frey, J. H. (2008). The interview: From structured questions to negotiated text. In N. K. Denzin & Y. S. Lincoln (Eds.), *Collecting and interpreting qualitative data materials* (pp. 60–106). Thousand Oaks, CA: Sage.

Gluck, S. B., & Patai, P. (Eds.). (1991). *Women's words: The feminist practice of oral history.* New York, NY: Routledge.

Gubrium, J. F., & Holstein, J. A. (2003). *Postmodern interviewing.* Thousand Oaks, CA: Sage.

Gubrium, J. F., Holstein, J. A., Marvasti, A. B., & McKinney, K. D. (Eds.). (2012). *The SAGE handbook of interview research: The complexity of the craft.* Thousand Oaks, CA: Sage.

Holstein, J. A., & Gubrium, J. F. (Eds.). (2003). *Inside interviewing: New lenses, new concerns.* Thousand Oaks, CA: Sage.

Josselson, R., & Lieblich, A. (Eds.). (1993). *The narrative study of lives.* Newbury Park, CA: Sage.

Kvale, S., & Brinkmann, S. (2015). *Interviews: Learning the craft of qualitative research interviewing* (3rd ed.). Thousand Oaks, CA: Sage.

Lucas, S. R. (2014). Beyond the existence proof: Ontological conditions, epistemological implications, and in-depth interview research. *Quality & Quantity, 48*(1), 387–408.

van Manen, M. (1990). *Researching lived experience: Human science for an action sensitive pedagogy.* Albany: State University of New York Press.

Rubin, H. J., & Rubin, I. S. (2012). *Qualitative interviewing: The art of hearing data* (3rd ed.). Thousand Oaks, CA: Sage.

Seidman, I. E. (2013). *Interviewing as qualitative research: A guide for researchers in education and the social sciences* (4th ed.). New York, NY: Teachers College Press.

Silverman, D. (2011). *Interpreting qualitative data: Methods for analyzing talk, text, and interaction* (4th ed.). Thousand Oaks, CA: Sage.

Weiss, R. S. (1994). *Learning from strangers: The art and method of qualitative interview studies.* New York, NY: Free Press.

Interviewing Elites or Experts

Aberbach, J. D., & Rockman, B. A. (2002). Conducting and coding elite interviews. *PS: Political Science & Politics, 35*(4), 673–676.

Becker, T. M., & Meyers, P. R. (1974–1975). Empathy and bravado: Interviewing reluctant bureaucrats. *Public Opinion Quarterly, 38*(4), 605–613.

Delaney, K. J. (2007). Methodological dilemmas and opportunities in interviewing organizational elites. *Sociology Compass, 1*(1), 208–221.

Hertz, R., & Imber, J. B. (1995). *Studying elites using qualitative methods.* Thousand Oaks, CA: Sage.

Odendahl, T., & Shaw, A. M. (2002). Interviewing elites. In J. F. Gubrium & J. A. Holstein (Eds.), *Handbook of interview research* (pp. 299–316). Thousand Oaks, CA: Sage.

Focus Group Interviewing

Allen, L. (2006). Trying not to think "straight": Conducting focus groups with lesbian and gay youth. *International Journal of Qualitative Studies in Education, 19*(2), 163–176.

Belzile, J. A., & Öberg, G. (2012). Where to begin? Grappling with how to use participant interaction in focus group design. *Qualitative Research, 12*(4), 459–472.

Botherson, M. J. (1994). Interactive focus group interviewing: A qualitative research method in early intervention. *Topics in Early Childhood Special Education, 14*(1), 101–118.

Hennink, M. M. (2008). Emerging issues in international focus group discussions. In S. N. Hesse-Biber & P. Leavy (Eds.), *Handbook of emergent methods* (pp. 207–220). New York, NY: Guilford Press.

Ho, D. (2006). The focus group interview: Rising to the challenge in qualitative research methodology. *Australian Review of Applied Linguistics, 29*(1), 1–5.

Krueger, R. A., & Casey, M. A. (2014). *Focus groups: A practical guide for applied research* (5th ed.). Thousand Oaks, CA: Sage.

Linhorst, D. M. (2002). A review of the use and potential of focus groups in social work research. *Qualitative Social Work, 1*(2), 208–228.

Madrid, E. (2000). Focus groups in feminist research. In N. K. Denzin & Y. S. Lincoln (Eds.), *Handbook of qualitative research* (2nd ed., pp. 835–850). Thousand Oaks, CA: Sage.

Peek, L., & Fothergill, A. (2009). Using focus groups: Lessons from studying daycare centers, 9/11, and Hurricane Katrina. *Qualitative Research, 9*(1), 31–59.

Interviewing Children

Alderson, P., & Morrow, V. (2011). *The ethics of research with children and young people.* Thousand Oaks, CA: Sage.

Christensen, P., & James, A. (2008). *Research with children: Perspectives and practices* (2nd ed.). New York, NY: Falmer Press.

Danby, S., Ewing, L., & Thorpe, K. (2011). The novice researcher: Interviewing young children. *Qualitative Inquiry, 17*(1), 74–84.

Daniels, D. H., Beaumont, L. J., & Doolin, C. A. (2007). *Understanding children: An interview and observation guide for educators*

(2nd ed.). Boston, MA: McGraw-Hill Higher Education.

Eder, D., & Fingerson, L. (2003). Interviewing children and adolescents. In J. A. Holstein & J. F. Gubrium (Eds.), *Inside interviewing: New lenses, new concerns* (pp. 33–53). Thousand Oaks, CA: Sage.

Fine, G. A., & Sandstrom, K. L. (1988). *Knowing children: Participant observation with minors*. Newbury Park, CA: Sage.

Gibson, J. E. (2012). Interviews and focus groups with children: Methods that match children's developing competencies. *Journal of Family Theory & Review, 4*(2), 148–159.

Graue, M. E., & Walsh, D. J. (1998). *Studying children in context: Theories, methods, and ethics*. Thousand Oaks, CA: Sage.

Greene, S., & Hogan, D. (Eds.). (2005). *Research children's experiences: Approaches and methods*. London, England: Sage.

Hart, R. A. (1997). *Children's participation: The theory and practice of involving young citizens in community development and environmental care*. London, England: Earthscan.

Lewis, A., & Lindsay, G. (1999). *Researching children's perspectives*. Buckingham, England: Open University Press.

Melton, G., Ben-Arieh, A., Cashmore, J., Goodman, G., & Worley, N. K. (Eds.). (2013). *The SAGE handbook of child research*. Thousand Oaks, CA: Sage.

Moore, T., McArthus, M., & Noble-Carr, D. (2008). Little voices and big ideas: Lessons learned from children about research. *International Institute for Qualitative Methodology, 7*(2), 77–91.

Spratling, R., Coke, S., & Minick, P. (2012). Qualitative data collection with children. *Applied Nursing Research, 25*(1), 47–53.

Thorne, B. (2001). Learning from kids. In R. M. Emerson (Ed.), *Contemporary field research: Perspectives and formulations* (2nd ed., pp. 224–238). Prospect Heights, IL: Waveland Press.

Observing

Angrosino, M. V., & Mays de Perez, K. A. (2000). Rethinking observation: From method to context. In N. K. Denzin & Y. S. Lincoln (Eds.), *Handbook of qualitative research* (2nd ed., pp. 673–702). Thousand Oaks, CA: Sage.

Bogdan, R. C., & Biklen, S. K. (2006). *Qualitative research in education: An introduction to theory and methods* (5th ed.). Boston, MA: Allyn & Bacon.

Delamont, S. (2001). *Fieldwork in educational settings: Methods, pitfalls, and perspectives* (3rd ed.). London, England: Falmer Press.

DeWalt, K. M., & DeWalt, B. R. (2001). *Participant observation: A guide for fieldworkers*. Walnut Creek, CA: AltaMira Press.

Emerson, R. M., Fretz, R. I., & Shaw, L. L. (2011). *Writing ethnographic fieldnotes* (2nd ed.). Chicago, IL: University of Chicago Press.

Guest, G., Namey, E. E., & Mitchell, M. L. (2013). *Collecting qualitative data: A field manual for applied research*. Thousand Oaks: Sage.

Wolcott, H. F. (2005). *The art of fieldwork* (2nd ed.). Walnut Creek, CA: AltaMira Press.

Wolcott, H. F. (2008). *Ethnography: A way of seeing* (2nd ed.). Lanham, MD: AltaMira Press.

Documents and Material Culture

Hodder, I. (2000). The interpretation of documents and material culture. In N. K. Denzin & Y. S. Lincoln (Eds.), *Handbook of qualitative research* (2nd ed., pp. 703–715). Thousand Oaks, CA: Sage.

Latham, K. F. (2014). Experiencing documents. *Journal of Documentation, 70*(4), 544–561.

Roberts, B. W., & Vander Linden, M. (2011). *Investigating archaeological cultures: material culture, variability, and transmission*. New York, NY: Springer.

Tilly, C., Keane, W., Kuechler, S., Rowlands, M., & Spyer, P. (Eds.). (2006). *The SAGE handbook of material culture*. Thousand Oaks, CA: Sage.

8

Issues That Arise in the Field

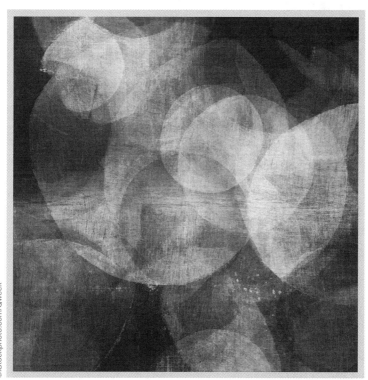

©iStockphoto.com/Qweek

Working in the field with real people with lives and commitments raises questions. These concerns or worries typically focus on preparing to gather data, getting comfortable in the setting, identifying and creating the data, doing fieldwork in another language, modifying the design as the project unfolds, systematically reflecting on the process, and deciding when to end the study. This chapter addresses these worries through posing eight questions that you may encounter while doing qualitative research:

1. How do I prepare to gather data?

2. How can I get comfortable in the field?

3. What are the data?

4. How do I turn sights, sounds, and objects into data?

5. Two languages: Which do I use?

6. How can I change my research plan?

7. What do I reflect on?

8. How do I leave the field?

HOW DO I PREPARE TO GATHER DATA?

Qualitative researchers think about how to get ready to gather their data. As described in Chapter 6, access and entry are not casual or random encounters. Although serendipity does play a part in the success of entry, at that point the researcher has already made decisions that influence the encounters. The conceptual framework (see Chapter 5) is a road map the researcher uses to guide data gathering. Reading, hanging around, and talking informally with people are all ways to build familiarity with the setting or subject and to start filling in the framework. Background and a road map can prepare researchers for the changes they most likely will make, the roadblocks they surely will encounter, and all the surprises and challenges they will face.

Marla, Ruth, and Anthony have read and reflected on their questions to develop *conceptual frameworks* that evolve as their work progresses (see Chapter 5). Their reading, reflection, and frameworks give their studies a purpose. This, in turn, shapes their understanding and implementation of the various data-gathering techniques.

Our Characters

Marla is aware of current problems in health care for poor women, and she wants to link her findings with action to improve their health care. Because Marla is doing a critical case study, she and her team use multiple methods to examine a few specific cases. She starts with participant observation, because her action research design requires that she include participants in the data gathering. From her initial observation and informal interviews, she learns what questions are important to women in the community served by the clinic, and she finds volunteers to form a collaborative research team. Together, they frame the specific questions and determine the data-gathering techniques.

For his compressed ethnography of the community arts program, **Anthony** also uses multiple techniques, but he focuses on the interactions he sees in the community regarding the arts. Anthony has learned about some exemplary community arts programs in other cities, so he has a sense of what high-quality community arts programs can be like.

He also gathers demographic data about the local community to inform his evaluation. Anthony knows that the director needs information to improve the program, so he plans to gather data on the activities and events offered and on what the community may need and be receptive to in the arts. He narrows his focus as he learns.

Ruth began with a foundation of knowledge from her work in the summer camp. To prepare for fieldwork, she reads extensively on children with disabilities. She hangs around an after-school center that happens to serve all children, including a few who use wheelchairs. Because of her experience as an athlete and her background in psychology, she becomes intrigued with the idea of wheelchair-bound children and physical activity. Therefore, she expands her reading to broaden her understanding of "bodied-ness." She chooses a phenomenological study, relying on interviews. Her focus is on words and the meanings they convey.

HOW CAN I GET COMFORTABLE IN THE FIELD?

You have negotiated entry and are finally in the field, ready to gather data. What do you actually do in the setting, however? Although you may feel awkward and self-conscious, try just acting naturally as activities and conversations unfold. What you learn in these first few forays will generate new sources for further interviews and observations. You will find you can connect with people, and details will fit together. Sometimes the setting is unfamiliar to you, so you may have to make a conscious attempt to get comfortable in it. We have found that certain strategies help.

Establishing some comembership (described in Chapter 6) is one such strategy. Another is building a genuine interest in the activities of the organization or the individual. Observing an activity that is routine to the organization or an individual and asking questions about that activity is a common strategy.

You might find a *grand tour* of the setting helpful, whether your focus is an organization or an individual. Sometimes this is quite literally a tour—of the building, the office, or the neighborhood. Other times, it is a "tour" of the participant's understanding of his or her lived experience. The tour introduces you to the participants' worlds; it provides a shared experience (albeit small) that can shape future interviews and observations. The informal questions and answers exchanged are often more intriguing than a formal interview in someone's office.

When we interview principals, for example, we start by asking them to show us around the schools. The principals' commentaries, as well as what they choose to highlight, tell us much about them and their priorities and leadership. During one such grand tour, a principal stopped regularly to pick up discarded candy bar wrappers on the stairs, saying, "Someone could slip on this." This same man always addressed students with respect and interest. These early impressions of him as a caring and sensitive person were corroborated by data we continued to gather. Similarly, what we learned on grand tours of inclusive schools guided our interviews and sharpened our observations in individual classrooms.

Getting Comfortable

- Be yourself; do not assume an artificial role.
- Establish what you have in common; ask for a "grand tour."
- Get involved in ways that fit.
- Pay attention to the "underground."

For example, during the grand tour of a high school, we observed unusual camaraderie among students, teachers, and security guards in the lunchroom. Our fascination with this scene pushed us to explore student–adult relationships in other areas of the school.

The grand tour can be especially important when the setting is unfamiliar to you. When studying humane societies and zoos, grand tours helped us establish the particular philosophies of the different groups. One zoo director emphasized the importance of holding all the animals in habitats that are as close to nature as possible. She pointed out undusted cobwebs hanging from doorframes that were allowed to remain because they were "natural." In another site with a similar stated philosophy, the director squashed spiders in an immaculate cage area. We wondered why spiders were not considered part of nature! These actions suggested avenues for exploring the depth of staff beliefs about nature and apparent contradictions between espoused values and values in practice.

Likewise, grand tours of the training facilities for cardiopulmonary resuscitation (CPR) and advanced cardiac life support studies not only familiarized us with settings that were unfamiliar but also shaped our actions. In hospitals, for example, we learned where and when the procedures of interest were likely to be performed, what equipment was available, who actually performed the procedures, and where we were (and were not) welcome. From these tours, we discovered new questions to ask and identified limitations to the studies. We got a sense of what kinds of protocols or checklists might or might not be possible. For example, witnessing a Code Blue (cardiac arrest) was unlikely, so we reasoned that we would have to rely on records made by staff who were present for such dramatic events. Because we saw how busy nurses were during these emergencies, we realized that they could not do much data gathering for us. We had to modify our design and data-gathering techniques.

Specific actions and stances in a setting are related to the researcher's degree of involvement with participants. Are your participants sources of information or active collaborators? The degree of involvement with participants depends on the design of the study, how long you anticipate being in the setting, and the willingness of participants (see Chapter 6). If your only interaction is to be a single interview, act fairly formal and appreciative. If you will be conducting iterative interviews with participants, building a more friendly relationship over time is important. This depends, of course, on the personality of the person being interviewed. For example, a student of ours interviewed a famous ballet master during the course of a year, but their relationship remained respectfully formal. Another student interviewed African American women educators who lived and worked in Africa. With some, she developed strong, intimate relationships; others were distant and formal.

In cases in which participants are directly engaged in gathering data, the relationship is collaborative. When we conducted a long-term, state-funded evaluation of teacher assistance teams, we worked closely with department of education personnel who managed the program. We designed the evaluation together. They felt that it was their study, with us supplying technical assistance. We acted accordingly, consulting with them as each step unfolded. Team leaders filled in the case status records, which were our main sources of data. These forms were delivered to the program directors, who relayed them to us for processing and analysis. When the lengthy printout sheets were ready, we sat together with the program personnel to interpret analyses. Over time, these personnel became our colleagues and friends.

Because the observer is also the observed, the researcher's actions soon become part of what we call the *underground*. Word spreads through the informal channels in a setting about how the researcher behaves and what the study is about. These stories of what the researcher is up to go through several iterations as people add their interpretations in the retelling. Awareness of the underground's messages can be a source of comfort—or discomfort—to the researcher. By the time we called the principal of the third school in our inclusion study, the underground had pegged us as "OK." On the phone, the principal was especially cooperative and told us, "I hear you all are pretty good, that you know schools." The hospital underground repeated for months the story of how one of us successfully filled in for a nurse in a simulated Code Blue (cardiac arrest). In another study, we found out that we were referred to as "the doctors," a pun both on our advanced degrees and on the fact that we were conducting a study.

Negative feedback from the underground also can reveal problems or misunderstandings. We have learned at times that, in the eyes of participants, we behaved gratuitously or as if we were saviors from the ivory tower. In one study, accusations by his colleagues that we were playing favorites with a director filtered out to us. Had we not been aware of these negative feelings and made an effort to address them, we would have most certainly gathered limited (or even skewed) data. As it was, we cannot be certain that we still did not have problems, but we were aware of them, and they revealed conflicts in the setting.

We have learned to keep our ears tuned in to any hints from the underground. Any organization or individual has secrets and closes doors to a researcher. As we have already made clear, participants in the study have a right to their privacy. Still, many of the "secrets" are more or less transparent in the underground, tacitly hidden from outsiders but nonetheless apparent to the astute researcher.

Although an underground is not readily accessible (thus its label), participants often try to communicate messages, both positive and negative, in feedback through the underground. Part of our work in the field, therefore, is to discover and gain access to the underground. Whenever we hear references to us or our work, we dig around to find the details behind the reference. For example, when a participant slipped and called one of us "doc," we probed to find out what he meant and who else used that nickname.

As you become comfortable (or try to become comfortable), you are apt to make promises to participants. We have learned to be careful about making promises in the field. Although we adamantly contend that the participants should have access to final reports, we consider carefully to whom we promise raw data or field notes, and we seldom promise editing rights. Collaborative efforts, however, do not require promises, just comfort in working together.

WHAT ARE THE DATA?

Beginning researchers often ask what to look for and how to know what are data and what are not. Gathering everything will not help analysis, but how do you know what is relevant and what is important? We believe that to be a good qualitative researcher, you need to develop sensitive eyes and ears, like an artist's or a detective's. This eye (or ear) detects both the figure and the ground or the detail within the whole. You can *see patterns* where others see only individual items. It is a *"both-and"* kind of thinking. In the classical field dependence test, you see the faces as easily as you see the vase, or the old woman as easily as the young woman.

One way to see the figure and ground equally is to train your eyes to draw a mental boundary around the field and then separate out activities, actors, and places. How do the three spheres relate? Which actors are involved in which activities and in which places? Are all actors active? Is activity occurring in all places? Does one activity, actor, or place stand out at one time and as something else at another time? Where do they intersect? This field dependence–independence exercise can clarify your focus.

Developing a sensitive eye or ear is a mixture of skill and craft. Qualitative researchers are focused but remain open to surprises and serendipity. Most important, they develop comfort with ambiguity because although the data may be concrete, their meaning and, therefore, their appearance change. Data do merge and emerge. Try not to settle for the first explanation. You identify themes, but be willing to abandon them to create new ones when the originals no longer serve your purpose. Seek relationships, but do not force fit anything.

Often, the relevant data are obvious: the size and enthusiasm of a crowd attending an event, the effectiveness of a math teacher whose students are applying the proof he has just demonstrated, and the reasons why people say they attended the famous author's lecture. Equally important, however, *data are sometimes unobtrusive:* the worn carpet leading to the teacher's desk, the sticky glass covering the museum exhibit, and the soda cans and candy wrappers left outside the computer room door. The sensitive eye picks up less obvious aspects of material culture that might be relevant data.

Less obvious data often reveal another story. For instance, during our CPR study, we noticed that instructors passed and certified nearly everyone who attended the course, even though most of the students failed the test based on Red Cross standards. Although we knew that these students had not mastered the technical skills to save a life, they readily told us about their pride in accomplishment, their confidence in their ability to save a life, and their readiness to perform CPR if necessary. These unanticipated data suggested an alternative outcome from the training: the confidence, rather than the skill, to perform. In another instance, a student told us about an evaluation of a training program for entry-level office workers. Her interviews indicated that the program was having minimal effect, but over the duration of the program, she observed that participants' dress became

What Are the Data?

- Pay attention to what is going on.
- Write down your intuitions and first impressions.
- Do not focus too quickly.
- Do not try to "get it all."

increasingly formal and businesslike. The meanings of these observations are open to varying interpretations, but both proved to be relevant data.

Some students tell us that they do not need to seek out data, that as they spend time in their settings, participants offer unsolicited information. People answer unasked questions, explain unquestioned actions, and point out what they consider important scenes or activities. Usually, these data can be relevant. Still, we caution any researcher to filter these offerings through a critical eye, scrutinizing their centrality and accuracy. We remember an art teacher gushing over a quilt he claimed was designed by a group of students to represent their diverse cultures. He gave us pictures of the finished quilt and insisted that it was a marvelous illustration of the progress this multicultural mix of students had made in accepting one another. We noted that no one else mentioned the quilt, so we began to ask about it. Although everyone remarked on its beauty, few indicated that it symbolized any strides in intercultural communication. Some even intimated that the teacher had designed it and done most of the work. Experiences like this have taught us to question unsolicited information.

HOW DO I TURN SIGHTS, SOUNDS, AND OBJECTS INTO DATA?

You create data when you record in *field notes* or *interview transcriptions* what you have seen and heard. These sights, sounds, and objects become, in effect, artifacts that you refer to when you analyze, interpret, and write about what you have learned. The sounds and sights on audiotapes and videotapes are data, just as the words you write in field notes are data. Try to take notes that record as completely as possible what you learn in the field. The notes should contain descriptions of settings, people, activities, dialogue, and emotions. They definitely should include your impressions and commentary (see Chapter 7). These records are objects. As objects, they are data that may be labeled, categorized, and organized; that is, they may be analyzed and interpreted. Recall the examples of how Marla, Ruth, and Anthony turn what they see and hear into data in Chapter 8.

We try to document as much as we can while we are in the field, but writing field notes while observing or interviewing can be overwhelming, requiring an ambidextrous researcher who also has two heads. Sometimes, taking notes is awkward, inappropriate, or just plain impossible. Still, we have to be sure that we capture what we witness. Whatever the status of our field notes, we make time as soon as possible afterward to complete them, filling in details we could not write down in the moment. Sometimes, we escape to an empty corner or a women's room to complete our notes. At other times, this filling in must wait until we are in our car after an interview or observation. Sometimes, we have no choice but to leave the task until we are alone in the evening. The sooner we can complete the notes, the fresher our memories are and, thus, the richer and more accurate the field notes.

Turning Sights, Sounds, and Objects Into Data

- Take field notes assiduously.
- Record interviews or take detailed notes.
- Write these up diligently.
- Discuss data with your colleagues.
- Share examples with your community of practice.

A cautionary tale comes from our experience with a doctoral student who failed to word process his field notes after each observation, both formal and informal. When we read a draft of his findings, there was scant evidence that he could bring to support the claims (themes) that he asserted were present in the setting. The themes appeared to be impressions with little concrete detail. In our attempt to help him, we asked to see the data, his field notes, and interviews. Sadly, he could not produce a written record that was usable by others, but he claimed that he had a box of notes on scrap paper. We sent him back to produce tangible evidence ("data") that could support his findings.

Whenever possible, we try to record sessions in the field. In interviews, this record is especially useful to capture quotes accurately while we are attending to the conversation. If we are moving around or listening to several activities occurring at once, a recorder clearly will be of no use. When we can make recordings, they serve to corroborate our notes. Sometimes, we choose not to fully transcribe the interview; we listen to the recording only to confirm or fill in what we have written or remembered. Whenever using a recorder, the unbreakable rule is to obtain permission for its use. A hidden recorder is never acceptable.

Recording can raise concerns. For whatever reasons, some people fear having their spoken ideas recorded. A doctoral student who was studying professional development and the advancement of women working on assembly teams at a car factory was repeatedly refused interviews if she used a recorder. The women, who were more than willing to speak to her without a recorder, expressed fear that supervisors would hear their voices as they told their stories and would somehow hurt them. The student respected their wishes and simply took notes. Unexpectedly, her study revealed a company whose supervisors regularly encouraged and supported women to use their training to assume more responsibility and leadership, but the women were still apprehensive that their words would be misunderstood or misused.

In some cases, people in a setting do not allow us to take notes. We remember a dramatic example that taught us to be sensitive to the idiosyncratic needs of the participants. During the grand tour of a school, we were standing near the mailboxes in the main office, scribbling away. A teacher entered, shouting that someone had stolen the bag containing her medications from her desk. We continued to take notes. The teacher turned to us and nearly screamed, "You stop writing down what I'm saying. It's none of your God-damned business!" The moral of the story: Do not worry about writing down everything that happens!

We have known people who fear recorders because they have difficulty articulating their ideas. For example, on reading a transcript of an interview, one participant implied that the recording had misinterpreted him: "Sure, I may have said that. But that's not what I meant!" Others report feeling foolish when they read transcripts of their words: "I sound so stupid, I keep repeating myself"; "I didn't realize I use 'um' so much. Um, I must have said 'um' twenty times on this page alone"; or "I don' wan' ya ta use no tape. Make me soun' lak I don' know nuttin'. I jus neva had 'nuf learnin' lik y'all has." Rendering speech into writing can pose difficulties.

For these reasons, we negotiate with participants about sharing the transcripts. If we want to use a quote, we make contextual decisions as to whether or how we will edit the words. Some idioms and accents or the presence of numerous "ums," when transcribed, obscure the actual message you are hoping to convey by using the quote. For example, the last person quoted above was a perceptive and intelligent custodian with valuable insights about the organization we were studying. After hearing his response, we transformed his spoken words into standard English because we felt it was ethical to respect his preferences. Our intent was never to make him appear ignorant. We also feared his accent would reveal his identity and wanted to ensure his privacy. In each case, you must make a considered judgment about the effect of editing a transcript. Be diligent to document what decisions you make and why.

TWO LANGUAGES: WHICH DO I USE?

Because we live and write in the United States, we presume that the outcome of your research will be presented primarily in English, and the analysis that follows flows from this assumption. Note that this issue was briefly discussed in Chapter 7 regarding translation of data gathered in one language into another. Many complex and fascinating circumstances surround interviewing and language. Sometimes the researcher conducts an interview in a language other than her primary language; for example, a student from Uganda or Taiwan interviews in English, or a German graduate student interviews American doctors about socialized health care. Another circumstance is when the researcher interviews in her primary language, which is not English; for example, a Puerto Rican researcher interviews in New York City in Spanish. A third is when both interviewer and participant are fully and fluently bilingual, so they slip between the two languages during the interview. You may think of other configurations. Because these researchers work in the United States, they must figure out ways to represent what they have learned in English.

Ideally, the interview is conducted in the language that both the participant and the interviewer feel most comfortable to communicate in. If the researcher is fluent in the language the participant prefers, there are fewer issues to deal with than if she is not fluent. Fluency enhances the understanding of specific terms as well as deeper knowledge of cultural meanings. The researcher understands subtle and idiomatic uses of phrases and terms. Without such fluency, however, she may not fully comprehend connotations or may not make connections with the assumed knowledge that comes from membership in a cultural or linguistic group. We recommend that the researcher conducting interviews in a language other than her primary one be aware of the potential to miss nuanced meanings. The researcher could engage someone fluent in that language to help with the analysis and interpretation of data.

Two Languages

- Use the language most comfortable for participants.
- Plan time to translate it into English.
- Include examples in the original language with your translations.
- Use phrases or words in the original language that are particularly evocative.

When a researcher conducts interviews in a language other than English, at some point they must be translated into English if she works in an English-speaking context. In this case, the researcher's workload increases enormously. Depending on the researcher's fluency in English, the task of transcribing an interview in Spanish, for example, and then translating it into English doubles the work. We know of no shortcuts to this process except for the fully bilingual person who, when analyzing, can apply English categories to Spanish texts, for example. Moreover, when analyzing and presenting the research, additional considerations arise.

- If you have translated from another language into English, what constitutes the direct quotes?

- Can you use translated words as a direct quote?

- How do you signal that a translation is accurate and captures the subtle meanings of the original language?

Marla and her team conduct several interviews in Spanish, which is Marla's primary language, although she is fluent in spoken English. They do not fully translate all the tapes into English. Instead, they listen to them several times and then select segments for translation. They decide that, in the final report that Marla must submit for her class, they will provide an appendix that includes examples of interview segments in both Spanish and English, showing the reader how they have translated them.

As our society becomes more multicultural, an increasing number of people are fully bilingual. In a research setting, they may move from one language to another, depending on setting and topic. One principal we interviewed spoke about the children in Spanish, the pedagogical and organizational issues in English, and community politics in Spanish.

HOW CAN I CHANGE MY RESEARCH PLAN?

Marla, Ruth, and Anthony find that the data-gathering process is not linear, clear, or rigid. As they enter their settings, they get confused. As they spend more time on their projects, they *modify their data-gathering techniques*. **Ruth** is unsure about what to look for at the beginning. Eventually, she decides to use interviews to learn about the life experiences of children in wheelchairs. But after she meets Katrine, she adds another disability: deafness. After reflecting on her informal interviews with the health care team in the clinic, **Marla** realizes that her techniques must include the poor women of the community who are affected by the problems she is concerned about. **Anthony's** early observations and survey returns reveal that people in the community may not understand that the program is available to them, so he holds several focus groups to explore both community interests and ways to "market" the programs.

In another example, our reading, reflection, and conceptual framework for the study of inclusive classrooms helped prepare us to gather data. At the outset, our purpose was to learn how children with disabilities were doing in these settings. We assumed that our observations would focus exclusively on these children. As we read more about inclusive education, and as we sat and watched in classrooms, we realized that we needed to look at how all children were learning in inclusive schools, so we broadened our observational focus.

WHAT DO I REFLECT ON?

You will directly encounter the phenomenon of reflexivity as you gather data. No matter how unobtrusive you try to be, you cannot help but become a part, however small, of the setting. Marla's presence in her site is obvious and interactive because she is working as a volunteer and collaborating with others for data gathering, but neither Ruth nor Anthony is invisible in his or her setting. The children get used to Ruth, but her presence adds an external dimension to each interview. At a large public performance, Anthony may not be noticed as an evaluator, but he is, in fact, a member of the audience. You are part of the social world you study, and you affect that world. How people in that world respond to you is often as informative as the answers to your questions or what you see through observations. Your presence in the field is inseparable from the outcome or product of data gathering. As we have noted many times, including your reactions and impressions as observer or interviewer comments in your field notes is a crucial element of documenting the processes and decisions of your work.

Reflexivity also involves those observed. The families of Ruth's children react to her too. They may see her as an intrusive student from the ivory tower who could never understand their realities. They might also assume that she is interested because she or someone close to her has a disability. They might even believe that she is a "spy" from some conservative coalition that is protesting increased funding for special education. Their hypotheses grow out of their personal backgrounds and beliefs, as well as what Ruth looks like and what they see her do. Similarly, Anthony's audiences create ideas and explanations for his presence and questions.

Because they are researchers with specific purposes, and not casual observers, Anthony and Ruth test their reflexive reactions (their emergent hypotheses) as they gather data. They form hypotheses based on initial data and then revise those working understandings in light of additional data. They continue to watch, ask, and listen. They become analytical and reflective during the data-gathering processes. Ruth monitors her reactions. She then examines these reactions to determine to what extent her own fears, sophistication, or dislikes shape her impressions. At the same time, she considers how the children's values and prejudices might be interacting with hers to influence their acceptance or dismissal of her. Because she tries to be aware of reflexivity, Ruth's observations are multifaceted in that she questions her role, constructs hypotheses, and tests impressions against additional data.

Changing the Research Plan

- Hold on to your conceptual framework.
- Be prepared for the unexpected.
- Consider the unexpected and modify your plan.
- Talk with advisors and your community of practice.
- Record why you changed your plan.

Reflexivity

- Pay attention to your intuitive insights.
- Note how people react to you.
- Think about what these reactions might mean for the study.

As part of their reflections, Marla, Ruth, and Anthony examine the contexts they study. **Anthony** considers the history of community involvement in this area of the city.

- How have residents reacted to other activities and events like the arts program?
- What are the demographics of the community?
- Has anything happened recently that might influence the way in which residents respond to the arts center?

Marla also seeks out information she may not know already about the community. She asks what the clinic workers have viewed as problems in the past and if any unique history exists that she should know about. Based on what **Ruth** observes at the after-school program early in her study, she might ask the following:

- How long has this group been together?
- Have children come and gone?
- Has the group had other observers?
- How was she introduced?
- Are the children predominantly of a different gender or ethnic group than Ruth?

As researchers, all three recognize that their interviews and observations, as well as the material culture available to them, are embedded in a larger context and place in time. They make this larger context and history a part of their data gathering.

HOW DO I LEAVE THE FIELD?

As you gather data, you will notice that, wittingly or not, you are analyzing them. In fact, the early stages of data analysis occur simultaneously with data gathering. You see patterns emerge and you gather more data to check out the possible patterns. You identify a category, and then you ask questions to elucidate. Finally, this ongoing analysis signals when you have enough data.

In principle, because it is heuristic, *field research is never complete*. New data are constantly being generated and new discoveries can always be made. In practice, fieldwork is seldom a one-shot event or a single episode. An ethnography calls for long-term immersion. A phenomenological study requires iterative interviews. A study of sociolinguistic patterns requires identifying and collecting instances of speech or text. Case studies might necessitate successive observations and interviews with several persons. For almost all studies, follow-up visits or phone calls are necessary.

At some point, however, you become aware that you can make sense of the people or settings you have been studying, that you can tell a coherent story about what you have learned. You realize that the data seem redundant, that your major insights are supported and explicated, or that you just plain know you have answered your questions. Maybe you have completed the contracted number of visits or funding has run out. The strange has become familiar. Time has come to leave the field.

Leaving the field may simply mean that you do not return to a site or seek another interview. If you have been in the field for only a short while, chances are you have not established deep or intimate relationships that will be ending. If, however, you have built relationships, leaving the field can be a bit like "breaking up," to use a dating metaphor (Ball, 1990). If the parties became close, ending fieldwork can be painful. Jonathan Kozol relates such pain as he says good-bye to his participants in *Amazing Grace: The Lives of Children and the Conscience of a Nation* (1995).

Often, we have continued, on a different level, relationships that we have built with participants in our studies. There is no longer a study to bring us together; we are just friends. One such personal friend is the director of a teacher assistance team program we evaluated several years ago (Rallis, 1990). Our partnership (Rossman and Rallis) as friends and coauthors began when one of us was the evaluator of the other's program. We came to know each other as we spent time together in the field of the project. Although that project ended, we continue to spend time together and still work together. Leaving the field, then, does not always mean ending relationships.

Whatever the relationships a qualitative researcher encounters, we have to think about the impact we might have had on participants. It may be more than we suspect. Siskin (1994) tells of a high school student who was deeply moved by the attention the interviewer paid her during a 30-minute interview. The student said she told the interviewer stuff she would not reveal to parents, teachers, or social workers. Later, at a crisis in her life, she asked if she could talk to the researcher again. Delamont (1992) argues that the qualitative research experience qualitatively changes both the researcher and the researched—that neither will ever be quite the same again.

DISPOSITIONS AND SKILLS

Our characters are facing the challenge of thinking on the run—of making decisions while working in the field. Once again, it is those principles of good practice that help them answer questions that arise in the field. Because of the ambiguous nature of qualitative research, they can never anticipate all the questions that will arise. As they prepare and become more comfortable in their new roles as researchers, they remember that their strong good sense about other people will serve them in good stead. As they figure out what the data are and how to record them diligently, they engage in the systematic inquiry that marks their work as ethical, trustworthy, and credible. The principles also guide them to know when and how to leave the field. They discern when they have enough data to tell a coherent and meaningful story. They know that the time to analyze and interpret (to write the story) has come. Analyzing and interpreting is the subject of Chapter 10.

Leaving the Field and Ending the Study

- Set some boundaries.
- Negotiate the boundaries with participants.
- Inform people that you will be leaving the site or ending the study.
- Keep some doors open.

ACTIVITIES FOR YOUR COMMUNITY OF PRACTICE

Study Questions

- What issues arise in your study? How might your community of practice help you with these?

- What issues arise that seem cross cultural? How do you reflect on them?

- How will you plan to end your study? What protocols should you observe?

Small-Group and Dyad Activities

Solving the Problems of the Field

On several 3" × 5" cards, describe issues you have faced. In your small group, take turns drawing these cards from a box. As each card is read aloud, brainstorm strategies to help with the issue or problem.

FURTHER READINGS

Janesick, V. J. (2011). *"Stretching" exercises for qualitative researchers* (3rd ed.). Thousand Oaks, CA: Sage.

deMarrais, K. B. (Ed.). (1998). *Inside stories: Qualitative research reflections.* Mahwah, NJ: Lawrence Erlbaum.

Weis, L., & Fine, M. (Eds.). (2000). *Speed bumps: A student-friendly guide to qualitative research.* Albany: State University of New York Press.

CHAPTER

9

Our Characters' Data

©iStockphoto.com/Qweek

This chapter presents data gathered by Ruth, Marla, and Anthony for their small-scale qualitative research projects. We note here that these data are authentic; they are drawn from actual studies that students in our qualitative research classes have conducted. We show how our characters begin the process of gathering data that will help them respond to their research questions. Our characters generate a variety of data, including field notes from observations and transcriptions of interviews. Note that the data we present have been "cleaned up" for ease of reading. Original field notes are often quite messy, with arrows, underlining, and questions all over them. While we could present some data this way, we believe that providing examples of good, well-developed field notes and interview transcripts is more useful for learning. Also, we caution you to consider carefully with whom you might share your raw field notes as they are likely to reveal identities.

We begin with a reminder about each student's study, its purpose and genre, and how it is evolving and changing over the course of the project. Throughout we comment on the quality of the data gathered and make suggestions for improvement. The text of the interviews and the field notes are formatted in regular type; the comments of Ruth, Marla and her team members, and Anthony are in **bold**. As noted above, in all instances, our characters have word-processed these excerpts, elaborating points where necessary and adding observer comments **(OCs)** at the end of several excerpts. You also will find our comments interspersed throughout the interviews, field notes, and analyses in *italics*. In these, we do three things: (1) we make suggestions for improvement, (2) we applaud a particularly skillful or effective example, and (3) we discuss alternatives our characters might have considered. We also comment at the end of each excerpt about the overall quality of the work and how it links to emerging insights and interpretations. These comments are italicized and bracketed.

ANTHONY'S DATA

Anthony is returning to the university for an advanced degree in public policy. On graduating from college, he volunteered as a community development worker around issues of water quality and housing. When funding for this project was cut, he applied for a legislative internship in Washington, D.C., to serve as a staff member on a joint committee on arts and education. His interest in evaluation and policy studies springs from these experiences. He learned firsthand, when his project's funding was cut, the effects of policy decisions on community members and their advocates. He hopes that his work will inform the policy-making process through the provision of more effective, thoughtful, and detailed information.

The purpose of his study is to describe and evaluate the effectiveness of a program designed to bring arts to members of the community. He uses a compressed ethnographic design to describe the culture of the program. As part of his responsibilities to the funding agency, Anthony will write an evaluation report to inform the agency and decision makers concerned with the arts. Bringing arts to the community means providing actual, usable opportunities for people who live in the neighborhood to both appreciate and create various forms of art.

The elements of a community-based program are many and complex. As Anthony has explored his topic and problem, he has decided to focus on specific elements of the program: participation at center events, staff and participant attitudes toward the activities, and views of nonparticipating community members about the program. His overarching question is "How is *participation* defined through the culture of the program?" He documents participation through observation and logs kept by staff members. Attitudes toward the program are obtained through two techniques: (1) in-depth interviews and (2) a survey. Anthony has made some preliminary decisions about how many participants and nonparticipants to interview and survey. He decided, given the resources available, to survey participants as they attend activities and to invite active participants to be interviewed. He further decides that interviewing 10 to 15 "actives" would give him an in-depth portrait of their involvement and views about the program, as well as their views on participation.

Field Notes 1

10/10. 12:15–1:00 p.m. Community Arts Center Office I'm sitting in the office of the Center because I want to get a sense of the "culture" of the Center and its community, so I figured here is a good place to start. I chose the noon hour because I thought people might stop by during their lunch hours. The Center is housed in a three-story commercial building that used to be some kind of store. The first floor is an open space, so they use it for large classes and the gallery. The office is at the back of this space. I ask Dionne *[Who is this person?]* what is upstairs and she tells me there are several smaller rooms used for classes and storage. The third floor is a dance studio—she says it is used also for rehearsals. *[Anthony might have asked what kind of rehearsals.]*

The room seems to be overflowing with papers. On the side walls are file cabinets. A big table is pushed up against the wall next to the door—it's spread with papers. On the wall above is a cork board. Schedules and such are tacked on it. The room has two desks. Dionne—late 30s?—is sitting at one. She is the assistant director/secretary. She answers phones, knows the schedules. Welcomes people when they enter. The door is open. A somewhat balding man enters. He is carrying a brown paper bag.	*[What kind of papers? Documents can often reveal important aspects of the culture.]* **She is a jack-of-all-trades to this organization—knows everybody and where everything is.**
D: "Hey there, Gene. So how did the gum work go? Was the dentist gentle?"	**Is she just nosy or does she care? Is this a regular routine? His bringing her lunch?**
G: "I survived. Got some catching up to do. Thought I'd see what's happening and if I can help on anything." He opens the bag, takes out two steaming cups of soup and a loaf of bread. "It's their version of minestrone today."	
D: "Smells good. Thanks. Actually, you can do the registrations for Heather's class." Gestures to the computer on the other desk. Gene begins working on the computer. Both sip soup and tear off chunks from the loaf.	*[Who is Heather? What does she teach?]* *[Anthony might want to note what the job is—to give an idea about the kind of folks who use the center; give more of a description of these women—age? ethnicity? clothing?]*

(Continued)

(Continued)

It's quiet until two women enter.

D: "About time you two came by. You need to try on your costumes. They're in the back room—way upstairs."

W1: "I got a job! Aren't you going to ask me what it is?"

W2: "Yeah, she's part of the labor force now. Wonder if she'll have time for us anymore."

D: "Well, congratulations! But don't forget you're still Stella to us." Five of us now crowd the relatively small office. Stella perches on Gene's desk; her friend takes the other folding chair. Conversation turns to what happened over the weekend in the neighborhood. Enter an elderly man. He looks a little timid. "I understand you have some drawing classes."

Is Stella her name or the role she has in the play?

[Can he capture any of the conversation?]

They seem really comfortable with each other.

D: "You're just in time to sign up for Barney's watercolor class. It'll meet in the late afternoon. How does that sound?"

EM: "I don't know. Do I need experience?"

D: "Now, honey, you've got all the experience you need for this class. You can fill out this paper and try some of this bread. What brings you to us?"

EM: "My granddaughter keeps telling me I need to get what she calls 'an interest.' I think she's worried about me. Always wanted to paint. . . ." Dionne assures him he is in the right place. He takes a chunk of bread and joins us. He tells us his name is Leo. D starts telling him how important it can be to learn to paint. She tells him about the Center.

She is really a master at making people feel comfortable.

Food may play a part in this culture.

[This is a chance to hear the values and beliefs of the center.]

A tall artsy-looking woman comes in. Everyone's attention turns to her and she sort of "takes over" the room. She's babbling on about getting ready for her afternoon class of kindergartners. She says something to the two women and to Gene. She helps herself to a gulp of D's soup. She opens a closet and gets materials—finger paints today. Another gulp of soup. She tosses instructions to D and leaves.

[What is "artsy"?] **I find out later that she does a mixed-media class for 5- and 6-year-olds. They are in a morning kindergarten in the nearby elementary school. Their mothers bring them to the group while they go to Heather's pot-throwing class. How can she teach the class? She seems so disorganized herself.**

The woman who teaches the pottery class, Heather, comes into the room. She brings a large bag filled with various equipment, including her lunch. She joins us, turning the talk to the outdoor craft show planned for this month.

[Anthony's comment here is a bit judgmental.]

Time's up. I thank everyone for letting me listen and take notes. I talk to Dionne for a minute, arranging to observe a class. She also gives me some advice on the survey. *[Elaborating on this advice would be helpful.]* I may follow up today by interviewing Gene.

OC: There seems to be a lot of interaction and joking around with one another in the office. I was particularly impressed with how much Dionne knows about everyone and how, without skipping a beat, she greeted the elderly man and made him feel welcome there. There's something intriguing that goes on around food here.

[Anthony's early field notes provide strong detail and capture the dialogue well. As with many beginners, however, the field notes are uneven. Anthony is learning that "paying attention" with the level of focus and concentration necessary for excellent field notes is hard work. Although he does not indicate so, he may have felt somewhat uncomfortable just sitting there, taking up space in an already crowded office. His OCs at the end of the field notes are astute. He has important insights into the culture of the program very early on. This is often the case, although the researcher may not realize it at the time. As Anthony reviews these early field notes and his commentary on them, the insights become clearer.]

Field Notes 2

11/3. 4:00–6:15 p.m. Watercolor Class

The class is a watercolor workshop. The 12 students (5 males, 7 females) have been together for 3 weeks (this is their 4th lesson). The instructor (Barney) signaled it was time to begin class by turning on a slide that showed an impressionist painting. He explained that they would learn a new technique, but he wanted to talk about impressionist painting first. He asked the class to give their "impressions" of the painting. I could hardly hear him, even though the room is not large. Class members responded: "old-fashioned"; "shadows"; "soft"; "bright colors"; "people look like they are going to move."

I'm not sure who it was. Maybe a Seurat.

Not sure the class knew what he wanted. Were enthusiastic but seemed mildly confused.

[Anthony is having some difficulty sorting out what are descriptions and what are his comments on the actions he observes. Note that he includes in his field notes, "I could hardly hear him"; this might be better here as an observer's comment.]

B: "Yes, that's all true. He accomplished that effect by using quick, short brushstrokes . . . almost like little dots." Barney spoke a few sentences about the brushstrokes and colors the painter used. He stood at the front of the room with his arms immobile at his side, stiff and dull.

Can this guy paint, let alone teach painting?

I think it would have been better if he had used a large print of the original or a poster. Anything but a slide. I can't tell what he's trying to demonstrate.

(Continued)

(Continued)

S: "Yeah, I heard Monet did that. But this doesn't look like Monet."	**I wonder if this is part of a curriculum and he is just using it because he thinks he is supposed to. He doesn't seem to have a handle on the point he's trying to get across.**
B: "OK, let's get to work. Today, you'll need the fat brushes, sponges, and a cup of water next to your colors." Suddenly Barney loosened up and became an artist. He began to demonstrate a technique with sponges and water. He didn't talk a lot, but his hands flew across the paper and between the paper and the materials. The class gathered around. Almost as quickly as he began, he turned away from the easel and told them to try it.	**He was almost dancing!** **He didn't even ask the group if anyone had questions about what he just did, but he wandered among them, pointing out things, making suggestions, and answering questions.** *[Observer comments on pedagogy; could lead to important insights; detail is good.]*
People worked at their easels. The room was quiet. Not much talking except with Barney. People seemed absorbed in their painting. *[How does he infer "absorbed"?]*	**The behavior norms must be established already. Everyone knows what they are supposed to do, where the materials are, and how to interact with each other and Barney. The atmosphere is very ordered but comfortable. Industrious is the word.**
After sitting at the side of the room, I wandered around looking at the paintings. Finally, I whispered a few questions about how they learned to do certain procedures, if this was their first watercolor class, and how many paintings they had worked on in this class. With one exception, this was everyone's first class. They practice different techniques, but they are each working to complete one full watercolor.	**I feel as if I'd seen two different people in Barney. What was that attempt to teach about impressionism at the beginning of the class?**

OC: Barney is an enigma to me! He seems to be an effective instructor but I'm just not sure. I wonder what he thinks about participation in this class. He's gotten people to come to take it, but do they really relate to the stuff about Impressionism? I'll have to follow up on that when I interview him.

[These field notes were difficult for Anthony to take, although he is able to capture details and the flow of action. He is a bit judgmental, however, in his observer's comments. With feedback from Kent and other class members, he will reflect on this, seeking to understand what was difficult about Barney and the class for him. This process is important for Anthony's growing skills in being reflexive. His notes to himself at the end of the field notes to identify areas for further investigation; this helps keep him on track with his questions.]

Interview 1

11/8 Interview with an active participant. Gene is a writer in his 50s, works out of his own home, was selected because he is very active in Center activities. Director mentioned that they want to get him on the advisory board. Q = interviewer's question; A = respondent's answer; OC = researcher's comments added after transcribing the interview.

Q: Gene, thanks so much for agreeing to the interview this afternoon. You know I'm interested in the programs at the Center and how participants feel about those programs. You're pretty active, which is why I wanted to talk with you. Tell me about why the arts are important to you. *[Good "grand tour" question.]*

A: Oh, there are lots of reasons. For one thing, it's my life! I'm a writer, you know. People need ways to express themselves, to communicate. The arts provide such an alternative to the boob tube! And a way for different generations to relate to one another.

Q: Can you give me an example of that? *[Helpful follow-up question.]*

A: One that comes to mind right away is the outdoor crafts show that was here last month. Did you see the pot-throwing demonstration that my friend Heather had? At one point, she let people come up and try it and all ages were interested. A couple of those punk teenagers really got into it! It was wonderful!

Q: Yes, I saw—

A: What I was going to add was about the clothesline art show where my sister took her daughter, who's 24, and our father, who's in his 80s. They had a great time talking about the scenes of the neighborhood and city that the local artists had painted. That, to me, is one of the great values of the arts—seeing families together appreciating or doing.

Q: Doing? Talk about doing. *[Asking for elaboration.]*

A: There was Heather's pottery booth, but there's always some sort of class at the Center that teaches you how to do the painting, pottery, silversmithing. Oh, I almost forgot! Once a season we have a play. There's this marvelous stockbroker—a guy who just split up with his wife—who comes and acts and it's *so* important for him.

Q: Why is *doing* important in the arts? *[Good probing question.]*

A: Because it's a way to express yourself. I write, but I need other ways too. That's why I take the painting. Oh, and another reason arts are so important is because we learn through them; we learn to do things we hadn't done before.

Q: It would be helpful if you could give me some specific examples. *[Excellent request for detail.]*

A: Take my friend Jack, the stockbroker. He had done some acting in high school and college but never really taken a class or studied it. So what did he really know? He was a natural, that's all. But in preparing the play each year, we bring in a professional actor to work with our community actors. Jack's told me several times how much he learns from these sessions.

Q: You've been telling me some ways that people participate. What are other ways people participate in the Center? *[Too vague.]*

A: I'm not sure I know what you mean.

Q: Well, if they don't want to paint or throw a pot or act in a play, what else can they do?

A: Don't you know? They come to activities like the clothesline art show or the crafts show. Or, once we had a dance group give a performance . . . people came to that. I've even been asked to read some of my poetry . . . but I'm not sure I'm ready yet.

Q: Why not?

A: Well, these are my neighbors, and I'm not sure I want them to . . .

Q: Do you think they may not value it as much as you?

A: You mean value my writing? Yeah, maybe that's it. Poetry's really personal.

Q: I've learned from interviews with other community members that it matters a lot to them to have people like you and Heather right here; they say it's uplifting. I think it makes them feel good about their community. What do you think?

A: Well, I can understand that, but when it comes to sharing my poetry in a public forum, it makes me feel a little strange.

Q: I've also heard that many parents appreciate having the after-school classes for their kids. *[Asking for corroboration of a perspective he has heard from others.]*

A: Yes, I think it's important. Some of these kids might not get exposure to art without them.

Q: Why is that?

A: Well, you know art isn't that important in schools any more. And parents are so busy, too. It's hard to find a place for the arts in lots of people's lives.

Q: And you feel the Center provides a place?

A: Definitely! It's wonderful for *all* of us.

OC: I think I'm beginning to get some insights into the various ways of participation in the arts program. This was great! I'll need to flesh out "ways of participation" in some kind of concept map to help me understand it better. Then I might share it with someone like Gene.

[We agree with Anthony's impression of this interview. He asked for elaboration and specific, concrete details from Gene. This will help him build a typology of "ways of participation." The discussion about Gene reading his poetry aloud was a bit delicate, not something Anthony had anticipated, but he handled it with tact.]

Interview 2

11/15 Interview with nonparticipant community member. Sal is in his 30s and married. He and his wife both work in a local company. Two nights a week, Sal goes to night school, so it was tough scheduling this interview. I had met him when I brought around the surveys last Saturday. He was outside repairing the front steps.

Q: So how's that loose riser doing?

A: I think I've got it fixed. I hope so, 'cause I wouldn't have a chance to get back to it for a couple of weeks. So what questions do you have for me?

Q: You know I'm doing a study of the Arts Center. I've talked with both participants and nonparticipants. You told me you've never really done anything there. Is that right?

A: Yeah. I don't really have time. I hardly had time to fill out that questionnaire you left! Boy was that long!

Q: Sorry! But I appreciate it. So you really don't have much free time?

A: Hell no! I do a lot of overtime at work and then there's these classes I'm taking. . . . My wife's taking one, too. I'm really busy.

Q: When you do have some free time, what do you do?

A: Well, there're some other couples that me and my wife are friends with, and we might go to a movie on a Saturday night. I visit my folks; they live down by the shore. I *love* to go to ball games, but I only got to one this summer. Guess I don't have time even for that anymore, what with the upkeep on this place and everything else.

Q: Well, I've been noticing that you've got an incredible CD collection and it's all different kinds. Some jazz, some New Age, some rock, some classical, some bluegrass. That's quite impressive! *[Picking up on some aspect of the arts that clearly has value to Sal.]*

A: Aw, well, you know. I used to play the guitar a bit. Ah, the classical guitar. I really miss it sometimes.

Q: You must miss it. When did you last do anything with your music?

A: Well, it's been a long time since I played. The wife and I used to go to some clubs when we were first married. But, no time, no money now. You know, sometimes I wish I could've played my guitar for a living rather than trying to be what everybody else says I should be. Ah, but that's just a dream.

Q: Do you ever get a chance to talk to musicians, professional or otherwise? *[Asking for elaboration on the place of music in Sal's life.]*

A: There was a time when my friends were all musicians, so we'd talk about it a lot. Now, our friends are from work. I don't know what happened to those old guys who played.

Q: You know, the Arts Center had a concert in the early summer. I don't remember the details on it, but did you hear about that? Did you go?

A: I didn't know they had concerts. *[This is important data; information about the program may not reach some community members.]* You mean like, somebody came and played the piano or guitar or some instrument? You don't mean some symphony?

Q: Well, no. It would have to have been one or two people because it's a small room.

A: Hmmm. That's cool.

Q: If you'd known about it, would you have gone?

A: I don't know. There's the time thing.

Q: What might help you learn about offerings at the Center—assuming that some-day you might have time?

A: Oh, I don't know. I don't even really read my mail these days. Judy takes care of all that. Does the Center send out announcements?

Q: Yes, it does.

A: Well, she must throw them away because I never see them. But she's busy too.

Q: Again, is there any way the Center could get to you?

A: When I finish my degree, that's a different story. Right now, I'm not sure I'd even want to know if Andres Segovia were playing!

OC: Clearly, the Center and its program of offerings are not part of Sal's everyday life. This interview felt difficult, but we did establish that Sal loves music. I also learned that he doesn't get information about the Center's activities. If he knew about some of the offerings, he might take advantage of them. I'll have to check up on how they disseminate information about what's happening. Obviously, Sal is not one of the "drop-ins."

[Anthony is learning that interviewing people who do not participate and have little knowledge about the community arts program is, indeed, difficult. He did well to pick up on Sal's interest in music, however. This may be an important insight for the program staff to consider. Also, Anthony should pursue this idea of "drop-ins."]

MARLA'S DATA

Marla is an experienced health care professional who, early in her career, helped build a clinic in a Central American village. She sees herself as an activist and hopes to improve the U.S. health care system for poor women, so she has come to the university for a master's degree in public health. Although she is not certain about the specific aspect of health care that she wants to attack, she is sure that the recipients of the care should take part in posing the questions. Her greatest concern has been how the people in her study are affected by the health care system, so she has involved the study participants in seeking answers and determining how the answers could be used. Her experiences as a Latina in the United States have taught her that collaboration is more effective than competition for changing any system. She is intrigued by the experiences of poor women but does not want to impose her views on them. She has chosen, therefore, a participatory action research strategy. Through volunteering at the clinic where she used to work, Marla has identified a small group of women who live in the neighborhood and are committed to discovering ways to improve health services and to take action. The possibility that research can be coupled with action appeals to her proactive nature. She believes that the world can be changed for the better.

As it has unfolded over the semester, Marla's study has two purposes: (1) to facilitate a team of women that engages in participatory inquiry about health care services and (2) to summarize the processes of this inquiry and what the women discover, and then to report it to Professor Kent for the course requirements. As often occurs with participatory action research, Marla feels torn between activism with the community and the demands of the academic world.

As the study has evolved, she and her team have focused on three women whose experiences in obtaining health services are problematic. To satisfy the requirements of the course at the university, the study results in mini descriptive case studies of these three women. For Marla's personal work in the clinic and with the community, she hopes that the study will lead to action intended to change the clinic to better meet poor women's needs. Midway through the study, several possible courses of action have been identified by the women and Marla.

Early on in this participatory action research, in dialogue with one another, Marla and her team identified *failure to return for follow-up visits* as a major problem, one shared by the women and by clinic staff. They decided to identify three women who live in the community, had visited the clinic within the past 6 months, and were willing to share their experiences with health services. Together, the team talked about strategies for dialogue with the women and developed an initial set of guidelines. The following excerpts from interviews were conducted by Marla. The observation notes were taken at the health clinic by team members Julia and Aida. Marla, as a volunteer, has been doing informal participant observation. She makes notes about these experiences when she returns home in the evening. The team has reviewed the interview transcriptions and observations. You will see the researcher's comments and our comments throughout the excerpts. Remember, the team members' comments are in **bold** and our comments are in *italics*.

Interview 1

10/22 Interview with Teresa, woman who used clinic but didn't come back. Done in Spanish and translated. Open-ended questions. M means me (Marla); T means Teresa; MC means my comments added while transcribing. About one-half hour.

M: You've heard about the group of women I am with? We're talking with women like you who've lived in the neighborhood for a year or more. We want to know about what kind of services are important to you. Especially health services. Tell me a little bit about yourself. Do you like living here? *[Good beginning; acknowledges that Teresa has recently moved here from the Island.]*

T: It's not so bad. I mean, I have a job. There's food. And the kids. There's lots for them to do. You know, they aren't always hanging around.

M: So, life's maybe a little better here . . . for you?

T: Oh yeah, it's better. Not the weather, but you know, we have more. I never had a wash machine before.

M: So taking care of the clothes is easier?

T: Yes, I even iron the girls' dresses. **[MC: I want to get to health, but I'd rather she brought it up.]**

M: What else do you have here that is important, that maybe you did not have before?

T: Oh, things . . . you know . . . like . . . um . . . oh! Supermarkets! So many choices. You don't have to get just what is at the little market. I don't know if that's so good. (laughs) The kids, you know, eat not so good: lots of potato chips and stuff.

M: Do you ever worry about their health? Or yours?

T: Yeah, but what can I do? I take them to the clinic when I have to. You know, I have to for the school, with all those shots. And the dentist clinic.

M: What about you? Your health?

T: Oh, I don't get sick. **[MC: I know she used the clinic once. Doesn't she remember that? Maybe she doesn't consider that to be sick?]** *[Marla's OC is a bit judgmental.]*

M: So you're pretty tough?

T: (smiles) Maybe so! I don't get so sick.

M: If you did, what would you do?

T: I guess I'd call my cousin. She lives the block over. She'd come help me with the children. **[MC: I wonder if she just doesn't see the clinic and doctors as an option.]**

M: Do you think you'd ever need a doctor? Would you ever use one?

T: Oh, I don't know about doctors. I just don't know. **[MC: I wait here for a few seconds. I'm hoping she will tell me what she means.]** *[Wait time is often needed to allow the person being interviewed to collect her thoughts.]* I think the kids need them for the shots. . . . But I just don't know about doctors. **[MC: Not sure if she means she doesn't trust them or if she doesn't know about doctors—what they are for?]**

M: Do you know anything a doctor could do for you? How to use one?

T: Umm . . . no.

M: But you used the clinic yourself once. Did a doctor help you then?

T: The clinic . . . yes. But I didn't see a doctor. I mean you don't see a *doctor* at the clinic. Do you?

M: Do you remember who treated you? What they said? What they did?

T: I remember. I had red spots on my skin. A nice woman looked at it. She gave me cream. It went away.

M: Did you ever go back? Did they tell you to come back?

T: Maybe. But I had the cream. The red came back once, so I used what was left. Why should I go back?

M: Did the woman who treated you seem to know what she was doing? Did she explain everything to you? **[MC: I should not have asked her both of these questions at once, but I want her to talk in general about the experience at the clinic.]** *[Marla's politics are showing here; she could have asked a more neutral question about the service.]*

T: I guess so. She told me how to use the cream. I didn't ask her anything else.

M: Can you think back to the whole visit to the clinic . . . and tell me why you came, what you were thinking about as you were there, as you waited, how you explained your problem, how you were treated? Just kind of tell me the whole story. *[Excellent question.]*

T: I didn't have to wait too long. And it was pretty comfortable. I was kinda scared, 'cause I didn't know what the place was like. I came because my boss noticed the red. He told me to come. I didn't know. They were real nice, but they acted like I should have known what to do. I didn't know how to fill out the papers they gave me. **[MC: I realize how much she does not know. I guess we need to let people know!]** Yolanda, she's my oldest daughter, she was with me. She helped me. I got called into a room. Everything was real clean. The woman in the blue blouse came in. Asked me so many questions. She was real smart. I don't think she was a doctor. She said her name was Sara, not doctor somebody. I didn't understand all that she said. But I liked her. And the cream worked. **[MC: Ah, she's talking. It sounds as if the clinic is not an integral part of the community. She would not have come if her boss had not told her to. Now I have specific questions. Let's see if she would go back.]**

[This is a good preliminary, getting-to-know-you interview. Marla has asked about Teresa's experiences and probed to discover her knowledge about the clinic's services. She also has asked some leading questions, ones that indicate where her political interests lie. Because Marla's work is explicitly oriented toward political action, such questions are consistent with her paradigm. She might want to consider whether she is allowing Teresa to fully express her own views, however. From this interview, Marla has developed some insights into how the clinic is perceived by Teresa and has identified strands to follow up on in subsequent interviews.]

Interview 2

10/23 Interview with Yvette, young woman who visited clinic about 6 weeks ago with some breathing problems. Didn't come to scheduled follow-up visit. Researcher = Marla; Woman = Yvette.

Researcher: Tell me about the first time you went to the clinic. *[Good beginning question.]*

Woman: Well, I had to walk over from the bus stop and it was raining . . . really pouring. I had two bags of groceries and it felt like they weighed a ton! It was hard . . . so hard. That stupid girl behind the desk—she acted like I wasn't even there. Looked right through me. Just yammered on the phone.

Researcher: Yeah, getting to the clinic isn't very easy. I had to take two buses to get here.

Woman: So what do you want to talk with me about?

Researcher: Well, all about the clinic and how you feel about it. Seems like when you first went, you didn't feel too welcome when you got there, right? *[This could be a leading question, but Marla is asking for corroboration of an impression she has.]*

Woman: Yeah, it was pretty uncomfortable.

Researcher: Tell me about that some more. *[Excellent elaboration question.]*

Woman: Well, that stupid girl. . . . You know. If I wasn't having so much trouble breathing, I think I would have left.

Researcher: What happened? What'd she do?

Woman: When she finally got off the phone—and it was her boyfriend, I think—she asked me a million questions and typed them into her stupid computer. Then she had me sit back down and fill out one of those long information sheets . . . you know, the ones that ask you if you sleep at night, how often you have a glass of water . . . questions that don't have anything to do with my breathing.

Researcher: Did you fill it out?

Woman: Most of it. Some of it seems pretty stupid. Then I had to sit there and wait. Seemed like forever. I almost got to see a whole episode of *As the World Turns!* Then the nurse called me in.

Researcher: So you finally got to see a doctor?

Woman: No! I changed into one of those little white things and sat in an examining room but there was no TV in there! (laughs)

Researcher: Well, what did you do?

Woman: There was a magazine with recipes that was lying there. Something about eating "light and healthy."

Researcher: And then the doctor came in?

Woman: No, it was one of those . . . what do they call them? Physician's assistants?

Researcher: And what did he do? *[This series of questions assumes a linear storytelling mode; the woman might respond more fully if she could structure the narrative herself.]*

Woman: Oh, it was a "she" and she was okay.

Researcher: What did she do?

Woman: She examined me and asked me some questions about my "lifestyle."

Researcher: What did she mean?

Woman: Kinds of foods I eat, about my apartment, alcohol, where I work.

Researcher: Did she help you? *[Marla has asked a series of yes/no questions; she could ask for more elaboration.]*

Woman: She said she thought it might be asthma but because it's not really bad, she wanted to try something to prevent it. So she gave me an inhaler.

Researcher: Did she tell you how to use it?

Woman: Yeah, I was supposed to breathe it four times a day.

Researcher: Did she give you any special instructions?

Woman: Just that I had to be sure to do it regularly.

Researcher: Did it help?

Woman: No. I finally gave up. It seemed more trouble than it was worth. I did it for about a week. You know, I'd carry it in my pocketbook to work and I'd pull it out and I'd puff on it. People around me would laugh. The supervisor asked me to go into the back when I had to do it. He didn't like it; thought it might make the customers nervous. It just got to be more trouble. And, I wasn't breathing any better.

Researcher: Did you ever think about going back to the clinic again to get something else?

Woman: Naw, it's so far, and it takes so much time. It just didn't seem worth it.

Researcher: What could the clinic do to make it better? *[Excellent question to elicit her hopes for the clinic.]*

Woman: Sure! Open a branch right next to where I work. And cut down on all the wait time. Maybe hire more people or get more efficient. I don't even have any kids yet and I can't find time. How do they think they can serve people with big families? It's gotta be easier. Oh yeah, one more thing: Hire people to work behind the desk who are nice. People like us. People from the neighborhood. You know, I tried to call them once but I got put on hold forever, and when I finally got a real person, she made me feel ignorant, like I shouldn't have been asking the question.

Researcher: Well, this has been real helpful. I might come and talk with you again. Would that be okay? And we'd like to ask you if you'd be interested in joining a group of women who meet once every 2 weeks—right near here—to talk about the ways the clinic can serve them better. Think you might be interested?

Woman: I'll think about it.

[This interview helps Marla and her team to establish more fully the experience of being placed in the impersonal bureaucracy of the clinic with its "wait time" and requests for information. It also depicts how this woman left the clinic with insufficient understanding about her asthma and the use of the inhaler. This is important infor-mation for the team to probe more deeply in order to explore the reasons why women do not feel comfortable returning to the clinic for follow-up care. In a subsequent team meeting, they hypothesize that (a) the woman was not told clearly that she should return (information) and (b) she may have felt depersonalized there because of her class, gender, or ethnicity (institutionalized oppression).]

Field Notes 1

10/10. 6:46 p.m. Clinic. Observation by Julia Waiting area is about 12' × 15' with col-orful (red, blue, orange, black) plastic-covered chairs arranged in groups around the room. TV hanging from ceiling in north corner. Piles of magazines around. Smell of over-brewed coffee coming from the dispenser in the corner mixed with smell of Vicks cough drops and cheap perfume. Receptionist sitting behind counter working at her computer. It's quiet. Three groups here. One's a mother, father, and three kids. Talking Spanish. Father's arm is around mother; little girl on mother's lap. Other two playing with puzzle on floor. Kids look close together in age; maybe 4 to 6? One on lap about 2? Little girl is coughing, sneezing, looks like she's got a fever. *[What does it mean to look feverish?]* Two old men, unshaven, drab-colored baggy clothes. One is dozing off; the other is smiling at the little kids. Both drinking coffee from dispenser in the corner. **[Here to see a doctor or just to watch TV? May be homeless.]** Young girl obvi-ously pregnant wearing short, tight dress, lots of jewelry and makeup. Long hair pulled back in a clip. Guy with her is much older, dressed flashy (polyester suit, earrings, long, stringy hair in ponytail, cowboy boots).

7:01 p.m. Nothing's really happened.

7:03 p.m. Door opens from back and tall woman with arm in sling walks out; stops at reception desk, makes another appointment, leaves.

7:06 p.m. Middle-aged man comes out; dressed in jeans and sweatshirt; talks with receptionist, appears to pay bill, leaves.

7:10 p.m. Nothing happening. **[These people have been here waiting for at least a half an hour! I'm going to have to leave soon; I hope something happens soon.]**

7:15 p.m. Two physician's assistants (PAs) wearing blue jackets come out from room behind counter. One calls for the Ariaga family; the other for Lucy. Father stays with two kids playing with puzzle; mother carries little girl into back area. Father pats mother's arm as she leaves. Lucy pushes herself up; her man continues his reading, pays no attention at all. *[Focus is on interaction between clients rather than clinic staff and clients; might want to redirect or refocus based on this interest.]* **[People seem comfortable here: reading, watching TV, playing with games; almost like a hotel lobby.]** *[Excellent descriptions: positive, neutral, nonjudgmental.]*

7:21 p.m. Still quiet; we're just sitting here!

7:23 p.m. Woman comes in; 30-something; curly brown hair, dark eyes; drags in resistant preadolescent girl; registers with receptionist and takes seat. Girl's eyes are sullen; mother touches her arm, she jerks it away. Mother picks up *Good Housekeeping;* girl picks up *People.*

7:30 p.m. No changes; I have to leave.

OC: (added later) I continue to wonder what the old men were there for and what the interactions in the examining rooms were like, especially for the mother and her little girl and the pregnant girl. Seemed like a long time to wait; I wonder if that's typical. I'm curious about the receptionist too; she seemed okay with the men (a little flirty?) but was cool with the women. Wonder what's going on there.

[These field notes are detailed, specifically around the passage of time. Because the team knows that clinic visits can entail seemingly endless waiting, these field notes are useful as data describing waiting. They also identify gender issues as having a potential role in the experiences of women who use the clinic.]

Field Notes 2

11/3. Clinic Observation. Early Evening (5:30 p.m.). Observation by Aida The place is buzzing. Three people waiting for the receptionist. She's tied up with one of the PAs who's trying to explain something to her. Moving around the room clockwise, I see three guys—late teens, early 20s—wearing jeans and leather jackets. They're talking together—complaining about how there's no smoking allowed. Next is a woman whose photo I've seen in the community newspaper. She's really attractive *[Who defines attractive? What does it mean? Is it culturally defined?]*, in her 40s, tall, and has on a charcoal gray tailored suit, high heels, earrings, and a bracelet. **[I think she is**

principal of the school.] Beyond her chair are two old men. They are pretty creepy: mesmerized by the TV, grubby clothing. All I hear from them is an occasional grunt or chuckle. *[Again note the use of "creepy"; does the team define this?]* One spills coffee on his already-stained pants.

Two kids are sitting doing puzzles. They keep arguing softly and every now and then break into laughter. **[Are they alone or waiting for someone else's parent?]**

Bang! The door to the back rooms is thrown open. Short middle-aged woman with wild hair comes storming out. She's yammering away, a mile a minute, but I can't understand. What language is that? A man in one of those blue shirts comes out with her **[I think this one is a doctor; he's an Anglo]**, trying to calm her down and tell her to be patient but he's not having much luck. Turns to receptionist, asks her something. I see them roll their eyes. Receptionist brings up something on the computer screen; PA shows it to the woman. She yells at him and turns to leave, charging out through the doors. He shrugs and walks back into the examining rooms. **[Who does he think he is? She really seemed upset, and I'm not sure he tried all that hard.]**

Everyone was really quiet listening to this and watching. After she leaves, a couple of people exchange looks and shrug their shoulders. The two old men lean over and whisper to each other; then they go back to their TV show. **[I can't really hear what the old men say but guess it has to do with the woman.]**

Woman in her 30s, looking really tired, comes in carrying two shopping bags from Food Lion. Waits at receptionist's desk for several minutes. Looks exasperated. I can hear her hacking cough all the way across the room. Woman taps her foot. **[Impatient?]** Finally talks with receptionist; her tone is belligerent. Receptionist is "all business." *[What does this mean?]*

I've been here 45 minutes, with no halt in the action. Gotta go now.

[These field notes focus on interactions and capture some of the action that takes place in the clinic. Lots of terms were used that will need to be fleshed out for the field notes to be more concrete and detailed: "attractive" and "creepy," for example. They also further identify potential issues of role, class, gender, and ethnicity as important analytic insights. These will be focused on more fully as the study progresses.]

Field Notes 3

11/9. 9:00 p.m. Clinic Observation Marla's tape recording, made (with permission of PAs and receptionist) in the reception area. Two PAs and the receptionist are present. A woman, 40ish, enters.

PA1:   Want some coffee?

R: Naw, might keep me up. Ha. Ha.

PA2:   Jeez, we need to organize these files. I can't find anything here.

R: That's because you don't know where to look! There's a system.

PA2:   So, if it's your system and no one else can figure it out, what good does it do? How am I supposed to serve my patients if I can't find anything?

R: Oh, I'm sorry, I didn't see you. Can I help you?

W: That person tell me to give you this.

R: Who?

W: That one in the blue blouse. Over there.

R: Hey, Randy. What's this?

[Pause, maybe 40 seconds. Background noise.]

W: Please. I need to get home.

R: Randy, a little help here.

PA2:   So, what do you want me to do? I'm trying to make sense of your system.

R: Let's see . . . I see you need another appointment.

W: But what I do now?

PA1:   Give it to me, Tina. Let's see . . . give Mrs. Lee the prescription. Mrs. Lee, can you take this to the pharmacy tomorrow morning and get it filled? But for now . . . don't we have some samples lying around?

[Pause. Background noise.]

PA1:   Here you go. I'll give you a couple of tubes, in case you can't get to the pharmacy tomorrow. And be sure to make the appointment with Tina.

R: The PA needs to see you in 3 weeks. How about December 1? That's right after Thanksgiving. Ten in the morning? Good. I wrote it on this card for you, Mrs. Lee.

W: Thank you.

[Pause. Background noise.]

PA2:   OK, I found what I was looking for. So, Tina, what did you want?

[This tape recording captures an ambiguous interaction that could depict deeper patterns in the clinic, specifically indicating how some health care professionals view women patients. This is an example of a "naturally occurring" discourse that Marla and her team can analyze using sociolinguistic tools of discourse analysis to interpret this exchange. They will need considerably more data like these to begin to feel confident in their analyses, but this excerpt is an excellent start.]

RUTH'S DATA

Ruth is an undergraduate student majoring in psychology. She is also an avid athlete. At the university, she has been goalie for the lacrosse team and often works out in the gym early in the morning. For the past several years, she has worked in a summer camp for children with disabilities. She enjoys working with children, especially through athletics, and helped design a 3-day wilderness course for deaf children. She volunteers one afternoon a week in a local elementary school and, through her qualitative research project, at the Culverton After School Center. She has found that her qualitative research, linked to phenomenological traditions, has deepened her understanding of the lived experiences of students with disabilities. When designing her study, she anticipated doing some observing at the center but wanted to focus her data gathering on in-depth interviews. She has found that interviewing children can be challenging and exciting, as noted in Chapter 7.

Recall that the purpose of Ruth's phenomenological study is to uncover the deep inner meaning of *bodied-ness* for children with physical handicaps. She hoped that her study would produce rich cultural description through stories of these children's relationships with sports. The *central concept of bodied-ness* would be explicated through the children's words and her interpretations of the meanings they express. Her initial design has changed over the course of her research. She began by volunteering at the Culverton After School Center where she knew children with physical disabilities who attended regularly.

While observing at Culverton's pickup basketball games, she noticed that one of the "regulars" is an early adolescent girl—Katrine—who is profoundly deaf. Her skills in basketball are quite impressive. Ruth, because of her experience with the wilderness program for deaf students, becomes fascinated with this young woman and asks her to participate in the study. At this point, she has conducted two of the series of three interviews recommended by phenomenological methodologists with Mark, a boy who uses a wheelchair, and one of the three with Katrine. She has also interviewed one parent and one teacher.

In this section, we offer sample transcripts of Ruth's interviews and field notes. Recall that the text of the interviews and the field notes are formatted in regular type; Ruth's comments as the researcher are in **bold;** our comments are in *italics*. Ruth has word-processed all of these excerpts, elaborating points where necessary and adding OCs at the end of each excerpt. These observer comments are indicated by **OC**. Some of Ruth's comments were added while transcribing and word processing her interviews and observations; other notes were made at the time. In some cases, the timing is unclear. Below are selections from the field notes Ruth has taken while observing at the center 2 afternoons a week. These are followed by excerpts from interviews she has conducted with Katrine, who is in the eighth grade, and Mark, a fifth grader.

Field Notes 1

9/24. Culverton After School Center I got there at about 3:00 p.m. Took some notes then wrote these afterward. Tried to take myself back into the scene, like Kent said.

Culverton After School Center is housed in an old reconverted elementary school building. The entrance looks like the entry to almost any old school you know: linoleum tiles underfoot, yellowish lighting, coats hanging on wall hooks, boots and shoes strewn across the floor, backpacks dropped in piles. I enter soon after the children, so their noise and chaos linger. Patsy, one of the aides, makes a futile attempt to push the droppings toward the walls so the pathway is clear. I can see hand smudges on the cream-green walls. Already, I feel the familiar warmth and moderate grime of a place where children are moving too fast to be orderly and too busy to wash. *[Excellent description.]*

I enter the large room to the left, where snacks are spread out on a table. I estimate about 25 to 30 kids from about second grade to middle school age. One group has already gobbled up the snacks and is heading to the closets that hold the gym equipment. I see one boy squirt a juice box all over the wall and floor in the corner. Nobody but me catches his act. He giggles and sprints away. **[I wondered how much juice and other food-stuff coated these walls! Yuck!]** Actually, only half of them are going to the gym. The other half are going to the art room. A few are carrying books. Later I found out that they probably went to the "quiet room" to read. There is also a game room.

I look for the kids in wheelchairs. I know that there are eight in all. Three (Amanda, Mark, and Jill) are with the group going to the gym. Another (Winnie) is in the art room. Sammy usually goes to the reading place so he's probably there. I can't see **[and didn't find out]** where the other three are. So far, the ones I see seem to be part of the crowd of kids. I can pick them out, but they don't *stand* out. I decide to follow the kids going to the gym. **[Already I'm thinking about how I can get to talk to the girls and boys in wheelchairs. I don't want to be too formal, at least not at first. Right now, I'm just standing there.]** A boy throws a ball at me, nearly hitting me in the nose. He calls to me, "We need another person on our side. Wanna play?" So I drop my notebook and join in. I see that Amanda is on the other team. She's in the middle of their players. Jill is off to the side: She doesn't go onto the court. She looks like she's going to cheer. I see that Mark is on our team. I start to watch Amanda play, but the ball comes to me, and I get into the game. I do notice that she makes two baskets. *[Ruth captures both actions and dialogue here.]*

After the game, I get to talking to the kids. They ask me who I am. I tell them I'm a student at the university, and I want to see what they do at the center. They ask a dozen questions. **[Most I *can* NOT even answer!]** Then I ask them to introduce themselves. **[Their identities are on the attached sheet.]** We talk about playing basketball, and they tell me about the league they belong to. One laughs about how it's the only league where kids do wheelies on the floor. **[I'm surprised that Amanda is their captain. I want to find out about that. And I wonder how she learned to play.]** The talk is moving fast so I can't get it all. Then we play some more.

When it's time for parents to come, I walk to the entrance with Amanda. She is kidding me about my team losing. I hand over her coat from its hook, and she wheels out.

OC: This was my first try at observing and recalling afterward what I saw. I took some notes while there, but it seemed real awkward to be writing in a notebook all the time. I just wanted to get involved with the kids, like at the elementary school. But I really had fun. The kids are terrific and seemed to like having another adult around. *[Ruth is being reflexive about her role at the center.]* I am already fascinated by how these kids manage to get a basketball game going. I don't know what data these notes are, but I think I'm getting a sense of the Center and the kids.

[Ruth's field notes are very well done. She describes the setting so that the reader can visualize it; she notes actions and movement from setting to setting, and she notes some of the conversation that occurs as the children go about their activities. Recall that her initial field notes, taken at the center, have been word processed and elaborated after the observation. In part, her ability to create rich field notes comes from this discipline of allocating time after an observation to fill in remembered details of action and dialogue.]

Field Notes 2

10/3. Culverton After School Center I arrive a bit later than usual, so the entry hall is empty except for the backpacks and jackets. That familiar school smell is in the air—salty food, mustiness, floor wax, all mixed with a hint of cleanser. The kids are already in their activities. I can hear the basketball game in progress; I'm told there's one nearly every afternoon. I head for the gym. The game is in full swing. I can sit on the side and take these notes.

Everyone is so engaged in the game that it takes me a minute to realize again that two of the players are in wheelchairs. **[They look so at home on the court!]** I recognize Amanda—she's wheeling to guard a large (bulky, not tall) boy who just missed getting the ball. Curtis got it and takes off. Suddenly, a tall—I mean, really tall, nearly six feet—girl streaks in from nowhere and steals it. She's lovely. *[What does she mean by "lovely"?]* **[Jill has wheeled over next to me and whispers, "That's Katrine. Isn't she wonderful?"]** Katrine passes the ball to Mark (he's in a wheelchair and was on my team both times I played before). Mark takes the ball and, holding it cradled in his lap, wheels down the court after Amanda, Katrine, and the other two. He pats his head three times. **[I find out later this means that Amanda will set up a pick for Katrine, who will cut to the basket.]** He passes the ball to Joey, who feeds the ball to Katrine. She grabs the ball, nearly fouling Curtis, dribbles once, and puts it in for two. **[Wow! I'm out of breath.]**

The large boy (I think he's called Diego) walks over and says something to Mark, who is off the wall by now. Mark wheels his chair around and bangs into the wall—vehemently. **[What's going on here?]** Amanda calls out, "Mark, get over here!" So he quickly wheels back in place. He's ready to take a pass again from Katrine. And it happens all over again: Mark's "carry" down the court, the signals, the setup, the basket by Katrine. This time

Diego calls out something **[I cannot make it out],** and Mark wheels over and bumps him. They nearly scuffle, but Joey and Curtis break it up. Joey actually wheels Mark away from Diego. Both Joey and Curtis give Diego "the cold shoulder." *[Again, specifics of body language would help describe "the cold shoulder."]* Diego struts off.

Almost as if there had been no interruption, the court action starts again. Curtis has the ball. He dribbles through Amanda's blocking and passes to another boy I do not remember, who shoots and misses. Joey gets the ball. This time, Joey carries it down the court and passes to Mark. **[Did I catch a signal from Katrine? I think she touched her shoulder twice, but I'm not sure it was a signal.]** Mark shoots and gets two! Katrine steals the ball on the inbounds pass and drops it into the basket again. Again, Jill whispers to me about how she admires Katrine. **[The action is so fast, I'm sure I'm missing a lot.]** I notice that Mark "carries" the ball a lot and that Katrine makes a lot of baskets. They are almost partners. In fact, their team seems to be a tight unit. Jill has interpreted some of their signals for me. **[Do they know each other well? Play a lot together? I see them use hand signals a lot—it seems part of their play. Have they worked this out before?]**

After about 20 minutes of action, they take a break. Most of the kids get their water bottles from the side near where I'm sitting. Jill tells them how good the game is and asks one of the girls **[I don't recognize her]** if she is feeling better. **[I guess she was sick last week.]** Joey and Mark are laughing together about some shared amusement. Then Joey goes over to Amanda and Katrine and the other girl and begins to bother them. I can't catch what he is saying, but they seem annoyed. *[How does she know this?]* I hear Amanda say, "Oh, grow up, will you?" Mark wheels over to the wall and rams it with his wheelchair. Joey grabs the back of his chair and wheels him onto the court again, calling out, "Come on, let's get started." Curtis says he has to go home now, so Amanda asks me if I want to play. I put down my pad and pencil and join them.

We play for about another 45 minutes. I am amazed with how fast they all are. Amanda truly seems to enjoy herself. Mark is always in motion—whether or not there is court action. And he's noisy—he's always calling out to the other kids. That's one way I learned their names. But I noticed that he still uses the hand signals. That tall girl, Katrine, is sooooo good; she really knows basketball and knows how to keep things moving. She's fascinating. When the session is over, I stay behind with Jill and Joey to put away the balls while the others walk to the front. They are talking about how Katrine played last Friday on the middle school team.

OC: I need to find out more about Katrine. Who is she? I also need to find out about how they came to use those hand signals. Another follow-up: Mark and that large boy (Diego?)—seems to be some tension there.

[Ruth's field notes are exceptionally "alive." They take the reader into the action of the basketball court, as if we were in the gym with her. Her descriptions capture the

actions: what people are doing and how it looks. As we have commented in this set of notes, however, Ruth needs to work on providing more specific detail: What does she mean by "lovely," "the cold shoulder," "annoyed"? These terms clearly mean something to her but are open to various interpretations by others. As she gets feedback from Kent, her skills will grow.]

Interview 1

10/5. Second Interview With Mark At his home in the Heights section. Early evening. Only his aunt is at home. In the first interview, I got to know him pretty well. Seems like a neat kid but sometimes a real pain at the Center—teasing the girls, bumping his wheelchair into the walls (I think on purpose), yelling out a lot. Need to focus on what he likes about playing in that pickup game after school.

Ruth: Good game, today, eh?

Mark: Yeah, not bad.

Ruth: How do you think you played?

Mark: Sometimes I do better. I didn't make any baskets today.

Ruth: I noticed you banging your wheelchair sometimes.

Mark: Oh, that. Yeah.

Ruth: What's going on when you do that?

Mark: I got pretty mad at Diego today.

Ruth: Why? What did he do?

Mark: Aw, he thinks he's so big.

Ruth: What do you mean, "big?"

Mark: Big! He's older than me and he's always letting me know.

Ruth: So you mean older, not taller? *[Asking for clarification.]*

Mark: Nope. . . . Not really. . . . I guess I mean both.

Ruth: Talk to me about that.

Mark: Naw. [pause] Well, you know, I bet I'm taller than he is but he doesn't know that. . . . because of *this*. [Bangs arms of wheelchair]

Ruth: But I've seen you play. *I've* been on your team and you make a lot of baskets.

Mark: Yeah, more'n Diego.

Ruth: So who's the better player?

Mark: No contest! I am! [laughs]

Ruth: Do you really think so?

Mark: Yeah, most of the time, I'm better.

Ruth: Say I were sitting in the stands watching the game and you're playing better than Diego. What would I see you doing? *[Excellent probing strategy.]*

Mark: Silly! I'd make more baskets!

Ruth: Oh, come on. You know basketball is much more than making baskets, Mark. Give me a break! What else would I see you doing? *[Another excellent probing question.]*

Mark: I have the ball more often. . . . That's Diego's problem: He's all over the place so he never gets the ball.

Ruth: So how do you get the ball?

Mark: I use my wheels. I can move faster. I'm The Dominator! *[She could have probed here, asking him how.]*

Ruth: So your wheelchair actually helps?

Mark: Well, I don't know. I just know that I use it. **[Sense of agency????]**

Ruth: What's it feel like being better than him? *[Awkwardness here; she should have asked him to elaborate.]*

Mark: Cool!

Ruth: Yeah, I'll bet. *[She is assuming that she knows what he means by "cool."]* You're better than Diego, but are you the star?

Mark: No! I said I'm The Dominator!

Ruth: But what does that mean? *[Here she asks him to elaborate.]*

Mark: I told you: I control the ball on the floor.

Ruth: Then you're really the Floor General, right?

Mark: Yeah, man.

Ruth: How do the other kids feel about that?

Mark: That's the problem with Diego; he doesn't want me to be. He wants it all for himself. But the other kids? . . . I guess they've figured that that's how to use me. And anyway, it's only an after-school league; it's not like it's the high school team.

OC: Interviewing Mark was tough. He's bright and cute but bounces all over in his wheelchair. Seems a bundle of energy all the time. It was hard getting him to be more reflective. I wonder if I should continue this with him. He talks better when we're doing something together, like hanging out around the Center practicing layups. Maybe this idea of three long interviews won't work with him. Frustrating.

[Interviewing 10- and 11-year-olds has real challenges. Ruth is learning that she will have impressions about Mark's life and worldview, but these are only glimpses into a complex life experience. When an interview does not go as well as a beginning researcher hopes, she may be inclined to doubt the whole process. Ruth's reflections about whether she has chosen a genre and design that make sense for research with children are important for her to ponder and consider. This is part of her learning in the field: learning not only about the children and their experiences with "bodied-ness" but also about qualitative research methods and assessing the usefulness of specific techniques for exploring her topic. Although not aware of it yet, Ruth is beginning to understand that what we learn in a study is always partial and incomplete. Learning to live with that ambiguity will become a disposition that Ruth embodies as she finalizes her project.]

Interview 2

10/9. First Interview With Katrine She *is* the star! Her interpreter's here. I know some signs but not a lot. Katrine has some oral language; that helps, but Joanie makes it easier.

Ruth:	Thanks for agreeing to talk to me. You know that I'm real interested in how you feel about basketball and how you got to be so good. I've talked with Mark some and been around the Center.
Katrine:	Yeah, I've seen you. You don't play too bad yourself. **[I'm trying to keep eye contact with K rather than with her interpreter. Not as hard as I thought because K speaks okay.]**
Ruth:	Thanks. So what started you in basketball?
Katrine:	Well, I've got four older brothers and they'd take me outside to the driveway where our dad put up a hoop. We'd shoot for hours. That started when I was real little . . . like around 4.
Ruth:	So this was a way you hung out with your brothers?
Katrine:	Yeah. That was about the only time they'd pay attention to me. And it was neat! I loved it. I had my four big brothers all to myself!
Ruth:	I've got a brother, but he never played basketball with me!
Katrine:	Oh, but I was really good!

Ruth: When did you know you were really good?

Katrine: I guess I've always known. They wouldn't have played with me if I couldn't have kept up with them. At least after they taught me the basics.

Ruth: Do you remember how they taught you? *[Good question; asking her to recall early experiences.]*

Katrine: Boy, it seemed like a lot of drill but . . . they were pretty patient with me.

Ruth: Do you remember anything specific? *[Another good question; asking for details.]*

Katrine: They were bigger than me, so they always had the ball. I got tired of them always having it. So they had to teach me how to steal the ball. That worked pretty well when I was little and could wiggle in between them. Now I'm nearly 6 feet and it's not so easy! [laughs]

Ruth: Other ways you knew you were good? *[Ruth has shifted away from exploring how Katrine's brothers taught her; she could have probed more here.]*

Katrine: Well, my mom talked to me about basketball camp when I was 10. That was a clue. You know, I just play here because I like the other kids. It's not like playing over at the middle school.

Ruth: I wondered because I've seen you here a lot, and you're really much better than the others.

Katrine: Well, I got to know Amanda and Mark and some of the others because my mom works and I have to come here when I don't have practice over at the school.

Ruth: So you see this as practice?

Katrine: Yeah. Maybe. I think it's a different kind of drill. Some of the kids are in wheelchairs, so it's all different. And sometimes I know I'm teaching them, too, but I try not to let it show.

Ruth: When I watch you on the court, it seems like you really enjoy playing. Is that true?

Katrine: [Big smile] Yeah. Here it's okay to be tall. Other places, people stare at me or make jokes. Sometimes, if I'm not looking, I don't get the jokes, but I can see it in their faces.

Ruth: I was wondering about your hearing. *[A delicate topic to bring up.]*

Katrine: It's OK to call me deaf! I am, just like I'm tall.

Ruth:	**[This felt weird to me—embarrassing]** OK. OK. Sorry. Are there any times when being deaf is a problem on the basketball court?
Katrine:	Well, sure! You've got kids out there in wheelchairs—they can't move around too well—and you've got me—I don't hear so well!! Somehow we make it work. [Big smile]
Ruth:	What about on the middle school team? *[Not being specific enough; unclear exactly what Ruth means here.]*
Katrine:	I'm just as good there, too. **[K sounds defensive; not a good question.]**
Ruth:	Oh, I know. What I meant is . . . on the school team, how do the other kids signal you when they're passing and you're not looking? What do they do?
Katrine:	It depends. Actually, I've got pretty good peripheral vision, so I can keep my eye on everyone else. That's one of the things that makes me a good player; I know how to pick up signals. My brothers taught me, and my mom says it's easier for me because I'm deaf. And you know, she told me about hearing a couple of girls sitting on the risers during a game. My mom was right in front of them and heard one say to the others something about how my being *deaf* made me a better player. When she told me, I hooted.
Ruth:	Do you think it does?
Katrine:	Well, you know, I'm not sure. It sure isn't a handicap.
Ruth:	Do you think of yourself as having a disability?
Katrine:	I'm not sure. That word is pretty weird, and deaf people don't like it much. I just don't think of myself that way. **[Need to probe how she feels about being deaf.]**

OC: Interviewing K was a pleasure! She seems poised and confident. I wonder if some of that comes from being so good at basketball. *[Beginnings of analysis here; trying to make connections.]* It felt awkward when I asked about playing on the middle school team; she got defensive and it was a bad question. *[Good critical reflection.]* Sometimes it was slow, with the interpreter going back and forth, but it worked okay. I'm glad I could keep eye contact with K rather than Joanie, though it was hard at times. The idea of *agency* keeps coming to mind. *[Important analytic insight.]*

[There are real differences in the reflectiveness and openness of Mark and Katrine. Katrine is mature and articulate; Mark is less interested in and less able to reflect on his lived experience. This makes phenomenological interviewing particularly challenging with younger children. Should Ruth pursue a more substantial study on this topic, she might well decide to focus on older children or to alter her methods of gathering data.]

ACTIVITIES FOR YOUR COMMUNITY OF PRACTICE

Study Questions

- What are Marla's, Ruth's, and Anthony's decisions about observing?

- How do Marla, Ruth, and Anthony take field notes? What different strategies do they use?

- What feedback would you give them about their interviewing? What might they do to improve?

Small-Group and Dyad Activities

Evaluating Field Notes

You have read samples of Marla's, Ruth's, and Anthony's field notes in this chapter. In small groups, critique their field notes, paying particular attention to the following:

- How the notes link to their research questions

- How carefully the events or activities are documented

- What is missing

- Where they may become judgmental

- Where they may jump to conclusions

- The techniques they use to deal with potential biases

- How they capture participant voices

Critiquing the Characters' Interviews

Refer to the interview transcripts in this chapter. As a whole group, critique their interviews, paying particular attention to the following:

- How their questions link to their research questions

- How thoughtfully they followed up

- In what ways they pursued intriguing but unanticipated ideas

- Where they may have become judgmental

- Places they could have probed for more details

- In what ways they guided or did not guide the interview

- How well the transcription seems to have captured the tone and nuance of the interview

- How fully they seem to have captured participant voices

Role-Play Interviews

Role-play the following interviews that our characters have conducted:

- Marla interviews the clinic director about perceived effects of welfare reform on the clinic.

- Anthony interviews Barney, the watercolor instructor.

- Ruth interviews Mark's mother.

Writing Activity

"First Days in the Field": Observing

This activity provides you with the opportunity to engage in systematic observation, write up that observation, and receive feedback on the clarity, detail, and usefulness of your field notes. Because the production of field notes is an integral part of many qualitative studies, learning how to do it is important.

Situate yourself comfortably so that you can closely observe the setting. Note its physical arrangement, the time, the date, who is present (just enumerate if you don't know them), and any particulars that would enliven a description of the setting and events. Record the interactions that you observe in field notes. These are typically verbal interactions coupled to actions (e.g., a teacher talking with a class of students; students' verbal or behavioral responses). If you are particularly interested in something specific (e.g., gender differences in interaction patterns), be sure that your notes record those analytic categories. Your focus during this first phase should be holistic, trying to get a sense of the setting and the patterns in it. Remember to be specific and concrete.

Conversations should be recorded as nearly verbatim as possible. If you paraphrase, indicate so. Develop a coding system that indicates either a direct quote or a paraphrase. Also use a code to indicate your personal reactions to or questions about what you observe.

After about 30 minutes (or when there is a natural conclusion to what you are observing), leave the setting and find a quiet place where you can look over your field notes and add important information or personal reactions you do not have time to record during the observation. Edit the field notes for clarity (handwriting is often difficult to decode when done quickly) and completeness. Note questions that arose or intriguing possibilities that you would like to pursue during your next observation. Identify puzzles or questions that could be integrated into an interview. When you have access to a computer or word processor, enter the field notes but preserve the originals. This will provide further opportunity to edit the field notes for clarity and completeness. Develop a code to replace the names of participants with pseudonyms and use these in the word-processed file.

(Continued)

(Continued)

The written memo of this observation should do three things. First, it should describe the setting in sufficient detail to take the reader "into the setting." Second, it should identify two or three interesting themes or ideas that you might pursue in subsequent observations. These themes or ideas should be supported with paraphrases and direct quotes from your field notes. Be sure that you use pseudonyms for the participants. Finally, you should reflect on the process and identify any difficulties you encountered. These could be personal feelings: for example, self-consciousness, or it could be logistical difficulties: being unsure of what to focus on or being unable to write fast enough. Taking field notes is difficult and tedious, requiring discipline and concentration. And it takes practice.

10

Analyzing and Interpreting Data

Analyzing and interpreting qualitative data is a complex and exciting process of bringing meaning to the piles of data you gather. A single piece of data by itself carries no real meaning. You assign meaning to the pieces as you label, code, and categorize; build analytic descriptions; compare and contrast; find patterns; construct themes; and consider alternatives. The process is both iterative and sequential, and it requires several activities: (1) fully knowing the data (immersion), (2) organizing these data into chunks (analysis), and (3) bringing meaning to those chunks (interpretation). Following Wolcott (1994) and the conventions in the field, we refer to these three distinct activities as analysis but also note that formal analysis (often conflated with coding data) can be understood as a single step in the process. Throughout the analysis process, you become deeply immersed in interview transcripts, field notes, and other materials you have collected; you systematically organize these materials into salient patterns and themes; you bring meaning so the themes tell a coherent story; and you write it all up so that others can read what you have learned.

One way to think about analysis is that it begins at the same time a study does, or at the conceptualization stage. The conceptual framework of the study, the research questions, the strategy for research and design, and the genre to which your study links—all of these provide preliminary foreshadowing of the analysis. Think of analysis as an ongoing and emergent understanding of what you are learning, a process that relies on both *inductive and deductive reasoning*. Saldaña (2015) offers four approaches to analytic thinking: (1) *deduction*—you have an idea of what you are looking for, (2) *abduction*—examining the possibilities and selecting those you want to pay attention to, (3) *induction*—discovering what is going on in what you see and hear, and (4) *retroduction*—reconstructing what happened (see pp. 22–23). We suggest that you will use all four in your analytic process.

Early decisions shape your study. At the beginning of a study, your understanding of the phenomenon you are interested in is preliminary and formalized in the conceptual framework, as we have noted throughout the previous chapters. This framework provides sensitizing concepts that focus the researcher's attention on some facets of the phenomenon of interest and "suggest directions along which to look" (Blumer, 1954, p. 7) for potential coding categories. As you gather data, this framework guides and constrains the data you collect. Moreover, decisions you make in the field focus and refocus the analysis as you discover important but unanticipated ideas and shift emphasis in interviews or observations. All this is part of data analysis and interpretation.

Two metaphors are useful for understanding data analysis. Imagine a closet full of clothes; these are your data. You can organize the clothes by color (blue slacks and sweaters together), by type (all the slacks in one pile), by season for use (heavy winter clothing), or by fabric (cottons all on the same shelf). Each organization (your analysis) is valuable and justifiable, depending on your purpose. As another metaphor, picture a child's playroom filled with toys. Some are dolls, others are trucks and cars, and still others are puzzles and crayons. The child could pull all the red toys together into one pile and the green ones in another. The child could then re-sort the toys into ones that move (trucks and trains), those that can be used to build (Tinkertoys and Legos), or those for drawing with (pencils, markers, and crayons). Data analysis is a similar process of sorting, categorizing, grouping, and regrouping the data into piles or chunks that are meaningful. Be aware that some of the data may fall into more than one category. Plan to group and regroup your data several times throughout the analysis process. One grouping may be deductive as you organize with a plan in mind; another grouping may be either abductive or inductive as you see what

Analysis is . . .

- immersion—knowing the data.
- categorizing and coding—organizing chunks.
- interpretation—meaning making (generating themes).

you have in your data. You may even want to reflect and explain how and why you grouped as you did (retroductive). Each grouping allows you to see different aspects of the data, enriching your understanding and insight into what you have learned.

Throughout a study, you are describing, analyzing, and interpreting data, although different activities may be more focused and instrumental at various times. A particular interview may reorient the direction that your study takes. Observations yield important insights that you pursue in subsequent observations or interviews. This emergent learning (discussed in Chapter 1 and illustrated in Chapters 7, 8, and 9) is the hallmark of qualitative inquiry: *You learn as you go.* The way you organize that learning (the descriptions you provide and the categories and themes you develop) is analysis. The meaning you make of these chunks is interpretation, defined as "a process of insightful invention, discovery or disclosure" (van Manen, 1990, p. 79).

ANALYSIS HAPPENS

The overall analysis strategy in a qualitative study is based on several decisions: when you formally analyze, how open ended or prefigured the analysis is, the genre to which your study links, as well as many other decisions. All your decisions contribute to producing thick descriptions that serve as the foundation for your analyses. Various qualitative methodologists take stands on when and how; we offer our views below.

Analysis Is Ongoing

Many methodological writers present two options for formal analysis: (1) ongoing analysis and (2) analysis at the end of data gathering. As we stated earlier, we believe that analysis starts when you frame the research questions. Experienced fieldworkers tend to describe and analyze as they go. They reflect formally about the data, ask analytic questions, and write descriptive and analytic memos throughout a study. Some beginners find it easier to focus on building relations with participants and gathering data, holding off on formal description and analysis until the end of the study. However, we recommend that everyone try to do some analysis as the study unfolds; it makes final analysis easier and less daunting. Keep in mind the following pointers to facilitate analysis, whether ongoing or toward the end:

- Refer regularly to your conceptual framework—remember that you chose to study this topic or these people for a reason—but be open to new insights. Theories you have identified as relevant can inform and shape preliminary categories.

- Keep your questions in mind. Remember what you are trying to learn. Stay connected to the qualitative genre framing your study.

- Modify your data gathering based on what you are learning, not on chance. Ask analytic questions as you go along.

- Document your decisions at every step in a log that can be used as an audit trail.

- Write all the time. Note down hunches, thoughts, and impressions; write descriptive and analytic memos. Keep a journal and reread it from time to time, or write a letter or e-mail to a friend (be sure you keep a copy).

- Talk your ideas through with people. Develop a community of practice or talk with the participants. Be open to their critique; they often see alternative views you may be missing or are unable to see.

- Read and read and read what others have said about the topic. Use the research literature, movies, novels, poems, and art to gain insight.

- Be creative. Use metaphors, create images, draw pictures, and draw concept maps. Think about how you might characterize what you are learning: What is it like? What images does it evoke?

In addition, practice good management skills for keeping the data organized and accessible. Management facilitates analysis, whether done concurrently or at the end. Discipline yourself to log the day's activities, noting the date, what you did, names, times, and places. This documentation can aid your analyses as well as serve as an audit trail. Transcribe your interviews and type and clean up your field notes immediately. Consider creating tables or matrices to record and store data according to research questions, initial codes or categories, theoretical perspectives, dates, or any other organizing tactic. Table 10.1 illustrates a matrix designed to organize data in response to the research questions: What formal and informal organizational routines allow school counselors to take on leadership? How do school counselors contribute to constructive leadership practices through those routines?

Assign identification codes to the materials you have collected so you can easily locate the data as you analyze it (and so that you can easily cite where the data that you use in writing up come from). Write down attendance at events, chronologies, and descriptions and maps of settings. Do not rely on your memory, which, several months into a study, more than likely will fail you. Build in time in quiet places for note taking. One of our students diligently went to a nearby Dunkin' Donuts shop after each data gathering session to log his activities and write notes about his impressions. Such practices pay off by keeping the data intact, complete, organized, and accessible. They are invaluable for defining categories for data analysis, planning further data collection, and especially for writing the final report. Be diligent in these management tasks!

Manage your data—don't rely on your memory.

Categorical or Holistic Analysis

Qualitative methodologists tend to recognize two sets of overall analytic strategies, one emphasizing the development of analytic categories, the other focusing more on description. Do not think of these strategies as mutually exclusive. They blur into

TABLE 10.1   Formal and Informal Interconnected Routines

Routine	Functions	Leaders and Followers	Leadership Distribution	Tools	Designed by
Building consultation team meeting	Responding to crisis (drug use, mental health problems, truancy issues, teen pregnancy, etc.)	School counselors, administrators, social worker, school psychologist, nurse, security officer, and English language learner teacher	Collaborated, coordinated collective	Weekly meeting agendas	School administration
Site-based management team	Main instrument for decision making on student achievement-related issues and aims to redistribute decision-making authority.	Administrators, teachers, students, school counselors, staff members, parents, and community members.	Collaborated, coordinated collective	School climate survey	School administration
Office visits	School counselors come together with the teachers and the administration on an as-needed basis to discuss individual students' issues.	School counselors and other school members (on an as-needed basis)	Collaborated, coordinated collective	Various	School counselors and other school members (on an as-needed basis)
Prescriptive math and introduction to geometry classes	Solving systemic problems in math education	School counselors and math teacher	Collaborated, coordinated collective	Achievement data on math and student perception data	School counselors and math teacher
Postsecondary planning	Investigate the barriers that prevented students from applying to college during their graduation year.	School counselors and outside institution (Lake Shore Technical College)	Collaborated, coordinated collective	Postsecondary placement data	School counselors
Teen screen routine	Mental health checkups to identify problems in their early stages	School counselors and outside institution (Mental Health Wellness Coalition)	Collaborated, coordinated collective	Statewide data on suicide rate	School district

Source: Aysen Kose, "Analysis of school counselors' leadership practices through the lens of distributed leadership" (January 1, 2010). *Electronic Doctoral Dissertations for UMass Amherst.* Paper AAI3427547. http://scholarworks.umass.edu/dissertations/AAI3427547

one another, but one may be emphasized in the analysis. A dissertation by one of our students illustrates the distinction between categorical and holistic analysis because she included the products of both analytic strategies. For her phenomenological study of elite female athletes, Burton (2002) interviewed eight women who competed in the Olympic Games. She analyzed her interviews through the categories of lived experience—body, time, space, and relationships (van Manen, 1990)—and wrote a chapter explicating these themes across the womens experiences. When she read this categorical analysis, however, she realized that her writing had lost the individual voice of each woman, so she performed a more holistic analysis. The result was eight minipor-traits that captured each woman's experience as an individual whole. She incorporated these as an additional chapter in her dissertation.

Categorizing strategies identify similarities and differences across the data, coding and sorting them into appropriate categories. These strategies require decision rules to help guide the assignment to particular categories. Generally, these rules should be articulated in the design, but, as with nearly all other aspects of analysis, you will modify and add to them. The emphasis, overall, is on the development and presentation of ana-lytic categories. Often categories are generated from the theories in which the conceptual framework is grounded. For example, Ruth may use categories from talent development theory (e.g., *practice, parent support, praise*) or from self-determination theory (e.g., *skills, knowledge, beliefs*). Another approach to this strategy is grounded theory, which uses the constant comparative method to identify, refine, and contrast analytic categories with the aim of generating mid-level theory to explain the phenomenon of interest (see Charmaz, 2014; Glaser & Strauss, 1967; Strauss & Corbin, 2015). Grounded theory pri-marily uses inductive reasoning—that is, "the patterns, themes, and categories of analysis come from the data; they emerge out of the data rather than being imposed on them prior to data collection and analysis" (Patton, 1980, p. 306). As we have noted, however, even grounded theorists work with conceptual frameworks. As humans, we do not enter our studies with blank slates.

In contrast and with a somewhat different emphasis, *holistic strategies* describe con-nections among the data in the actual context—a place, an event, a person's experience, a text. The result is a narrative portrait of an individual or program. Holistic analysis is especially useful when you want to capture a person's experience in a setting. A doctoral student is studying how a young man with intellectual disabilities (Dan) experiences his first job. While she uses self-determination and self-efficacy theory as a guide for data collection and analysis, she wants to give voice to Dan. So she paints a holistic portrait that illustrates what she identifies as his major theme: *I can do it if I have directions and times to practice.*

Your purpose (see Chapter 1) helps frame your analysis. If your intent is more focused on description, you are likely to conduct a holistic, contextualized analysis. Details coalesce, connections are made, and you build a narrative. If you intend to compare and contrast, you will seek categories and themes by which you code the data. You then look at

Data Connection

- Assigning codes and categorizing
- Identifying patterns and themes

differences and similarities across categories. If your study aims to forecast or predict, you usually stipulate analytic categories or indicators at the conceptualization phase.

In practice, actual studies fall somewhere along a continuum, as with the assumptions you make about social science and society (see Chapter 2). All studies are shaped and therefore guided by the conceptual framework and its embedded theories, but the degree to which you confine yourself to this frame varies. Most studies are more or less open ended or prefigured; few are all one way or the other. Remember that the process of qualitative inquiry is an interweaving of inductive and deductive thinking. *All researchers enter the field with a perspective.* This perspective is usually articulated in the conceptual framework. Theories that inform this framework offer focus, questions, and potential categories and themes. At the same time, qualitative researchers remain open to the unexpected and let the analytic direction of the study emerge.

We combined categorical analysis with holistic analysis in our study of inclusion in a large city school system. We conducted cross-school analyses using categories such as leadership, teacher–student interactions, and professional development opportunities. We also wrote mini–case studies of each school, elaborating the inclusionary structures and practices we saw. Like Burton (2002), we saw that combining the two analytic strategies can enrich interpretation. Still, the product of either strategy can stand alone.

Whether you stipulate precise analytic decisions before data collection or begin the process during data collection depends on the study's genre and its duration. Generating categories of data to collect, or cells in a matrix, early in your study can be an important focusing device. Tightly structured, highly organized data gathering and analyzing schemes, however, often limit flexibility and hide the unusual or the serendipitous—the paradox that can lead to insights. Try to find a balance between efficiency considerations and flexibility.

Thick Description

Whatever strategies you use, the foundation of analysis and interpretation is thick description. Thick description details physical surroundings, time and place, actions, events, words, people, and interactions on the scene. This deep description generates insights that lead to identifying patterns and can suggest or hint at intentions and meaning. Thick description makes analysis and interpretation possible, and it allows your readers to see what you see. In taking field notes, be sure you have as much detail as possible, because without the details, the descriptions will be thin and too weak to support strong interpretations. Think of your descriptions as building a pathway or map, so that someone else can see how you made your interpretation.

In discussing thick description, Geertz (1973) relates the philosopher Gilbert Ryle's example of two boys contracting the eyelids of their right eyes: the movements are identical, but how can we tell if one is a twitch or a wink? A thick description would suggest, because of its focus on context and history, that it was one or the other. Such description

> Analysis is pattern identification over awareness of detail.

> Thick description makes analysis and interpretation possible.

is necessary to further the researcher's interpretation and make clear to a reader what is actually happening. Thick description helps answer the following analytic questions:

- What is the nature of this act?
- What is happening here?

Note, however, that there is "no such thing as 'pure description'" (Wolcott, 1994, p. 13). As you gather data and begin to record them in narrative form, you pay attention to some features of the social world and not to others. What you choose to note and describe will depend on the purpose and conceptual framework. For example, in his descriptions of life on the designated Asian and Pacific American floor of a university residential hall, one of our students, Gerry, focused on the residents' experiences living in a culturally safe space where they could express their heritage. His rich narratives captured images of comfort in expressing opinions without having them labeled as Asian, of not having to explain the food they preferred to eat, of not being the butt of Asian jokes, and the narratives were detailed enough to reveal subtle differences across various ethnic groups.

Quantifying Qualitative Data

Some qualitative researchers analyze and present data in the form of numbers, thereby quantifying qualitative data. In some cases, this can be a useful exercise. For example, Anthony presents some of his observational data in the form of tallies. Such quantification can lead to insights into frequencies of observed events or the use of particular vernaculars in speech. Usually, quantification is performed when the frequency or amount represents an important *quality* of the phenomenon. Descriptive statistics can provide evidence for qualities of an event or activity. In general, however, quantification does not do justice to the power and heuristic value of qualitative data—often a single occurrence can carry profound importance. We advise that you present qualitative data as narratives, stories, themes, or patterns, thereby fully developing the evocative power of words. Counting (tallies, frequencies) can be used to supplement the narrative but should not take the lead. Other qualitative researchers, of course, disagree with our stance. The original work of Miles and Huberman (1984) offered useful variations on the quantification of qualitative data. All three editions of the texts (Miles & Huberman, 1984, 1994; Miles, Huberman, & Saldaña, 2014) are filled with matrices and charts that provide models for structuring your analyses and can be very useful in making patterns visible.

Analysis Related to Qualitative Genres

Analysis is shaped also by the genre framing your study. *Phenomenological studies* are primarily open ended, searching for the themes that express meaning in participants' lives, and typically rely on interview data. Broad categories are sought (either inductively or deductively), building subthemes that elaborate the topography of meaning communicated by the participants. **Ruth's** study focuses on the sports experience of children with physical disabilities. Focusing questions capture the children's feelings of shame or joy in sports activities, how their families support their independence, and the meanings associated with "differentness." These questions provide preliminary categories on which Ruth can rely as she begins to analyze the data. (Ruth's analysis is elaborated in Chapter 11.) A feminist phenomenological study would search for the deep meaning of women's experiences. The conceptual framework would elaborate important categories for data gathering and analysis: (a) women's experiences of patriarchy, (b) how oppression plays out in their lives, (c) specific instances of discrimination because of gender, and (d) what strategies the women use to confront or acquiesce to domination. Just as in Ruth's case, the research questions (as stipulated early on and then modified) provide a starting place for analysis.

Ethnographies usually begin with broad domains (e.g., participants in or locations for specific social interactions) for gathering data that then shape analysis, and they are balanced between structure and openness. Ethnographies rely on participant observation data (captured in extensive field notes), interview data (both formal and informal), and material artifacts. Central to ethnographic studies is the concept of culture with its norms and patterns. Although vague and ambiguous, the concept focuses attention on widely shared and deeply held beliefs extant in a cultural group. The questions posed by Erickson (1986) that we mentioned in Chapter 4 offer a possible starting point for both data collection and analysis. Another recommendation is to focus on the following to prompt analytic insights:

- Members' Terms of Address and Greetings

- Everyday Questions and Answers

- Members' Descriptions (Not Prompted by an Interview Question)

- Members' Stories

- Members' Terms, Types, and Typologies

- Indigenous Contrasts

- Members' Explanations and Theories (see Emerson, Fretz, & Shaw, 1995, pp. 112–126)

Anthony's study focuses on program staff's and community members' beliefs about the arts, participation in events and activities, and the value of the program to the community. These categories—arts, participation, and value—are guides for his analysis. (See Chapter 11 for details on Anthony's processes of data analysis.) A critical ethnography would search for the class-, race-, or perhaps gender-based structures of domination that shape participation by community members. The critical ethnographer would search for evidence of hegemony or paternalism in the program, asking whose conception of the arts is expressed in the program and how participation is defined. Analysis would focus on ways by which community members reproduce or resist possibly elitist and exclusionary ideas inherent in the program.

Analysis following sociolinguistic genres deconstructs natural conversations and speech contexts to understand the meaning of what is said and the rules for interaction. Interpretation of discourse depends on features of the social context (e.g., setting and activity) as well as features of the speaker and the audience (e.g., gender, background, and ethnicity). Sociolinguists look at more than actual words. They consider moves, turns, tone, exchanges, repetitions, stories, code switches, and paralinguistic cues. They also look at nonverbal actions such as gestures, body language, and movements. Their analyses of these features tend to be holistic: How do they fit together to make meaning? The relationship between form and function of the speech events or moves cannot be assumed. Rather, particular meaning is investigated: What does *this* speech event, *this* turn taking, mean in *this* context to *these* people? Intent and purpose are crucial for the assigning of meaning to any discourse. Sociolinguistic analysis can be categorical, as it constructs taxonomies and searches for communication rules. Statements can be categorized, for example, as compliments, bribes, threats, insults, and so on. Still, a particular rule will not apply in all settings. Identical statements can take on altered meaning in different settings. A threat can become a joke: "Your eyes will fall out if you look at me!" **Marla** does some microanalyses of the conversations between the women patients and the male physician's assistant at the clinic. Although his words are caring, his moves reveal inattention (e.g., the physician's assistant asks while perusing a stack of mail, "So, how long have you felt this pain?").

Case studies are uniquely intended to capture the complexity of a particular event, program, individual, or place, and they rely on multiple kinds of data. Case studies use both categorizing and holistic strategies. They focus holistically on the organization or the individual. The conceptual framework and research questions, however, stipulate this broad focus more closely. A case study of an organization would specify the elements of interest, for example, leadership, decision making, and informal communication. These categories then provide the initial ways for thinking analytically and for a first cut on coding the data. A critical case study assumes that the case exemplifies oppression and domination in specific ways. Marla assumes a feminist and class-based perspective with her interests in poor women's health. As her project unfolds, she and her team focus on the ways in which clinic services are structured to perpetuate middle-class values that exclude the poor women's choices in health care. (This collaborative process is detailed in Chapter 11.)

Overall analysis, then, proceeds logically and systematically from decisions made early on. It does not begin de novo at some point in the study. Decisions made about the specific strategy, assumptions about knowledge and truth, and the genre most congruent with these decisions all forecast analysis. Whether you analyze as you go or hold off until the end of a study, whether you have stipulated analytic categories at the conceptualization stage or let them emerge, and whatever the qualitative genre framing the study, the processes of analysis are similar. We next discuss the generic processes of analyzing and interpreting qualitative data and then present specific strategies for analyzing interview data, field notes, and objects of material culture.

GENERIC ANALYSIS

Data analysis is the process of bringing order, structure, and meaning to the mass of collected data. It is time-consuming, creative, and fascinating. Analytic procedures typically fall into the following eight phases:

1. Organizing the data

2. Familiarizing yourself with the data

3. Identifying categories

4. Coding the data

5. Generating themes

6. Interpreting

7. Searching for alternative understandings

8. Writing the report

As we have mentioned previously, the process, while systematic and documented, is not necessarily linear. You are likely to move iteratively back and forth between and across phases. Data analysis and interpretation have parallels with the *creative process* (Bargar & Duncan, 1982), which entails immersion, incubation, insight, and interpretation. During organization and familiarization, you *immerse* yourself in the data, becoming deeply involved in words, impressions, and the flow of events. Then, let the data sit on the back burner of your mind—that is, let them *incubate*. This leads to *insight* about the salient themes and meaning embedded in the data. You then code and recode the data in instrumental ways, developing the *interpretations* that are written in the final report. Be prepared for the amount of time analysis and interpretation take, generally two or three times the hours spent gathering the data. Thus, for a 90-minute interview, plan for 3 to 4 hours of making decisions about data reduction, description, category generation, and coding.

Data analysis can be considered a process of data reduction—you *reduce* the piles of data you have collected (see, e.g., Luker, 2008). Each phase entails *data condensation* (Kvale, 1996)—as the reams of collected materials are synthesized into manageable elements—and interpretation—as you bring meaning and insight to the words and actions of the participants. Think of data condensation as analogous to the difference between

Data condensation . . .

- is the process of synthesizing material into smaller chunks or clusters.
- requires judgment about the salience and power of the data to "tell the story."

a novel and a poem on the same topic. The novel provides great descriptive detail; the poem synthesizes the essence of the experiences depicted in the novel. All analysis entails making judgments about how to reduce the massive amounts of data collected. Writing about ethnography, Emerson et al. (1995) note that "the ethnographer selects out some incidents and events, gives them priority, and comes to understand them in relationship to others" (p. 168). Doing so systematically and with the research purpose in mind is essential.

Organizing the Data

As a preliminary step, inventory on note cards the data that you have gathered. You also might perform the minor editing necessary to make field notes retrievable and generally "clean up" what seems overwhelming and unmanageable, if you have not already done so. We cannot emphasize enough how important it is to do this cleaning up and organizing as you go along. It saves time, creates a more complete record, and stimulates analytic thinking. Be sure that you know where and when you took field notes, who was there, and what the event was. Check to be sure that interview transcriptions are dated and you are sure whom you interviewed. This may seem simplistic and obvious. In a long study, however, you may find that you forgot whom you interviewed or when the interview took place. These details will be important when you are writing the findings as you will need to identify where the quotes came from and which observations or artifacts you refer to.

Tools for Organizing

- Note cards
- Highlighter pens
- Post-it notes
- File folders
- Software

Also, be sure that you have written down hunches and analytic ideas throughout the study. This shapes and refines your thinking and provides insights for analysis. At this time, you also could enter the data into one of several software programs for web applications for analysis and data management. The data generated by qualitative methods are voluminous. Be prepared for this sheer volume. Find a way to store the data so you know where different pieces are and so they are safe. As analysis proceeds, however, be confident that your organizational scheme will change.

The organization schemes you settle on must include a way to track your thinking (choices of categories and coding, creation of themes, and developing interpretations and meaning) that leads to what you will report as findings. Lincoln and Guba (1985) talk of *audit trails* that trace the progress from raw data to final product. However you choose to organize and keep records, some clear documentation is essential both as evidence that you have conducted systematic inquiry and to support the trustworthiness of your study.

Our Characters **Ruth**'s preliminary organization is very simple. Because she is relying primarily on interviews, she keeps her transcripts in files identified by the children's names. As she becomes more confident about the salient themes, however, she reorganizes segments of data into those themes. She then creates folders (or files in a software program) for the themes. As she writes the final report, she relies on this thematic organization, which pulls together data from five children and their families (see Chapter 11).

Anthony initially organizes his data by the various data gathering techniques he uses. He has one folder for interviews and others for the survey returns and observations. As he gets more deeply into analysis, however, he also organizes the data into events based on his reasoning that telling the stories of participation and beliefs about it is best depicted through concrete incidents. His observations at arts events (the opening of the gallery and a dance exhibition) and his interviews with people who attend them are all in one folder (see Chapter 11).

Marla's strategy is similar to Anthony's. She initially organizes the data by source: (a) her observations, (b) field notes of team meetings, and (c) interviews with prospective team members. She and her team then reorganize the data into salient themes. They also develop files for data about the three women on whom they focus in depth. These files contain the team's notes, transcriptions of interviews, and the women's journals. Because she has chosen to study the verbal interactions of the women, her files include sociolinguisitc analyses. She tracks naturally occurring interactions and conversations (e.g., between women patients and physician assistants), coding for dialogic and univocal discourse (see Chapter 11).

Familiarizing Yourself With the Data

Read, reread, and once more read through the data. This intense and often tedious process enables you to become familiar in intimate ways with what you have learned. What if you have not transcribed all your interviews? How can you read through them? Students often ask whether they must transcribe all the interviews they have conducted. We usually temporize, saying "It depends." There is no substitute for transcribing interviews. It familiarizes you with the data, provides leads for further data gathering, provokes insights, and stimulates analytic thinking. Transcribing is not a mere technical exercise. However, not all people are visual learners; some learn better when they listen. If you are an oral learner, you are probably better served by listening, listening, and listening again to tape-recorded interviews. You might even listen to them in your car as you drive. You can then note passages that you will transcribe selectively (not while driving, please). However you choose to do it, you must become intimately familiar with the data. This takes extraordinary discipline.

Identifying Categories and Generating Themes

These phases of data analysis are the most difficult, complex, ambiguous, creative, and fun, but few descriptions of this process are found in the methodologic literature. We present them together because they are practically inseparable and iterative: codes inform categories and categories suggest codes; categories contribute to creation of themes and themes suggest further categories. Thoughtful analysis demands a heightened awareness of the data; a focused attention to those data and how they might connect; and an openness to the subtle, tacit undercurrents of social life. There is much confusion, especially among beginners, about the difference between a code,

Familiarize

- Review and review the data.
- Let the data "incubate."
- Review and review again.
- "Live" with the data; you must know the data intimately— there is no substitute.

a category, and a theme. "A code is a word or short phrase that symbolically assigns a summative, salient, essence-capturing, and/or evocative attribute to a portion [of your] data" (Saldaña, 2013). Categories are groupings of these codes that represent some segment of your data that is relatively discrete (a variable, if you will). As you begin to see patterns, you interpret meaning and construct themes. A *theme* is a declarative phrase or sentence describing a process, a connection, or an insight. Think of a theme as an abstraction that explains the pattern you see in or across categories. In a theme, you often state an argument regarding your interpretation.

Typically, a qualitative study begins with some preliminary categories to focus on data gathering, as noted above. These categories typically are drawn from the conceptual framework as key constructs or notions that you wish to understand more fully, and they are then elaborated in interview questions and guidelines for observations. Note, however, that the choice of categories and which data you place in each category is quite personal. You may organize your clothing by fabric, while someone else might do it by color. Categories provide direction for data gathering. Themes, in contrast, emerge as linkages, patterns, processes, and possible explanations begin to appear within and across categories.

Thematic analysis typically requires the deep familiarity with the data that comes from categorizing. For example, a study of undergraduate women of color in an engineering program at a major university (Sosnowski, 2002) generated categories such as the following:

- Early experiences with mathematics
- The role of teachers and mentors
- The role of mother

These categories were clearly identified early on in the study as important ones to explore with the young women. The researcher sorted excerpts from interviews and observations into those categories. A more subtle analysis, however, revealed a preliminary theme: *Developing self-efficacy is important*. The researcher did not explicitly ask the young women about this topic, yet she found evidence throughout the data that she interpreted as revealing this theme. The theme then informed further, more nuanced subcategories.

Inductive analysis searches for salient categories within the data themselves. The researcher may identify indigenous categories (the emic view). Indigenous categories are those expressed by the participants; the researcher discovers them through analysis of how language is used. This strategy is illustrated in a study of ways by which students are labeled in an urban high school (Rossman et al., 1988). The researchers used categories that came from the actual words of the two disciplinarians: *nut case, hot babe,* and *good kid*. These emic categories were seen as distinct from the analyst-generated categories (*good citizen, loyal,* and *teacher's pet*) that we describe next.

Your analysis also may be more *deductive*, relying on categories you have developed through the literature or through previous experience that are expressed in the conceptual

Indigenous categories are those expressed by participants.

framework. In reading related literature, you identified what other researchers found salient about the topic; what they wrote (the categories they used) can be a preliminary guide. Similarly, if you identified theories that inform your topic or question, you can use categories articulated in those theories. During focused analysis, possible new categories may seem salient, either identified in the data (but unanticipated) or through further reading of the literature. You can then comb the data using these new categories to find whether they stand up and are an important additional element. These categories represent the etic view and are often referred to as *analyst-constructed categories* (see Patton, 2002). Such categories do not necessarily correspond directly to the categories of meaning used by the participants. Both indigenous and analyst-constructed categories are often presented as typologies (classification schemes) in matrices. Patton (2002) cautions against allowing these matrices to lead your analysis. Instead, use them to generate sensitizing concepts to guide further explorations: "It is easy for a matrix to begin to manipulate the data as the analyst is tempted to force the data into categories created by the cross-classification to fill out the matrix and make it work" (p. 469).

> **Analyst-constructed categories do not necessarily correspond directly to the categories of meaning expressed by participants.**

Developing the etic view (the researcher's view) has been critiqued as a kind of imperialism through which the researcher's meanings (categories) are privileged over those of the participants. Patton (2002) notes that analyst-constructed categories may well "impose a world of meaning on the participants that better reflects the observer's world than the world under study" (p. 460). With this criticism in mind, we note that typical qualitative studies provide a blend of analyst and indigenous categorizations.

Theme generation takes the analysis to a deeper, more integrative level. *What is a theme?* One of our students described a theme as a declaration of the sense you are making of the data and categories. van Manen (1990) defines the concept as follows:

1. *Theme is the experience of focus, of meaning, of point.* As I read over an anecdote I ask, what is its meaning, its point?

2. *Theme formulation is at best a simplification.* We come up with a theme formulation but immediately feel that it somehow falls short, that it is an inadequate summary of the notion.

3. *Themes are not objects one encounters at certain points or moments in a text.* A theme is not a thing; themes are intransitive.

4. *Theme is the form of capturing the phenomenon one tries to understand.* Theme depicts an aspect of the structure of lived experience. (p. 87)

Source: Van Manen, M. (©1990). Researching lived experience: Human science for an action sensitive pedagogy. Albany, NY: SUNY Press.

Images, words, and emotions sift through your mind as you read through field notes or listen to interview tapes, coding, and categorizing. During this immersion process, your task is to identify recurring ideas or language, patterns of beliefs and actions that signal something more subtle and complex than categories. Mindful of the research questions but open to the serendipitous, the researcher follows his intuition that suggests a deeper way to understand and interpret the data. Since a theme implies some claim or assertion as a result of the process, themes take the form of a declarative statement. This phase of data analysis is extraordinarily challenging; however, without it, the analysis remains thin and underdeveloped. Generating themes is an art; recall the discussion of data gathering techniques as art in Chapter 7. Just as you uniquely implement data gathering, so, too, are analysis and interpretation an expression of your individual understanding of the phenomenon you study.

> **Generating themes is an art.**

The work of several students in one of our introductory qualitative methods classes provides examples of the thinking behind their analysis and interpretation phases. Sara, a doctoral student in higher education, was interested in how young professionals became socialized in an era of public social networking. She studied the Facebook content of a group of masters' students who held entry-level positions in student affairs at a large state university. Her large categories included *content control* and *identity construction*. The theme she built from her data was "Young emerging professionals establish appropriate professional identity through controlling the content on their Facebook pages." Her paper elaborated how they accomplished both control and identity construction.

Another student in that class, Cheryl, wanted to learn how students in the school of engineering experienced their internships. She asked, How did they gain knowledge and make meaning from their experience? Using holistic analysis of her interview data, she wrote miniportraits of each participant as an intern. She articulated two common themes across these portraits: (1) "interns relied on external influences to help them find meaning, purpose, and direction for their experience" and (2) "interns built self-confidence by overcoming challenges." A third member of the class, Javad, used a theoretical framework for assessing teacher learning environments to analyze his data on a teacher professional development project in Afghanistan (Ahmadi, 2010). The theoretical framework provided his categories: (a) *learner centered*, (b) *knowledge centered*, (c) *assessment centered*, and (d) *community centered* (Bransford, Brown, & Cocking, 1999). His themes indicated that the project did not meet these criteria for an effective teacher learning.

Dan and John had quite different experiences. Dan, a community college transfer student advisor, wanted to understand the enrollment process that his students follow in order to gain entrance (i.e., transfer) to the university. In the course of carrying out the study, he "underwent" (de la Torre, 2010, p. 1) the process of gaining access for himself. Doing so gave him the insight that if *he* experienced such gatekeeping, what did students face? He offered the following analysis:

I use the analogy of a door, with accompanying movement to open and movement to close, as a way of describing impressions gained during the study. Those colleagues who participated in interviews, and shared the forms of interaction that they have with students, implied a kind of door-opening as they conveyed proce-dural information in conjunction with contextual guidance and support. On another level, those institutional colleagues whom I sought out for collaboration in the study seemed to convey a kind of door-closing in the way they responded (more often did not) to my overtures for contact. (de la Torre, 2010, p. 1)

Similar to Dan's attention during analysis to his data collection experience, John attended to his personal reactions to the words of his participant as he transcribed and identified categories. John interviewed school superintendents to learn how they built and maintained—and described—relationships with the district school board. He recognized a pattern of responses across the interviews that seemed to indicate a script, a set of expected answers—what they were supposed to say. His insight was that their words indicated a kind of "dance" superintendents engage in with their board members. He called his insights "working hypotheses" that he needed to explore further in future studies.

We have encouraged you to critically scrutinize your decisions throughout analysis. When you articulate a theme or preliminary finding, ask yourself these questions:

- Where did the theme come from? What data support this idea?

- How am I representing it? Will others (participants, readers) see it as I do?

- What learning does the theme convey? What surprises?

- What makes the theme worth presenting?

Answering these questions contributes to the trustworthiness of your sense-making, your analyses.

We have found that *concept mapping* helps in developing categories and making con-nections for theme building. In this exercise, you brainstorm what are the important ideas that recur. We suggest that you put down the ideas on paper and then draw arrows to show how you think they relate to one another. Figure 10.1 illustrates a preliminary con-cept map that uses interview quotes as key ideas. (A concept-mapping activity is provided at the end of this chapter.)

Look for recurring words that participants use to describe something. Try some anal-ogies. Talk with your community of practice. Set yourself the task of relating the three or four important ideas that you are learning from your study. All these strategies help both category and theme identification.

Both categorization and thematic analysis are often thought of as an unambigu-ous enterprise of coding data. As we note next, coding is the formal representation of categorizing and thematic analysis; it does not precede or invalidate the necessity of deeper analysis.

FIGURE 10.1   "My Success Is My Mother" Concept Map

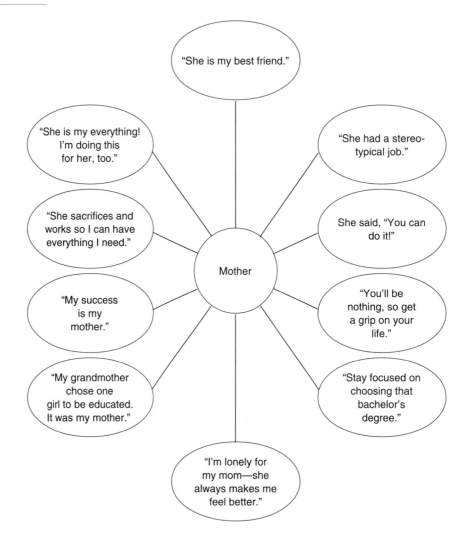

Source: Sosnowski, N. H. (2002). *Women of color staking a claim for the cyber domain: Unpacking the racial/gender gap in science, mathematics, engineering and technology* (Unpublished doctoral dissertation). University of Massachusetts Amherst, Amherst, MA.

Coding

As Marla notes in the vignette at the beginning of this chapter, coding is the formal representation of analytic thinking. It is not, however, simply a "bookkeeping" task. It is complex and iterative. Coding entails thinking through what you take as *evidence* of a category or theme. Categories are concepts, or abstractions. A code is "a word or short phrase that captures and signals what is going on in a piece of data in a way that links it to some more general analysis issue" (Emerson et al., 1995, p. 146). In coding the data, you will have to be clear about what words or phrases illustrate and elaborate each concept. For example, consider the following:

- What do Marla and her team take as evidence of gender discrimination in the clinic?

- What does Anthony judge to be a perspective on participating in arts events?

- How does Ruth decide which stories told by the children show joy?

Because abstractions are ephemeral and vague, your task is to make them concrete through snippets and segments of data. These decisions on what constitutes evidence of a category should be solid and grounded in the data. As noted in Chapter 3 in the discussion of trustworthiness and earlier in this chapter under organizing your data, the grounds for these decisions should be clear to anyone who reads your work; they should not be capricious or insupportable.

Plan to code your data more than once, because thinking in terms of evidence stimulates insights, often generating new categories or seeing categories collapse. The first coding should be simple and elegant, only four or five large categories initially. Then recode the data, refining those categories or adding new ones. These "big-chunk" categories may well become the major sections of the final report, the chapters of the story you want to tell about what you have learned.

The *mechanics of coding* vary, depending on your style and what works for you. Despite this age of software alternatives, many researchers use hard copy and code the data by hand. Anthony formats his word-processed data with wide margins on the right-hand side. He codes the data by bracketing chunks and writing a word representing a category in the margin. He could use symbols instead of words, but he needs to use a scheme that is simple and clear to him and to others. Marla plans to use highlighter pens to indicate categories. If you should use this option, have plenty of copies of the data handy because blocking over with highlighters gets messy. Both Marla and Anthony then make lists on 5 inches × 8 inches cards, on which they note particular categories. This process pulls together in one place all the instances of, for example, strong participation, in Anthony's case. He lists that evidence of participation is found in an interview, with whom the interview was conducted, and on what page the instance is found. One of his 5″ × 8″ cards is summarized in Table 10.2. He indicates interviewees by their initials (ML), the interview by number (1, 2, 3 . . .), and the pages on which he has found evidence of strong participation. He lists field notes by date and page numbers. Evidence found in material culture is listed by date and type.

We recognize that computer tools may be helpful in the coding phase (as well as earlier in the organizing phase), especially if you have large amounts of data or are working

Coding . . .

- is the formal representation of analytic thinking.
- links data to the conceptual framework.

TABLE 10.2   Anthony's Data Summary Form

	Interviews	Field Notes	Material Culture
Category: "strong participation"	ML 1: 14, 17 JB 2: 2, 14, 30	10/3: 9–11, 15 10/7: 18–22, 24, 27	10/3: attendance, receipts
	DE 1: 3–4, 6, 11	10/12: 2–3, 5, 18	10/7: center log
	JC 3: 5, 7–9		10/9: meeting minutes
	JE 1: 2–4, 8, 19		
	KG 2: 7, 15–17		
Category: "involvement in decisions"	DE 2: 5 JE 1: 14–15	10/1: 1–3, 5, 7 10/9: 6, 8–10	10/9: meeting minutes
	FR 4: 16–17, 22	10/22: 3–6, 18, 22	
	JB 2: 2–3, 17		

with a team of researchers collecting data. We argue that software programs that claim to assist in data analysis actually only assist in managing data and in the mechanics of coding. Since analysis and interpretation require insight, judgment, and creativity, no software can substitute for the human mind. Qualitative software programs can make it easier for a researcher or a team of researchers to assemble masses of data in common codes and quickly find data within categories. Software also can assist in combining and relating categories, recoding, clustering, and memo preparation. In general, the software can help researchers ask questions of data they have coded, but remember that it is the researcher's mind that does the analytic and interpretive work. Recommended software includes ATLAS.ti, Ethnograph, MAXQDA, and NVivo (URLs for purchasing or downloading trial copies can be found at the end of this chapter; because technology develops rapidly, any URLs and references to software packages will be quickly out of date). If your study is small scale (as in most dissertation research), you might carefully consider the time associated with learning and using new software.

Interpretation

- Sense-making
- Telling a story
- Not rule bound
- Reliant on thick description

Interpretation

At some point, your thematic analysis moves to a higher level of integration and synthesis to find meaning beyond the specifics of the data. "Interpretation is an art; it is not formulaic or mechanical" (Denzin, 1994, p. 504). As you interpret your analyses, you are putting together a story. "Interpretation means attaching significance to what was found, making sense of findings, offering explanations, drawing conclusions, extrapolating lessons, making inferences, considering meanings, and otherwise imposing order" (Patton, 2002, p. 480). Again, you draw on your conceptual framework. You connect the way you understand and interpret the data with a larger concept, research, or theory. To facilitate this process, ask yourself the following questions:

- What is going on here?

- What is the essence of the phenomenon?

- Of what is this phenomenon an example?

- How is the phenomenon related to broader concepts or theory?

- What is the story these data tell?

Your task is to turn what you have learned into something that makes sense to others, something you can communicate to a relevant community of discourse. Denzin (1994) calls the interpretive process moving from the field to the text to the reader, *a complex and reflexive process*. In this light, interpretation is storytelling. What you have seen in the field, what you heard participants say, symbols and signs you have noted, all come together into an experience that has meaning for the participants and for you. Interpretation is capturing that meaning and expressing it so that it fits into a larger picture. "A good interpretation takes us into the center of the experiences being described" (Denzin, 1994, p. 504, paraphrasing Geertz, 1973).

> Finding the meaning or essence in phenomena is multidimensional. Making something of a text or of a lived experience by interpreting its meaning is more accurately a process of insightful invention, discovery or disclosure—grasping and formulating a thematic understanding is not a rule-bound process but a free act of "seeing" meaning. (van Manen, 1990, p. 79)

The process follows the hermeneutic circle. You analyze the parts to see the whole; seeing the whole further illuminates the parts.

Thick description is, as we have already mentioned, at the heart of the interpretive–hermeneutic process—thick description makes interpretation possible. You must provide enough description to allow the reader to understand the interpretation, to see how you made it. The details in the description form the evidence, the logic. They build the argument. At the same time, the explanation, the lessons, the linkages revealed in the interpretation serve to clarify the descriptions and illuminate the details.

Because interpretation tells a story, your "emphasis is on illumination, understanding, and extrapolation" (Patton, 1990, p. 424). Remember that qualitative research does not aim to uncover a unitary, totalizing interpretive Truth (see Denzin, 1994). Kvale (1996) identifies "three contexts of interpretation" (p. 213): (1) *participants' understanding*, (2) *commonsense understanding*, and (3) *theoretical understanding*. As you build *your* story, you will find that you move through these three contexts.

Approach the data with humility.

"The fieldworker
renders the data
meaningful."

(Emerson et al.,
1995, p. 168)

**Alternative
Understandings**

- What are
  other plausible
  interpretations?
- How does your
  argument stand
  up to these?
- Is your argument
  well supported
  by the data and
  analyses?
- Is your argument
  credible?

Remember that you are not seeking to determine a single causal explanation, to predict, or to generalize. Instead, you aim to tell a richly detailed story that respects these contexts and connects participants, events, experiences, or discourses to larger issues, theories, or phenomena.

Searching for Alternative Understandings

As you put forward your interpretations, you will have to challenge the very patterns that seem so apparent. You must search for other plausible explanations. Alternative understandings always exist, so you will need to search for, identify, and describe them and then demonstrate how your interpretation is sound, logical, and grounded in the data. The search for alternative understandings is not a solo enterprise. Ask your participants whether they agree or have different understandings. Ask your community of practice if your story makes sense and if it can offer alternatives. Search the literature to see if relevant theories (your community of discourse) correspond to, extend, contradict, or deepen your interpretations (see Kvale, 1996).

For example, Anthony remarks that high attendance and the party atmosphere at the gallery opening indicate the pleasure and enjoyment people have in seeing the displays. He recalls reading Erving Goffman (1959), about the *presentation of self in everyday life*, and questions whether the actions of the participants might not be the result of expectations—that is, they think that they are supposed to enjoy themselves. When he discussed this with his colleagues, Marla wondered whether the food and friendship, not the art, were a possible explanation.

Recall that you are building an argument or interpretation about what you have learned in the field, an argument that is more compelling than the other alternatives. This argument builds logical relationships among your assertions, documents them with evidence, and presents a summation of your conclusions that relate to what is known in the literature. You are evaluating the plausibility of your interpretations and testing them through the data. This entails a search through the data, during which you challenge your interpretations, search for negative instances of the patterns, and incorporate these into your story. That Anthony notes a pattern of participation and pleasure across events supports his first explanation.

Part of this process is to *assess the data for their credibility, usefulness, and centrality* to your major points. Although rigorous procedures can be set up to determine if a participant is consistently truthful, a more reasonable stance is to approach the data with humility, noting that the data are what participants said to you in interviews or what you observed, rather than making broad assertions that imply Truth (with a capital *T*). You also need to consider whether the data are useful in illuminating your questions and whether they are central to the story that is unfolding. Some data are just more relevant than others. Your task is to make decisions diligently about what is significant and what is not.

Involving a critical friend and your community of practice is imperative at this point. They can be useful for identifying your "blind spots" and for suggesting different ways of seeing the data, for questioning your interpretations, and for ensuring that you are not excluding data that hint at an intriguing counterexample. Their job is to tell you whether the sense you have made of the data makes sense to anyone else. Don't be surprised—or hurt—if they criticize your analyses!

Writing the Report

Writing about qualitative data cannot be separated from the analytic process. In fact, it is central to that process because, in the choice of particular words to summarize and reflect the complexity of the data, the researcher is engaging in the interpretive act, lending shape and bringing meaning to massive amounts of raw data. The interpretive process illuminates the multiple meanings of events, objects, activities, experiences, and words. Writing reveals these discovered meanings to the reader, so writing must include description. What you write reveals the pathway to your interpretations and findings; it shows the reader how you made inferences, reached conclusions, and found the story in the data. Because the writing process is so crucial, we discuss it fully in Chapter 12. For now, we turn to a brief discussion of three specific analysis strategies drawn from cognitive anthropology, phenomenology, and narrative analysis for analyzing interview data.

WRITING IN-PROCESS ANALYTIC MEMOS

We cannot overstate the importance of writing analytic memos throughout the process. Marla, Ruth, and Anthony came to rely on their memo writing to help them organize their data and generate themes. At first, Ruth resisted writing "as too much work." But she came to see that "the more I sit with the data, the more I actually want to start writing. Certain themes almost pop out." Marla talks about how she can "hear a theme" when she rereads her memos. She also shares them with her team, who often find something she has missed.

Whether analysis is ongoing or focused toward the end of data gathering, composing short memos (to yourself, your advisor, a critical friend, your community of practice, or a scholarly audience) about emergent insights, potential themes, methodological questions, and links between themes and theoretical notions is invaluable. These short narratives are called *memos* by convention and can be constructed in formal memorandum format. They also can be letters written to yourself, to a critical friend, or to inform an academic committee about your progress. This writing process encourages analytic thinking and demands that the researcher commit emerging ideas to paper. There is no substitute for the thinking and reflecting that go into these memos. "As the ethnographer turns increasingly from data gathering to the analysis of field notes, writing integrating memos which elaborate ideas and begin to link or tie codes and bits of data together becomes absolutely critical" (Emerson et al., 1995, p. 162).

Methodologic memos focus on in-process design, methodology insights, and new directions. They serve as a kind of monitoring of your design as it unfolds, providing documentation of design decisions. Methodologic memos may focus on the following:

- What should I observe next?

- What questions should I ask to follow up on this event? (Emerson et al., 1995, p. 103)

- Whom else should I interview?

- What artifacts might be relevant?

In these memos, the researcher discusses what data have already been gathered, summarizing key activities and outlining future directions.

Thematic memos bring together the data from across several sources on an emerging theme. Working across interviews and field notes, for example, the researcher brings together a short discussion of a theme: What it means to participants, what evidence is available to document and elaborate the theme, and what additional sources of data might be useful for developing the theme. Thematic memos may respond to the following questions:

- What theme is emerging?

- What are its elements?

- Where do I have evidence (data) to support the theme?

- What disconfirming or contradictory data do I have at this point?

- What other data might help elaborate the theme?

- Why is this theme important?

Theoretical memos develop a theme in light of theoretical writing on the topic. Building on a thematic memo, the researcher integrates the thematic discussion with theoretical concepts or principles that might help elaborate the theme and situate it within a discourse community. Theoretical memos could address the following:

- How does this theme link to a particular theory?

- How does this theme elaborate the theoretical concept or principle?

- How does it contradict or question a theoretical idea?

- What other theoretical perspectives might provide insight?

In-process analytic memos should be written in an exploratory, open-ended narrative style. Ideas and assertions about the data and their interpretation should be put forward tentatively with lots of questions still to be answered. Although some argue for writing such memos to a scholarly audience (e.g., see Emerson et al., 1995), we argue against such formality. It precludes the creative insights that can emerge when writing to one's self or a critical friend and can unduly constrain exploring possibilities. Be natural in this writing, be creative, and document assiduously—but explore. Above all, write (see Table 10.3.).

STRATEGIES FOR ANALYZING INTERVIEW DATA

Three strategies for analyzing interview data offer refinements in the generic process detailed previously. Grounded in different genres of qualitative research, they provide different insights into the analytic process.

Analyzing Ethnographic Interview Data

Ethnographic interviews take many forms. Some are formal, with the researcher setting up a specific time and place to "talk" with the participant. Others are informal, occurring during more naturally occurring fieldwork. In addition, "talk" between participants may be recorded in field notes. All these materials are potentially useful for constructing a thematic understanding of the culture of interest. Typically, analysis of these materials as part of an ethnographic study proceeds with thematic analysis as described above. The researcher searches for indigenous meanings as represented in talk. "Ethnographers begin to construct members' meanings by looking closely at *what members say and do* . . . paying particular attention to the words, phrases, and categories that members use in their everyday interactions" (Emerson et al., 1995, p. 112). Specific questions to guide analysis include the following:

- What are people doing? What are they trying to accomplish?
- How, exactly, do they do this? What specific means or strategies do they use?
- How do members talk about, characterize, and understand what is going on?
- What assumptions are they making?
- What do I see going on here? What did I learn from these notes?
- Why did I include them? (Emerson et al., 1995, p. 146)

An example of a table-based analytic memo is provided in Table 10.3.

Analyzing Phenomenological Interview Data

Phenomenological analysis requires that the researcher approach the texts with an open mind, seeking what meaning and structures emerge. This stance can be characterized as

Table 10.3 Analytic Memo on Juanita's Interview

Surprises	Interesting Thoughts	Themes to Pursue	Key Themes
Having the opportunity to interview Juanita's mother who was visiting from Puerto Rico	When asked about what income level they would categorize themselves in, mom indicated "high." Juanita indicated "middle."	High school was the pivotal for Juanita to pursue engineering. Outreach and MEP programs are critical for attracting women of color.	Income level and outreach programs
Juanita's mother wanted her to be an artist—to have fun in college. She feels that engineering is too much hard work and doesn't leave time for leisurely, typical college experiences. Juanita is an artist and a track athlete.	Juanita and her colleagues have indicated their sadness about the state of recruitment and retention.	The way teachers teach science and math and the inherent power that comes with their positions greatly influence what girls choose to pursue for further studies. Juanita asked, "Why don't many teachers know really how to teach these subjects, even though they have expert knowledge about their subject areas?"—good question! Often, they get hired because of their expertise and research.	Present status quo for women in IT outside interests (art and sports), and teachers' pedagogy in teaching math and science
Juanita is the only Latina in the chemical engineering program. She doesn't want to be considered an "oddity" because she is the only Latina. She says that people think she is white until they hear her speak.	Juanita has a very strong family connection that has supported her and been an internal motivation for her. She has three brothers; two are engineers and one is a doctor. She is accepted no matter what career she chooses.	Juanita and her mother are extremely close. Both mother and daughter expressed this closeness a number of times. Juanita said, "She is my #1 friend and supporter." The mother says that she misses her very much; they are friends. In my interview, the affection and closeness they shared was exceptional and quite moving.	Isolation—being the only one among many boys, mom—daughter best friends, and strong family connections (influences to be an engineer)
Although an all A student in PR, she has had disappointing test grades at the COE. Her GPA is 3.25, which she considers good for engineering but wants to aspire to a higher level.	Juanita's family is highly educated. One grandfather was an engineer and the other a teacher. Both parents are in highly paid professional positions.	The family support is really becoming an important theme for my research. What happens when there is no family support? Maybe the support of a teacher or a mentor can also make a profound difference.	Parents/family members as role models and strong aspirations in spite of disappointments

Source: From Sosnowski (2002). Adapted with permission.

"deliberate naivete" (Kvale, 1996, p. 33). Phenomenological interview data may be analyzed in several ways, but always the focus is on the development of themes. "When we analyze a phenomenon, we are trying to determine what the themes are, the experiential structures that make up that experience" (van Manen, 1990, p. 79). The first strategy is meaning condensation, through which long interview passages are distilled into shorter statements, retaining fidelity to the original words of the interview participant. The researcher then constructs a narrative description of the phenomenon of interest.

The second strategy is meaning categorization. The researcher codes long interview passages into categories: What does this passage reveal or explain about the phenomenon or experience being described? (see van Manen, 1990). Kvale (1996) notes that the categories "can be developed in advance or they can arise ad hoc during the analysis; they may be taken from theory or from the vernacular, as well as from the interviewees' own idioms" (p. 192). (Although Kvale asserts that these categories can then be counted and presented in tables, we disagree.) Categorization provides an organizational structure for narrative presentation of phenomenological interview data. A third strategy is narrative structuring, which follows the natural organization of the interview to reveal a story. A fourth is meaning interpretation, in which the researcher puts forward "more or less speculative interpretations of the text" (Kvale, 1996, p. 193).

These strategies closely parallel the discussion above of the generic processes of qualitative data analysis. A final step is to validate your analyses by checking with the participants to see if they agree, extend, or dispute your judgments of what is important and interesting.

Analyzing Narrative Interview Data Gathering narrative data (the stories people tell about their lives) is an increasingly popular qualitative research genre that we linked to phenomenological inquiry in Chapter 4 because of its deeply psychological orientation. We separate it out, however, believing that it merits direct attention. Although there are many different strands of narrative analysis, all proceed on the assumption that people make meaning of their lived experiences by narrating those experiences. Some narratives are organized chronologically, others are structured around episodes, and still others are hypothetical narratives. The analysis of narrative data can be highly structured or open ended. In the former, the researcher looks for structure in the narrative, focusing on the abstract (a summary), orientation (place, time, and participants), complicating action (sequence of events), evaluation (meaning of the action), resolution (what happened), and coda (return to the present) (this discussion is adapted from Riessman, 1993).

Consider the excerpt from an interview Marla and her team conducted with one of the women on whom they focus in depth. In Table 10.4, Marla has analyzed the structure of the narrative, indicating where the abstract, orientation, and complicating action occur. She also analyzes the theme apparent in it: *being ignored*. Both structure and content form the basis for the analysis. In writing up the research, both are included.

TABLE 10.4   Narrative Analysis Using Marla's Data

Researcher:	Tell us about the first time you went to the clinic.	Abstract
Woman:	Well, I have to walk over from the bus stop and it was raining . . . really pouring. I had two bags of groceries, and it felt like they weighed a ton. It was hard, so hard. That stupid girl behind the desk, she acted like I wasn't even there. Looked right through me. Just yammered on her cell phone.	Orientation Complication Action *Being Ignored*

A less structured analytic strategy focuses on the thematic content and searches for examples of being ignored in other interviews with this woman and in interviews with other women. This and other themes become the major organizing scheme for writing up the research. Recall the discussion above of narrative structuring; the parallels should be clear.

Analyzing Voice-Centered Interview Data Gilligan recommends four readings in her voice-centered interview process (see Brown & Gilligan, 1990). Each reading listens for a different voice of the self, each telling a different story. The first reading establishes the who, what, when, where, and why of the story. In the second reading, the reader listens for the self: Who is the narrator? How does the narrator speak about himself or herself? The third and fourth readings look for relational voices: the care voice and the justice voice. The result is an understanding of the contrapuntal voices describing the lived experience of the self. Rogers (2000) suggests four layers of analysis: (1) restorying, (2) relational dynamics, (3) languages of the unsayable, and (4) figurative thought. She links the research questions, these multiple layers of analysis, and an unfolding theoretical story about the unique qualitative data of the study. "This method, itself in a process of evolution, seeks to clarify how cross-case analyses can be used to build theoretically compelling stories of human development" (Rogers, 2000, p. 56).

Analyzing Sociolinguistic Data

The field of sociolinguistic research is broad, encompassing several distinctive analytic strategies. For introductory purposes, we focus on two approaches: (1) discourse analysis and (2) semiotics. Both rely on naturally occurring "talk" and "text" as data.

Discourse analysis is a "heterogeneous range of social science research based on the analysis of recorded talk" (Silverman, 1993, p. 120). It is frequently concerned with how social issues such as power, gender relations, or racism are expressed in talk. The analytic strategy is thematic, noting instances in which the social issue of interest is expressed and negotiated. The talk may be between, for example, a social worker and a client, a teacher and pupil, or a manager and worker, all naturally occurring speech interactions. In these examples, an obvious focus is on how power relations are negotiated and understood by the participants.

Gee (1999) offers six analytic tasks that build understanding of discourse networks, a constellation of communication patterns:

1. Semiotic Building. Using cues and clues to construct meaning in the immediate moment.

2. World Building. Using cues and clues to understandings of reality.

3. Activity Building. Using cues and clues to understand the meaning of various actions.

4. Socioculturally Situated Identity and Relationship Building. Using cues and clues to understand the identities and relationships that are relevant to the interactions.

5. Political Building. Using cues and clues to understand the "nature and relevance of various 'social goods' such as status and power." (p. 86)

6. Connection Building. Using cues and clues to understand how the present interaction is shaped by interactions in the past and future. (pp. 85–86)

Source: From Gee, J. P., Copyright © 1999 Routledge. Reproduced by permission of Taylor & Francis Books UK.

These analytic tasks can provide a framework to make sense of texts and talk.

Another example of discourse analysis is illustrated in the work of a student (Truxaw, 2001) in one of our classes who was interested in the nature and role of teacher discursive intervention in a middle school math class. She taped episodes of classroom discourse (defined as "purposeful talk on a mathematics subject in which there are genuine contributions and interactions"; Pirie & Schwartzenberger, 1988, p. 460) and coded to identify univocal exchanges (those that convey meaning) and dialogic exchanges (those that generate meaning; see Table 10.5). Truxaw's analysis of a similar text suggests a teacher role of initiation and follow-up encouraging student responses that expand or clarify (see Table 10.6). This analysis reveals a more dialogic interaction as students introduce a new way of understanding, dividing a whole into fractions.

Semiotics, the study of sign systems and their relationship to human behavior, relies on three central concepts:

1. Signifier

2. Signified

3. Sign

TABLE 10.5   Math Class Discourse I

1	T	Okay, go ahead and tell us.	I	Question
2	G4	We did one and a half. We divided 6 by 4.	R	Answer
3	T	Oh, did you divide that mentally in your mind or did you do it out on a piece of paper?	F I	Asks to clarify
4	G4	Mentally	R	
5	T	Mentally. So you take six and you divide it by four and you got . . . ?	F I	Asks to expand
6	G4	Well, we got one remainder, two. And then we split . . . And then	R	Expands
7	G3	. . . and that would be two fourths. And then two fourths can go down to one half. And we have a one and a half.	R	Expands
8	T	Wow. Do you all agree, girls, that that's how it's done?	F/I	Comment/question
9	C	Yes	R	Answer

Source: From Truxaw (2001, pp. 15–16). Adapted with permission.
Coding: T, teacher; C, class group response; G, girl student; B, boy student; I, initiation; R, response; F, follow-up; E, evaluation.

TABLE 10.6   Math Class Discourse II

1	T	Go ahead.	I	
2	G	Um, well, first we cut one donut into fourths because we didn't know that we had one donut remainder left. So once we cut it into fourths, then we had another donut left and we cut that into fourths (inaudible) . . . and that made one and two fourths.	R	Explanation of their strategy
3	T	So they each have one and two fourths donut which also equals one and . . . ?	F I	Accept question
4	C	One half	R	Answer
5	T	One half	F	Accept
6	T	And what was the other way (student name)? You said you had another way.	I	Asks for expansion
7	G4	Well, I just realized that . . . I had to do something . . .	R	
8	T	Are you sure?	I	
9	G4	. . . I think one and five tenths because you could divide the half into more than quarters . . . then more and more and more and get a really big number.	R	New meaning

Source: From Truxaw (2001, p.16). Adapted with permission.
Coding: T, teacher; C, class group response; G, girl student; B, boy student; I, initiation; R, response; F, follow-up; E, evaluation.

The signifier intends to convey meaning; the signified is the meaning conveyed; together they are the sign. A red octagonal traffic post is a *signifier* that motorists should come to a full stop (the meaning conveyed—*signified*); together they constitute the *sign* of traffic control. A red cross on the side of a van is a *signifier* (the Red Cross organization); the meaning conveyed is about rescue, health, or humanitarian interests. Together they constitute a *sign system* about health and caring. The American flag is often the focus of study for semiotic historians who note the varying meanings the symbol has taken on over the years: from the rallying point of a new nation to the object of burning during the Vietnam War to the display of pride and strength after the terrorist attacks on the World Trade Center and the Pentagon on September 11, 2001.

Semioticists are interested in the extent to which people vary in their understanding of and conformity to the meaning conveyed in sign systems. Thus, analysis identifies a significant sign system in the setting of interest and explores the extent to which various groups and subgroups understand and conform to the meaning of the sign system. For example, Anthony might conduct a semiotic analysis of a community crafts fair sponsored by the center. He would note signifiers such as the artists' clothing and the location of booths displaying their work. Focusing on clothing in the context of the event, his analysis might suggest that the *signifiers* (clothing), are conveying meaning about "presentation of self in everyday life" (what is *signified*) (Goffman, 1959), as some artists considered themselves "costumed" for the event. He would probe more deeply to understand which artists consider the fair a form of theater and which see it as an economic opportunity. Together, the clothing and its meaning constitute a *sign system* that Anthony could interpret as expressive of the deep ambivalence of artists to economic realities. Looking at booths (*a signifier*), Anthony could see meaning about a tacit hierarchy among the artists (what is *signified*) that is established according to the location of the booths. Together, the booths and their meaning of hierarchy constitute a *sign system* about social relations within the artistic community.

STRATEGIES FOR ANALYZING FIELD NOTES FROM OBSERVATIONS

As noted in Chapter 7, observations range along the prefigured/open-ended continuum. Some are tightly structured, relying on checklists to record types of actions or interactions and their frequencies. Others are holistic, recording the flow of events in the setting and captured in detailed descriptive field notes. Analyses guided by checklists entail counting the distribution of actions and interactions, interpreting these as indicators of a specific theme. Anthony uses checklists to document interactions between potters and community members at the crafts fair. He records the number of times community members go to the potter's wheel and the interactions between potter and community members. His checklist is depicted in Table 10.7. He makes slash marks (/) for each person or interaction as a running tally of presence, interactions, and actions. Anthony will interpret these data based on his judgments about whether these actions

TABLE 10.7   Anthony's Checklist of Actions

Time	# Around Wheel	Interactions	Actions
9:00–9:30 a.m.	////	Questions: //	Touching pots
		Comments: //	Picking up glazes
9:30–10:00 a.m.			

and interactions represent interest on the part of community members, how intense that interest is, and how it links to other aspects of the program.

Holistic observation field notes are a running record of events. To supplement his checklist, Anthony wrote down as much as he could about the environment and the ebb and flow of activities. He drew a simple map of the small park where the crafts were displayed, noting the surrounding shopping and residential areas. He included as much detail as he considered relevant. As happens with many beginners, when he first tried to write a running record, he was overwhelmed by the enormity of the task. There are so many sights and so many actions to try to write down! Following Kent's advice, he let events unfold. Now his field notes are more focused, depicting actions and interactions between a few community members and the craftspeople. He reads through these notes, writing codes in the margins where there is evidence of intense interest and involvement.

STRATEGIES FOR ANALYZING MATERIAL CULTURE

Material culture is composed of the unspoken and expressive. It has been called the "mute evidence" (Hodder, 2000, p. 703) of a cultural group. Because it expresses deep beliefs and values through written texts and artifacts, however, it is, in fact, quite eloquent. Analyzing such materials proceeds from the assumption that understanding what people do (or what they produce) tells the researcher as much as what people say that they do. For example, worn tiles in front of the chick-hatching exhibit in a museum indicate interest, empty beer cans in the recycling bin suggest alcohol consumption patterns, a coffee urn in the office suggests conviviality, and shortcuts across a lawn show preferred walking paths. Material culture, whether written or actual objects, provides the researcher with insights into actions and their meanings in a setting.

Analysis of material culture may be the most interpretive analytic act in qualitative research. No protocols or specific guidelines for such analysis are available. The techniques the semioticist uses to analyze signs may be useful in the analysis of material culture. Researchers emphasizing material culture write about the hermeneutical processes of searching for patterns in cultural artifacts, identifying contexts in which the artifacts were produced and had similar meanings, recognizing similarities and differences, and applying relevant theories to illuminate the analysis (Hodder, 2000). The resulting interpretations (working hypotheses) that explain patterns cannot be subjected to strict verification procedures. Instead, credibility is determined by the fruitfulness of the theory applied, the trustworthiness of the researcher, the depth of engagement in the field (Hodder, 2000), and the support for the interpretation from the relevant discourse community.

Thus, analyzing such materials involves higher levels of inference and interpretation than with interview or observation data. In interviews, participants may more directly express meaning for events, but with material culture, you must infer that meaning. It is, therefore, a risky business, but one that can enrich a qualitative study. Remember Marla's question about her observations that copies of *Quick and Healthy Cooking* disappear? She does not know how to interpret this information so she checks with someone in the setting. Inferring meaning entails making judgments about whether the cultural artifacts you have gathered corroborate interpretations based on other data, elaborate on those interpretations, or contradict them (Rossman & Wilson, 1994).

For example, as Anthony interviews community members about their involvement in planning the arts events, he learns that participants feel excluded from decision making. He then reviews minutes of the advisory board meetings, looking for evidence of how community members' preferences are included in their deliberations. He discovers that dance events, the most preferred activities, have not been on the agenda for the past three meetings. The artifacts of the program (its records) corroborate participants' views. When he interviews the director of the program, he learns that this individual has a strong commitment to participatory planning. The evidence Anthony collects, however, contradicts this view. In this case, Anthony interprets his data as providing some evidence of a disjuncture between the rhetoric of the program (being participatory) and its reality.

DISPOSITIONS AND SKILLS

Our characters grow in their understandings of the principles of good practice as they work through the complex process of analyzing their data. The tension they encounter is finding a balance between the minutiae of daily research experience (data) and the general assertions (theory) that move analysis beyond the specific. They have to find a balance between inductive and deductive reasoning. They begin to see that they could organize the data in many ways: by color, season, or fiber. They learn that each way yields important insights, but the schemes on which they settle are uniquely their own. They immerse themselves in the data, searching for story lines that make sense and that represent the data (what they have learned) fully, accurately, and ethically. In this sense, they build grounded theory. At the same time, however, they draw on existing theory to provide analytic insights. Aware that analysis and interpretation are creative acts, they articulate the logic guiding their decisions.

Immersion, incubation, insight, and interpretation are the phases of creative insight involved in analyzing qualitative data. This chapter has depicted the generic processes that qualitative researchers work through, whatever the genre framing their inquiry: (a) organizing, (b) familiarizing, (c) building categories, (d) coding, and (e) searching for alternatives. As they work through these processes, they are mindful of the final product: a written representation of what they have learned. This is the focus of Chapter 12; Chapter 11 presents examples of our characters' analyses that will lead to their final products.

ACTIVITIES FOR YOUR COMMUNITY OF PRACTICE

Study Questions

- What decisions does a qualitative researcher make about analysis?

- How does the qualitative genre shape analytic approaches?

- How does analysis link back to the study's conceptual framework?

- What are the basic phases in generic qualitative data analysis?

Small-Group and Dyad Activities

Everyday Taxonomies

Choose one common activity or setting that is familiar to each member of the group, such as a pickup basketball game, the kitchen pantry, a clothes closet, or bookshelves. Each person individually depicts the way he or she classifies the articles or events in the setting. The classification or taxonomy can take any useful form (diagram, chart, table, descriptive narrative) as long as it shows how the items are related. Once the depiction is complete, the individual writes a statement that explains the organization (e.g., the game consists of individual moves, exchanges, team decisions, and time-driven actions). Then, together, they discuss the various ways people have organized the activity or setting. What similarities and differences appear? What reasoning do people give for their classification schemes? Which schemes seem to make sense to others and which do not? In what other ways might the items be organized?

Generating Categories

Use the 3″ × 5″ cards on which were recorded issues identified previously (see activity in Chapter 9). Individually create categories into which you can cluster the issues. With your colleagues, list all the categories generated. Together, winnow these down to four or five generic categories. One colleague can then write the four or five category terms on newsprint and hang them on the walls. Copy onto a Post-it note one issue that you judge to be particularly illustrative of each category. Stick your notes on the appropriate newsprint. With a partner, ask each other the following questions:

- How were the categories generated?

- Are these the right categories?

- Are some categories missing?

- Are the right terms used to label them?

- How do you select items to include? To exclude?

Identifying Themes in the Characters' Work

Work in three groups. One group is Marla, another Anthony, and the third Ruth. Each group reviews the field notes and interview transcriptions presented in Chapter 8 for its character. Generate themes and provide supporting evidence from the data for the assertion associated with each theme. Suggest possible theoretical frameworks to further support the themes. Share your preliminary analyses with the other two groups.

Writing Activity

Writing an Analytic Memo

Take one theme or idea that you are developing about the setting and "flesh it out." Provide some narrative about the theme and some evidence to support the ideas. The memo could include questions that you want to pursue in a next round of data collection, questions that puzzle you, or leads on which to follow up. The memo also might include a concept map. It can be shared in your community of practice.

FURTHER READINGS

Generic Analysis

Anfara, V. A., Jr., Brown, K. M., & Mangione, T. L. (2002). Qualitative analysis on stage: Making the research process more public. *Educational Researcher, 31*(7), 28–38.

Atkinson, P., & Delamont, S. (2005). Analytic perspectives. In N. K. Denzin & Y. S. Lincoln (Eds.), *The SAGE handbook of qualitative research* (3rd ed., pp. 821–840). Thousand Oaks, CA: Sage.

Auerbach, C., & Silverstein, L. B. (2003). *Qualitative data: An introduction to coding and analysis.* New York: New York University Press.

Bowen, G. A. (2006). Grounded theory and sensitizing concepts. *International Journal of Qualitative Methods, 5*(3), 1–9.

Charmaz, K. (2014). *Constructing grounded theory* (2nd ed.). London, England: Sage.

Cohen, L., Manion, L., & Morrison, K. (2011). *Research methods in education* (7th ed.). New York, NY: Routledge.

Miles, M. B., Huberman, A. M., & Saldaña, J. (2014). *Qualitative data analysis: A methods sourcebook* (3rd ed.). Thousand Oaks, CA: Sage.

Patton, M. Q. (2015). *Qualitative research and evaluation methods* (4th ed.). Thousand Oaks, CA: Sage. (See Part III, chaps. 8 and 9)

Richards, L. (2014). *Handling qualitative data: A practical guide* (3rd ed.). Thousand Oaks, CA: Sage.

Roulston, K. (2010). *Reflective interviewing: A guide to theory and practice.* Thousand Oaks, CA: Sage.

Ryan, G. W., & Bernard, H. R. (2000). Data management and analysis methods. In N. K. Denzin & Y. S. Lincoln (Eds.), *Handbook of qualitative research* (2nd ed., pp. 769–802). Thousand Oaks, CA: Sage.

Saldaña, J. (2013). *The coding manual for qualitative researchers* (2nd ed.). Thousand Oaks, CA: Sage.

Samure, K., & Given, L. M. (2008). Data saturation. In L. M. Given (Ed.), *The SAGE encyclopedia of qualitative research methods* (Vol. 1, pp. 195–196). Thousand Oaks, CA: Sage.

Witz, K. G. (2007). "Awakening to" an aspect in the other: On developing insights and concepts in qualitative research. *Qualitative Inquiry, 13*(2), 235–258.

Wolcott, H. F. (1994). *Transforming qualitative data: Description, analysis, and interpretation.* Thousand Oaks, CA: Sage.

Yesh, C. J., & Inman, A. G. (2007). Qualitative data analysis and interpretation in counseling psychology: Strategies for best practices. *The Counseling Psychologist, 35*(3), 369–403.

Analyzing Phenomenological Data

Gubrium, J. F., & Holstein, J. A. (2003). *Postmodern interviewing.* Thousand Oaks, CA: Sage.

Kvale, S., & Brinkmann, S. (2014). *Interviews: Learning the craft of qualitative research interviewing* (3rd ed.). Thousand Oaks, CA: Sage.

van Manen, M. (1990). *Researching lived experience: Human science for an action sensitive pedagogy.* Albany: State University of New York Press.

Smith, J. A., Flowers, P., & Larkin, M. (2009). *Interpretative phenomenological analysis: Theory method and research.* London, England: Sage. (See chap. 5)

Analyzing Ethnographic Data

Bogdan, R. C., & Biklen, S. K. (2006). *Qualitative research in education: An introduction to theory and methods* (5th ed.). Boston, MA: Allyn & Bacon.

Emerson, R. M., Fretz, R. I., & Shaw, L. L. (2011). *Writing ethnographic fieldnotes* (2nd ed.). Chicago, IL: University of Chicago Press.

Erickson, F. (1986). Qualitative methods in research on teaching. In M. C. Whittrock (Ed.), *Handbook of research on teaching* (3rd ed., pp. 119–161). New York, NY: Macmillan.

Madden, R. (2010). *Being ethnographic: A guide to the theory and practice of ethnography.* Thousand Oaks, CA: Sage.

Madison, D. S. (2011). *Critical ethnography: Method, ethics, and performance* (2nd ed.). Thousand Oaks, CA: Sage.

Wolcott, H. F. (1994). *Transforming qualitative data: Description, analysis, and interpretation.* Thousand Oaks, CA: Sage.

Wolcott, H. F. (2008). *Ethnography: A way of seeing* (2nd ed.). Walnut Creek, CA: AltaMira Press.

Analyzing Sociolinguistic Data

Gee, J. P. (2014). *Introduction to discourse analysis: Theory and method* (4th ed.). New York, NY: Routledge.

Holstein, J. A., & Gubrium, J. F. (2011). *Varieties of narrative analysis.* Thousand Oaks, CA: Sage.

Labov, W. (1982). Speech actions and reactions in personal narrative. In D. Tanner (Ed.), *Analyzing discourse: Text and talk* (pp. 219–247). Washington, DC: Georgetown University Press.

Lindlof, T. R., & Taylor, B. C. (2011). *Qualitative communication research methods* (3rd ed.). Thousand Oaks, CA: Sage.

Silverman, D. (2000). Analyzing talk and text. In N. K. Denzin & Y. S. Lincoln (Eds.), *Handbook of qualitative research* (2nd ed., pp. 821–834). Thousand Oaks, CA: Sage.

Silverman, D. (2015). *Interpreting qualitative data: Methods for analyzing talk, text, and interaction* (5th ed.). Thousand Oaks, CA: Sage. (See chap. 5)

Tilley, S. A. (2003). "Challenging" research practices: Turning a critical eye on the work of transcription. *Qualitative Inquiry, 9*(5), 750–773.

Analyzing Artifacts and Material Culture

Hodder, I. (2000). The interpretation of documents and material culture. In N. K. Denzin & Y. S. Lincoln (Eds.), *Handbook of qualitative research* (2nd ed., pp. 703–715). Thousand Oaks, CA: Sage.

Neuendorf, K. A. (2002). *The content analysis guidebook*. Thousand Oaks, CA: Sage.

Software for Analysis

ATLAS.ti for Windows [Computer software]. Berlin, Germany: ATLAS.ti Scientific Software Development. Trial copy retrieved from http://www.atlasti.com

Basit, T. N. (2003). Manual or electronic? The role of coding in qualitative data analysis. *Educational Research, 45*(2), 143–154.

Dedoose (Version 5.0.11) [Computer software]. Los Angeles, CA: SocioCultural Research Consultants, LLC. Retrieved from www.dedoose.com

Ethnograph (Version 6.0) [Computer software]. Colorado Springs, CO: Qualis Research. Retrieved from http://www.qualisresearch.com

Friese, S. (2014). *Qualitative data analysis with ATLAS.ti* (2nd ed.). Thousand Oaks, CA: Sage.

Kaefer, F., Roper, J., & Sinha, P. (2015). A software-assisted qualitative content analysis of news articles: Example and reflections. *FQS: Qualitative Social Research, 16*(2). Retrieved from http://www.qualitative-research.net/index.php/fqs/article/view/2123/3816

Lewins, A., & Silver, C. (2014). *Using software in qualitative research* (2nd ed.). Thousand Oaks, CA: Sage.

MAXQDA (Version 10) [Computer software]. Marburg, Germany: VERBI Software. Trial copy retrieved from http://www.maxqda.com

NVivo (Version 8) [Computer software]. Doncaster, Victoria, Australia: QSR International. Trial copy retrieved from http://www.qsrinternational.com

Rademaker, L. L., Grace, E. J., & Curda, S. K. (2012). Using computer-assisted qualitative data analysis software (CAQDAS) to re-examine traditionally analyzed data: Expanding our understanding of the data and of ourselves as scholars. *Qualitative Report, 17*(22), 1–11.

Weitzman, E. A. (2000). Software and qualitative research. In N. K. Denzin & Y. S. Lincoln (Eds.), *Handbook of qualitative research* (2nd ed., pp. 803–820). Thousand Oaks, CA: Sage.

11

Our Characters' Analyses

This chapter presents the products of our characters' labors. They have diligently gathered data and begun to make sense of them. Each follows a different analytic path, but all engage in asking questions of their data, identifying salient themes, coding the data, and interpreting them. This process is iterative, as the researcher cycles back and forth from snippets of data to larger categories and thematic ideas, back to the data to see if they "fit." To this process, our characters bring a range of resources, which may include

- direct experience of life and events in the setting;

- sensitivity toward the concerns and orientations of members;

- memory of other specific incidents described elsewhere in [their] notes;

- [their] own prior experience and insights gained in other settings; and

- the concepts and orientation provided by [their] own profession or discipline (Emerson et al., 1995, p. 146).

In **Ruth**'s case, the analysis process entails reading and rereading the data, noting broad themes that emerge through that work. Her sample field notes and transcripts are reformatted with broad right-hand margins where she writes a term to indicate a theme (Anthony also follows this formatting). She then writes a brief analytic memo in which she develops the theme of *agency*. Writing analytic memos, as indicated in Chapter 10, is an important part of developing insights into the topic. In Ruth's case, this memo is very much a work in progress.

Marla's process is collaborative. She and the women in her study read and reread and discuss possible themes that have relevance for their lives. Marla then takes these insights and does some preliminary coding of field notes and transcripts. She shares these with the women, and they make revisions. Based on these revisions, Marla writes a preliminary summary of what they have learned. This, too, is in the form of an analytic memo. This becomes a "working document" for the women to read, discuss, and revise. Because of her commitment to collaborative work, Marla's process is more iterative and complex than either Ruth's or Anthony's. Therefore, we include a second memo that reflects on the participation of and changes in the team members themselves.

With his focus on the culture of the arts program, **Anthony** relies on his three guiding questions to analyze the data. As you recall, he has data from multiple sources: (a) observations, (b) interviews, (c) surveys, and (d) documents. He elaborates subquestions from the guiding questions and codes the data with terms for these subquestions. He then develops a summary of one guiding question for his analytic memo.

ANTHONY'S ANALYSIS

Ethnographies usually begin with broad domains for gathering data that then shape analysis, and they are balanced between structure and openness. Central to ethnographic studies is the concept of culture. Tough, vague, and ambiguous, the concept focuses attention on widely shared and deeply held beliefs extant in a cultural group. Anthony's study focuses on program staff's and community members' beliefs about the arts, participation in events and activities, and the value to the community of the program. These categories (arts, participation, and value) are guides for his analysis.

Anthony initially organizes his data by the various *data-gathering techniques* he uses. He has one folder for interviews, others for the survey returns and observations.

As he gets more deeply into the analysis, however, he reorganizes the data into themes, based on the original evaluation questions about the extent of participation by community members; ways of participating; and the value of the program to staff, local artists, and both participating and nonparticipating community members. His observations at events and in the program office, the surveys he has administered, and his interviews with participants and nonparticipants are brought together to help him respond to the evaluation questions. Anthony identifies an overarching theme (*a culture of inclusion*) to depict the ways in which the program is integrated into the community.

As presented in Chapter 10 (see Table 10.7), Anthony has used checklists to document interactions at events. Table 11.1 shows the checklist he constructed while observing interactions between potters and community members at an outdoor crafts show. He has recorded the number of times community members went to the potter's wheel and the interactions between potters and community members. He has made hash marks (/) for each person or every interaction, as a running tally of presence, interactions, and actions. He also records instances of data that describe perspectives on *ways of participating* (see Table 11.2). For his analytic memo, Anthony presents and interprets some of these data to depict participation.

Anthony will elaborate these data with details from interviews with active participants and those less active, seeking to build a grounded understanding and explanation for his central concept (*participation*) and how that is fostered by a *culture of inclusion*. A summary table of Anthony's preliminary analysis of this concept is presented in Table 11.3.

Analytic Memo: What Participation Means

The community arts program office buzzes with people and ideas. Located in an aging storefront building just across from the little park, it sits at the center of the community. People are in and out all day long and well into the evening. Attendance at events and enrollment in classes is high. How has this program succeeded in building such strong links to its community? Three critical elements of the program stand out: (1) there is a strong belief in involving community members in all aspects of the program, (2) a variety of activities and events is offered, and (3) it is staffed by community members and the location is ideal. This analytic memo begins with detailing attendance and enrollment and then elaborates on the *culture of inclusion* that characterizes the program.

TABLE 11.1   Actions at Pottery Exhibit, 10/17

Time	# Around Wheel	Interactions	Actions
9:00–9:30 a.m.	////	Questions: //	Touching pots
		Comments: //	Picking up glazes
9:30–10:00 a.m.			

TABLE 11.2   Participation

Theme	Data Source
Types of participating	
Watching and asking questions	ON, pottery exhibition (10/17)
Attending classes	ON, watercolor class (11/3)
Giving readings	I, Gene (11/8)
Attending concerts (wanting to)	I, Sal (11/5)
Helping out at the office	ON, office (10/10)
Value of participating	
Brings families together	I, Gene (11/8)
Lets people experiment and take risks	ON, office, Elderly Man (10/10)
	ON, watercolor class (11/3)
Gets teenagers off the streets	I, Gene (11/8)
Expressing self	I, Gene (11/8)
	ON, office, Elderly Man (10/10)

Note: ON, observation notes; I, interview.

TABLE 11.3   Culture of Inclusion: Knowing and Being Known

Knowing and Being Known	
Observation, 10/10:	Details of life
D: "Hey there, Gene. So how did the gum work go? Was the dentist gentle?"	
G: "I survived. Got some catching up to do. Thought I'd see what's happening and if I can help on anything."	Sharing food
He opens the bag and takes out two steaming cups of soup and a loaf of bread. "It's their version of minestrone today."	
D: "Smells good. Thanks. Actually, you can do the registrations for Heather's class." Gestures to the computer on the other desk. Gene begins working on the computer.	Helping out
Observation, 10/10:	
W1: "I got a job! Aren't you going to ask me what it is?"	
W2: "Yeah, she's part of the labor force now. Wonder if she'll have time for us anymore."	Details of life
D: "Well, congratulations! But don't forget you're still Stella to us."	

(Continued)

TABLE 11.3   (Continued)

Knowing and Being Known	

Observation, 10/10:

EM:	"I don't know. Do I need experience?"	
D:	"Now, honey, you've got all the experience you need for this class. You can fill out this paper and try some of this bread. What brings you to us?"	Reassurance Sharing food
EM:	"My granddaughter keeps telling me I need to get what she calls "an interest." I think she's worried about me. Always wanted to paint. . . . "	Sharing food

D assures him he is in the right place. He takes a chunk of bread and joins us.

Attendance Records from the program office and results from the survey of instructors indicate that most classes offered by the center are fully enrolled: 82% of all classes this year have enrolled at least 10 people (the minimum number needed). Instructors indicated that attendance in classes is generally good (the exception being the class on "WomanPause," which had 100% each session). Observations (crafts show, classical guitar concert, clothesline art exhibit, and indigenous dance) indicate that community members attend regularly and in high numbers. Estimates ranged from 175 to more than 200 in attendance. For the concerts, these estimates were obtained by counting rows and numbers of seats in rows for the concerts; for the outdoor shows, by counting people around an exhibit and multiplying by the number of exhibits, with some estimate of "large" or "small" groups. This is a crude way to estimate but the results were corroborated by program staff.

From the interviews, the ways people participate and the value that participation has for them are being documented. Community members have mentioned that they can watch closely an artist at work and ask him questions or allow him to comment; they particularly mention that this casual atmosphere makes asking questions easy. Many talk about the classes they or their children have attended. A few help out in the office, but several noted that they feel they can "drop in" to the office to see what is happening. A few even mention that a cup or a bite of something is always available for them when they do.

The value of the program to them is that the variety of activities gives them ways to express themselves or appreciate the work of others. Some mentioned that they can take risks and try out new things. In the case of a man who came into the program office, he mentioned that he had always wanted to paint (ON, 10/10), and the class in watercolors would let him try this out. One artist who teaches poetry writing said that the program brings families together and even involves youth in important ways (I, 11/8). (Note that "ON" means observation notes; "I" indicates an interview.)

A Culture of Inclusion   The program is clearly successful, although not without challenges. Program staff, instructors, and community members have built a *culture of inclusion* that makes the community feel that the program belongs to them. This is accomplished through actions and interactions that suggest that people feel known and welcomed in all program activities. Ways of *being known and welcomed* include (a) the accessibility of the center and its office (dropping in is easy); (b) awareness of program staff and "regulars" in the program office who know details of their lives (to drop in is to belong); (c) sharing of food, including offering it to "newcomers" who come in ("come eat with us"); and (d) everyone being asked to help out in small and large ways (ON, 10/10). For example, two women from the community came into the office to share the good news about one of them getting a job. Others there were congratulatory but suggested that the woman would be missed if she no longer dropped in regularly. When an elderly man entered the program office to ask about a painting class, the staff person reassured him that he needed no prior experience, invited him to share a large loaf of bread on the table, and facilitated his signing up for the watercolor class. These observations suggest that those who are integral to the program's functioning (staff and community members alike) take quite seriously the notion that the program is to welcome and serve *all* the community.

Next steps are to continue gathering data about attendance, complete the surveys of community members, and locate additional people (participants and nonparticipants) for interviews. The interviews with less active people are proving to be especially useful for identifying ways the Center can reach out more effectively; these will be incorporated in the final report under Recommendations.

[This in-process memo by Anthony is well done. He provides sufficient evidence to support his themes, but at times his points are a bit unclear, such as when he discusses attendance. He indicates the broad themes for his subsequent data gathering and analysis and is beginning to flesh out the concept of culture of inclusion. This may well be the most insightful aspect of Anthony's evaluation. However, he will have to continue to document participation to satisfy the requirements of the evaluation contract.]

RUTH'S ANALYSIS

Phenomenological studies are open ended, searching for the themes of meaning in participants' lives. Broad categories are sought, with subthemes, to elaborate the topography of meaning. Phenomenological analysis requires that the researcher approach the texts with an open mind, seeking what meaning structures emerge. The first step in reducing text is to read the interview transcripts (and related observation field notes, if gathered) and mark those passages that stand out as interesting. Through her growing understanding of the phenomenon, the researcher develops an intuitive sense of what is "interesting." An essential part of the process is then to examine those passages to discern and identify what prompted this initial interest. The researcher might then check with participants to see if they agree with the emerging analytic themes. Each transcript is unique; the meaning of the experience of interest will emerge from that transcript. The identified important passages of interest are then assigned codes that represent themes. Using these words to organize the data, the researcher generates a profile, or a narrative, depicting the meaning of the phenomenon for the individual.

Ruth's study has focused on the meaning of "bodied-ness" for children who have physical disabilities. As the study has evolved, Ruth has identified the concept of *agency* to capture the children's feelings about their lives, particularly in terms of participating in sports activities. Related themes focus on how their families support their *independence* and the meanings associated with *differentness*. These themes are broad and provide preliminary categories on which Ruth can rely as she begins to analyze the data.

Ruth's preliminary organization is very simple. Because she relies primarily on interviews, she keeps her transcripts in files identified by the children's names. As she becomes more confident about the salient themes, however, she reorganizes segments of data into those themes. She then creates folders containing copies of relevant quotes for each theme. As she writes the final report, she relies on this thematic organization, which pulls together data about the children and their families. Tables 11.4 through 11.6 show Ruth's preliminary coding and analysis about the theme of agency.

Following is an example of the preliminary analysis Ruth does with her data. Kent has asked the students to write analytic memos periodically. These help organize the data, provide insights into the topic, and identify areas for further data gathering. Ruth wrote this memo after several observations at the center and four of the six planned-for interviews. She develops the theme of *agency*, pulling together snippets of data and elaborating her interpretations. She is well aware of her partial understanding of the complexities of the children's lives.

TABLE 11.4   Preliminary Coding: Agency (Mark's Interview, 10/5)

Mark: I use my wheels. I can move faster. I'm The Dominator!	
Ruth: So your wheelchair actually helps?	
Mark: Well, I don't know. I just know that I use it.	
Ruth: What's it feel like being better than him?	Agency: Sense that he can be good while using a wheelchair
Mark: Cool!	
Ruth: Yeah, I'll bet. You're better than Diego, but are you the star?	
Mark: No! I said I'm The Dominator!	
Ruth: But what does that mean?	
Mark: I told you: I control the ball on the floor.	
Ruth: Then you're really the Floor General, right?	

TABLE 11.5   Preliminary Coding: Agency (Katrine's Interview, 10/9)

Ruth: When did you know that you were really good?	
Katrine: I guess I've always known. They wouldn't have played with me if I couldn't have kept up with them. At least after they taught me the basics.	Agency: Sense of being strong and powerful; relationships with brothers (acceptance???)
Ruth: Do you remember how they taught you?	
Katrine: Boy, it seemed like a lot of drill, but they were pretty patient with me.	
Ruth: Do you remember anything specific?	
Katrine: They were bigger than me, so they always had the ball. I got tired of them always having it. So they had to teach me how to steal the ball. That worked pretty well when I was little and could wiggle in between them. Now I'm nearly 6 feet and it's not so easy! (laughs)	
Ruth: Other ways you knew you were good?	
Katrine: Well, my mom talked to me about basketball camp when I was 10. That was a clue. You know, I just play here because I like the other kids. It's not like playing over at the middle school.	

TABLE 11.6   Agency: Acceptance

K's interview (10/9):

"They were pretty patient with me." (p. 3)

"It [being deaf] sure isn't a handicap." (p. 5)

M's interview (10/5):

"I guess they've figured out how to use me." (p. 4)

Field notes (10/3):

"Mark takes the ball and, holding it cradled in his lap, wheels down the court after Amanda, Katrine, and the other two. He pats his head three times. I find out later this means that Amanda will set up a pick for Katrine, who will cut to the basket." (p. 9)

On Agency

Mark is the point guard—the floor general—of an after-school basketball team. Katrine is the star center. Both have what society calls "disabilities." Mark uses a wheelchair and has to be helped to use the bathroom. Katrine is profoundly deaf and has been so since birth.

Mark has been called "crippled." Katrine has been told that she daydreams and is stupid. Both have survived the cruelty of their peers and adults, and they have built lives that are strong and powerful. How? Through a sense of *agency*.

Agency is defined as action, as having an effect, as being able to influence events. Children with physical disabilities, living in an able-bodied world, can feel marginalized, different, or weird. Some cannot get into a building because it lacks ramps; others do not hear the bells ring announcing the end of a class. The hearing and ambulatory world is indifferent to their differences. Within this indifferent or downright hostile world, Mark and Katrine have come to feel that they are accepted and have power as individuals—power to shape events, to have an effect, to be accepted in the world. They have a sense of agency.

This preliminary analytic memo develops the theme of agency that I have identified in the data gathered up to now. Using quotes from interviews and observation field notes, as well as my own interpretations, I elaborate on the concept of agency as Mark and Katrine have taught me about it.

Sense of Efficacy Integral to the meaning of *disability* to both Mark and Katrine is a sense of efficacy—the capacity to act on the world in positive ways. Katrine was taught in her early years that she could compete with her brothers. They drilled into her the basics of basketball, developing her natural talents. As she grew (both in height and in skill), she could play nearly evenly with them. She could steal the ball and throw jump shots, playing two-on-two with them. All these early experiences helped build a sense of efficacy.

Mark has learned that his quickness with his arms and his ability to see opponents' moves make him quite effective as a point guard, even using a wheelchair. He calls himself "the dominator," which suggests that he relishes this leadership role on the court.

Acceptance For both Mark and Katrine, a sense of agency comes in part from being accepted and valued by their peers. This is played out (no pun intended) on the basketball court, where both feel that they have important roles to play that are recognized and valued by others in the team. Mark describes his role on the team as setting up plays and controlling the movement of the ball. He calls himself "the dominator," suggesting that his role is a powerful one. He notes that the other kids "have figured out how to use me." He feels like he's a valuable contributor. In an observation (10/3), I wrote that Mark decides the plays and works the ball from player to player, calling out their names as he passes:

> Mark takes the ball and, holding it cradled in his lap, wheels down the court after Amanda, Katrine, and the other two. He pats his head three times. **[I find out later this means that Amanda will set up a pick for Katrine, who will cut to the basket.]** He passes to Joey, who feeds the ball to Katrine. She grabs the ball, nearly fouling Curtis, dribbles once and puts it in for two.

The team has decided that plays will be signaled using hand gestures, a mark of respect for Katrine. In the first interview with her, Katrine mentioned this: "That's one of the things that makes me a good player; I know how to pick up signals. My brothers taught me, and my mom says it's easier for me because I'm deaf." Katrine has turned what society calls a disability into a strength; the team honors and values this capacity in her.

Next Steps These ideas are just now coming together. I have become fascinated with Katrine and Mark and how they view their worlds. It is difficult to get Mark to elaborate on how he feels about his role on the court as someone who uses a wheelchair, but it has been easier with Katrine. I plan to do one more interview with Mark (at the center) and two more with Katrine. She is quite open about her deafness and how it has shaped her life; Mark is less so.

[Ruth's preliminary analytic memo brings together her insights about these two children and the data that support these insights. She will have to tease out more fully what she means (and what she infers Mark and Katrine mean) by agency, efficacy, and acceptance. Is efficacy distinct from agency? What is the role of a sense of acceptance in the development of Mark's and Katrine's worldviews? These are questions for Ruth to consider as her study and analysis proceed.]

MARLA'S ANALYSIS

Case studies are uniquely intended to capture the complexity of a particular event, program, individual, or place. They focus holistically on an organization or an individual. The conceptual framework and research questions help narrow a broad focus more closely into categories of interest. These categories then provide the initial ways for thinking analytically and for a first cut on coding the data. Marla and her team have assumed a critical stance, focusing on oppression and domination in specific ways. They assume a feminist and class-based perspective, examining ways by which clinical services are structured to depersonalize poor women and their choices in health care.

The strategy of Marla and her team is similar to Ruth's, although more iterative and collaborative. Marla has assumed responsibility for organizing and managing the data. She initially organizes the data by source: (a) observations, (b) field notes of team meetings, and (c) interviews with women. She and her team meet regularly for dialogue and analysis. They read the data independently and then bring their insights to the team meetings. As their understanding evolves, they reorganize the data into salient themes. They also develop files for data about the three women on whom they focus in depth. These files contain the team's notes, transcriptions of interviews, and excerpts from the women's journals. Marla, as "chief scribe" of the group, creates a set of tables that summarizes data around emerging themes (one such table is presented in Table 11.7). For her first analytic memo, she writes about the theme, as well as the team's process in analyzing these data collaboratively.

TABLE 11.7   "Waiting"

> "That stupid girl behind the desk—she acted like I wasn't even there. Looked right through me. Just yammered on the phone." (Int w/Yvette, 10/23, p. 1)
>
> "When she finally got off the phone—it was her boyfriend, I think—she asked me a million questions and typed them into her stupid computer." (Int w/Yvette, 10/23, p. 3)
>
> "Then I had to sit there and wait. Seemed like forever. I almost got to see a whole episode of *As the World Turns*!" (Int w/Yvette, 10/23, p. 3)
>
> "These people have been waiting here for at least a half an hour!" (OC, Obs, 10/10, p. 2)
>
> "Still quiet; we're just sitting here!" (OC, Obs, 10/10, p. 2)

Memo 1: Collaborative Analysis: The Process and Some Preliminary Insights

Analyzing data together is hard work. My team and I have met weekly for the past 7 weeks. We have read over the data we are gathering before these meetings and then come to the meeting ready to talk about what we discover. After that, we go home, read through the data again, and come back to share those insights. The team has been terrific! They are really committed to doing this work, even though it means lots of reading and thinking. And they are continuing to interview the three women and do some observations at the clinic.

We've had some interesting discussions. One centered around the theme of *waiting*. We all agreed that the data we had from the women, our own experiences, and what we observed show that there are lots of ways that people who use the clinic are made to wait. Take Yvette, for example. She talked about how the girl at the desk made her wait while she was on a personal phone call. And she talked about sitting and watching TV for a long time before she was called in to see one of the PAs or doctors. The field notes have mentioned several times about people who had to sit and wait and wait and wait.

The discussions we've had about this have to do with "why" questions. We've disagreed about the reasons why women have to wait. We all have our own hypotheses, but we haven't really explored this deeply with the three women. Aida says that she thinks that it has to do with race. I think it has to do with class and gender. For example, we have all seen that the receptionist responds differently to men than to women, and she always listens to the PA. Julia believes it is that the doctors are so busy that they can't see the patients sooner. It is just in the nature of health clinics not to see people quickly. We are all concerned about this waiting because it may be one of the reasons why the women don't come back to the clinic. The next step in our process will be to discuss these possibilities with the three women in some depth.

[This early memo describes the preliminary data analysis done by Marla and her team and identifies the next steps, as asked for in Kent's course requirements. The team has focused on waiting as a persistent issue for the women. This insight comes from their own previous experiences in clinics, the data from the women, and their observations. They are beginning to hypothesize that this expectation of several lost hours at the clinic might be a deterrent for the women to return for follow-up care. Although not providing much supporting data (in the form of quotes from interviews and field notes), this memo hints at the complexity of collaborative data analysis: the need for full involvement, balancing alternative insights and perspectives, and honoring the views of all team members. The next memo Marla writes shows the evolution of the team's process from inquiry and reflection to a commitment to take action, an essential element of participatory action research.]

Memo 2: Taking Action

We have come a long way, my team and I. We have gathered data and involved the three women in the process of reflecting on their experiences, identifying possible reasons, and discussing various courses of action that we, as committed women, can take.

One idea that has become very important is how the three women feel like they are not real people when they come into the clinic. Some of this has to do with all the time they spend waiting, some has to do with having a man examine them, and some has to do with speaking English. We have discussed all this with them in two sessions, where we talked through what we were collectively learning and asked them what actions they might take. The three women all commented on how going through this process with us has made them feel like they could take some action. They talked about the need to change the clinic, in small ways at first, to make it *their* clinic. In one of these meetings, Yvette talked about her oldest daughter, who goes to Eastside Community College for a degree in human services. One of her instructors talked about the need for bilingual workers in community health clinics to serve as liaisons and interpreters with clinic patients. Her instructor is committed to changing social service agencies to better meet the needs of the people they are supposed to serve. One idea that came out of this discussion was to ask the instructor to work with the manager of the clinic to have people like Yvette's daughter placed there for some of their internship work. We agreed that this kind of action might make the clinic more responsive to the needs of poor people, especially women.

Another idea that has come out of these meetings is to ask for an appointment with the Director of Health Clinics for the city. His office is downtown, and he may not agree, but the women (Yvette, Teresa, and Maria) and all the members of our team feel that, as a group and based on our action research, he might listen to us. We want to talk with him about what we have learned and see if he can develop a plan for assigning staff to the neighborhood clinics. We talked about how this might be a good time to try to meet with him because of the big grant that the city just got to help rebuild poorer neighborhoods.

We are also planning to meet with the Healthy Women/Healthy Children group that has formed in The Heights. It is an advocacy group that is trying to change health care services to women and children, and it is close to us. We can join forces with this group and learn what its strategies are for getting bureaucracies to listen.

I am feeling a bit overwhelmed by all the work ahead of us. But I'm really pleased that the women continue to be as involved as they are. They are coming to learn that the clinic is *their* clinic. They understand now how it works and want to take action to make it work for them.

[Marla's second memo describes the process of determining to take action that is central to participatory action research. It might have turned out otherwise. The women might have continued to feel distant and marginalized from the clinic, or they might have felt that taking action would come to nothing. But through the process of dialogue, research, and reflection, they have come to a place of commitment to action. Although Marla's work for the qualitative research course will soon end, her work with these women, and others like them, will continue for a long time.]

DISPOSITIONS AND SKILLS

Anthony, Ruth, and Marla's use of memo writing contributes to their growing sense of competence with the principles of good practice. Their memos highlight their decision making and the logic behind those decisions, as well as their sensitivities to the subtle undercurrents in the field. At this point, memo writing can help our characters begin to see if—and when—they have enough data to support their conclusions. They are ready to start writing their final projects. They are demonstrating their understanding of the key dispositions and skills that they have practiced over the course of their projects:

- Comfort with ambiguity

- Capacity to make reasoned decisions and to articulate the logic behind those decisions

- Deep interpersonal or emotional sensitivity

- Ethical sensitivity of potential consequences to individuals and groups

- Political sensitivity

- Perseverance and self-discipline

ACTIVITIES FOR YOUR COMMUNITY OF PRACTICE

Study Questions for Students

- How do researchers analyze ethnographic data?

- How do researchers analyze phenomenological data?

- How do researchers analyze sociolinguistic data?

- What strategies do they use for analyzing field notes from observations? For analyzing material culture?

Small-Group and Dyad Activities

Analyzing Analytic Memos

Divide into three groups representing Marla, Ruth, and Anthony. In your group, examine the analytic memo(s) that your character has written. Discuss the following questions:

- What do you imagine was the character's process in constructing the themes?

- What is the supporting evidence provided by the character for a theme?

- What advice would you give your character to strengthen this analytic memo?

- What do you see as your character's next steps?

Developing Criteria for Judging Your Project

Throughout the book, we have presented several principles for the sound, thoughtful, and ethical conduct of qualitative research projects. One is that there should be *integrity* in the assumptions of the paradigm in which you situate yourself. Those driving the conceptual framework and expressed in the design, implementation, and writing up of the project should be congruent. Another principle is that, in your final write-up, your *thinking should be clear* to the reader.

- Where did this project begin?

- What questions drove it initially?

- How did these change?

- How did you then design the project?

- What changes did you make?

- What prompted these changes?

(Continued)

(Continued)

Yet another set of principles rest on the *clarity of your interpretations*.

- Are they supported by evidence from your work?

- Have you examined other possible interpretations?

- How do you incorporate the interpretations of the participants, if they differ from yours?

In your small groups, first share progress on your project. Focus specifically on issues, problems, or worries that you have identified. Then turn the discussion to some criteria or standards that you would apply to your own work and to that of your colleagues.

- What would you look for, if you were reading the final papers?

- What would convince you that a project had been thought through and conducted carefully, sensitively, and thoughtfully?

- How might you structure the writing of the final report to demonstrate this?

- How would you like *your* project to be evaluated?

- What considerations would you bring to that evaluation to ensure that the project is evaluated sensitively and thoroughly?

Develop some criteria for all projects and for yours specifically. Then share these with the large group.

12

Presenting the Learnings

Anthony, Marla, and Ruth are at the final step in the research process. They have collected and analyzed their data. They have made their interpretations. They have moved from field texts of notes and documents to research texts of codes, categories, and memos, and finally to interpretive texts. They are ready to present what they have learned. Whether for class, for the participants in their studies, or for other audiences, they have options for how to present their findings. They also have a variety of ways to organize the presentation of their material. How they choose to present and organize their findings depends on their purposes, the questions they posed, and to whom they are presenting. As Marla suggests, they may need to prepare more than one presentation if they have several audiences.

Like the three students, you are also at the presentation stage. You have turned your data into information that has become your knowledge, and now you want to share this knowledge with others. Whatever you have learned, chances are that you do not want it to be ignored, relegated to a dusty shelf or forgotten file. You want your work to make a difference, to be used by some audience. You are at the final stage of the heuristic discovery process. Once again, you rely on your sense of becoming a good qualitative researcher to consider the prevailing context and to design an engaging and useful presentation of your findings. The format you decide on could be anything from a formal written report to a multimedia demonstration, depending on what you have discovered, who your audience is, and the extent of your resources.

Your *knowledge and practice of key dispositions and skills* are just as important at the end as they were at the start of the study. To finish the project, you have to know when you have enough data. Political sensitivities will, in part, shape your choice of presentation. Just as the entire research process has been conducted with deep interpersonal and ethical sensitivity, so should the final report reflect this sensitivity (whatever form it takes). You are careful that the findings do not deliberately hurt anyone (although this is often challenging to predict). You are diligent about grounding the findings in data (rather than impressions or conjectures), and you articulate the logic behind any decisions. Your audiences have to be able to *see* or *hear* how you reached your conclusions. Throughout this process, you are reflexive—that is, you remain acutely conscious of yourself as the author of the presentation.

This chapter explores the possibilities and challenges frequently faced in this final step in the research. Although we introduce various ways to present the work, we recommend including some form of writing because writing demands that you articulate and clarify the findings. Writing, especially analytic descriptive writing, is essential to the discovery process. We discuss purpose and voice, and we offer a detailed example of the evolution of a formal written report (a dissertation) as a play. We suggest several strategies for organizing the material, as well. Finally, we review the potential uses for research in light of the general dispositions and skills that have been presented throughout the book. We hope that you are beginning to integrate these into your practice as a qualitative researcher.

PRESENTATION

Sharing what has been learned (the findings) draws from both systematic and creative ways of thinking. Consider two tasks: (1) engaging your audience and, at the same time, (2) convincing them that the findings are credible and trustworthy. To accomplish the latter, you will need to demonstrate how your work has been "systematic, analytical, rigorous, disciplined, and critical in perspective" (Patton, 1990, p. 433).[1] To engage your audience, your work could well be "exploring, playful, metaphorical, insightful, and creative" (Patton, 1990, p. 433). Fortunately, today, given the Internet, an almost limitless variety of ways, other than a traditional written report, exist to enliven how you share your findings. The options you choose may well be shaped by audience (politics and ethics again) and purpose, but consider creating your own medium. In today's technology-dependent world, audiences often respond more directly to multimedia presentations or online formats, so considering alternatives to a written report has merit.

Audience and Purpose

As you consider how to present the findings, have an audience in mind. Consider these questions:

- Who cares about what you have learned?
- Who should know about this?
- What interests them?

Different groups have different norms and expectations, so knowing at least something about the audience matters. Academic audiences want a term paper, thesis, or dissertation; they also read scholarly journals and monographs. Sponsors feel that they have contracted to get a full report. Popular audiences read magazines, books, autobiographies, blogs, and websites. All of these audiences also watch videos, listen to tapes, and get news and other information from the Internet. The particular audience will, at least to some extent, shape the format and medium of your presentation. Consider creating more than one product to avoid the impossible task of believing that you have to say everything to everyone at the same time (Richardson, 1994).

For our three students, the professor and their classmates provide the first and most obvious audience: their community of practice (remember that this includes the professor). But Kent has already told them that he will accept alternative formats, depending on other audiences for their work.

A second audience for **Anthony**'s evaluation is program staff and the funders. He most likely will produce an evaluation report, but he may find that an oral briefing supplemented with PowerPoint slides, perhaps including video clips, is more meaningful for them. However, Anthony would be wise to (and most likely contracted to) offer a brief executive summary or abstract that summarizes the essential findings, the conclusions, and recommendations (if any) and that outlines the procedures he used (to establish reasons for confidence in the findings). People are more likely to read the summary than the report, and they will *need* a written summary if they did not require a full report. If Anthony's clients request an oral briefing, he may consider (depending on his resources) preparing a multimedia presentation drawing on the various arts represented in the center to tell the history of the arts center in the community.

Marla has several very different audiences. She hopes to change the behavior of the barrio women who might need the clinic's services, so these women are an immediate audience. She and her collaborators are planning a series of newsletters using information from their case studies. The newsletters will be readable and will be distributed in places where barrio women will find them and read them—she is aware that not everyone has Internet access. She also hopes to influence clinical practices and procedures to be more responsive to clients. Thus, another audience is the clinic staff and board of directors. Marla's team may communicate its findings to the staff through formal and informal conversations. The women will orally brief the board and leave with them an executive summary. Beyond the clinic-related audiences, Marla envisions telling the story of poor women's health care so that a greater society can comprehend, and perhaps address, this aspect of poverty and the disenfranchised and disempowered. A book of the case studies sold on the popular market is a possibility for reaching this broad audience.

Ruth's audiences are less easily defined. She wants her story about the turning points in the athletic lives of children with disabilities to reach people who work with these children, but she does not want to limit her audience to special educators. She submits her story to an online journal for teachers. She knows that she would like to also reach parents and maybe the general public, so she considers writing a script for a video that would capture the story visually as well as in words. Her roommate, a student of cinematography, has already explored possibilities for producing a documentary.

Ruth, Anthony, and Marla consider how to present their information so that it will be used. They think about their *purposes*. Do they aim to

- explain?
- describe?
- influence?
- change behavior?
- entertain?
- advocate?

Marla is concerned about action; Anthony's intent is to influence decision making and to improve the program; and Ruth wants to tell a story. Most of their ideas break the paradigm of the traditional, linear, attempting-to-be-objective, written report. They assess the learning preferences of intended and potential audiences and design their presentations accordingly, choosing what they hope will be the most effective medium.

Possible Formats

Presenting what you have learned is a form of knowledge dissemination. Options for disseminating knowledge used to be limited to a few traditional media: written material, television, film, and radio. Today, media are more developed and variegated, and you can now choose from a whole world of technological applications. Use the following list as a stimulus for thinking about ways you could present your findings:

- Paper
- Descriptive essay
- Journal article or monograph
- Analytic memo or report
- Magazine or newspaper article
- Webpage
- Social media posts
- Individual conference presentation
- Conference symposium or roundtable discussion
- PowerPoint presentation
- Newsletter
- Story, novelette, or play
- Poem
- Biography or autobiography
- Documentary film or video
- Handbook
- Letter to editor
- CD/DVD/interactive video
- Interactive website
- Topical blog or wiki
- Teleconference
- Imagine other possibilities

Examples of these formats, even the more unusual, abound. Pore over articles in journals in your area or on your topic to find potential models or to spark your imagination. Attend relevant conferences to observe both the good and the bad. Borrow ideas from other fields such as film and literature and journalism. We had a doctoral student who presented her findings from a study of first-year teachers in the form of a novel (Chatman, 1990). Bolman and Deal (1993, 1994) and Bolman, Deal, and Rallis (1995) have shared the cumulative findings from years of work in educational organizations in a series of novelettes focusing on a principal, a teacher, and a school board. Wolf (1992) presents a fictionalized account, actual field notes, and an article published in an academic journal in *A Thrice Told Tale*. Another student used findings from a study of student teachers to prepare a handbook that could be used to guide student–teacher supervisors. An accomplished photographer who studied the meaning of a chapel in the lives of students and teachers at a boarding school exhibited the photographs that comprised part of her findings; the photographs were also included in her dissertation (Fisk, 1996). Research on teaching, learning, cognition, and technology culminated in the production of the now classic Jasper Series[2] of interactive videos to enhance children's problem-solving processes in math and science classes.

Advances in technology suggest multiple new avenues for dissemination. Several students have produced videos that supplement their written work with visual compositions. One, whose dissertation compared leadership transition periods with change of command in the military, developed a video to accompany his written material. Bulletin boards can display findings of several related studies. The Internet is a natural pathway, as wikis, blogs, and other websites are increasingly popular ways to disseminate findings. Graphics packages offer new and alternative means to display findings. The use of hypertext allows interaction with audiences. The variety of methods in teleconferencing enables researchers to share information and take live questions from remote audiences.

Because so many different possibilities for presentation exist, a few *cautionary notes* are in order. Be sure you have a reason for the medium you have chosen if you are using an alternative format. Don't use technology just because it is there and you are fascinated with it or because you think that it will show that you are very current. Surely you have yawned as "talking heads" on a video screen imparted so-called knowledge that would have been more interesting to read. Used with prudence, however, technology is a powerful way to share what you have learned.

VOICE

The voice you choose to tell your story (to relate your discoveries) is as likely to determine the impact you will have on the audience as the findings themselves. Voice engages the reader. It conveys passion and interest—or a lack of it. Boring texts and dull presentations are those in which individual voices have been suppressed and homogenized through professional socialization into the "omniscient voice of science" (Richardson, 1994, p. 517). Boring texts are not read and dull presentations are not listened to.

Your presentation, written or oral, need not be dull. You have spent time in the field, looking, asking, listening, and reading. You have interpreted events, activities, conversations, and objects and constructed your own meaning or understanding of them. Remember who you are, why you undertook the study, and the decisions that grounded your inquiry (Richardson, 1994). The story is *yours* to tell, even if the story is about another or others. "The Other who is presented in the text is always a version of the researcher's self" (Denzin, 1994, p. 503). As the storyteller, you choose the voice.

Voice implies subjectivity, not clean, scientific objectivity.   "All texts are biased, reflecting the play of class, gender, race, ethnicity, and culture, suggesting that so-called objective interpretations are impossible" (Denzin, 1994, p. 507). You choose a voice that allows you to reveal yourself, to articulate your biases. Establishing who you are frees you to tell the story of the "Others." Ruth, for example, will blend the first and third persons as she writes about the children she has come to know:

> Amanda is a champion basketball player. She captains her winning team with enthusiasm, joy, humor, and lots of practice. She told me, "I guess anything is possible . . . as long as we're all patient. I know I'll never walk and chew gum at the same time, but I *can* wheel and dribble at the same time!" Amanda is a 12-year-old who uses a wheelchair. I met Amanda and her teammates as a part of my study of how children in wheelchairs see themselves as athletes.

Choosing a voice is tricky because the voices of the researcher and the participants become enmeshed. Brown and Gilligan (1990) refer to the "polyphony of human discourse" (p. 3) and the self behind the self. As has Jonathan Kozol in his moving works about the lives of children, Ruth situates herself in direct relationship with her participants. Readers of her stories will know why she became fascinated with the athletic lives of children with physical disabilities and how she discovered the concept of "bodied-ness." Anthony will use the third person to tell the history of arts in the community, but his voice will not be that of an abstract, disembodied observer. He will use the words of the artists and the community members, spoken to him, to tell the story.

The trick is to *balance the various voices* without allowing your own voice to take over so that the story is about you rather than the subject. We caution you not to "bare your soul" in an autobiographical or confessional piece (Van Maanen, 1988). Our position is that you claim your authorial (and interpretive) voice, but you are not the center; you are not the focal point of the story. As Dara Rossman Regaigon (personal communication, March 3, 1997) notes, "The 'I' of your writing is the sun illuminating the object; it is not the object itself." You want the reader to engage with what you have learned, not with an egocentric revelation of your learning process.

Voice is especially important because *authorship gives power*. Although power lies in the knowledge produced by the study, the mode of representation chosen by the author augments that power. For example, people who read Ruth's story or watch the documentary will recall vividly Amanda and her triumphs, *as Ruth has represented them*. For many people, Amanda will come to symbolize *all* children in wheelchairs. The author's version of reality is powerful, but power also lies in how the participants speak *through* the authorial voice. The author has to be vigilant that she is accurately and ethically representing the voice she has chosen. Marla and her research team hope to use the power of their learnings to precipitate change. Because they speak *for* the women they have studied, they must be extra careful. To avoid misrepresentations, they rely on the fact-filled newsletters about the health problems they have identified as common to women in the barrio. Their oral report is filled with direct quotes. If they write a book, it will be coauthored and will enable the women to tell their own stories.

Finding the right balance of voice can take *many, many drafts*—and then some more. An example comes from a painful memory of writing the portrait of the principal of a restructuring school (Rallis, 1992). The first draft was overly focused on the author and what she saw; it told more about her than about the principal. Early critiques of the manuscript pointed out that she dominated the text,[3] so she was able to shift the focus. Several drafts later, she captured the "self" of the principal she had shadowed and learned about, keeping her "author self" in the background. Still, she recognized that what she saw and heard constituted her evidence, her foundation for the principal's self she describes, so she kept her voice present.

> Ken seems to belong in his school. Whether we walk into the building during the day or for an evening concert, whether we join a group of teachers in a meeting or passing through the halls, Midway High is Ken's domain. The atmosphere reflects his personality: calm and orderly and enthusiastic. Like most comprehensive high schools, Midway is a large and complex organization whose operations are shaped by multiple agendas and constantly reshaped by immediate and arising needs. Yet, Ken is not a slave to these agendas and needs. In my week with Ken, I have seen him balance emerging needs with existing priorities, without breaking the natural momentum of school life. (p. 5)

Knowing your audience and having decided on a format and voice, you can organize an engaging presentation of what you have learned.

AN EXAMPLE

What follows is an illustration of how you can present your data in both a formal academic style and a livelier manner. Woo (1999) developed a strong dissertation describing and analyzing the experiences of six Asian American young women attending a high school in New York City. Recently, she has experimented with expressing the findings in different formats. She has been working on a play that depicts the internal struggles and social and academic pressures these young women face. The thick description and analysis that follow are adapted from that dissertation (with her permission). The skit (Woo, 2000) is a work in progress. We present both to show how creative presentations of your data can be quite engaging and reach different audiences. The first two sections below, "Thick Description" and "Analysis," come from her dissertation (Woo, 1999). The final section on her work comes from her unpublished, work-in-progress play (Woo, 2000).

Thick Description: Starr

"Most Asian people get good grades. If we do something like cut class or walk in the hallway without a pass, we're not going to get in trouble . . . because they know we are good students. We get away with a lot of things."

Starr was 18 years old and a senior at Green High School. Of the six participants in the study, Starr appeared to exemplify most fully the stereotypical image associated with the model minority. Starr's modest "preppy" attire—faded but neat blue jeans, pastel sweater set, tennis shoes, metal-framed glasses, and ponytail—and slender physique of 5 feet 3 inches and 110 pounds evoked 1950s images of girls. I first met Starr while she was working as an assistant in the deans' office at Green High School. In speaking with one of the deans about my research, she suggested Starr as "the perfect person to be in your study."

In describing her family, Starr said that her parents immigrated to the United States in 1985 but that she did not join them until 1990 . . . Starr's father was a chef in a Chinese restaurant. Her mother worked as a seamstress for a time; more recently, in addition to her role as a housewife, she had served as a part-time manager of the apartment building in which they lived. On the weekends, Starr worked as a part-time hostess in the same restaurant as her father. Starr estimated that her family's annual household income ranged between $10,000 and $20,000. Starr said that she spoke Chinese (Cantonese and Mandarin) and English both at home and in school.

During our first interview, I asked Starr about her plans for the future. She told me that she had recently received an early admissions letter to one of the most competitive state universities. Starr indicated that the school's strong academic reputation and the relatively low tuition of the state university system made it the college she most wanted to attend, and thus she was pleased with her acceptance. While a student at the university, she hoped to study business and ultimately establish an import/export business with mainland China. In addition, Starr said that she enjoyed her English classes and hoped to pursue this subject as well.

As a student at Green High, Starr was quite accomplished. As part of her six-class course load for the semester, she was enrolled in two Advanced Placement (AP) classes, math and English. Starr explained that if she scored at least a "three" (out of a possible five) on each AP exam, she would receive college credits that could be applied toward her undergraduate degree. Starr said that earning AP credit before beginning college was important, for it decreased the time and expense she would incur as an undergraduate (Woo, 1999, pp. 71–72).

Analysis: "It's Not Easy Being a Member of the Model Minority"

Although Starr's life seemed to epitomize success, her experiences also underscored the two-edged sword of being perceived as a member of the model minority. Without exception, teachers and school administrators described Starr as "the perfect student," "a good kid," "hardworking, cooperative," and "earning high marks." In addition, Starr was respected by her classmates, had developed a close network of friends, and had anticipated a bright future in college and beyond. Yet Stacey Lee (1996) argues that the model minority stereotype is harmful because it assumes that all Asian Americans are successful:

> The model minority myth [is] viewed negatively [because it] overlooks both the struggles and the ultimate achievements of individuals. . . . Some Asian Americans internalize the model minority myth as the standard by which they measure their self-worth, thereby establishing expectations which do not allow for different definitions of success and personal satisfaction. (p. 125)

In keeping with this, although Starr appeared to "have it all," it was clear that she also struggled to maintain the appearance of being a perfect student. Starr admitted during our second interview that she had recently decided not to register for the upcoming AP calculus test:

> I didn't study enough in the first semester. I didn't always do my homework. This semester I've been more serious about studying. But I am still afraid I will not score at least a three, so I am not going to take the exam. As long as I get a 90% or better grade in the class, my parents will never know that I did not take the AP Calculus test. I am not going to tell them. I don't want them to get mad. I don't want to waste their money.

Starr's decision not to take this test can be seen as a response to the stresses she experienced as a result of being perceived as a member of the model minority. Starr feared others' reactions—especially her family's—and her own, if she failed the exam (Woo, 1999, p. 73).

Play: Scene Based on a Doctoral Dissertation With Six Asian American Girls

Setting. A 1,055-student high school in New York City. The demographics of this setting are noteworthy as the school is committed to "ensuring that the student population consists of equal numbers of individuals from four major racial groups." Thus, selection of the incoming freshman class occurs via personal application and interview. Final selection is made with particular attention paid to the overall racial composition and targets 25% white, 25% black/African American, 25% Asian American, and 25% Hispanic.

Six Asian American female students meet twice monthly with a school counselor. For one reason or another, each girl has been encouraged to participate in the group. The group's goals are twofold: (1) to provide the girls with a "safe space" to express their concerns and (2) to encourage group members to see one another as resources when working through life's challenges. Cans of soda, bags of cookies and potato chips, and napkins and paper plates are spread on the table.

Characters

Ms. B: Young, white, female, 30ish-year-old, fast-talking, New York-born and
                 -bred social studies teacher and school counselor

Starr: 18-year-old senior—slender, modest metal glasses, hair in ponytail, and
                 preppy attire of faded khakis, pastel sweater set, and tennis shoes

Courtney: 17-year-old sophomore—gangly, tomboyish

Alli: 16-year-old junior—sturdy, stocky build. Theatrical, punk-rockish appear-
                 ance, baggy pants with frayed hems, Doc Martin shoes, form-fitting
                 T-shirt, blond streak in hair, and heavy dark makeup circling the eyes

Scene I

Ms. B: Hi girls! Sorry I'm a little late. You know how busy those halls can get
                 between classes. Oh great, I see you've helped yourselves to the snacks.
                 Great, I could use a soda myself. Give me a few minutes and we'll get
                 started.

*[Ms. B places her things on a table behind her, plugs in the tape recorder, centers the
microphone, and reaches for a can of soda.]*

                 That's better. 'Kay, when we met last time, we were just beginnin' to talk
                 about our parents. Anyone wanna continue?

Courtney: Yeah, I'll go. I don't see what the big deal is. I mean, my ma doesn't worry
                 about me. Like this weekend, me and my boyfrien' hooked up and we
                 went clubbin'. I didn't get home till after 4 a.m. No biggie. Knew I had
                 to be at work at 9 a.m. in the mornin' so I caught a coupla zzzs, took a
                 shower, and went to work. I guess my ma trusts me ta do the right thing.

Starr: Oh my God! I mean, oh my God! Out till 4 a.m.? My mom and dad
                 would never let me do that. They say that only bad girls stay out that
                 late partyin'.

Courtney: Are you sayin' I'm one of those girls?

Starr: I'm not, but my parents do, so I never get to go out. I come straight home
                 after school and do my homework. Then I help my ma shop, prepare the
                 food, and clean the house. My ma works all day and I want things to be
                 nice when she gets home. Since my dad's [working at the restaurant all
                 the time], she wants me to be around to visit relatives and to help with
                 chores. I don't wanna go out and hang out with friends; my ma needs me
                 at home.

Alli: Well, well (snaps gum). If we don't have a case of yin and yang. I mean, look at what we got. One of y'alls can go out till all hours of the night and raise hell till dawn, while the other can't even walk around the block without her folks' permission. Surprise, surprise. The funniest thing is that you both think that what you're doing is okay.

Starr: Alli, you don't know. I mean, your family and mine are different. Your ma works in real estate, she speaks English. My ma works in a sewing factory. She doesn't want me wearing makeup; she's worried about my future. None of my parents went to college and they want to make sure that I graduate, get a good job, get married, get a house, and have a family.

Alli: So they've brainwashed you into thinking ya want the Asian American dream? Well, lah-dee-dah! What if that's not what you want? (Woo, 2000)

ORGANIZING THE REPORT

Despite the alternatives presented above, many researchers must still produce formal reports. In the report, you synthesize your discoveries for public consumption. The report is the critical stage in the transformation of data into knowledge, so the organization is a reflection of your analysis and interpretations. Metaphorically, if during analysis you organized your closet (data) by fiber, your report is likely to be organized by fiber (recall Chapter 10). Several models for organizing your report exist:

- A chronology of events
- A descriptive life history of an individual
- Themes
- A composite ("day in the life of")
- Critical episodes
- Miniportraits

Each model is not exclusive. You may find that blending the models works for you. But all require thick description and serve to generate theory.

Chronology

A common organizational strategy is to present events chronologically—that is, in the order they happened. This strategy is especially powerful if the story lies in its history. Anthony chooses to describe the development of the community arts program chronologically because he has discovered that the community has a rich history of artistic expression, beginning with community murals drawn on sidewalks outside a building that housed an after-school program. The core of local artists behind these early works have remained in the community and most recently initiated the effort to establish the center. Anthony's history of arts in the community culminating in the current activities is a compelling story of community activism and involvement.

Life History

The chronology strategy also may be useful if your focus is an individual. A phenomenological study, an ethnography, or a case study may result in a descriptive life history. Here, you present an account of one person's life, framing the description with analytic points about the significance of that life in light of your questions and the genre. Ruth could write life histories about the children she has studied.

Themes

Another common organizational strategy is thematic. Meaningful themes that have emerged from your data form the backbone, or structural framework, of your report. The bullets in the executive summary that Marla and her partners offer the clinic's board of directors are the themes that dominated their interviews and observations. We saw in Chapters 10 and 11 that one theme was *being ignored*. Marla's oral presentation and a full report, were she to write one, would define the themes, providing rich details, examples, and quotations. We organized our report on inclusive schools around themes such as *supports for* and *barriers to professional development*. This general theme was broken down into categories such as *principal activities*, *central office attitudes*, *available resources*, and *community involvement*.

Composite

Sometimes, findings are best presented as a composite or a "day in the life of X." The portrait of Ken, the principal of a restructuring school, follows Ken through meetings and interactions of what is called a typical day for him. The day described is actually a composite of the several days during which he was shadowed. All the events around which the day in the report was organized actually occurred but not necessarily during the same day. Yet, on balance, the day described seems typical and real.

You also may present a composite individual drawn from data about several different people. The principal, Lee (Rallis & Goldring, 2000), and the teachers, Maggie and Don (Rallis & Rossman, 1995), are composite characters. Their every act and thought are drawn from real principals and teachers in our data sets, but no one principal or teacher was exactly like Lee, Maggie, or Don in everything he or she said, thought, or did. We present these composites as real because they represent the actual teachers we interviewed, observed, or surveyed.

When Marla and the women on the research team collaborate to write a book about women's health issues, they might create composite women from their case studies. The strategy is effective because readers could be overwhelmed by the number of cases necessary to cover all the issues poor women encounter when dealing with health services.

Critical Events

Critical episodes in the life of a person, event, or program provide another organizational structure. Ruth organizes her journal article around critical episodes because all her children have experienced at least one event that defined their relationships to athletics and sports. She tells the stories of her wheelchair-bound children around these critical episodes. For example, she depicts Amanda by describing the afternoon when she and another friend in a wheelchair were left alone in a gymnasium to wait for one parent to pick them up. The parent was delayed. To avoid boredom, the two girls started "fooling around" with a basketball, and Amanda "discovered her talent." Ruth relates a comparable crucial episode for each participant.

Portraits

Multiple cases, critical episodes, or composites may be organized and presented as portraits (see Lawrence-Lightfoot & Davis, 1997) or miniportraits of individuals or institutions. Like their painted counterparts, written portraits yield a rich and textured impression of the subject over an extended but limited period. Ruth's stories of the children, organized around critical episodes in their lives, are actually miniportraits of each child. The reader can *see* the children and can *touch* their development through the pages on which Ruth describes their experiences.

In sum, writing is an active part of the learning process. It stimulates thinking and is part of the analysis. Through writing, you generate knowledge. Findings gain clarity when you articulate them in writing. Writing up your findings is a process in itself: You write, revise, rewrite—and then you write again. You make discoveries along the way as you continue to unravel the mysteries in your data. Writing draft after draft helps you find your voice and refine the message. At best, writing is interactive. You read and work with the text to produce successive drafts; you seek feedback from your community of practice or others; and you leave it and return with revisions (remember the discussion of the creative process in Chapter 10). In short, writing is not simply sitting down at your word processor and tapping on the keyboard.

As a final word about presenting your contribution, we suggest that you be sure to tell people what you are writing about and why and how you did the study. Give your audience sufficient background about the context of the study, but do not drown them in details. Also, provide enough data in the body of the report to support your conclusions and interpretations. We urge you to play with metaphors: swim with the dolphins, leap into the unknown, open your eyes to see in the dark, hold onto the safety bar and enjoy the roller coaster ride, and so on. Finally, trust the process, and discoveries will emerge.

USING THE DISPOSITIONS AND SKILLS
TO GENERATE USEFUL KNOWLEDGE

However organized, and however represented, what you have learned can be used by others to generate knowledge. Your challenge is to write or present something that is true to what you have discovered and that also appeals to a specific audience. Beginners are often concerned about the number of research reports that sit on shelves gathering dust. Yet they are also dismayed at what seems like the crass "packaging" of their work necessary to enhance its potential usefulness to various audiences. Remember that the principles of good practice free you to consider multiple and alternative ways to present what you have learned. Your goal is to communicate so that others may use what you have discovered.

Audiences might use your work to solve problems and to enlighten, legitimize, or transform their lives. Your reporting can provide information that is *instrumentally useful* in decision making or program redesign, as in Anthony's case and maybe Marla's. So, too, your work may *enlighten* as you consciously decide to contribute to theory. For example, you may directly stipulate links between practice and theory. Sometimes, your contribution happens in a less planned manner, as with Ruth's study. In addition, your work may serve *symbolically*, expressing and legitimizing new understandings for the way things are. Ruth's vivid images of children in wheelchairs playing basketball have high symbolic value. Finally, your work may serve as a tool that *transforms*. Marla and her colleagues hope that their action research will change women's lives and improve the health services available to them. The newsletters could be an "intervention" that sparks behavior changes regarding their health.

You anticipate and plan for certain uses for your work, but do not be surprised at unexpected uses—some that you might not be comfortable with. Someone might find a way to misuse the information that you generate. Although mindful of potential negative uses, you understand that you cannot control them all. You let go. Because your research has been conducted thoughtfully, ethically, and systematically, your contribution sheds light on some small corner of the world.

ACTIVITIES FOR YOUR COMMUNITY OF PRACTICE

Study Questions

- Who is the primary audience for your study?

- Which possible formats for presentation appeal to you and will do justice to your topic?

- What are the trade-offs in alternative reporting formats?

(Continued)

(Continued)

- What voice will you use in crafting your report?

- What are the typical organizing schemes for written reports?

Small-Group and Dyad Activities

Alternative Formats to the Written Report

In a small group, select a film, photographic essay, PowerPoint presentation, fictional narrative, portrait, online Internet conference, website, or other alternative format for reporting findings from qualitative research. Display these as an exhibit for the larger group, and discuss with your colleagues the advantages and disadvantages of each.

Audience

In your small group or dyad, discuss the intended and potential audiences for your study, as well as the intended and potential uses for your study. Explore alternative formats for presenting your findings.

NOTES

1. Although Patton also expresses these ideas in the third edition of his book (2002, see p. 513), we prefer the earlier phrasing.

2. The Jasper Series was produced by the Learning Technology Center, Peabody College, Vanderbilt University, Nashville, Tennessee. The interactive videos introduce the character Jasper, who encounters specific problems (e.g., whether he has enough gas or how to get an injured bird to the veterinarian) he must solve. Sufficient data and information to solve the problem are embedded in the body of the video, and students are asked to advise Jasper.

3. Sharon Rallis thanks Carolyn Evertson, Ted Sizer, Pat Wasley, and Paula Evans, among others, for their critique of the early manuscript (Rallis, 1992).

FURTHER READINGS

Hughes, C. (Ed.). (2003). *Disseminating qualitative research in educational setting: A critical introduction*. Maidenhead, UK: Open University Press.

Keen, S., & Todres, L. (2007). Strategies for disseminating qualitative research findings: Three exemplars. *Forum: Qualitative Social Research*, 8(3). Retrieved from http://www .qualitative-research.net/index.php/fqs/ article/view/285/625

Van Maanen, J. (1995). *Representation in ethnography*. Thousand Oaks, CA: Sage.

Wolcott, H. F. (2009). *Writing up qualitative research* (3rd ed.). Thousand Oaks, CA: Sage.

References

Adelman, C., Jenkins, D., & Kemmis, S. (1983). Rethinking case study: Notes from the second Cambridge conference. In *Case study: An overview. Case Study Methods 1* (Series). Melbourne, Victoria, Australia: Deakin University Press.

Ahmadi, J. (2010). *Evaluation of Afghanistan HEP teachers' professional development.* Unpublished manuscript, University of Massachusetts, Amherst.

Allport, G. (1937). *Personality: A psychological interpretation.* New York, NY: Holt.

Argyris, C., & Schön, D. A. (1974). *Theory in practice.* San Francisco, CA: Jossey-Bass.

Ball, J. S. (1993). Self-doubt and soft data: Social and technical trajectories in ethnographic fieldwork. In M. Hammersley (Ed.), *Educational research: Current issues.* London, England: Paul Chapman.

Ball, S. (1990). Self-doubt and soft data: Social and technical trajectories in ethnographic fieldwork. *Qualitative Studies in Education, 3*(2), 157–171.

Bandura, A. (2012). On the functional properties of perceived self-efficacy revisited. *Journal of Management, 38*(1), 9–44.

Bargar, R. R., & Duncan, J. K. (1982). Cultivating creative endeavor in doctoral research. *Journal of Higher Education, 53*(1), 1–31.

Barone, T., & Eisner, E. (2006). Arts-based educational research. In J. L. Green, G. Camilli, &

P. B. Elmore (Eds.), *Handbook of complementary methods in education* (3rd ed., pp. 95–108). New York, NY: Routledge.

Bishop, R. (2011). Freeing ourselves from neo-colonial domination in research. In S. R. Steinberg (Series Ed.), *Transgressions: Cultural studies and education* (Vol. 66, pp. 1–30). Rotterdam, Netherlands: Sense.

Blumer, H. (1954). What is wrong with social theory? *American Sociological Review, 18,* 3–10.

Blumer, H. (1969). *Symbolic interactionism.* Englewood Cliffs, NJ: Prentice Hall.

Bolman, L. G., & Deal, T. E. (1993). *The path to school leadership.* Newbury Park, CA: Corwin Press.

Bolman, L. G., & Deal, T. E. (1994). *Becoming a teacher leader.* Thousand Oaks, CA: Corwin Press.

Bolman, L. G., & Deal, T. E. (2013). *Reframing organizations: Artistry, choice, and leadership* (5th ed.). San Francisco, CA: Jossey-Bass.

Bolman, L. G., Deal, T. E., & Rallis, S. F. (1995). *Becoming a school board member.* Thousand Oaks, CA: Corwin Press.

Booth, W. C., Colomb, G. G., & Williams, J. M. (2008). *The craft of research* (3rd ed.). Chicago, IL: University of Chicago Press.

Bransford, J., Brown, A., & Cocking, R. (1999). *How people learn: Brain, mind, experience, and school.* Washington, DC: National Academies Press.

Bredo, E., & Feinberg, W. (1982). *Knowledge and values in social and educational research.* Philadelphia, PA: Temple University Press.

Breuer, J., & Freud, S. (1955). Studies on hysteria (A. Strachey & J. Strachey, Trans.). In J. Strachey (Ed.), *The standard edition of the complete psychological works of Sigmund Freud* (Vol. 2, pp. 19–305). London, England: Hogarth Press. (Original work published 1885)

Brinkmann, S., & Kvale, S. (2015). *InterViews: Learning the craft of qualitative research interviewing.* Thousand Oaks, CA: Sage.

Brissett, N. (2011). *A critical analysis of Jamaica's emerging educational policy discourses in the age of globalization* (Unpublished doctoral dissertation). University of Massachusetts, Amherst.

Brown, L., & Durrheim, K. (2009). Different kinds of knowing: Generating qualitative data through mobile interviewing. *Qualitative Inquiry, 15*(5), 911–930.

Brown, L. M., & Gilligan, C. (1990, August). Listening for self and relational voices: A responsive/resisting reader's guide. In M. Franklin (Chair), *Literary theory as a guide to psychological analysis.* Symposium conducted at the annual meetings of the American Psychological Association, Boston, MA.

Burgess, R. G. (1984). *In the field: An introduction to field research.* London, England: Allen & Unwin.

Burrell, G., & Morgan, G. (1979). *Sociological paradigms and organizational analysis.* London, England: Heinemann.

Burton, L. J. (2002). *The development of talent in United States female Olympians: A phenomenological approach* (Unpublished doctoral dissertation). University of Connecticut, Storrs.

Butz, D., & Besio, K. (2004). The value of autoethnography for field research in transcultural settings. *The Professional Geographer, 56*(3), 350–360.

Caine, R. N., & Caine, G. (2013). The brain/mind principles of natural learning. In T. B. Jones (Ed.), *Education for the human brain: A road map to natural learning in schools.* Lanham, MD: Rowman & Littlefield.

Caine, R., Caine, G., McClintic, C., & Klimek, K. (2008). *The 12 Brain/Mind Learning Principles in Action* (2nd ed.). Thousand Oaks, CA: Corwin Press.

Charmaz, K. (1995). Grounded theory. In J. A. Smith, R. Harré, & L. van Langenhve (Eds.), *Rethinking methods in psychology* (pp. 27–49). London, England: Sage.

Charmaz, K. (2002). Qualitative interviewing and grounded theory analysis. In J. F. Gubrium & J. A. Holstein (Eds.), *Handbook of interview research: Context and method* (pp. 675–694). Thousand Oaks, CA: Sage.

Charmaz, K. (2005). Grounded theory for the 21st century: Applications for advancing social justice studies. In N. K. Denzin & Y. S. Lincoln (Eds.), *The SAGE handbook of qualitative research* (3rd ed., pp. 507–535). Thousand Oaks, CA: Sage.

Charmaz, K. (2014). *Constructing grounded theory* (2nd ed.). London, England: Sage.

Chatman, R. (1990). *Fresh roses* (Unpublished doctoral dissertation). Vanderbilt University, Nashville, TN.

Cleaver, F. (2012). *Development through bricolage: Rethinking institutions for natural resource management.* New York, NY: Routledge.

Crano, W. D., Brewer, M. B., & Lac, A. (2015). *Principles and methods of social research* (3rd ed.). New York, NY: Routledge.

Creswell, J. W. (2009). *Research design: Qualitative, quantitative, and mixed methods approaches* (3rd ed.). Thousand Oaks, CA: Sage.

Creswell, J. W. (2013). *Qualitative inquiry and research design* (3rd ed.). Thousand Oaks, CA: Sage.

Cronbach, L. J. (1975). Beyond the two disciplines of scientific psychology. *American Psychologist, 30*(2), 116–127.

Delamont, S. (1992). *Fieldwork in educational settings: Methods, pitfalls, and perspectives.* London, England: Falmer Press.

Delaney, K. J. (2007). Methodological dilemmas and opportunities in interviewing organizational elites. *Sociology Compass, 1*(1), 208–221.

Demerath, P. W. (1996). *The social cost of acting "extra": Dilemmas of student identity and academic success in post-colonial Papua New Guinea* (Unpublished doctoral dissertation). University of Massachusetts, Amherst.

Denzin, N. K. (1989). *Interpretive interactionism.* Newbury Park, CA: Sage.

Denzin, N. K. (1994). The art and politics of interpretation. In N. K. Denzin & Y. S. Lincoln (Eds.),

Handbook of qualitative research (1st ed., pp. 500–515). Thousand Oaks, CA: Sage.

Denzin, N. K., Lincoln, Y. S., & Smith, L. T. (Eds.). (2008). *Handbook of critical and indigenous methodologies.* Thousand Oaks, CA: Sage.

Dicks, B. (2013). Action, experience, communication: Three methodological paradigms for researching multimodal and multisensory settings. *Qualitative Research, 14*(6), 656–674.

Douglas, J. D. (1976). *Investigative social research: Individual and team field research.* Beverly Hills, CA: Sage.

Duckworth, E. R. (2006). *"The having of wonderful ideas" and other essays on teaching and learning* (3rd ed.). New York, NY: Teachers College Press.

Elliot, J., & Keynes, M. (1991). *Action research for educational change.* Philadelphia, PA: Open University Press.

Emerson, R. M., Fretz, R. I., & Shaw, L. L. (1995). *Writing ethnographic fieldnotes.* Chicago, IL: University of Chicago Press.

Empirical. (n.d.). In *Merriam-Webster's online dictionary* (11th ed.). Retrieved from http://www.merriam-webster .com/dictionary/empirical

Erickson, F. (1986). Qualitative methods in research on teaching. In M. C. Whittrock (Ed.), *Handbook of research on teaching* (3rd ed., pp. 119–161). New York, NY: Macmillan.

Erikson, E. (1958). *Young man Luther.* New York, NY: W. W. Norton.

Erikson, E. (1963). *Childhood and society* (2nd ed.). New York, NY: W. W. Norton.

Evertson, C. M., & Green, J. L. (1986). In M. C. Whittrock (Ed.), *Handbook of research on teaching* (3rd ed., pp. 162–213). New York, NY: Macmillan.

Fisk, D. B. (1996). *Empowerment through place: Participatory architecture and education at Concord Academy* (Unpublished doctoral dissertation). University of Massachusetts, Amherst.

Flick, U. (2014). *An introduction to qualitative research* (5th ed.). London, England: Sage.

Foucault, M. (1977). *Discipline and punish: The birth of the prison* (A. Sheridan, Trans.). New York, NY: Vintage Books.

Freire, P. (1970). *Pedagogy of the oppressed.* New York, NY: Seabury Press.

Gage, N. L. (1989). The paradigm wars and their aftermath: A "historical" sketch of research on teaching. *Educational Researcher, 18*(7), 4–10.

Gall, M. D., Borg, W. R., & Gall, J. P. (1996). *Educational research* (6th ed.). White Plains, NY: Longman.

Gall, M. D., Gall, J. P., & Borg, W. R. (2007). *Educational research: An Introduction* (8th ed.). New York, NY: Pearson.

Gallagher, S. (1992). *Hermeneutics and education.* Albany: State University of New York Press.

Gatson, S. N., & Zwerink, A. (2004). Ethnography online: "Natives" practicing and inscribing community. *Qualitative Research, 4*(2), 179–200.

Gee, J. P. (1999). *Introduction to discourse analysis: Theory and method.* New York, NY: Routledge.

Geertz, C. (1973). *The interpretation of cultures: Selected essays.* New York, NY: Basic Books.

Geertz, C. (1983). Blurred genres: The reconfiguration of social thought. In C. Geertz (Ed.), *Local knowledge: Further essays in interpretive anthropology* (pp. 19–35). New York, NY: HarperCollins.

Genre. (n.d.). Retrieved from https://en.wikipedia.org/wiki/Genre

Glaser, B. G., & Strauss, A. L. (1967). *The discovery of grounded theory: Strategies for qualitative research.* Chicago, IL: Aldine.

Gleick, J. (1987). *Chaos: Making a new science.* New York, NY: Viking Press.

Goffman, E. (1959). *The presentation of self in everyday life.* Garden City, NY: Doubleday Anchor.

Gubrium, J. F., & Holstein, J. A. (Eds.). (2002). *Handbook of interview research: Context & method.* Thousand Oaks, CA: Sage.

Gubrium, J. F., & Holstein, J. A. (2003). *Postmodern interviewing.* Thousand Oaks, CA: Sage.

Guillemin, M., & Gillam, L. (2004). Ethics, reflexivity, and "ethically important moments" in research. *Qualitative Inquiry, 10*(2), 261–280.

Hammersley, M., & Atkinson, P. (1983). *Ethnography: Principles in practice.* London, England: Routledge.

Hammersley, M., & Atkinson, P. (2007). *Ethnography: Principles in practice* (3rd ed.). London, England: Routledge.

Hemmings, A. (2006). Great ethical divides: Bridging the gap between institutional review boards and researchers. *Educational Researcher, 35*(4), 12–18.

Hine, C. (2000). *Virtual ethnography.* Thousand Oaks, CA: Sage.

Hodder, I. (2000). The interpretation of documents and material culture. In N. K. Denzin & Y. S. Lincoln (Eds.), *Handbook of qualitative research* (2nd ed., pp. 703–715). Thousand Oaks, CA: Sage.

Holman Jones, S. (2005). Autoethnography: Making the personal political. In N. K. Denzin & Y. S. Lincoln (Eds.), *The SAGE handbook of qualitative research* (3rd ed., pp. 763–791). Thousand Oaks, CA: Sage.

Holstein, J. A., & Gubrium, J. F. (1994). Phenomenology, ethnomethodology, and interpretive practice. In N. K. Denzin & Y. S. Lincoln (Eds.), *Handbook of qualitative research* (1st ed., pp. 262–272). Thousand Oaks, CA: Sage.

Holstein, J. A., & Gubrium, J. F. (Eds.). (2003). *Inside interviewing: New lenses, new concerns.* Thousand Oaks, CA: Sage.

Hostetler, K. (2005). What is "good" education research? *Educational Researcher, 34*(6), 16–21.

Jewitt, C. (Ed.). (2009). *The Routledge handbook of multimodal analysis.* London, England: Routledge.

Johnson, J. M. (1975). *Doing field research.* Beverly Hills, CA: Sage.

Jorgensen, D. L. (1989). *Participant observation: A methodology for human studies.* Newbury Park, CA: Sage.

Kahn, A. (1992). *Therapist-initiated termination to psychotherapy: The experience of clients* (Unpublished doctoral dissertation). University of Massachusetts, Amherst.

Kant, I. (1956). *Critique of practical reason* (L. W. Beck, Trans.). New York, NY: Liberal Arts Press. (Original work published 1788)

Kaye, W., & Rallis, S. F. (1989). Educational aspects: Resuscitation training and evaluation. In W. Kaye & N. Bircher (Eds.), *Cardiopulmonary resuscitation* (pp. 177–222). New York, NY: Churchill Livingstone.

Kennedy, M. M. (1979). Generalizing from single case studies. *Evaluation Quarterly, 3*(4), 661–678.

Kidder, T. (1993). *Old friends.* Boston, MA: Houghton Mifflin.

Knapp, M. L., & Daly, J. A. (2011). *The SAGE handbook of interpersonal communication* (4th ed.). Thousand Oaks, CA: Sage.

Knight, P. (2002). *Small-scale research: Pragmatic inquiry in social science and the caring professions.* London, England: Sage.

Kose, A. (2010). *Analysis of school counselors' leadership practices through the lens of distributed leadership* (Unpublished doctoral dissertation). University of Massachusetts, Amherst.

Kozol, J. (1995). *Amazing grace: The lives of children and the conscience of a nation.* New York, NY: Crown.

Krueger, R. A., & Casey, M. A. (2015). *Focus groups: A practical guide for applied research* (5th ed.). Thousand Oaks, CA: Sage.

Kvale, S. (1996). *Interviews: An introduction to qualitative research interviewing.* Thousand Oaks, CA: Sage.

Lareau, A. (1989). *Home advantage: Social class and parental intervention in elementary education.* New York, NY: Falmer Press.

Lave, J., & Wenger, E. (1991). *Situated learning: Legitimate peripheral participation.* Cambridge, England: Cambridge University Press.

Lawrence-Lightfoot, S., & Davis, J. H. (1997). *The art and science of portraiture.* San Francisco, CA: Jossey-Bass.

Learn. (1993). In L. Brown (Ed.), *New shorter Oxford English dictionary* (Vol. 1, pp. 1554–1555). Oxford, England: Clarendon Press.

Learning. (1993). In L. Brown (Ed.), *New shorter Oxford English dictionary* (Vol. 1, p. 1555). Oxford, England: Clarendon Press.

Leavy, P. (2015). *Method meets art: Arts-based research practice.* New York, NY: Guilford Press.

LeCompte, M. D., & Schensul, J. J. (2010). *Designing and conducting ethnographic research: An introduction.* Lanham, MD: AltaMira Press.

Lee, S. (1996). *Unraveling the "model minority" stereotype: Listening to Asian American youth.* New York, NY: Teachers College Press.

Legacy. (n.d.). Retrieved from http://www.legacyproject.org/guides/lifeintquestions.html

Lewin, K. (1948). *Resolving social conflicts: Selected papers on group dynamics.* New York, NY: Harper & Row.

Li, P. P. (2012). Toward an integrative framework of indigenous research: The geocentric implications of yin–yang balance. *Asia Pacific Journal of Management, 29*(4), 849–872.

Lightfoot, S. L. (1983). *The good high school: Portraits of character and culture.* New York, NY: Basic Books.

Lincoln, Y. S., & Guba, E. G. (1985). *Naturalistic inquiry.* Beverly Hills, CA: Sage.

Luker, K. (2008). *Salsa dancing into the social sciences: Research in an age of info-glut.* Cambridge, MA: Harvard University Press.

Luttrell, C., & Quiroz, S. (with Scrutton, C., & Bird, K.). (2009). *Understanding and operationalising empowerment* (Working Paper 308). London, England: Overseas Development Institute.

MacIntyre, A. (1981). *After virtue.* Notre Dame, IN: University of Notre Dame Press.

van Manen, M. (1990). *Researching lived experience: Human science for an action sensitive pedagogy.* Albany: State University of New York Press.

Mann, C., & Stewart, F. (2004). Introducing online methods. In S. N. Hesse-Biber & P. Leavy (Eds.), *Approaches to qualitative research: A reader on theory and practice* (pp. 367–401). New York, NY: Oxford University Press.

Manusov, V., & Patterson, M. L. (2006). *The SAGE handbook of nonverbal communication.* Thousand Oaks, CA: Sage.

Markham, A. N. (2013). Remix culture, remix methods: Reframing qualitative inquiry for social media contexts. In N. Denzin & M. Giardina (Eds.), *Global dimensions of qualitative inquiry* (pp. 63–81). Walnut Creek, CA: Left Coast Press.

Markham, A., & Baym, N. (2009). *Internet inquiry: Conversations about method.* Thousand Oaks, CA: Sage.

Marshall, C., & Rossman, G. B. (2016). *Designing qualitative research* (6th ed.). Thousand Oaks, CA: Sage.

Maslowe, A. (1970). *Motivation and personality.* New York, NY: Harper & Row.

Merriam, S. B. (1998). *Qualitative research and case study applications in education* (Rev. ed.). San Francisco, CA: Jossey-Bass.

Merriam, S. B., & Tisdell, E. J. (2015). *Qualitative research: A guide to design and implementation.* San Francisco, CA: Wiley.

Meyerhoff, M., & Strycharz, A. (2013) Communities of practice. In J. K. Chambers & N. Schilling (Eds.), *The handbook of language variation and change* (2nd ed.). Oxford, England: Wiley. doi:10.1002/9781118335598.ch20

Miles, M. B., & Huberman, A. M. (1984). *Qualitative data analysis: A methods sourcebook* (1st ed.). Beverly Hills, CA: Sage.

Miles, M. B., & Huberman, A. M. (1994). *Qualitative data analysis: A methods sourcebook* (2nd ed.). Thousand Oaks, CA: Sage.

Miles, M. B., Huberman, A. M., & Saldaña, J. (2014). *Qualitative data analysis: A methods sourcebook* (3rd ed.). Thousand Oaks, CA: Sage.

Milner, H. R. (2007). Race, culture, and researcher positionality: Working through dangers seen, unseen, and unforeseen. *Educational Researcher, 36*(7), 388–400.

Murray, W. E., & Overton, J. (2003). Designing development work. In R. Scheyvens & D. Storey (Eds.), *Development fieldwork: A practical guide* (pp. 17–35). London, England: Sage.

Nasar, S. (1998). *A beautiful mind: The life of mathematical genius and Nobel laureate John Nash.* New York, NY: Simon & Schuster.

Newman, D. L., & Brown, R. D. (1996). *Applied ethics for program evaluation.* Thousand Oaks, CA: Sage.

Noddings, N. (1984). *Caring: A feminine approach to ethics and moral education.* Berkeley: University of California Press.

Noddings, N. (1995). *Philosophy of education.* Boulder, CO: Westview Press.

Organisation for Economic Co-operation and Development. (2013). *New data for understanding the human condition: International perspectives.* Retrieved from http://www.oecd.org/sti/sci-tech/new-data-for-understanding-the-human-condition.pdf

Pallas, A. M. (2001). Preparing education doctoral students for epistemological diversity. *Educational Researcher, 30*(5), 6–11.

Patton, M. Q. (1980). *Qualitative evaluation methods.* Beverly Hills, CA: Sage.

Patton, M. Q. (1990). *Qualitative evaluation and research methods* (2nd ed.). Newbury Park, CA: Sage.

Patton, M. Q. (1997). *Utilization-focused evaluation: The new century text* (3rd ed.). Thousand Oaks, CA: Sage.

Patton, M. Q. (2002). *Qualitative research and evaluation methods* (3rd ed.). Thousand Oaks, CA: Sage.

Patton, M. Q. (2015). *Qualitative research & evaluation methods: Integrating theory and practice* (4th ed.). Thousand Oaks, CA: Sage.

Pe-Pua, R. (1994). Advances in the development of indigenous social research methods. *DLSU Dialogue: An Interdisciplinary Journal for Cultural Studies, 27*(2).

Peshkin, A. (1988). In search of subjectivity—one's own. *Educational Researcher, 17*(7), 17–21.

Piaget, J. (1948). *The moral judgement of the child* (M. Gabain, Trans.). Glencoe, IL: Free Press.

Pink, S. (2011). Multimodality, multisensoriality and ethnographic knowing: Social semiotics and the phenomenology of perception. *Qualitative Research*, *11*(3), 261–276.

Pink, S. (2012). *Situating everyday life.* London, England: Sage.

Pirie, S. E. B., & Schwartzenberger, R. L. E. (1988). Mathematical discussion and mathematical understanding. *Educational Studies in Mathematics, 19,* 459–470.

Polanyi, M. (1962). *Personal knowledge.* Chicago, IL: University of Chicago Press.

Popkewicz, T. S. (1984). *Paradigm and ideology in educational research: The social functions of the intellectual.* London, England: Falmer Press.

Price, S., Jewitt, C., & Brown, B. (Eds.). (2013). *The SAGE handbook of digital technology research*. Thousand Oaks, CA: Sage.

Punch, M. (1994). Politics and ethics in qualitative research. In N. K. Denzin & Y. S. Lincoln (Eds.), *Handbook of qualitative research* (1st ed., pp. 83–97). Thousand Oaks, CA: Sage.

Rallis, S. F. (1990). *Learning disabilities identification process: Final evaluation report.* Providence,

RI: Department of Education, Office of Special Needs.

Rallis, S. F. (1992). *Connecting the conversations about change: Portrait of a principal as a leader.* Providence, RI: Brown University, Coalition of Essential Schools.

Rallis, S. F., & Goldring, E. B. (2000). *Principals of dynamic schools: Taking charge of change* (2nd ed.). Thousand Oaks, CA: Sage.

Rallis, S. F., & Militello, M. (2009). Inquiry-minded school leaders: Evaluation as inquiry, inquiry as practice. In K. E. Ryan & J. B. Cousins (Eds.), *The SAGE international handbook on educational evaluation* (pp. 253–272). Thousand Oaks, CA: Sage.

Rallis, S. F., & Rossman, G. B. (with Phlegar, J. M., & Abeille, A.). (1995). *Dynamic teachers: Leaders of change.* Thousand Oaks, CA: Corwin Press.

Rallis, S. F., & Rossman, G. B. (2001). Communicating quality and qualities: The role of the evaluator as critical friend. In A. P. Benson, D. M. Hinn, & C. Lloyd (Eds.), *Visions of quality: How evaluators define, understand, and represent program quality* (pp. 107–120). Oxford, England: JAI Press.

Rallis, S. F., & Rossman, G. B. (2002). Mixed methods in evaluation contexts: A pragmatic framework. In A. Tashakkori & C. Teddlie (Eds.), *Handbook of mixed methods in the social and behavioral sciences* (pp. 491–512). Thousand Oaks, CA: Sage.

Rallis, S. F., Rossman, G. B., & Gadja, R. (2007). Trustworthiness in evaluation practice: An emphasis on the relational. *Evaluation and Program Planning, 30*(4), 404–409.

Rawls, J. (1971). *A theory of social justice.* Cambridge, MA: Belknap Press.

Reed-Danahay, D. E. (Ed.). (1997). *Auto/ethnography: Rewriting the self and the social.* Oxford, England: Berg.

Reflexive. (1993). In L. Brown (Ed.), *New shorter Oxford English dictionary* (Vol. 2, p. 2522). Oxford, England: Clarendon Press.

Reflexivity. (1993). In L. Brown (Ed.), *New shorter Oxford English dictionary* (Vol. 2, p. 2522). Oxford, England: Clarendon Press.

Rein, M. (1970). *Social policy: Issues of choice and change.* New York, NY: Random House.

Rennie, D. L. (2012). Qualitative research as methodical hermeneutics. *Psychological Methods, 17*(3), 385–398.

Richardson, L. (1994). Writing: A method of inquiry. In N. K. Denzin & Y. S. Lincoln (Eds.), *Handbook of qualitative research* (1st ed., pp. 516–529). Thousand Oaks, CA: Sage.

Riessman, C. K. (1993). *Narrative analysis.* Newbury Park, CA: Sage.

Rogers, A. G. (2000). When methods matter: Qualitative research issues in psychology. In B. M. Brizuela, J. P. Stewart, R. G. Carrillo, & J. G. Berger (Eds.), *Acts of inquiry in qualitative research* (pp. 51–60). Cambridge, MA: Harvard Educational Review.

Rosenthal, R. (1994). Science and ethics in conducting, analyzing, and reporting psychological research. *Psychological Science, 5*(3), 127–134.

Rossman, G. B., Corbett, H. D., & Firestone, W. A. (1988). *Change and effectiveness in schools: A cultural perspective.* Albany: State University of New York Press.

Rossman, G. B., & Wilson, B. L. (1994). Numbers and words revisited: Being "shamelessly eclectic." *Quality and Quantity: International Journal of Methodology, 28*(3), 315–327.

Roth, W.-M. (2001). Gestures: Their role in teaching and learning. *Review of Educational Research, 71*(3), 365–392.

Roulston, K. (2010). *Reflective interviewing: A guide to theory and practice.* Thousand Oaks, CA: Sage.

Rubin, H. J., & Rubin, I. S. (1995). *Qualitative interviewing: The art of hearing data.* Thousand Oaks, CA: Sage.

Ryen, A. (2003). Cross-cultural interviewing. In J. A. Holstein & J. F. Gubrium (Eds.), *Inside interviewing: New lenses, new concerns* (pp. 429–448). Thousand Oaks, CA: Sage.

Sadker, D. M., & Sadker, M. (1994). *Failing at fairness: How America's schools cheat girls.* New York, NY: Scribner.

Saldaña, J. (2013). *The coding manual for qualitative researchers* (2nd ed.). Thousand Oaks, CA: Sage.

Saldaña, J. (2015). *Thinking qualitatively: Methods of mind.* Thousand Oaks, CA: Sage.

Schatzman, L., & Strauss, A. L. (1973). *Field research: Strategies for a natural sociology.* Englewood Cliffs, NJ: Prentice Hall.

Schön, D. (1983). *The reflective practitioner: How professionals think in action.* New York, NY: Basic Books.

Schram, T. H. (2006). *Conceptualizing and proposing qualitative research* (2nd ed.). Upper Saddle River, NJ: Prentice Hall.

Schratz, M., & Walker, R. (1995). *Research as social change.* New York, NY: Routledge.

Seidman, I. E. (1998). *Interviewing as qualitative research: A guide for researchers in education and the social sciences* (2nd ed.). New York, NY: Teachers College Press.

Seidman, I. E. (2006). *Interviewing as qualitative research: A guide for researchers in education and the social sciences* (3rd ed.). New York, NY: Teachers College Press.

Seidman, I. E. (2013). *Interviewing as qualitative research: A guide for researchers in education and social sciences* (4th ed.). New York, NY: Teachers College Press.

Shavelson, R., & Towne, L. (Eds.). (2002). *Scientific research in education.* Washington, DC: Committee on Scientific Principles for Education Research, National Research Council.

Silverman, D. (1993). *Interpreting qualitative data: Methods for analyzing talk, text, and interaction.* Newbury Park, CA: Sage.

Silverman, D. (2000). Analyzing talk and text. In N. K. Denzin & Y. S. Lincoln (Eds.), *Handbook of qualitative research* (2nd ed., pp. 821–834). Thousand Oaks, CA: Sage.

Silverman, D. (Ed.). (2010). *Qualitative research: Theory, method, and practice* (3rd ed.). London, England: Sage.

Siskin, L. (1994, November). *Seduction and desertion: Implicit promises in qualitative research.*

Unpublished remarks delivered at the Spencer Hall Conference on Teacher Development, London, Ontario, Canada.

Sociolinguistics. (2015). Retrieved from http://dictionary.reference.com/browse/sociolinguistics

Sosnowski, N. H. (2002). *Women of color staking a claim for the cyber domain: Unpacking the racial/gender gap in science, mathematics, engineering and technology* (Unpublished doctoral dissertation). University of Massachusetts, Amherst.

Spradley, J. S. (1979). *The ethnographic interview.* New York, NY: Holt, Rinehart & Winston.

Stake, R. E. (2000). Case studies. In N. K. Denzin & Y. S. Lincoln (Eds.), *Handbook of qualitative research* (2nd ed., pp. 435–454). Thousand Oaks, CA: Sage.

Strauss, A. L., & Corbin, J. (2015). *Basics of qualitative research: Techniques and procedures for developing grounded theory* (4th ed.). Thousand Oaks, CA: Sage.

Subedi, B., & Rhee, J. (2008). Negotiating collaboration across differences. *Qualitative Inquiry, 14*(6), 1070–1092.

Tannen, D. (1986). *That's not what I meant! How conversational style makes or breaks relationships.* New York, NY: HarperCollins.

Tannen, D. (1990). *You just don't understand: Women and men in conversation.* New York, NY: HarperCollins.

Taylor, S. J., & Bogdan, R. (1984). *An introduction to qualitative research: The search for meanings* (2nd ed.). New York, NY: Wiley.

Technique. (n.d.). Retrieved from http://dictionary.reference.com/browse/technique

Temple, B., & Young, A. (2004). Qualitative research and translation dilemmas. *Qualitative Research, 4*(2), 161–178.

de la Torre, D. (2010). *A door half-open, a door half-closed: Adventures in gaining access to college by students, . . . and others.* Unpublished manuscript, University of Massachusetts, Amherst.

Translating and transcribing data. (2008). In *Facilitator's manual for qualitative research skills.* Cambridge, England: Research Consortium on Educational Outcomes and Poverty. Retrieved from: http://manual.recoup.educ.cam.ac.uk/wiki/index.php/Transcription_%26_translation

Truxaw, M. P. (2001). *The nature and role of teacher intervention with respect to discourse in the middle school mathematics class: A case study using socio-linguistic tools.* Unpublished manuscript, University of Connecticut, Storrs.

Ulin, P. R., Robinson, E. T., Tolley, E. E., & McNeill, E. T. (2002). *Qualitative methods: A field guide for applied research in sexual and reproductive health.* Research Triangle Park, NC: Family Health International.

U.S. Department of Health and Human Services. (1979). *Ethical Principles and Guidelines for the Protection of Human Subjects of Research. The National Commission for the Protection of Human Subjects of Biomedical and Behavioral Research.* Retrieved from http://www.hhs.gov/ohrp/humansubjects/guidance/belmont.html

Utilitarianism. (1993). In L. Brown (Ed.), *New shorter Oxford English dictionary* (Vol. 2, p. 3534). Oxford, England: Clarendon Press.

Van Maanen, J. (1983). The moral fix: On the ethics of field work. In R. Emerson (Ed.), *Contemporary field research: A collection of reading* (pp. 169–187). Prospect Heights, IL: Waveland Press.

Van Maanen, J. (1988). *Tales of the field: On writing ethnography.* Chicago, IL: University of Chicago Press.

Vygotsky, L. S. (1978). *Mind in society: The development of higher psychological processes.* Cambridge, MA: Harvard University Press.

Walsh, R. A. (2008). Mindfulness and empathy: A hermeneutic circle. In S. F. Hick & T. Bien (Eds.), *Mindfulness and the therapeutic relationship.* New York, NY: Guilford Press.

Watson, J. D. (1968). *The double helix: A personal account of the discovery of the structure of DNA.* New York, NY: Atheneum.

Weiss, C. (1980). Knowledge creep and decision accretion. *Knowledge: Creation, Diffusion, and Utilization, 1*(3), 381–404.

Weiss, C. H. (1998). Have we learned anything new about the use of evaluation? *American Journal of Evaluation, 19*(1), 21–33.

Wenger, E. (1998). Communities of practice: Learning as a social system. *The Systems Thinker, 9*(5).

Westby, C., Burda, A., & Mehta, Z. (2003). *Asking the right questions in the right ways: Strategies for ethnographic interviewing.* Retrieved from http://www.asha.org/Publications/leader/2003/030429/f030429b.htm

Whyte, W. F. (1981). *Street corner society.* Chicago, IL: University of Chicago Press. (Original work published 1943)

Wolcott, H. F. (1994). *Transforming qualitative data: Description,* analysis, and interpretation. Thousand Oaks, CA: Sage.

Wolf, M. (1992). *A thrice told tale: Feminism, postmodernism, and ethnographic responsibility.* Stanford, CA: Stanford University Press.

Woo, K. A. (1999). *"Double happiness," double jeopardy: Exploring ways in which race/ ethnicity and gender influence self-perceptions in Chinese American high school girls* (Unpublished doctoral dissertation). Teachers College, Columbia University, New York.

Woo, K. A. (2000). Untitled. Unpublished play. Storrs: University of Connecticut.

Yin, R. K. (1994). *Case study research: Design and methods* (2nd ed.). Thousand Oaks, CA: Sage.

Yoder, F. E. (2009, November 17). *Protecting human subjects of research—the basics.* PowerPoint presentation at the University of Massachusetts, Amherst.

Index